Praise for *Jews of Florida*

"What Macaulay was to the history of the English, what Michelet was to the history of the French, Marcia Jo Zerivitz is to the history of Florida Jewry. She has salvaged the records of the past and turned the struggles and successes of the dead into a living, breathing narrative."

—Stephen J. Whitfield, professor emeritus of American Studies, Brandeis University

"Through exhaustive research and the collection of hundreds of oral histories, cultural anthropologist Marcia Jo Zerivitz reveals her landmark contribution with this book. By reading her stories, you become witness to the vitality and variety of the lives of Floridian Jews. You sense her commitment to maintaining their identity while she makes a deep footprint in every area of Florida history."

—Richard B. Stone, US ambassador and US senator from Florida

"I urge you to open this easily accessible volume with gigantic impact that illustrates the diamond quality of Marcia Jo's work. It contains truthful accounts in history written through real people, Jewish within a non-Jewish context. The research and groundbreaking sourcing is arrayed to help the reader understand the authenticity of what we read. Credibility is her foundation. Bury yourself in it deeply. Marcia Jo has produced a rich, definitive, accurate depiction from St. Augustine to the arrival of the first Jewish settlers in county after county in good writing, oozing from fine historical fact-finding wrapped with the soul of an author who has lived what she has written about thoroughly and well."

—Mark Talisman, chair of Project Judaica Foundation, founding vice chair of the United States Holocaust Memorial and Museum

"Marcia Jo Zerivitz's earlier book Jews of Tampa presented a compelling picture of Jews who were woven into the fabric of the community for more than a century. I have turned the pages of that book many times enjoying the images of people I know and respect. I was also surprised at what I learned. That book was thoroughly enjoyable. Now I look forward to her new book covering all of Florida."

—Honorable Samuel Bell, former member of the Florida Legislature

"Marcia Jo Zerivitz should take great pride in knowing that Jewish American Heritage Month, now celebrated each May, began with her work at the Jewish Museum of Florida. Her vision has not only influenced Florida's Jewish community but communities across our entire nation."

—Debbie Wasserman Schultz, US representative from Florida

Jews of Florida

JEWS *of* FLORIDA

— Centuries of Stories —

MARCIA JO ZERIVITZ

THE History PRESS

Published by The History Press
Charleston, SC
www.historypress.com

FRONT COVER IMAGES:
Top Left: Cardozo Hotel, Miami Beach, 1939.
Top Right: Morris Moses inspects a shipment of celery heading north, Sanford, 1926.
Middle Left: Fannie Moss in her Purim Masquerade Ball seashell costume, Jacksonville, 1918.
Middle Right: NASA astronaut wearing space suit and backpack designed by Harry Kaplan, Cape Canaveral, 1970.
Bottom Left: Carnival Cruise Lines, founded in 1972 by Ted Arison.
Bottom Right: Honeymooners Gertrude Katz Moses and David Moses on alligator, West Palm Beach, 1920s.

BACK COVER IMAGES:
Top Left: Synagogue Torah ark ornament, carved, painted, and gilded wooden pediment depicting the Ten Commandments, Torah crown, and lions of Judah as guardians, Pensacola, circa 1925.
Top Right: K. Kanner Dry Goods interior, left to right: Sophie, Samuel, and Kalman Kanner, Orlando, 1905.
Bottom Right: Citrus crate label reads "Florida" in Yiddish, Winter Haven, circa 1930. Museum of Florida History

This book is dedicated to the Jewish pioneers who settled in Florida and their families who preserved the photographs that tell us stories. Their perseverance to tame the hostile environment and commitment to their traditions made it comfortable for more Jews to follow and build a strong community that takes care of its own. This documentation of our collective historic memory helps ensure Jewish continuity.

First published 2020

Manufactured in the United States

ISBN-13: 978-1-4671-4253-3

Library of Congress Control Number: 2019914985

This book was published
with the generous support of
my friend Jonathan Symons.

Contents

Foreword
by Mark Talisman

We may have come on different ships, but we're in the same boat now.
—Martin Luther King Jr.

For in the end, it is all about memory, its sources and its magnitude, and, of course, its consequences.
—Elie Wiesel, *Night* (The Night Trilogy, 1962)

These two quotations are one side of the same coin. When at university I majored in history, not in so-called political science, or government at my school, or in the newly created subject of social relations either. Why history? Reviewing all the other concentrations, I found them to be only pieces of a missing whole, which I soon identified to be history—with its depth, breadth, and soul wrapped up in the realities lived out over and over the eons of human endeavors. It turned out to be fortuitous that I made that choice as I am always engulfed in it—what was and what happened—no matter where I find my assigned task at any given moment.

I do believe in Santayana's oft quoted words, "Those who do not understand history are [indeed] condemned to relive it!" Elie Wiesel, founding chairman of the US Holocaust Memorial Museum, with whom I served for years as founding vice-chairman, wanted the museum to be a truth telling of the impossible to tell—the Holocaust. To do so, he insisted we pay attention to the survivors of this unique event through their own words, images, and interviews first…living history, in other words. Then there is Martin Luther King Jr., whose simple words are filled with meaning needing no detailed explanation. Both geniuses and Nobel Laureates intersect, and their words explain the core of this wonderful book: the truthful accounts of history based on real Jewish people within a non-Jewish context.

I hope you will open this volume and bury yourself in it deeply. After more than forty years of knowing each other and happily working together, I just learned that Marcia Jo has been diligently doing the impossible. For her this is yet another task, but for many of us, it's a lifetime achievement, if possible at all. All the research and groundbreaking sourcing of unique history is arrayed to help the reader understand the authenticity of what we will soon read. Credibility is her foundation.

In this one book, there is a definitive inventory of this remarkable treasure—Marcia Jo's achievements, her many firsts, so much of which have been a devotion to all things Jewish. Reading this record, one feels compelled to say *dayenu*. But it was not enough. For me, just her encounter with Samuel Bell III while searching for funds for an early but vital project tipped me off that I was in for a treat! Without revealing the details of this amazing little story with gigantic impact, it illustrates the diamond quality of this major work Marcia Jo has labored to produce for all of its lucky readers!

This story is a perfect example of the *two* degrees of separation—Jewish and non-Jewish—that to me is the essence of the remarkable, rich, deep, and complicated history of our Jewish people. The geographic location, Florida, is equally remarkable, complicated, and rich with details that you will find yourself completely entangled in and delighted to learn. You will discover, buried within its recesses, tiny and huge concepts and surprises delighting the mind, mind's eye, and imagination—all of which will be opened wide by good writing that is oozing from fine historical fact-finding wrapped with the soul of an author who has lived what she has written about thoroughly and well.

One dependable source of this genre of history is the doctoral candidate thesis being published as a trade book. Then there is the writer who is filled with information finally ripe for organization in terms of its amazing breadth and depth. After decades, here is the opus ready to educate from your favorite reading chair. Check and recheck and use these newly revealed facts in conversation now for the first time with authority and accuracy. Finally, even in Florida, Jewish need not be a Wolfie's corned beef sandwich but instead the amazing story of Miami Beach from the get-go to satisfy those of you seeking the here and now.

Luckily for us, the readers, the combination modern storyteller and scholar has produced a rich, definitive depiction stretching from 1500s St. Augustine to long after the arrival of the small band of Hebrews to Pensacola in 1763. This journey continues on to the first Jewish settlers in county after county and follows the longest-continuing Jewish family in Florida—and on and on. I will not spoil the finds that fill this work of fine history with my dull versions of examples.

Marcia Jo has had her beloved husband's full support, so between her and Elliott, we are all very fortunate to have this well-organized, easily accessible book now in print for *you* to fully enjoy. Since it's not my job to list all the content within, please just glance over the table of contents before you enter this Jewish and general history work. You will be kibitzing about all you learn, which causes me to lovingly advise that you take care with how you approach your new interest so as not to stress your best friends. Invite them to begin reading for themselves! A must-have, this fine book details the history of Jewish people in the state with our nation's third-largest Jewish population—and now you will understand why!

Thanks, Marcia Jo, for all you have given us in a life well lived with much yet to be revealed, I am sure.

Mark Talisman Z"L
May 23, 2019, Washington, DC
(1941–2019)

Humanitarian, chair of the Project Judaica Foundation, founding vice-chair of the United States Holocaust Memorial Museum (1980–86), creator of the 1983 Smithsonian Institution's *Precious Legacy: Judaic Treasures from the Czechoslovak State Collections* exhibit (of Judaica stolen by the Nazis), creator/director of the Washington Action Office for the Council of Jewish Federations (1975–93), coauthor and support organizer for the 1974 Jackson–Vanik amendment to free Soviet Jews, creator/teacher of the Newly Elected Members of Congress program (1970s) at the Harvard Kennedy School Institute of Politics, consultant on democracy building, sculptor, baker, master gardener, and friend.

Acknowledgments

Thanks for the memories! As you will read in the introduction, this book is a result of my thirty-five years of statewide grassroots research into the hidden history of the Jews of Florida. Over those years, hundreds of people met with me as I traveled the state; they answered my questions and contributed their stories, photographs, documents, and artifacts. From genesis, this has been a team project.

My devoted and hardworking *MOSAIC: Jewish Life in Florida* traveling exhibit statewide task forces during the 1980s were especially participatory, and I owe them each a huge debt of gratitude. Some of them continue to stay in touch and send me materials—such as Doris Rosenblatt (Tampa and St. Petersburg), Dolly Williams (Tampa), Beverly Kaiman (Pensacola and Gainesville), Rabbi Stanley Garfein (Tallahassee), and Hazel Mack (archivist, Congregation Ahavath Chesed, Jacksonville).

In the beginning, Randy Nimnicht and Andy Brian, who were at that time the executive director and designer at the Historical Museum of Southern Florida, now HistoryMiami, taught me about translating what I collected into writing a museum exhibition. Robert Buck of Presentations South Inc. in Orlando contributed to my knowledge of how to develop an audience.

In the 1990s, when I began the process of creating the Jewish Museum of Florida, there were two people who guided me. Tom Freudenheim, assistant secretary of the Smithsonian Institutions and Seymour Fromer, cofounder with his wife, Rebecca, of the Judah L. Magnus Museum in Berkeley, California, gave me invaluable direction and set me on a course for success. I also want to especially thank Helene and Murray Dubbin, Ann Bussel, and Elaine Bloom for their thirty-five continuous years of advocacy.

As I gathered photographs for this book, I reached back to past collaborators Lisa Schwartz in Orlando and notably Todd Bothel, registrar at the Jewish Museum of Florida–FIU (Florida International University). Todd spent more than one hundred hours preparing many of the images for publication. A good neighbor Steve Mistretta was always ready to help me format challenging images. From Orlando, my *Kehillah* collaborator Roz Fuchs and *Florida Jewish Heritage Trail* coauthor Rachel Heimovics provided research assistance and documentation. Rachel, always the editor, has guided me through the *Chicago Manual of Style* and writing a glossary. Former public school principal and assistant superintendent Ann Scholl and my daughter, Marni Kerstein Odom, displayed true devotion by reading the manuscript for clarity.

I think of my Mom, who would be so proud to see this book become a reality; my original cheerleader and mentor, Sam Proctor (Gainesville); Marcia and Lewis Kanner (Miami); Sylvia Shorstein (Jacksonville); Pat Glickstein Haas (Jacksonville); Joe Wittenstein (Orlando); Norman Giller (Miami Beach); Burnett "Burnie" Roth (Miami Beach); and so many others who are no longer with us to see the results of their influences on my work.

Thank you to all my friends and family, especially Marni and Matthew, for encouraging me all the long way to making this book happen. My most important advocate is my husband, Elliott Zerivitz. He has been with me on this entire journey—listening and dreaming with me, sharing my excitement with each discovery and connection, editing, questioning, and taking good care of me so that I could be unconditionally devoted to Florida Jewish history.

And, of course, a huge thank-you to *everyone* who contributed photographs—from back in the MOSAIC days up to the present. Without the preservation of family photographs, our collective historic memory would be greatly diminished.

(Notes: All photographs are from the Collections of the Jewish Museum of Florida–FIU (Florida International University), originated by Founding Executive Director Marcia Jo Zerivitz, LHD (litterarum humaniorum doctor), unless otherwise credited. Mentions of the Jewish Museum of Florida-FIU are abbreviated as the JMOF-FIU. All towns and cities mentioned are in Florida unless otherwise indicated. Women's married names are in brackets.)

"For me, this is all about roots and memories to ensure Jewish continuity. Like cut flowers, Jews wither without our roots. Our collective memories are our roots."
—Marcia Jo Zerivitz

It is 1986, before cell phones, Google, and Wikipedia, and I am in Jacksonville, interviewing Rosalie and Robert Lee Coleman about his grandfather George Dzialynski. In 1857 George was the first boy born in Florida to a Jewish family that had planted roots in the state, and the family has continued to live here as Jews since 1850. I ask if they have any of George's personal possessions. Rosalie chimes in, "I have his pocket watch with Hebrew numerals that he carried his entire life! It's in the safety deposit box at the bank—and no one in the family knows I have it. Would you like to see it?"

I say, "Absolutely," and at the bank, I ask if our *MOSAIC: Jewish Life in Florida* project can borrow it for display in the traveling exhibition. She says "yes," and then in 1995, when I created the Jewish Museum of Florida on Miami Beach, I asked if she would donate it to the Collections. She said "yes." This is how the material evidence and collective historic memories of more than 250 years of Jewish life in Florida were retrieved—piece by piece.

Pocket watch with Hebrew numerals, owned by George Dzialynski, who was born and died in Jacksonville (1857–1937).

On the reverse is a bas-relief of Moses with the Ten Commandments. The family continues to live in Jacksonville and has seventy-five descendants in Florida, going into the eighth generation.

INTRODUCTION

Why This Book? Memory, Jews, and Stories

We Jews are a community by virtue of history memory.
We have been held together and upheld by common remembering.
—Martin Buber

Memory is life. Life is like a tapestry, woven from a sense of continuity with past generations and rewoven with our own experiences and memories.

Memory is retrieving history. History is more than names and dates. Rabbi Jacob Rader Marcus, founder of the American Jewish Archives, said, "History is a record of how people respond to their environment." History means to inquire about what is no longer, to study or find out—a narrative or story. The word *history* contains the word *story*. Jews are storytellers. We have a collective responsibility to tell the stories of the past to help ensure the future.

Scholar Rabbi Irving "Yitz" Greenberg, founding president of CLAL (the National Jewish Center for Learning and Leadership), taught me at a Young Leadership Retreat in Orlando in 1977, "If your memories are Jewish, you will be Jewish."

Stories engender or retrieve Jewish memories. ***In my book, I tell stories to preserve the memories and pass them on to the next generations to help ensure Jewish continuity.*** The stories enthuse us to take action in our own lives—to weave our own tapestries.

Who are the Jews? Jews are a people—a *family* of less than one-quarter of 1 percent of the world's population. I use the word *family* in my book more than five hundred times, more than any other word. A family is defined as having a common ancestor. The Jewish family descended from Sarah and Abraham about 4,000 years ago. They arrived in the land of Israel about 3,700 years ago. After the Romans took control there in 135 CE, Israel remained the spiritual homeland of the Jews. As a result of exile and expulsions, most Jews became a migratory people for 1,800 years until the modern State of Israel was founded in 1948.

One is born into the family or adopted through conversion. Like any family, there are rules or traditions to follow, some perhaps more than 3,000 years old. Through all the migrations, Jews have carried their traditions and passed them down through the generations—all the way to Florida more than 250 years ago.

Florida's greatest asset is its people, who for more than 500 years have been part of the flow of people arriving from all over the world and enriching the state. Throughout its history, Florida has served as a place of refuge, renewal, and rebirth—and a catalyst for innovation.

After discovery in 1513 and for the following 250 years, only Catholics could live in Florida. Jews joined other groups when they were allowed to settle in 1763. Florida's Jews overcame expulsions and exclusions and brought their visions of freedom and their creativity, leaving their footprints across the entire state. For the last 250-plus years, Jews have hugely influenced the shape and destiny of the Sunshine State. They have made contributions in every area of development—agriculture, business and industry, tourism, science, education, arts and culture, medicine, law, politics, sports, media, and more. At the same time, they have maintained their traditions and built institutions to help ensure Jewish continuity for future generations.

As of 2019 Florida is the third most populous state in the nation with about 21 million people. The state hosts the nation's third largest Jewish community, comprising about 3.4 percent of the total population or 714,000 people. From the state's beginning as "gentiles only," how did this happen?

The perception that Jews were late arrivals in Florida (think post–World War II Miami Beach!) parallels the belief that the Pilgrims from the *Mayflower* founded our nation in 1620. One-half century before the Pilgrims arrived, the Spanish were claiming sovereignty of the Florida colony of St. Augustine (1565), the oldest continental US city. Just as the British, French, and Dutch colonized the northeastern US, the Spanish colonized the southeast. And Jews, as *conversos*, might have been there!

We now know that Jews were in Florida, as Jews, 150 years before Miami Beach! Within these pages, you will meet some of those Jews who came to America and then chose to come to Florida.

You will be surprised and inspired by the contributions that Florida's Jews have made to effect change—to make the state, nation, and world better places.

How We Know

The grassroots project—*MOSAIC: Jewish Life in Florida* traveling exhibit. The research for the MOSAIC project helped propel the Florida Jewish community into the twenty-first century with the strength of knowledge of what came before. Until 1984 no one had comprehensively researched the hidden, rich Jewish history of Florida. There were no books on the broad subject: merely a paper written in 1955 about Greater Miami by Miami Beach Temple Emanu-El Rabbi Irving Lehrman, a paper written in 1956 by Jacksonville native and University of Florida professor of history Dr. Samuel Proctor, and a monograph written about south Florida in 1980 by Malvina W. and Seymour B. Liebman.

In 1984 a project team (comprised of Henry Green, Laura Hochman, Abe Gittelson, and me) was assembled to retrieve and record materials for a traveling exhibition called *MOSAIC: Jewish Life in Florida*. I was designated state coordinator to manage the research and train hundreds of volunteers in Florida communities to collect family photographs, documents, and artifacts and record hundreds of oral histories. I was also tasked with raising public and private funds to support the project. Our initial funding source was a grant from the Florida Humanities Council, and then continuing support was received from the State of Florida.

I am from West Virginia—and that turned out to be a good thing for getting our first line item in the 1987 Florida legislative budget. I found out that the chairman of appropriations was Representative Samuel P. Bell III from Daytona Beach. When I went to visit him to plead for funding for a statewide project about one ethnic group's history, he responded very enthusiastically. Sam Bell explained that when he was growing up as the son of a Methodist minister, he became friendly with a Jewish boy in his elementary school. Every day after classes ended, they visited his father in the church; got a *nosh* from his friend's *bubbe*, who lived across the street from the church; and then went to the nearby *shul* to play basketball in the church league. As he described the *shul* and its basketball court, I remarked that it sounded like my *shul* in Charleston, West Virginia. Sam Bell looked up from his desk and said, "I'm talking about B'nai Jacob Synagogue on Virginia Street."

I said, "That was my *shul*, and I was captain of the girls' basketball team!" Even more incredible, his young Jewish friend was my first husband! So that is how the MOSAIC project got its first state funding.

Retrieving Florida Jewish history was a perfect task for me—and became my passion. I live to learn something new every day. My children have always said I ask a lot of questions. I am curious about people's stories.

I had immersed myself in Jewish involvement within a misogynistic society. Throughout my life, I have been the first female to hold a great variety of positions after being repeatedly told, "Girls don't do this" or "Women have never done this before" or "Leadership is for men." Undeterred, I proceeded to become the president of everything in which I became involved, from youth groups to high school and university clubs and volunteer civic, Jewish, and activist groups and then as a professional.

In the early 1960s, when I was initiated into the adult Jewish communal service world in Orlando, an involved woman was recognized as "Mrs. husband's name." Inspired by the women's movement of the sixties, I questioned and challenged the male-only leadership custom and encouraged change. In the 1970s I was among the earliest women in the country to be a Jewish Federation president. When I attended national meetings, some men dismissively patted me on the head and said that I was confused: "You must be president of the Women's Division."

I transitioned from volunteer to professional in 1980, after my divorce, when I had to support my family and home. When hired for my first position in a nonprofit organization with an $18,000 annual salary, one of the male board members said publicly in a meeting, "That is a lot of money for a lady to make!"

Along my route, I was told time and time again that my goals could not be met, either because I was a female or because it had never been done before. Of course, this only reinforced my drive to succeed. I love the challenges of problem-solving and decision-making.

I've had role models along the way who motivated me to be the best I can be for women and the community. One example is former Israeli prime minister Golda Meir, whom I met shortly before she died in 1978. While serving on the first United Jewish Appeal (UJA) Young Women's Leadership Cabinet, I had an opportunity during a private meeting to ask Golda why she had gone to Palestine in 1921. She said, "I felt something was happening there, and I had to be a part of it. Jews have to help Jews—especially as Jewish women."

My journey to discover the Jewish history in Florida for a traveling exhibit and then create the JMOF had many doubters, but I knew it had to become a reality. The men in the field of American Jewish history had not taken Florida seriously, assuming we had no history. So I set out to change that. When I traveled alone around Florida in the 1980s—before the days of cell phones and laptop computers—to retrieve and document history and record stories—so many men told me that people would not talk to a woman about their lives or trust their precious family photographs to me.

Well, they did, and I learned that women should not take the word no personally and should keep up the struggle for whatever it is we want and what we know is the right thing to do—for ourselves, our families, our communities, and our people.

And how times have changed! Now women are identified by their own names (imagine that!) and achievements. Women can become executive directors and presidents of organizations—even rabbis and cantors! And these milestones are documented here throughout this history so future generations will have role models.

Ultimately, over eight years, I traveled more than 250,000 miles to thirty cities and rarely stayed in a hotel. I would get a lead, call someone in a community, and get an invitation to stay overnight—and to look at their family photograph albums, a great resource for documenting the story that was unfolding.

Asking questions is how I obtained the history: Who were the first Jews in your community? From where did they come? Why did they come to Florida? How did they make a living? What did they do to contribute to the community? How did they interact with the non-Jewish population? How did they maintain their Jewish traditions?

The stories flowed along with the material evidence that reflected a dynamic past of a proud immigrant people who came with nothing, worked hard, contributed and influenced much, and organized to retain the traditions of their heritage. Some did so with adaptations, and a few lost their past, but the culture survived and is thriving. This is the story of every American as each of us has immigrant origins—each family has experienced the acculturation process.

The Documentation Process

Marcia Jo Zerivitz creating a database to document the material evidence of the revealed history (on an Apple MacIntosh 512K computer), Orlando, 1987.

As I moved from community to community, I established volunteer task forces and worked from my outline of what we needed to tell the story. Each person's and each community's story became a part of the collective memory of the Florida Jewish experience. In Orlando, teen Hirsh Katzen taught me how to use the newly revealed Apple MacIntosh computer and set up a database. I entered each oral history, photograph, document, and artifact. With the entries, I could track the item and its date, description, community, source, and notes. This was before the days of Google and Wikipedia. This document became the basis for producing the traveling exhibit and was later used as the Collections inventory for the Jewish Museum of Florida–Florida International University (JMOF-FIU).

The Florida State Archives in Tallahassee made duplicate negatives (no digital at this date!) of the photographs. These are now also part of the JMOF's Collections and are available on the internet. In each community where we had a task force, we worked together to create an exhibit of that local history. At first these photographs and captions were simply on foam core, then we advanced to professionally fabricated modules that included artifacts. This process instilled a tremendous sense of pride and community as the local history emerged. *And I learned that* history *is* people.

Traveling Exhibit

***MOSAIC: Jewish Life in Florida* traveling exhibit, 1990.**

From this early collection, the team wrote an exhibit that was then designed and fabricated by museum professionals. The two-thousand-square-foot display opened in October 1990 in Miami at the Historical Museum of Southern Florida (now HistoryMiami) and traveled to ten other Florida cities (Orlando, Sarasota, Jacksonville, Tallahassee, Pensacola, Palm Beach, Fort Lauderdale, Tampa, Miami Beach, and Key West) all the way through 1994. Then the exhibit was displayed nationally (in Philadelphia and Washington). In each host community, educational programs focused on the pioneer immigrant experience and ethnic diversity. A multicultural curriculum was created and piloted in Miami-Dade County Public Schools; this curriculum is state endorsed and is now being used in both public and private schools throughout the state.

Birth of the Jewish Museum of Florida

As the exhibit traveled, enthusiasm mounted for a permanent museum that would continue to collect and mount exhibitions based on the Collections and that would relate to all ethnic groups. In 1992 I was selected as the founding executive director. A statewide board of directors was assembled, a strategic planning process executed with mission and vision statements and specific goals, and then a capital campaign planned and implemented. After considering several sites throughout the state, we selected a unique location at 301 Washington Avenue on Miami Beach because of its historical and cultural significance.

Congregation Beth Jacob, Miami Beach, 1940.

These buildings had been synagogues for the first Jewish congregation on Miami Beach (the first Orthodox one in the county). Because of antisemitic deed restrictions, when Jews began to settle on Miami Beach, the only area where they were *allowed* to live was south of Fifth Street. The structure on the left was built in 1929 and the one on the right in 1936 as a result of growth. These buildings at Third Street served as the centerpiece of Jewish life through the heyday from the 1950s through the 1970s.

Congregation Beth Jacob as restoration began to turn it into the Jewish Museum of Florida, 1992.

In the early 1980s, the neighborhood began to rapidly decline. The 1936 building was abandoned and fell into disrepair. MOSAIC Inc. arranged a long-term lease as the property at that time was not for sale. The structure, on the National Register of Historic Places, served as a synagogue for fifty years (1936–86). Designed by noted Art Deco architect Henry Hohauser, it featured a sloping floor, nearly eighty stained glass windows, a Moorish copper dome, Art Deco chandeliers, a marble *bimah*, and 7,200 square feet on three levels to house the museum, its Collections, and its administration. The museum raised the funds for the two-year adaptive reuse renovation (1993–95) with the assistance of the City of Miami Beach, the Miami-Dade County Cultural Affairs Council, the state of Florida legislature, and private and foundation funding. Ira D. Giller was the architect and contractor.

Rendering of the Jewish Museum of Florida after restoration of both buildings, Miami Beach, 2008.

The museum opened (in the building on the right) in April 1995. The restoration was the spark for the gentrification of the entire neighborhood and the designation of a historic area. The City of Miami Beach launched a streetscape project and spent millions of dollars on sewers, irrigation, paving, and landscaping with the museum as the centerpiece. This project may have been the first of its kind in the entire nation and provides a model for all ethnic groups to preserve their sites and cultural heritage.

As a result of its success, the museum outgrew its space for the Collections and areas to present more exhibitions. In 2005 the organization grasped the opportunity to purchase the three contiguous properties (the leased building on the right, the original 1929 synagogue [left], and the parking lot [not shown]) and began plans to expand. In 2007, after a restoration also completed by Ira D. Giller, the museum opened the second space, which added another seven thousand square feet. In 2008 the two historic buildings were connected with a glass enclosure to extend the space to fifteen thousand square feet and create a smooth transition between the former synagogues that house exhibitions.

Early in its history, the museum was awarded accreditation by the American Alliance of Museums, an honor achieved by only 5 percent of the nation's museums. We have earned many other recognition awards for our buildings as well as what we do in the buildings.

Collections of the Jewish Museum of Florida

The museum Collections are substantial in number, wide ranging in content, and geographically representative of all of Florida. The origin of the Collections is from the period during the 1980s when six thousand items were identified in Florida communities for consideration for the MOSAIC traveling exhibition. That exhibition contained more than five hundred photographs and two hundred artifacts that were on loan. When the decision was made to create a permanent museum, I contacted each lender about donating their items; most did.

The museum Collections draw crucial links between the social, political, economic, cultural, and religious aspects of Jewish life in Florida and the relationship of Jews to the dominant non-Jewish population. The Collections include materials pertaining to individuals, families, communities, organizations, and businesses and issues closely associated with the Florida Jewish population. These materials include photographs, oral histories, documents, ephemera, film and sound recordings, historic objects, religious objects, sculptures, textiles, works of art on paper, newspapers, and particulars used for research—and the restored 1929 and 1936 synagogues that now house the museum. The Collections dramatically reveal the propensity for ethnic stereotyping by illustrating the variety of political, economic, and religious trends within a single ethnic group that is geographically dispersed, and the Collections increase one's understanding of the practices and beliefs that separate Jews from other ethnic minorities.

To support the museum's mission of retrieving items for research, education, exhibitions, films, and publications, the Collections are inventoried according to themes: immigration, family, synagogue and institutions, community relations and responses to world events, and contributions to every area of development.

Museum Exhibitions

The core exhibit, *MOSAIC: Jewish Life in Florida*, is the original traveling exhibit, expanded and continuously updated as new items come into the Collections. The JMOF-FIU continues to create new exhibits on various topics related to Florida Jewish history and based on items in the Collections. Many of these original exhibits travel to other museums around the state and the nation—and even to Israel. In addition, temporary history and art exhibits are borrowed from outside sources. Permanent features include a timeline wall of Jewish history, a film depicting the Jewish history of Florida and the two building restorations, other films, and the Collections and Research Center.

The primary educational goal of the museum is to create an environment where young and old, residents and tourists can think, learn, absorb, and enjoy newfound or reaffirming information on the Jewish experience. Additionally, the museum encourages the discovery of how this history impacts and is impacted by the multicultural community, state, nation, and world.

Prior Publications

As the Jewish history of Florida was uncovered through the early and continuing research phases, I was engaged with producing exhibitions, articles, films, and publications. The books include *MOSAIC: Jewish Life in Florida*, a traveling exhibit catalog (with Henry Green), 1991; *Exploring Florida Jewish History: Family Activity Book*, a guide for multicultural students, 1998; the *Florida Jewish Heritage Trail*, a guide to 250 sites of Jewish historical significance in 44 cities (with Rachel Heimovics), Florida Department of State, 2000; two essays in *Jews of South Florida*, Brandeis University Press, 2005; *Jews of Greater Miami*, Arcadia Publishing, 2009; *Jewish Settlement in Florida*, a student curriculum; "Creating a Museum from a Grassroots Project," *Inspiring Action*, MuseumsEtc, Edinburgh, 2009; *Jews of Tampa* (with Rob Norman), Arcadia Publishing, 2013; and *Kehillah: A History of Jewish Life in Greater Orlando* (with Roz Fuchs), 2017.

I have explained the documentation process because it is *how* we know our *story* as reviewed in this book. Any ethnic group can emulate the process to help ensure its continuity by preserving its past to strengthen identity.

Photographs freeze a moment in history—they stay in your head and trigger their stories. I get asked all the time how I remember the names and dates of the people who comprise Florida Jewish history. Just like we collect images of our families and recall the memories attached to them, I recall the stories from the images I've collected—and I expect you will as well. I am optimistic that my passion for the images and their stories is contagious!

As you read, keep in mind that the 715 photographs I selected to illustrate the themes are a very small sampling of the Collections of tens of thousands held at the JMOF-FIU. The narrative is primarily drawn from responses to questions asked while recording more than 700 oral histories. This is our story—our collective historic memory.

PART 1

A Look at Early Florida Jewish History

From 1513 Through Statehood

Timeline of Florida Jewish History Created by Marcia Jo Zerivitz, LHD	
1513	Juan Ponce de León discovers Florida for Spain and only Catholics can live in Florida for the next 250 years.
1565	Jews as *conversos* are believed to be among the early settlers and soldiers of St. Augustine.
1763	England acquires Florida from Spain in the Treaty of Paris. For the first time, people other than Catholics—including Jews—are allowed. Alexander Solomons, Joseph D. Pallaccios, and Samuel Israel arrive in Pensacola as the first-known Jews to settle in Florida.
1769	Isaac Monsanto is expelled from New Orleans and settles in Pensacola.
1783	England returns Florida to Spain, which orders a census that reveals a Polish Jew David Moses is operating a hide store in St. Augustine. Needing settlers, Spain allows Jews to remain in Florida.
1820	Moses Elias Levy begins purchase of one hundred thousand acres in what is now St. Johns, Volusia, and Alachua Counties and organizes the first development corporation in Florida. In 1822 he builds Pilgrimage Plantation, a refuge for Jews that lasts until 1835. He publishes a plan to end slavery and also serves as the territory's first education commissioner.
1821	Lawyer Samuel Myers settles in Pensacola and becomes an alderman and an officer in the military. In 1822 his wife, Louisa Myers, gives birth to Virginia Myers, the first-known Jewish child born in Florida; the family relocates.
1836	West Point graduate Abraham C. Myers serves as Army quartermaster for the Second Seminole Indian War (1835–42). The City of Fort Myers is named to honor him.
1836	Raphael Jacob Moses opens a store in Tallahassee, later becomes a lawyer, and then practices in Apalachicola.
1837	David Levy Yulee, a son of Moses Elias Levy and considered the architect of Florida's statehood, is elected to the Florida Legislative Council (1837). He helps write Florida's Constitution (1838), is territorial delegate to the US Congress in 1841, is elected Florida's first US senator when Florida becomes the twenty-seventh state (1845), is the first person of Jewish ancestry to serve in the US Senate (1845–51 and 1855–61), and organizes the first cross-state railroad (1853). The town of Yulee (Nassau County) and Levy County honor his name.
1844	Emaline Miley settles in Tampa with husband and plants the first orange grove in area.

1850	Philip P. Dzialynski arrives in Jacksonville. His is the longest-known continuing Jewish family in Florida.
1856	Philip's sister, Helena D. Williams, gives birth in Jasper to Rachelle Williams, the first child born in Florida to a Jewish family (Dzialynski) that planted roots in the state and has continued to live here as Jews since 1850.
1857	The first Jewish cemetery in Florida is established in Jacksonville.
1857	George Dzialynski is the first boy in the Dzialynski family born in Florida (in Jacksonville).
1865	Floridian Jews serve in the Civil War. Judah P. Benjamin from Louisiana serves as attorney general, secretary of state, and secretary of war for the Confederacy (1861–65). At the end of the Civil War, he escapes from the Union Army by hiding in the Gamble mansion in Manatee County.
1869	Samuel Fleishman, longtime resident of Marianna, is murdered for giving credit in his store to freed slaves.
1871	Charles Slager serves as postmaster, sheriff, and tax collector of Hillsborough County.
1874	B'nai B'rith opens a chapter and becomes the first Jewish organization in Florida.
1875	Jacob R. Cohen helps write the charter for the town of Orlando and is elected an alderman. He later conducts the first statewide appeal for Jews in Palestine.
1876	Florida's oldest Jewish congregation, Temple Beth El, founded in Pensacola.
1879	Henry Brash elected mayor of Marianna, becoming the first known of nearly 200 Jewish mayors in Florida.
1880s	Jacksonville has the largest Jewish population in the state.
1880s	Morris Dzialynski of Jacksonville and Herman Glogowski of Tampa serve as mayors of their cities.
1880s	The earliest known Jewish school in Florida is established in Tallahassee.
1882	Temple Ahavath Chesed is founded in Jacksonville with Morris Dzialynski as president.
1884	Simon and Solomon Benjamin build Florida's first-known ice-making plant in Ocala.
1887	Congregation B'nai Zion founded in Key West with Morris Zion as president.
1888	United Hebrews of Ocala congregation is founded; its synagogue is the oldest extant in Florida.
1890	Dr. Louis Oppenheimer of Bartow establishes the local school system.

1891	A discriminatory peddler's tax is imposed in Key West, prompting most Jews to leave for Miami or Tampa.
1892	Jews settle in West Palm Beach, following the path of Henry Flagler's railroad to south Florida.
1895	Key West Jews raise funds for Cuban revolutionaries fighting for independence from Spain.
1896	The first permanent Jewish settlers arrive in the Miami area.
1897	Dr. Philip P. Phillips settles in Orlando, where he becomes the King of Citrus with an empire of five thousand acres.
1898	Gertrude Dzialynski Corbett is probably Florida's first woman lawyer admitted to the bar.
1900	There are six Jewish congregations in Florida.
1907	The first *brit milah* is held in Miami-Dade County (for Eddie Cohen, son of Ida and Isidor Cohen).
1910	Louis Brown is the first-known Jew to settle in Broward County.
1913	B'nai Zion is the first congregation in Miami-Dade County; it later becomes Beth David.
1913	The first Jews on Miami Beach are Jennie and Joe Weiss, who start Joe's Stone Crab Restaurant.
1931	The Brown family are the first-known Jews to settle in Boca Raton.
1933	David Sholtz of Daytona Beach begins his term as governor of Florida (1933–36).
1939	The German ocean liner *St. Louis* cruises off the coast of Florida before the US prevents European Jewish refugees from landing and forces their return to Europe, where 254 perish in the Holocaust.
1940s	Rear Admiral Ellis M. Zacharias of Jacksonville is the deputy chief of naval intelligence and conducts psychological warfare against the Japanese that leads to the US victory in the Pacific.
1943	Mitchell Wolfson serves as mayor of Miami Beach, the first of 17 Jewish mayors in that city. In 1949 he and Sidney Meyer start Florida's first TV station.
1953	Abe Aronovitz serves as mayor of Miami, the only Jew to serve in this office.
1957	Leonard and Julius Rosen develop Cape Coral in southwest Florida, a planned community with four hundred miles of canals.
1959	Approximately ten thousand Cuban Jews seek freedom in south Florida.

1960s	Jack and Jules Freeman plant the largest citrus grove in the world, covering twenty-four thousand acres (thirty-seven square miles) in Arcadia; they also develop San Carlos Park, a city in Lee County.
1966	The first US postage stamp of a living person is issued with the image of master clown Lou Jacobs of Sarasota.
1968	Marshall Warren Nirenberg of Orlando and a graduate of the University of Florida is awarded the Nobel Prize in Physiology or Medicine for deciphering the genetic code.
1970	Burton Young of Miami is elected the first Jewish president of the Florida Bar.
1975	Richard Stone of Miami Beach begins his term as a US Senator (1975–80), the second Florida Jew to hold this office.
1975	Arthur J. England of Miami begins his term as a justice on Florida's Supreme Court (1975–81); he becomes chief justice in 1978. More than 250 Jews have served as judges in Florida.
1976	Dr. Richard Hodes of Tampa is elected the first Jewish president of the Florida Medical Association.
1978	Isaac Bashevis Singer of Miami Beach is awarded the Nobel Prize in Literature.
1981	Raymond Ehrlich of Jacksonville begins his term on Florida's Supreme Court (1981–91); he becomes chief justice in 1988.
1984	The MOSAIC Inc. project is created to document Florida's Jewish history; the traveling exhibit evolves into the Jewish Museum of Florida.
1987	Gerald Kogan of Miami begins his term as a justice on Florida's Supreme Court (1987–98); he becomes chief justice in 1996.
1990	After 8 years of statewide research on 250-plus years of hidden Florida Jewish history, the traveling exhibit *MOSAIC: Jewish Life in Florida* begins its tour to 13 cities.
1990	Gwen Margolis of Miami becomes the first female Florida Senate president, the first in the nation.
1994	Florida is one of first states to mandate Holocaust education.
1995	Jewish Museum of Florida opens in the restored Beth Jacob Synagogue on South Beach.
1995	Miami Beach High School graduate Robert Rubin is appointed the seventieth secretary of the US treasury.
1997	Barbara Pariente of West Palm Beach becomes the second woman and first Jewish woman appointed to the Florida Supreme Court (1997–2019); she becomes chief justice in 2004.

2000	Susan and Stanley Rosenblatt of Miami win a $145 billion tobacco verdict, the largest civil damage award in US history.
2003	Governor Jeb Bush signs a bill designating each January as Florida Jewish History Month.
2004	Debbie Wasserman Schultz of Broward County is elected to the US Congress, the first Jewish woman to represent Florida.
2006	President George W. Bush signs a proclamation designating each May as Jewish American Heritage Month to honor contributions by American Jews to our nation. The Jewish Museum of Florida was the birthplace of this legislation, with the congressional effort led by Rep. Debbie Wasserman Schultz.
2012	The Jewish Museum of Florida becomes part of Florida International University (JMOF-FIU).
2012	Miami Beach High School graduate and Miami Dolphins football team owner Stephen Ross begins $25 billion Hudson Yards project in Manhattan.
2014	Journalist Steven Sotloff of Miami is murdered in Syria by the Islamic State of Iraq and Syria (ISIS).
2017	Using controlled-release fertilizer developed by Sarasota's Ed Rosenthal and the National Aeronautics and Space Administration (NASA), the first crop of lettuce is grown in space and consumed by astronauts.
2018	The St. Augustine Jewish Historical Society convenes the *Conversos* Conference.
2018	Tampa Bay Lightning hockey team owner Jeffrey Vinik begins a $3 billion, 52-acre project in Tampa with Cascade Investment (Bill Gates) to be completed in 2027; if successful, it will be the world's first WELL-certified community.
2018	Holocaust survivor Tibor Hollo opens the tallest building in Florida, eighty-five stories in Miami.
2018	David Wolkowsky donates his fourteen-acre Ballast Key property to the US Fish and Wildlife Service.
2019	Miami native Nikki Fried is elected commissioner of the Department of Agriculture and Consumer Services, the sixth Jewish member over the history of the Florida Cabinet.
2019	Robert Luck of Miami begins his term on Florida's Supreme Court.

Engraving of Juan Ponce de León arriving in Florida, 1513.
Tampa-Hillsborough County Public Library System.

The authoritative credit for finding Florida goes to Ponce de León because his voyages were made under official Spanish auspices, recorded, and recognized. He first reached the Florida coast, probably between today's Daytona Beach and Melbourne, on April 2, 1513; found the natives hostile; and named the new land La Florida after *Pascua Florida*, the Feast of Flowers at Easter time. On his second trip in 1521, he reached Tampa Bay.

Since this discovery was made by Spain during the Inquisition, only Catholics were allowed to settle in Florida for the next 250 years.

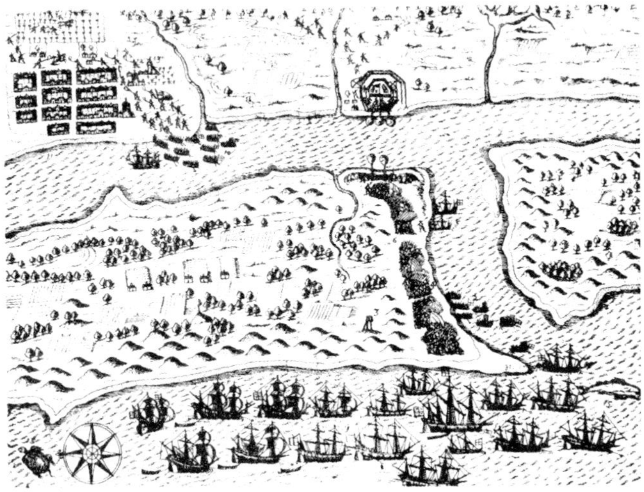

Drawing of St. Augustine Harbor, Florida, 1565. *Charlton W. Tebeau,* A History of Florida, *University of Miami Press, 1971.*

The nation's first permanent settlement was St. Augustine in 1565. In 1987 I met with Dr. Eugene Lyon, then the director of the St. Augustine Foundation, who shared microfilm containing the names of possibly Spanish Jewish people on lists of soldiers and settlers in Spanish Florida in the sixteenth century. He suggested that it was possible that these were *conversos.*

Following this lead from Dr. Lyon, I made many attempts with scholars to follow up on the hypothesis that the earliest Jews to land in what became the United States might have done so in St. Augustine in the sixteenth century—actually 89 years before the landing in New Amsterdam in 1654, the commonly accepted date of the first arrival of Jews, and 198 years before the first record of Jewish life in Florida.

If documented, this would rewrite American Jewish history.

Just as the settlement of St. Augustine in 1565 predates the first permanent English settlement of Jamestown, Virginia, in 1607, if *conversos* sailed with Ponce de León in 1513 (just as we know *conversos* sailed with Columbus in 1492 to escape the Inquisition) or arrived with Spanish admiral Pedro Menéndez de Aviles in 1565, they would predate the twenty-three Jews who came to New Amsterdam (which became New York) in 1654. In fact, why is the focus always New York? *Conversos* have been documented in New Mexico in the late 1570s, and historians in Texas say that *conversos* have been there since 1590. They may have also been in Florida even earlier. Time and again I got no response to my pleas.

Then, in 2015, with the celebration of the 450th anniversary of the founding of St. Augustine, I asked, "*Were Jews, as* conversos, *present at the founding of St. Augustine?*" By this time, there was a response. Rabbi Merrill Shapiro, who I'd known when we both lived in Orlando, had organized the St. Augustine Jewish Historical Society (SAJHS) in 2011 to research this very question!

This is what Rabbi Shapiro and the SAJHS have revealed through their research and collaboration with scholars.

St. Augustine was founded by Pedro Menendez de Aviles on September 8, 1565. ***There are six arguments, bolstered by circumstantial evidence,***

for the presence of conversos in St. Augustine during the first Spanish colonial period from 1565 to February 10, 1763—with the signing of the Treaty of Paris: (1) Pedro Menendez's taking on of 150–300 "undocumented" passengers before leaving the waters of Cadiz, Spain; (2) the dates of the Menendez sighting of land and the landing/claiming of Florida for Spain; (3) the choice of "Nombre de Dios" for the name for St. Augustine's Mission; (4) the directional orientation of graves found at Mission Nombre de Dios; (5) the presence of Chief Harbor Pilot Antonio Martinez Carvajal in 1577–78; and (6) the presence of notary Bernardo Nieto de Carvajal beginning in 1690.

Such endeavors were tightly controlled by the royal Casa de Contratacion at Seville, which meant that the number, names, and suitability of all the passengers were verified in part to guarantee compliance with all applicable laws and to assure that all taxes were properly remitted to the Crown. Prominent among those applicable laws was the decree forbidding travel to the New World by those who did not meet the requirements of Limpieza de Sangre, "Purity of Blood" statutes that forbid certain activities by those who had Jewish or Moorish ancestors.

Setting sail on June 27, 1565, the fleet soon encountered "contrary winds" and Menendez's flagship *Pelayo,* found anchored off Fort San Sebastian, the furthest point of the peninsula of Cadiz. It was reported that overnight an additional 150–300 passengers were taken on board before the ship and its fleet set sail across the Atlantic. The theory is that these passengers could not have met the requirements of Limpieza de Sangre because they were the descendants of Jews, perhaps even practicing Judaism in secret.

Hurricanes, storms, the loss of ships, and landings in Hispaniola and Puerto Rico may have meant these 150–300 additional passengers never made it to Florida. But the fleet did, sighting land on August 28, 1565, which marked the feast of St. Augustine of Hippo. Menendez named the land he saw "St. Augustin" but remained at sea, landing at St. Augustine on September 8, 1565.

Dr. Eugene Lyon, expert on the Menendez expedition and the founding of St. Augustine, is at a loss to explain why it took ten days to sail thirty-eight miles south from the May River to St. Augustine. However, recognizing that the dates provided belong to the Julian calendar, we must add ten or eleven days to transpose them into the Gregorian calendar that is now in use. Doing so demonstrates that St. Augustine was first sighted by Menendez on the First Day of Rosh Hashanah, the Jewish New Year. The fleet remained at sea and only came ashore on the day after Yom Kippur, the Day of Atonement. This has been regarded as strong evidence of some sort of Jewish influence over the founding of St. Augustine.

Only one of the sixty-eight Spanish missions in Florida stands out in a study of their names: Nombre de Dios established on September 8, 1565, at St. Augustine. All the others were named for saints or events in the life of Jesus. It has been suggested that the mission was named for the ancient ritual of Yom Kippur, the Day of Atonement during which the high priest in Jerusalem pronounced the ineffable "Name of God" or "Nombre de Dios."

In 1934 a gardener planting hedges on the property of Nombre de Dios found human remains. The Smithsonian Institution was called in, and a great many graves of Native Americans were found in the area. Most unusual in the experience of the Smithsonian and later researchers was the presence of two sets of graves. In the first set, the graves were oriented with the feet toward the cross on the altar of the church that stood in the midst of the cemetery so that during the Second Coming, the dead could rise from their graves and ascend the altar to the cross. A second set, most unusually, was oriented with the feet facing toward the east.

The Native Americans were most certainly not members of the so-called ten lost tribes of Israel. But the early Spanish believed that they were! It is suggested that the burial orientation, still a puzzle to researchers, was arranged by someone who knew that the Natives were actually descendants of the ten lost tribes and also knew that the proper way of Jewish burial was to orient the feet of the dead toward Jerusalem. That someone may well have been an early descendant of Jews living in St. Augustine in the last half of the sixteenth century.

Antonio Martinez Carvajal was the well-respected harbor pilot in St. Augustine, and his name appears on musters during 1577 and 1578. A copy of his letter to King Philip II asking for reimbursement of expenses as the harbor pilot in St. Augustine during this period is in the hands of the University of Florida Libraries. The Carvajal family in the New World was known to be of *conversos* descent.

The family of Luis de Carvajal, viceroy of New Spain, is well documented. They ran afoul of the Inquisition authorities, and the viceroy's sister was burned at the stake for practicing Judaism, burned while her brother, Luis, watched from the jail cell where he died a year later. While viceroy, Carvajal was most interested in developing the ports of the Spanish colonies, particularly as shipments of New World silver back to Spain became more numerous. Nepotism was common at the time. Researchers continue to work to link harbor pilot Antonio Martinez Carvajal with the family of the viceroy and thus make certain that he was of Jewish descent and living in St. Augustine during 1577 and 1578.

Taken individually, these suggestions of a Jewish or *conversos* presence in St. Augustine may be persuasive. But taken as a group, they bolster the claim that Jews first came ashore in what would be the United States of America at St. Augustine, Florida.

TRAITÉ DE PAIX
ENTRE
LE ROI,
LE ROI D'ESPAGNE
ET
LE ROI DE LA GRANDE-BRETAGNE,
Conclu à Paris le 10 Février 1763.
AVEC
L'ACCESSION DU ROI DE PORTUGAL.

A PARIS,
DE L'IMPRIMERIE ROYALE.
M. DCCLXIII.

Treaty of Paris, 1763. *Office of the Historian, Bureau of Public Affairs, United States Department of State, "Milestones: 1750–75."*

What we do know is that in 1763 (on February 10) the Treaty of Paris was signed between Britain, France, and Spain following the Seven Years' or French and Indian War, the final phase of a century-long Anglo-French struggle for colonial and commercial supremacy that led to our Revolutionary War.

On July 4, 2018, I visited the new Museum of the American Revolution in Philadelphia. The very first exhibit text panel stated, "After the treaty ending the Seven Years' War in 1763, Britain controlled over 20 colonies and provinces in North America…including lands in Florida. The people on these lands now found themselves under British rule."

Important to our story is that when Spain ceded Florida to Britain, people other than Catholics could finally settle there, including Jews. The French had turned over Louisiana to Spain the year before, and some Jews who feared Spanish discrimination polices moved from New Orleans to Pensacola in West Florida.

The immigration pattern of settlement for Jews in Florida follows that of Jews in America in general. The earliest were Sephardim (originated in Spain and Portugal), then Ashkenazim (from central and eastern

Europe) such as Prussian, German, and Polish Jews. Then there were Russian Jews followed by Jews from Cuba and Latin American countries, Holocaust survivors, and those from Israel, France, and other places in the world. During the twenty-first century, Jews have continued to settle in Florida, especially coming from places where their economic and religious lives are challenged.

Rabbi Jacob Rader Marcus, an inspiration for all those who research America's Jews, made an observation decades ago that applies to all the waves of immigration, including to Florida. "The American Jew has never been obscure. Ever since the days of their first arrivals, the 'high visibility' of Jewish women and men has been 'palpable.' They have always done business on Main Street." They share with other groups a wide diversity of roles—as farmer, rancher, peddler, merchant, educator, entrepreneur, policeman, baker, banker, scientist, architect, developer, professional, soldier and politician and Supreme Court justice defending democracy, Nobel prize recipient, builder of the cultural arts and sports, and supporter of civil and human rights, among others.

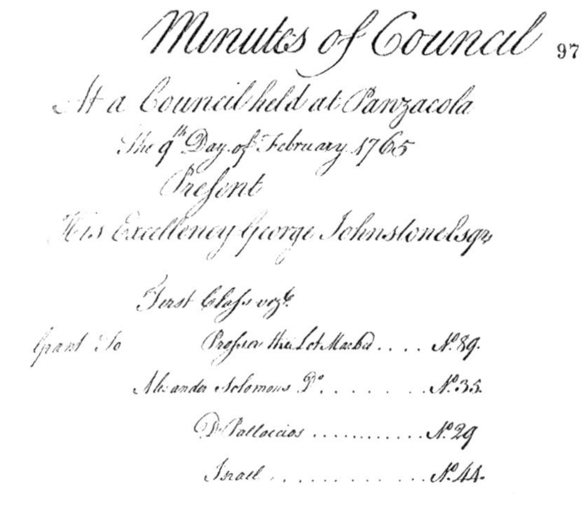
Minutes of Council 97
At a Council held at Panzacola
The 9th Day of February 1765
Present
His Excellency George Johnstone Esqr
First Class vizt
Grant To Professor the Sol Macbd .... No 89
Alexander Solomons Do ...... No 35
D. Pallacios .... No 29
Israel .... No 44

West Florida (Pensacola) Council Minutes, document indicating the land plat numbers purchased by the three first-known Jewish landowners in Florida, 1765. *The University of West Florida Historic Trust.*

Florida's earliest Jews (who could identify as Jews) arrived in Pensacola in 1763, when about 2 million people lived in the 13 colonies, including about 17,300 in Florida. Alexander Solomons, Joseph D. Pallaccios, and Samuel Israel bought property and stores. They sold wood and other goods to the British and settlers, both locally and to Jews in other southern colonies. Soon others joined them, including Isaac Mendes of Jamaica who arrived in 1766 and Samuel Judah in 1767.

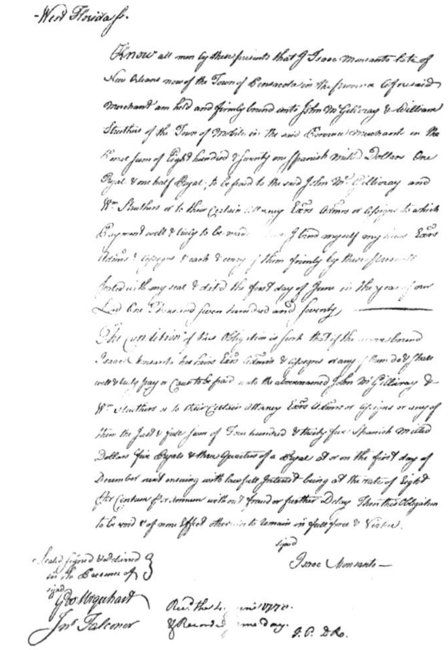

Loan document for Isaac Monsanto to purchase property in Pensacola, 1770. *The University of West Florida Historic Trust.*

Jews were expelled from New Orleans because France turned Louisiana over to the Spanish. Fleeing discriminatory religious laws, some joined other Jews already in Pensacola.

"They are to leave this province…before the end of the next month, the Jew Monsanto, for the reason that [he is] undesirable on account of the nature of [his] business and of the religion [he] profess[es]." Thus Isaac Monsanto, the earliest-known Jew in New Orleans, a slave dealer and wealthy merchant, was expelled by the Spanish governor in 1769 and settled in Pensacola. When Monsanto Company was founded in 1901, the founder chose the maiden name of his wife, a descendant of this Monsanto family.

There appears never to have been enough Jews in Florida during this period to form any religious organization. The economic frontier shifted frequently, and colonial Jews were constantly on the move.

In 1783 Florida reverted to Spain. During this second period, the Spanish did not insist on conversion to Catholicism as they encouraged settlement. Some Jews feared the climate and fled, and others continued to migrate to Florida. There were Jews in St. Augustine and Tallahassee. Jewish life between 1763 and 1821 is difficult to trace because the small population left no known records.

In 1821 the American government purchased Florida from Spain and Florida became a US territory. About 66,000 square miles in land mass, Florida is surrounded by water on three sides and rich in natural resources. Before air-conditioning became popular in homes post–World War II, it was very inhospitable due to the climate and mosquitos—and settlement was slow.

Modern rendering—based on Moses Levy's written instructions to his carpenter—of his house on Pilgrimage Plantation in Micanopy, 1822–35, 2002. *Drawing by Chris Monaco.*

Dr. Samuel Proctor, esteemed professor of history at the University of Florida for more than fifty years and the first University of Florida historian and archivist, told me, "by far, the most important Jewish personage to live in Florida during the territorial period was Moses Elias Levy."

An Orthodox Jew, Moses Elias Levy (1782–1854) took advantage of development opportunities in the new territory of Florida. According to Chris Monaco, author of *Moses Levy of Florida*, the Sephardic Abenyule family migrated to Morocco following the 1492 Spanish Inquisition. There, the name was translated to ibn Yulee. Moses was born in Morocco to Rachel and Eliahu Ha-Levi ibn Yulee, a government minister and royal merchant there. When the Moroccan sultan died in 1790 and the successor monarch turned against the Jews, the family fled to British Gibraltar, where the family assumed the name of Levy. Around 1800 Moses migrated to St. Thomas. There he married Hannah Abendanone (1803), and they had two sons and two daughters. Moses joined a relative of his wife, Philip Benjamin, in making a provisions company called Levy & Benjamin in Charlotte Amalie. As businesses grew, Levy made a fortune in the lumber exporting business, divorced his wife in 1815, and then moved first to Puerto Rico and then to Cuba. He became a contractor to the Spanish government, furnishing army supplies and lumber, and became interested in Florida.

Moses Levy was progressive, anti-assimilation, an advocate of the proto–Reform Judaism of the *Haskalah* (the Jewish enlightenment movement) and Bible fundamentalism (literal interpretation).

By 1820 Moses Levy organized the Florida Association, the first development corporation in Florida, and started buying Florida land (nearly one hundred thousand acres, averaging seventy-three cents an acre) in what are now Alachua, St. Johns, and Volusia Counties. His attorney was Alexander Hamilton Jr., the son of one of America's founding fathers and the US attorney for east Florida at that time. Levy became one of Florida's largest landowners. Near the end of his life, even after liquidating assets to pay debts, he still owned about seventy thousand acres in Orange, Clay, Alachua, Marion, Volusia, and Sumter Counties. Throughout his life, Levy literally observed the kosher laws and other limitations just as they were written in the Torah. He continually sought to improve conditions for Jews throughout the world. Moses Levy died in 1854 at the White Sulphur Springs resort in West Virginia and is probably buried on the grounds of the present-day Greenbrier resort—another West Virginia connection!

Etchings of what Moses Levy's sugarcane fields and mill could have resembled.

On May 4, 1822, nearly two months after he received his US citizenship, Moses Levy arrived in St.

Augustine on a schooner that was laden with Cuban sugarcane. He also brought tropical fruits, roots, and seeds to start his plantation.

That same year, he founded Pilgrimage Plantation, America's first Jewish communitarian settlement, in Micanopy, just south of Gainesville and the first distinct US town in the Florida Territory. Levy's one thousand acres were designated a refuge for European Jews fleeing the pogroms and restrictions of the post-Napoleonic era. It resembled a later *kibbutz*, where everyone worked the land and studied Hebrew.

I do get asked if Moses Levy had slaves. He was a vigorous advocate for the gradual abolition of slavery and the education and humane treatment of enslaved people—blacks and Jews. In his book, *Moses Levy of Florida*, Chris Monaco writes, "The number of slaves at Pilgrimage fluctuated from a low of ten to a high mark of 31—the total Levy held when he divested himself of all his slaves in 1839." Levy applied laws from the Hebrew Bible and published *Plan for the Abolition of Slavery* in London in 1828. He believed that slave families should be kept together and that children of slaves should be free at the age of twenty-one after they had completed a basic education with agricultural training. His ideas of abolition, if known, would have been threatening in the territory.

Frederick S. Warburg, of the German Jewish banking family, was Levy's partner and European recruiting agent and became a colonist at Pilgrimage himself. In addition to his home, Levy built houses for the settlers (who originally included twenty-three Jews and later more), a sugar mill, sawmill, cornmill, stable, and blacksmith shop.

Lake Wauburg, on the edge of Paynes Prairie in central Alachua County and within the original boundaries of Moses Levy's plantation, is the (misspelled) named for Warburg. Since 1918 the University of Florida has been operating it as a student and faculty recreational center.

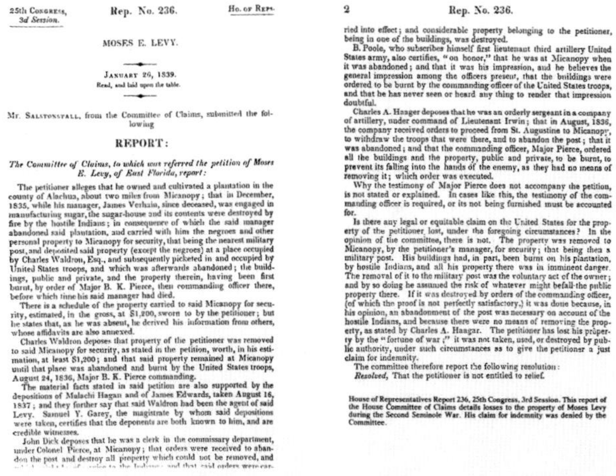

25th Congress, 3d Session. | Rep. No. 236. | Ho. of Reps.

MOSES E. LEVY.

January 26, 1839.
Read, and laid upon the table.

Mr. Saltonstall, from the Committee of Claims, submitted the following

REPORT:

The Committee of Claims, to which was referred the petition of Moses E. Levy, of East Florida, report:

The petitioner alleges that he owned and cultivated a plantation in the county of Alachua, about two miles from Micanopy; that in December, 1835, while his manager, James Verhain, since deceased, was engaged in manufacturing sugar, the sugar-house and its contents were destroyed by fire by the hostile Indians; in consequence of which the said manager abandoned said plantation, and carried with him the negroes and other personal property to Micanopy for security, that being the nearest military post, and deposited said property (except the negroes) at a place occupied by Charles Waldron, Esq., and subsequently picketed in and occupied by United States troops, and which was afterwards abandoned; the buildings, public and private, and the property therein, having been first burnt, by order of Major B. K. Pierce, then commanding officer there, before which time his said manager had died.

There is a schedule of the property carried to said Micanopy for security, estimated, in the gross, at $1,200, sworn to by the petitioner; but he states that, as he was absent, he derived his information from others, whose affidavits are also annexed.

Charles Waldron deposes that property of the petitioner was removed to said Micanopy for security, as stated in the petition, worth, in his estimation, at least $1,200; and that said property remained at Micanopy until that place was abandoned and burnt by the United States troops, August 24, 1836, Major B. K. Pierce commanding.

The material facts stated in said petition are also supported by the depositions of Malachi Hagan and of James Edwards, taken August 16, 1837; and they further say that said Waldron had been the agent of said Levy. Samuel Y. Garey, the magistrate by whom said depositions were taken, certifies that the deponents are both known to him, and are credible witnesses.

John Dick deposes that he was a clerk in the commissary department, under Colonel Pierce, at Micanopy; that orders were received to abandon the post and destroy all property which could not be removed, and

2 | Rep. No. 236.

ried into effect; and considerable property belonging to the petitioner, being in one of the buildings, was destroyed.

B. Poole, who subscribes himself first lieutenant third artillery United States army, also certifies, "on honor," that he was at Micanopy when it was abandoned; and that it was his impression, and he believes the general impression among the officers present, that the buildings were ordered to be burnt by the commanding officer of the United States troops, and that he has never seen or heard any thing to render that impression doubtful.

Charles A. Haager deposes that he was an orderly sergeant in a company of artillery, under command of Lieutenant Irwin; that in August, 1836, the company received orders to proceed from St. Augustine to Micanopy, to withdraw the troops that were there, and to abandon the post; that it was abandoned; and that the commanding officer, Major Pierce, ordered all the buildings and the property, public and private, to be burnt, to prevent its falling into the hands of the enemy, as they had no means of removing it; which order was executed.

Why the testimony of Major Pierce does not accompany the petition, is not stated or explained. In cases like this, the testimony of the commanding officer is required, or its not being furnished must be accounted for.

Is there any legal or equitable claim on the United States for the property of the petitioner lost, under the foregoing circumstances? In the opinion of the committee, there is not. The property was removed to Micanopy, by the petitioner's manager, for security; that being then a military post. His buildings had, in part, been burnt on his plantation, by hostile Indians, and all his property there was in imminent danger. The removal of it to the military post was the voluntary act of the owner; and by so doing he assumed the risk of whatever might befall the public property there. If it was destroyed by orders of the commanding officer, (of which the proof is not perfectly satisfactory,) it was done because, in his opinion, an abandonment of the post was necessary on account of the hostile Indians, and because there were no means of removing the property, as stated by Charles A. Haagar. The petitioner has lost his property by the "fortune of war;" it was not taken, used, or destroyed by public authority, under such circumstances as to give the petitioner a just claim for indemnity.

The committee therefore report the following resolution:

Resolved, That the petitioner is not entitled to relief.

House of Representatives Report 236, 25th Congress, 3rd Session. This report of the House Committee of Claims details losses to the property of Moses Levy during the Second Seminole War. His claim for indemnity was denied by the Committee.

US House of Representatives Report No. 236, 25th Congress, 3rd session, regarding Moses Levy's property losses during the Second Seminole War, 1839.

During the Second Seminole War (1835–42), Pilgrimage Plantation stood in the direct line of fire between opposing Native American tribes and US Army troops and was burned to the ground in 1835. This report of the US House Committee of Claims details losses to the property of Moses Levy. The committee denied his claim for compensation.

The plantation had been a continuing challenge, mostly due to its hostile, remote location. As prominent American Jewish educator and philanthropist Rebecca Gratz noted in an 1820s letter, "me thinks I would place foreigners in a more interior situation." Levy, reflecting on the collapse of his dream, said, "It is not easy to transform old clothes men into practical farmers."

Moses Levy, a proponent for free education in Florida and a charter officer of the Florida Education Society, helped establish Florida's earliest free public school, was the territory's first education commissioner, and served on a legislative committee investigating the establishment of the University of Florida.

He was a social activist and also played a vital role in the economic development of the area. In 2016 the Florida Department of State placed a historical roadside marker in Micanopy to honor his contributions in transforming Micanopy from a small trading post to a bustling town.

With the presence of the University of Florida, the area continues to be a hotbed of progressive thought and research. Levy aimed to bring European Jews to the swamps of northern Florida to escape antisemitism, and the university now boasts one of the nation's largest Jewish student bodies of any public institution.

It is noteworthy that the sons of relatives by marriage, David Levy Yulee and Judah Philip Benjamin, both became US Senators in the mid-1800s.

David Levy Yulee, first US Senator from Florida, architect of Florida statehood, and first US Senator of Jewish ancestry, Tallahassee, 1845.

Moses Levy's second son, David Levy (1810–86), moved to his father's Pilgrimage Plantation when he was seventeen years old. He helped run the operation for four years, then left to apprentice with a lawyer in Tallahassee, becoming a lawyer in 1836. He became heavily involved in politics through his roles as landowner, lawyer, and segregationist, the latter a cause of his estrangement from his father. His reputation as an orator and arbiter helped him get elected from St. Johns County to the Legislative Council of Florida in 1837. In 1838 he was a representative to the convention that framed Florida's constitution. In 1843 he was elected a Democratic territorial delegate to the US Congress, persuaded Floridians of the advantages of land grants, and worked incessantly—and successfully—to get Florida admitted to the Union as the twenty-seventh state.

In 1845 David Levy was chosen US Senator with less than 100 Jews within a state population of 66,500. It is important to note that he was the first person of Jewish ancestry in the US Senate, serving eight years before Judah P. Benjamin. In 1846 he legally added his family's Moroccan Yulee surname. Some think this was because Yulee sounded less Jewish than Levy, but in Washington, he was referred to as "the alien Jew delegate from Florida." Throughout his political career, he represented the views of the white, Southern, agricultural plantation system, first against the Seminole Indians and then against the Union.

In 1846 Yulee married Nannie Wickliffe, daughter of a former Kentucky governor. He bought five thousand acres near the mouth of the Homosassa River in Citrus County near the Gulf of Mexico for their home and established a plantation called Margarita. Sugarcane, cotton, and citrus were grown on the plantation, which operated for thirteen years with about one thousand slaves.

When I lecture, sometimes the question arises as to whether David Levy Yulee converted to Christianity. Samuel Proctor was emphatic that Yulee never converted. I have seen no documentation of Yulee converting from Judaism, but he and Nannie did raise their children as Christians. He had not converted when he was a politician (1837–61). There is factual evidence that he had not been baptized as late as 1872 from a letter his wife wrote to him on December 4 imploring him to be baptized along with their eldest son. This letter is in the David Levy Yulee Papers at the George A. Smathers Libraries, Department of Special Collections at the University of Florida. According to the *Jewish Floridian* dated June 24, 1932, Yulee remained and died a Jew.

Florida Railroad built by the "father of Florida's railroads" US Senator David Levy Yulee's company, 1861.

Senator Yulee had a great impact on Florida politically and economically. During the antebellum period, Yulee took advantage of land grants and the sale of stock to build Florida's first cross-state railroad. On March 1, 1861, his train left Fernandina on the east coast at 7:15 a.m. and reached the outskirts of Cedar Key on the west coast at 4:00 p.m., with eight stops in between. The railway was successful in transferring freight brought from Europe to the Gulf of Mexico in a more cost effective and safer route than water transport.

Yulee resigned from the US Senate when Florida seceded from the Union in early 1861. During the Civil War, Union forces burned down Yulee's Homosassa plantation (1864), and then his railroad lay in ruins. The family moved to another of his plantations, Cotton Wood, near Archer, a town he named and one of his railroad stops. Yulee had been close to Confederate president Jefferson Davis. Upon the fall of the Confederacy on May 22, 1865, some personal baggage of Jefferson Davis reached Cotton Wood. There is a legend that part of the Confederate treasury, under armed guard, also reached Cotton Wood. A soldier's letter indicates a discussion among the troops as to the distribution of the gold. One of Yulee's sons Charles Wickliffe Yulee wrote in an article of the 1909 *Florida Historical Magazine* (pages 29 and 30) that he buried two chests in a stable for his mother. Another historical mystery—what happened to the Confederate gold?

Three days after the arrival of the baggage, David Levy Yulee was imprisoned for nine months by federal troops for his support of the Confederacy. He rebuilt his railroad, its operation continuing until the 1930s. Nannie died in 1885, only two months after completion of their mansion in Washington, DC. David's spirit was broken, and he died the next year.

Florida's Levy County, the town of Yulee (in Nassau County near Jacksonville) and the Yulee Sugar Mill Ruins State Historic Site and Park in Homosassa are among the places in Florida named for him. The town of Fernandina Beach has a statue of Yulee. One of the Liberty ships built during World War II, the *David L. Yulee*, is named in his honor. Florida's Department of State included Yulee in the Great Floridians 2000 Program.

Judah P. Benjamin and the Florida connection: Gamble Mansion, Ellenton, 1865.

Representing Louisiana, Senator Benjamin served in the US Senate (1853–61) where his cousin David Levy Yulee preceded him there representing Florida. Benjamin then served the Confederacy as the secretary of war and state. Escaping retribution following the Civil War when a $50,000 reward was offered for his capture, Judah P. Benjamin disguised himself as a farmer seeking land and traveled south in a horse cart, arriving in May 1865 at the Gamble Mansion in Ellenton. According to Lillie McDuffee in the *Lures of Manatee*, Captain Archibald McNeill gave him "the best bedchamber, the large front room on the second story." From there, he watched for federal troops, and then a former Egmont Key lighthouse keeper helped him escape to the Bahamas, with some close calls to being identified. He eventually arrived in England (August 30, 1865), where he worked as a barrister (lawyer) for the next sixteen years. The Judah P. Benjamin Chapter of the United Daughters of the Confederacy rescued the Gamble Mansion from decay in 1923. A marker was placed (in 1942) in Sarasota noting his escape from federal forces.

Abraham Charles Myers, chief quartermaster during the Second Seminole War, 1835–42. *Fort Myers Historical Museum.*

Of interest to Florida Jewish history during this early period is Abraham Charles Myers (1811–89). He was born in South Carolina, a great-grandson of Moses Cohen, the first rabbi in Charleston. In 1833 he graduated from West Point. During Florida's Second Seminole War, as a 2nd lieutenant, he engaged in battle with the Seminole Indians. In 1849 he was made chief quartermaster of the Department of Florida and was stationed at Fort Brooke in Tampa with General David Emanuel Twiggs.

Myers became General Twigg's son-in-law in 1853 when he married Marion Twiggs. General Twiggs ordered a new fort to be built in southwest Florida on the Caloosa River. To honor Abraham Myers and please his daughter, he named it Fort Myers. The fort was abandoned in 1858 and reoccupied by federal troops from 1863–65. The southernmost battle of the Civil War occurred across the river in 1865 and is reenacted annually at the North Fort Myers Cracker Festival. The fort itself was disassembled and some of the wood used in construction of the first buildings in what would become the city of Fort Myers. A wall display at the Fort Myers Historical Museum relates the story of Abraham and Marion Myers.

Samuel Proctor estimated that the entire Jewish population of Florida at the time of the Civil War was about two hundred individuals. Florida's population was growing, attracted by fertile soil for cotton and tobacco, pasture for cattle, and trees for lumbering. The port cities developed—Jacksonville and Fernandina on the east coast and Apalachicola and Pensacola on the west coast—and Jews followed.

From the bits of data I've been able to find, it appears there were about 800 Jews in Florida by 1880 and 3,000 by 1900. The little information from this period that is available has either been donated by descendants of pioneer families and is now in the Collections at the JMOF-FIU or comes from the *American Israelite*, which began publishing in Cincinnati in 1854. The George A. Smathers Libraries at the University of Florida has a wonderful collection of Florida entries digitized for the period through 1900, compiled by Yael Herbsman.

Raphael Jacob Moses, Apalachicola, circa 1863.
Collections of Lewis Regenstein.

Samuel Proctor spoke to me of Raphael Jacob Moses (1812–93), a Sephardic Jew who lived in Tallahassee in 1836. When Moses heard of the economic development of the town of St. Joseph, he settled there. He obtained the position as secretary of the Lake Wimico and St. Joseph Railroad Company with a $2,000 annual salary. Moses remained there with his family, which included his parents, until a yellow fever epidemic and hurricane wrecked the town. He then turned to law and moved his family in 1843 to nearby Apalachicola. A persuasive public speaker, he moved into politics, and in 1847 Moses was elected as a Florida delegate to the Democratic convention. He and his three sons served in the Confederate army. Known to Generals Lee and Longstreet as the "honest commissary," Moses was tasked with carrying out the last order of the Confederate government: the delivery of $40,000 in gold bullion to Union forces to be used for the benefit of Confederate soldiers and hospitals. The US Government honored this request.

Emaline Quentz Miley, first-known Jewish settler in the Tampa area in 1844. Martha Parr's *"Homesteading in Hillsborough County,"* Sunland Tribune, *November 1941.*

At age eighteen, Jewish immigrant Emaline (1814–1907) married William Miley, who was not Jewish, only after he agreed to sell his slaves. They arrived in Thonotosassa (near Tampa) in 1844, one year before statehood. There, they cleared land, built a log cabin, and planted the area's first orange grove. Emaline survived the Indians, raised twelve children (her first born in Florida in 1847), and after William's death in 1862, expanded the groves. The family is buried in Thonotosassa, where there is a Miley Road.

PART 2

Who Are Florida's Jews?

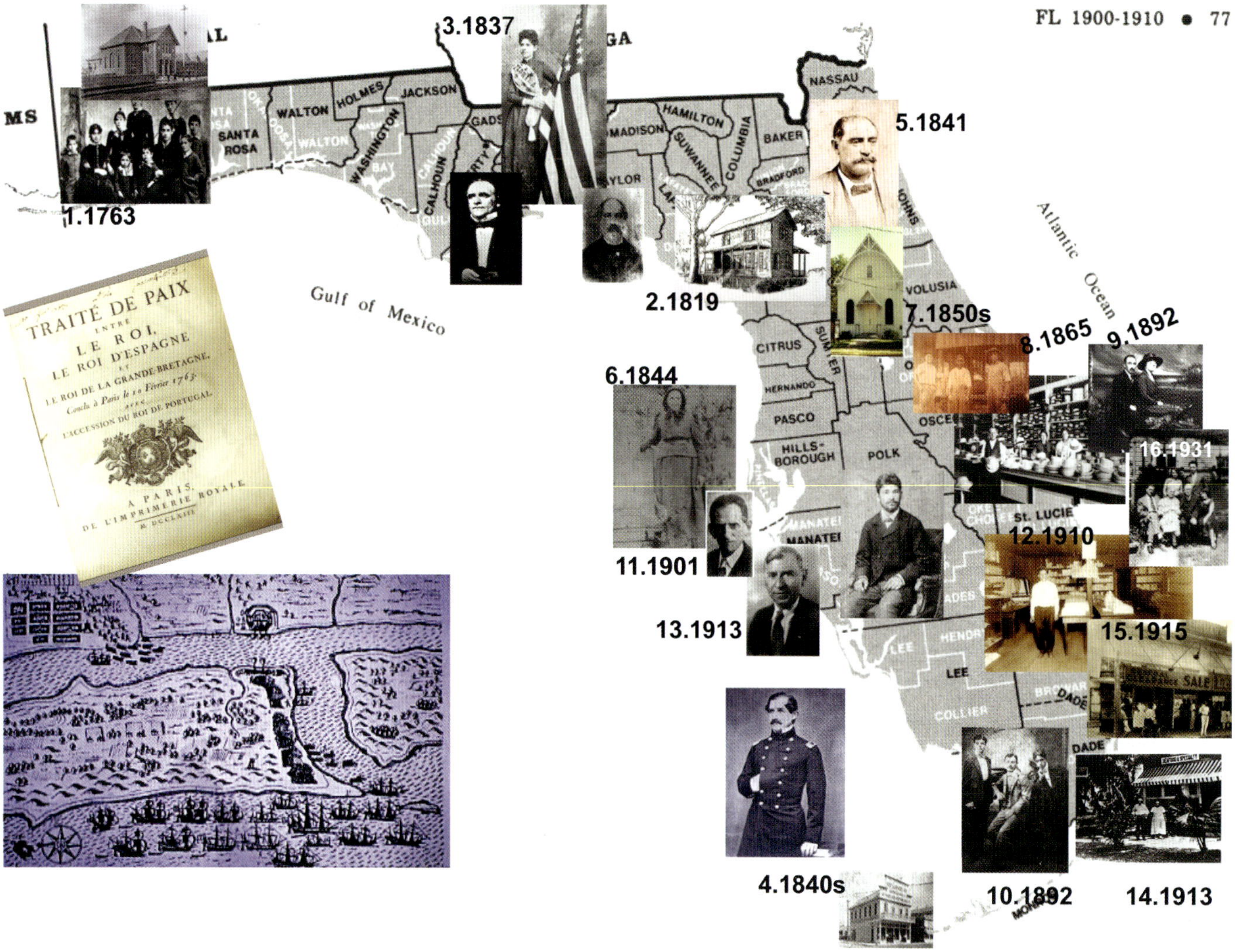

Map illustrating the sequence of the settlement of Jews in Florida.

We may have come on different ships, but we're in the same boat now.
—Martin Luther King Jr.

This powerful quote focuses us to forge a sense of unity among all the peoples who have come from diverse places around the globe. When the Florida Humanities Council first funded our MOSAIC project, their theme was "Making Florida Home" as almost everyone was from somewhere else. Even today, when some people die in Florida, they have their bodies shipped "up north" because they never felt that Florida was home. Only about 35 percent of Floridians were born here. (In most states, the average is 64 percent.)

Jews have been part of the eternal struggle of human beings to move forward and improve their lives and those of their families and their communities. Jews, as other people, have come to Florida seeking economic opportunity, favorable climate for health reasons, and an enhanced lifestyle. Some were assigned to the dozens of military bases, got "sand in their shoes," liked it, and came back to make it home.

I arrived at McCoy Air Force Base in Orlando as a military wife in 1965 and stayed—as I wanted to raise my children in Florida—on the water with palm trees and beautiful sunsets each evening. I was not pulling on snowsuits and boots. Even though John Denver sang "Almost Heaven, West Virginia," I felt even closer to heaven in Florida.

When I met Polish-born Yiddish writer and Nobel Prize winner Isaac Bashevis Singer on Miami Beach two decades later, he regaled me with his impressions of the palm tree and reminded me that the immigrants who came to Florida from all over the world did not come to forget their history, origin, or ethnic identities. They came for the freedom to grow in their own culture, in their own way of life, altered to their roots and hopes while becoming part of the whole of their new place.

I created this visual superimposed on a 1910 Florida map to tell a large story. The numbers of the cities with dates reflect the sequence of the earliest documentation I found of a Jewish settler in communities around the state. The photographs are of pioneers, mostly those who remained in those communities. It also shows (lower left) the first permanent settlement in North America, the harbor of St Augustine where *conversos* could have been among the soldiers and settlers in 1565. And it shows the 1763 Treaty of Paris that allowed Jews to settle in Florida—*as Jews.*

Here is a list of cities in order of settlement by Jews. The date is the year of the first known Jewish settler in that city, and the Jewish population today is in parentheses. Photographs that have been identified are listed after the population.

1. Pensacola 1763 (750): Temple Beth El, Gundersheimer Family

2. Micanopy 1819: drawing of the house of Moses Levy

3. Tallahassee 1836 (2,500): Miss Florida Mena Williams, US Senator David Levy Yulee (also shows Henry Brash in Apalachicola)

4. Key West 1840s (550): S. R. Davis's Dry Goods Store (also shows Abraham C. Myers in Fort Myers in Lee County)

5. Jacksonville 1841 (13,000): Philip Dzialynski

6. Tampa 1844 (23,000): Emaline Miley (This is forty-eight years before south Florida; in fact, there is no south Florida at this time!)

7. Ocala 1850s: Congregation B'nai Darom (also shows Saul Snyder in St. Augustine)

8. Orlando 1865 (31,000): the Shader brothers

9. Palm Beach 1892 (265,000 in County): Gertrude Katz Moses and David Moses, Joseph Schupler Hat Store

10. Miami 1892 (123,200): businessmen Jacob Schneidman, Isidor Cohen, and Marcus Frank

11. St. Petersburg area 1901 (36,000): Henry Schutz

12. Dania in Broward County 1910: Louis Brown

13. Sarasota 1913 (20,000): Phillip Levy and Marcus Weinkle in nearby Arcadia

14. Miami Beach 1913: Jennie and Joe Weiss of Joe's Stone Crab Restaurant

15. Fort Lauderdale 1915 (149,000 in Broward County): store of Abe Lehrman

16. Boca Raton 1931: the Florence and Harry Brown family (This area today has the state's largest Jewish population.)

CHAPTER 1

Early Immigration and Mobility around the State

During the period prior to Florida becoming a US territory in 1821, Jews who lived here came from somewhere else. The earliest-known recorded Jewish birth in Florida is of Virginia Myers, born in Pensacola on April 20, 1822, to Louisa and Samuel Myers. Samuel was an alderman and military officer, and the family soon relocated because of a yellow fever epidemic.

Throughout the nineteenth and early twentieth centuries, nearly all the Jews who came to Florida were immigrants from the old Jewish world. Coming to America and to Florida meant that for the first time, Jews could participate in and help grow the core of their host culture. Where they lived before, no matter what contributions they made, it was never possible for them to affect the essential nature of those societies. The Jews I am writing about who settled in Florida became part of the very substance of their communities—they made a difference that has helped change the very fabric of Florida. In their various roles over the centuries, Jews have struggled to maintain a balance between assimilation and maintaining the traditions of their culture.

When I visited the Immigration Museum at Ellis Island in 1990, the year it opened, I was captivated by the map of the ports of immigration. My own relatives who came from Austria, Poland, and Russia had arrived in America first through Castle Garden (1820–92) and then Ellis Island (1892–1954). They were greeted by the Statue of Liberty, with a pedestal plaque engraved, "Give me your tired, your poor, Your huddled masses yearning to breathe free." This was written in 1883 by Jewish poet Emma Lazarus. On the map, I found two ports of immigration in Florida! That validated many stories I'd been told while taking oral histories. During the early period in Florida statehood, ships brought immigrants directly from Europe to Florida at the port cities of Jacksonville and Key West—and the immigrants were greeted by palm trees and sand.

During Florida's territorial period (1821–45), I found no records of congregations or any Jewish institutions, yet a trickle of Jews continued to migrate to Florida. Michael Lazarus bought 150,000 acres of land at one dollar per acre (expensive for those days!) in the area of Daytona. Some names I found of Jews who were naturalized in St. Augustine are English watchmaker Lewis Solomon, English farmer George Levy, a farmer from South Carolina named Isaac Hendricks, and Hollander grocer M. Rodenberg.

Following statehood in 1845, immigrants from Germany, Prussia, Bavaria, Bohemia, and Austria straggled into north Florida towns in the aftermath of the 1848 European revolutions. Also, steamships sailing from New York to Savannah to Florida brought both new residents and tourists from within the US. Most who settled were merchants. Jacksonville was strategically located on the St. Johns River, so Jews probably came through that community as early as the 1820s.

This chapter discusses the earliest Jewish settlers who **stayed** in Florida and their mobility around the state.

The Moses Elias Levy family is no longer Jewish. ***So who is the longest continuing Jewish family in Florida? Answer: the Dzialynski family descendants are Floridian Jews into the eighth generation.***

Dzialynski Family

Rachelle Williams Cohen, daughter of Helena Dzialynski and Robert S. Williams, Tallahassee, circa 1877.
Ruby Diamond Collection, Florida State University Libraries, Special Collections and Archives.

George Dzialynski, son of Ida Erlich and Philip Dzialynski, with his sister Regina, Jacksonville, 1869.

The first known Jews born in Florida to a family who planted roots in the state and has continued to live here as Jews (since 1850) are Rachelle Williams [Cohen] in Jasper (1856–1936) and George Dzialynski in Jacksonville (1857–1937), who were first cousins with family origins in Prussia.

A wave of Jews arrived in Florida from Prussia during the mid-nineteenth century. This was a historically prominent German state that originated in 1525, located in northern Europe along the coasts of the Baltic and North Seas; it was dissolved in 1947. As a result of the Napoleonic Wars, Prussian Jews were officially emancipated in 1812, but in reality, over time, they faced growing restrictive policies and the denial of basic rights. Discrimination in the army, bureaucracy, and university remained the rule, so some Jews left to live in freedom with opportunities for their children.

Philip Dzialynski, Fort Meade, circa 1875.

Florida's "first family" was headed by Prussians Halena Liebsh and Aaron Dzialynski. The first to come to America and then to Jacksonville was their grandson Philip. He may have fought in the 1848 Polish Revolution. That same year, he emigrated at the age of fifteen. He was educated, was a Hebrew scholar, spoke eight languages, and began his life in Florida as a peddler. He soon opened a dry goods store and started saving money. Around 1850 he brought his father, Abraham; mother, Rosalie; four sisters; and four brothers to America. The family was at sea for fifty-seven days, and Rosalie died shortly after landing in New York. The nine Dzialynski children were all born in Prussia: Philip (1833–96), Helena (1836–1931), Johannah (1836–1900), Henry (1838–57), Morris A. (1841–1907), Jacob (1845–57), Dora, John (1847–1929), and Augusta. Abraham, Henry, and Jacob died of yellow fever in Jacksonville in October 1857.

According to Samuel Proctor, Philip Dzialynski was the first permanent Jewish resident to settle in Jacksonville, an important Florida town of about 1,500 people. In 1856 Philip married Ida Erlich who had come from Germany. They had two children who survived, George (1857) and Regina (1859) [Herzog]. When the Union troops invaded Jacksonville in 1862, Philip and his family took refuge in Madison, where Ida died in childbirth in 1864. Philip had a Jewish burial for Ida and then married Mary Cohen. Mary and Philip had four daughters and a son. When the family lived in Fort Meade for nineteen years, Philip diversified their livelihood—he became a cotton broker; owner of a hotel, drugstore, and livery stable; and one of the state's first citrus shippers. Some say he named a river *sholom*, the Hebrew word for peace, and it is known today as the Peace River. But his personal life was one of boom and bust due to the citrus freezes and yellow fever epidemics of the 1880s.

Mary and Philip's daughter Gertrude Dzialynski (1874–1931) graduated from Summerlin Institute in Bartow in 1888, wrote short stories and plays, and was the first-known female faculty member of the East Florida Seminary, one of the institutions that became the University of Florida. Not content, she studied law in night school in Tallahassee. She was probably Florida's first woman lawyer admitted to the bar in 1898 (likely at the local level after passing an exam given by circuit court judges), but the Florida Supreme Court's records indicate her admission in 1921. Gertrude opened a law office in Jacksonville, but as a woman it was challenging to get clients, so she became personal secretary to Napoleon Bonaparte Broward, aided in his campaign for governor, and stayed with him during his term (1905–9). She associated with a law firm in Jacksonville beginning in 1914 and married John Corbett in 1915. Gertrude served four years as deputy collector of the Internal Revenue Service of Florida with responsibilities for the enforcement of the new federal income tax, and then she was in charge of the Inheritance Tax Department. She was president of many organizations and active in Democratic Party and business affairs. In 1921 she helped found the Florida League of Women Voters. Professor and author E. Canter Brown Jr. referred to her as "Miss Dynamite" in an essay on women in the post–Civil War century.

Helena Dzialynski Williams, Tallahassee, 1890s.

Helena Dzialynski and Robert S. Williams in front of their home, Tallahassee, circa 1897.

In 1855 Helena married Robert S. Williams (originally Wolf in Prussia), an observant Jew who had fled Europe after the failure of the liberal revolutions of the 1840s. Williams had participated in the California Gold Rush in 1849 and then came east and settled in Jasper. After serving in the Civil War, he moved his family to Tallahassee, where he owned a cotton plantation and also became a merchant. Family legend is that when Union troops came to their home during the Civil War, Helena said, "Take anything you want, just don't take my *schmaltz*!" Robert inaugurated Tallahassee's first street lighting by placing kerosene lamps on street posts. Helena and Robert raised five daughters (Rachelle, Henrietta, Sippie, Ida, and Mena) who all married Jews. One groom was Jacob Raphael Cohen, who in 1877 married Rachelle Williams. Jacob's sister Mary had married his business partner, Philip Dzialynski, so Rachelle was part of his family by marriage. Ida married Jacob's brother Maurice Cohen.

Ruby Diamond, Tallahassee, 1910.

Mena Williams as Miss Florida, presenting the US flag at the inauguration of Florida Governor Edward Perry, Tallahassee, 1885.

Mena, already a third-generation Floridian Jew, was the first Miss Florida. The flag was spun from Tallahassee silk worm cocoons, and when she presented it to the governor, she made a speech about national pride and the newborn prosperity throughout our land. Mena married Julius Hirschberg of Jacksonville.

Ruby Diamond with Smiley Bruce, who drove Miss Ruby around for sixteen years in a 1963 Cadillac, Tallahassee, 1970s.

Sippie Williams married Julius Diamond of Tallahassee, who was in the seed and fertilizer business and donated some of his inventory to the poor for their own gardens. Their two children were Sydney and Ruby. Ruby Diamond (1886–1982) was a prominent supporter of Florida State University (FSU), from which she graduated in 1905 with a bachelor of arts degree in chemistry (when it was Florida Female College), and she was charitable throughout her community. Engaged to a Goodman boy who was killed in World War I, Ruby never married. She donated land valued at $100,000 to FSU, where the Westcott Building auditorium is dedicated to her. She was a founder of Temple Israel in 1937 in Tallahassee, where she was named honorary president on her ninety-fourth birthday. After the family home was sold, Miss Ruby, as she was known, spent the rest of her life living in hotel rooms. And like Miss Daisy (of *Driving Miss Daisy*), Miss Ruby had her own chauffeur, Smiley Bruce, to whom she was devoted; she left Bruce her car.

"The Dzialynski House,"
FORT MEADE, FLA.
Mrs. M. P. Dzialynski,
Proprietress.
Will be opened October 1st, 1883, for the accommodation of visitors and the traveling public generally.
— RATES. —
$2.00 per day. One Meal, 50c.
Livery Stable attached to the house.
PH. DZIALYNSKI, General Manager.
— ALSO —
The New York and Fort Meade Mercantile Company,
Under the management of PH. DZIALYNSKI,
Will open a general business at Fort Meade within the next sixty days.

Mary and Philip Dzialynski opened a hotel, The Dzialynski House, in Fort Meade, 1883. *George W. Hendry, Polk County, FL, Its Lands & Products.*

Fort Meade was the center for Florida cattle and attracted politicians, businesspeople, and travelers. Philip Dzialynski was a merchant in Madison, Fort Meade, Palatka, Bartow, and Tampa; one of Florida's first real estate agents; an organizer of the Tampa, Pease Creek, and St. Johns Railroad; and a politician. In 1877, with others, he created the Tampa and Fort Meade Telegraph Company that helped link Tampa to the outside world. He brought Jewish culture to the frontier, maintained a library of about 1,400 books, and even conducted religious services.

Morris Dzialynski became a civic and Jewish community leader, Jacksonville, 1914.

Morris Dzialynski (1841–1907) lived in several Florida cities but settled in Jacksonville, where he married Rosa Slager. He fought for the Confederacy during the Civil War, then sold carriages, buggies, and wagons and became an auctioneer. Very civic minded, Morris organized the city's first volunteer fire department and served as chief. He was one of the founders of the Children's Home Society of Florida, helped organize the first baseball club, and was master of the Duval Lodge of Masons. In 1881 Morris was elected as Jacksonville's first, and still only, Jewish mayor and served two terms. In 1882 he helped organize Florida's second Jewish congregation, Ahavath Chesed, and was elected its first president. He was elected municipal judge in 1895, a position he held until his death. His body lay in state at the city building, with all city offices closed and flags at half-mast. At Morris's funeral, Rabbi Pizer Jacobs quoted the *Florida Times-Union*,

"Never before has there been such a general expression of sorrow and regret over the death of any person."

Bertha Zadek Dzialynski and George Dzialynski, Gainesville, circa 1880.

In 1882 Philip's son George married immigrant Bertha Zadek (1864–1947), who was living with her aunt Pauline Braun in Gainesville. Bertha said, "He was perhaps the greatest catch," referring to the Dzialynski family. The couple went by boat to Sanford on the St. Johns River, which Bertha said was more beautiful than the Rhine, and resided in Fort Meade for about a decade. Then they moved to Tampa where they helped found the first congregation in 1894. Bertha and George had two daughters, Ida Clare and Ruth Hope [Leon], and finally settled in Jacksonville. Ida Clare married William Coleman, who had settled in Jacksonville in 1896; their seven children were Elsie, Hortense, Wilma, Ruth, Colson Perry, Robert Lee, and Carol. Bertha and George Dzialynski's grandchildren all remained Jewish. Six stayed in Jacksonville and produced fourteen great-grandchildren. Although there are no descendants today named Dzialynski, several great-grandchildren have remained in Jacksonville **and are still practicing Jews**.

In 1944, at the age of eighty, Bertha typed her two-hundred-page biographical memoir, *Within My Heart*, about a Prussian-born Jewish woman on the Florida frontier. She speaks about the acculturation challenges and how she drew strength from her heritage. The manuscript is in the JMOF-FIU Collections.

Jacob Raphael Cohen, Tallahassee, circa 1877.
Ruby Diamond Collection, Florida State University Libraries, Special Collections and Archives.

After opening Florida stores in Bartow, Fort Meade, and Fort Ogden, Jacob R. Cohen (1844–1901) settled in Orlando in the 1870s. He bought property and operated a general merchandise store. He became active within the small group of qualified voters who formed the government. In 1875 he helped write the Town of Orlando charter, was requested to act as secretary for the meeting of incorporation, and was elected an alderman. He remained in Orlando until he married Rachelle Williams in December 1877 and then relocated to Tallahassee. There he succeeded his father-in-law, Robert S. Williams, in business; bought property; was a leader of the Masonic Lodge, was on the city commission; and arranged for the first Jewish burial ground in the city cemetery. Cohen conducted the first statewide appeal for funds for Jews in Palestine, collecting $10,000, and was a delegate to the National Democratic Convention in 1901, the year he died. His funeral procession was the largest ever seen in Tallahassee up to that time.

Jacob Raphael Cohen (top left) became politically involved, Tallahassee, 1899.

US president William McKinley (front left) visited the Florida Legislature two years prior to his assassination. Governor William Bloxham is in the front right. Seated left to right are Mrs. Hanna, Mrs. McKinley, and Mrs. Bloxham. Senator Marcus Hanna is standing between Mrs. Hanna and Mrs. McKinley, Jacob R. Cohen is at the top left, Guyte McLendon is standing next to him, and General Richard Scarlitt is standing in front of him.

I obtained this photograph of Jacob Raphael Cohen—who was important in early Orlando political history and married into the Dzialynski-Williams family—from a relative in a West Palm Beach nursing home, Roberta Cohen Mendel. Finding such photographs and compiling them into the story of Jewish life in Florida was a continuing treasure hunt. Why did Roberta have this rare image? She was a granddaughter of Helena Dzialynski Williams. Her mother, Ida Williams, had married Maurice Cohen, a brother of Jacob! It's all in the family.

The story of this Floridian Jewish family is one of the American dream come true. They came out of European revolutionary strife and settled in Florida prior to the Civil War. Some served in that war, and then they all helped their communities and state rebuild. In the process, they sustained their Jewish heritage. **The family has seventy-five descendants and continues!**

The primary source for most of the stories I share with you is interviews with family members. For the Dzialynski family, I also obtained much from a doctoral paper of unknown authorship in our Collections and from Rabbi Stanley Garfein of Tallahassee, the Ruby Diamond Collection at the Strozier Library at FSU, Jacksonville's Congregation Ahavath Chesed archivist Hazel Mack, descendants Margaret Miller and Wilma L'Engle, and a speech that Ruth Hope Leon gave for the Jacksonville Historical Society around 1954. I spoke to this same group sixty-two years later.

During this early period of Florida settlement, everything was in the north. There was no south Florida until the end of the nineteenth century. The most important Florida cities for Jews in the nineteenth century were Jacksonville and Tampa. As economic conditions changed, Jews moved back and forth and around the areas. With only about one hundred Jews in Florida, it was common for Jews to marry relatives to ensure Jewish continuity.

Benjamin Family

Among the Jews who moved to Florida following the Civil War were members of the Prussian Benjamin family, who made many civic, business, and architectural contributions to their adopted state, primarily in Micanopy, Ocala, Jacksonville, and Orlando. They even invested in 1879 in the Silver Springs, Ocala, and Gulf Railroad that by 1891 connected to Homosassa on the Gulf of Mexico and northeast Florida. The railroad was a key factor in opening up central Florida to development. Their story illustrates the economic success and integration into the larger non-Jewish society and reveals the kinship, marriage, and business connections as well as the family migration pattern. Some in the family resided in Micanopy, a town founded by Moses Elias Levy.

Simon Benjamin settled in Florida in 1865, Ocala, circa 1895.

Born in the Prussian province of Posen, Simon Benjamin (1850–1931) came to Alachua County to establish a business in the village of Waldo. Simon stayed in Waldo until 1868, when he was "run out of town by the Ku Klux Klan," and moved to Ocala, where his brother Solomon joined him. Simon married Carrie Pinkussohn in 1880, and then when she died, he married her sister Ida in 1898.

East Florida Ice Manufacturing Co., built by the Benjamin family, Ocala, circa 1890.

In 1889 brothers Simon, Solomon, and Morris and other family members opened the first-known ice-making plant in Florida. It was located at the junction of two railways, which facilitated rapid transport. Imagine—this was a time when there were no refrigerators in which to store and preserve meats or electricity to operate them if they had existed. Many homes contained iceboxes, and they delivered ice on wagons to homes and businesses. Cattle was a large industry in this area, but there was no way to keep meat unless it was cooked or cured. In 1899 they added cold storage to the plant, where they could preserve eight hundred pounds of meat, stored in pigeonholes arranged around the walls. The temperature would be kept constant around the year to preserve the meat. This gave a tremendous boost to the cattle industry in Marion County.

In 1882 Solomon was president of the Board of Marion County Commissioners, and then Simon held that position in 1896. That same year Simon was on the school board and started immunizations. He served as president of the United Hebrews of Ocala congregation.

Simon Benjamin's family with his second wife, Ida, and their children, spouses, and grandchildren, Jacksonville, 1916.

After the great fire in Jacksonville in 1901, Simon Benjamin moved there, began a cigar and tobacco business and served as president of Congregation Ahavath Chesed. In the front row from left to right are Phyllis Meyer Benjamin (with Roy Jr.), Carol Moss Oberdorfer, Adolf A. Rothschild (son-in-law), Irene

Benjamin Rothschild, Rita Gutman Benjamin, Frances Benjamin, Babette Altmayer Benjamin. In the top row from left to right are Roy Benjamin, Morris Moss (son-in-law), Rosalie Benjamin Moss, Ida Benjamin, Simon Benjamin, Julien Benjamin, and L. Walter Benjamin.

Simon's son Roy Benjamin recalled stowing away on a troop train to Tampa to join the Spanish-American War. Simon also took the train—to bring him back! Roy apprenticed in New York and Albany, Georgia, before moving to Jacksonville where he became an architect who was acclaimed for his theater designs (see "Architects" in part 3, chapter 7). On a personal note, my husband's middle son, Don Zerivitz, is married to Joy Benjamin, a great-granddaughter of Simon and granddaughter of Roy; their two sons Benjamin and Teddy are fifth-generation Floridian Jews!

S. H. Benjamin Building, Micanopy, 1885.

Simon's younger cousin S. H. Benjamin (1854–1919) was in Micanopy by 1879 as a dry goods and furniture merchant. Records indicate he had several stores. In 1883 he gained fellow Prussian immigrant Jacob Katz as a business partner, and they purchased ten acres of land for $200. In 1885 they built the S. H. Benjamin Building, Micanopy's first brick building. It originally had two stories, but the second was destroyed by fire circa 1900. S. H. and Jacob continued in business in Micanopy and Jacksonville until 1901. This building most recently housed O. Brisky Books and is still in use.

Drawing of Evinston General Store and Post Office, structure built in 1882 by S. H. Benjamin as his warehouse, Evinston, n.d. *Ashley Wood.*

Records show that S. H. Benjamin purchased about one-and-a-half acres from the Florida Southern Railway for one dollar to build a warehouse across the road from the railroad depot in nearby Evinston. This is where he and Katz stored merchandise delivered by the train until he could arrange transport to his stores. That warehouse, on the National Register of Historic Places (1989), became a store and post office circa 1901 and is still in use, owned and operated by the Henry Deaver Wood family (not Jewish) since 1909. In 1977 the property was used as a set for the movie adaptation of Marjorie Rawling's short story "Gal Young'un."

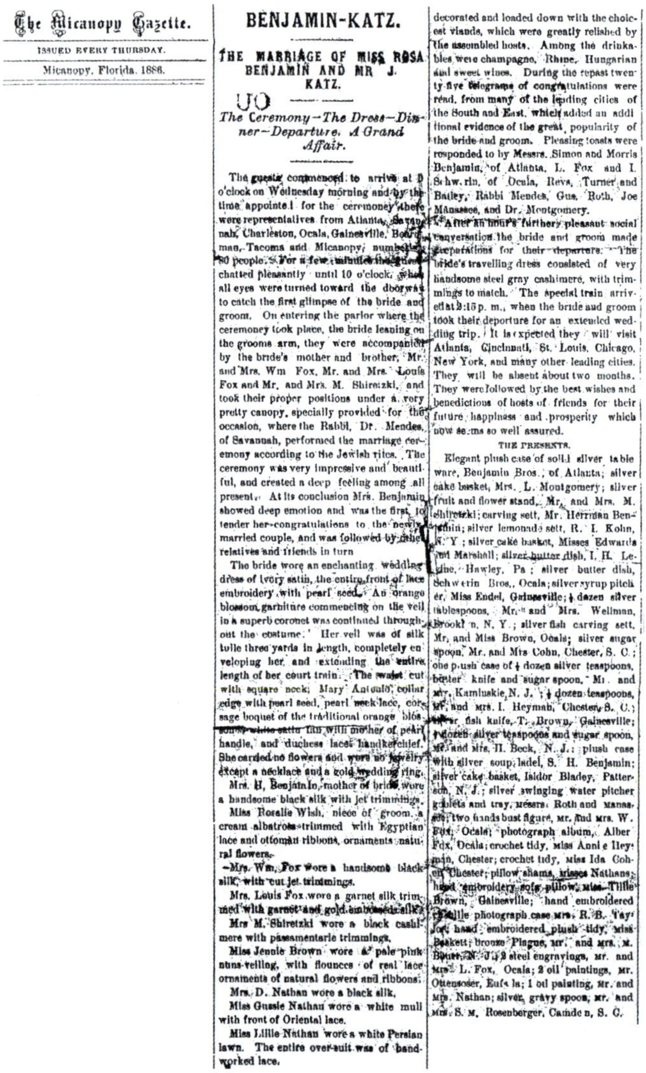

The Micanopy Gazette.
ISSUED EVERY THURSDAY.
Micanopy, Florida, 1886.

BENJAMIN-KATZ.

THE MARRIAGE OF MISS ROSA BENJAMIN AND MR J. KATZ.

The Ceremony—The Dress—Dinner—Departure. A Grand Affair.

The guests commenced to arrive at 9 o'clock on Wednesday morning and by the time appointed for the ceremoney there were representatives from Atlanta, Savannah, Charleston, Ocala, Gainesville, Boardman, Tacoma and Micanopy, numbering 80 people. For a few minutes the guests chatted pleasantly until 10 o'clock, when all eyes were turned toward the doorway to catch the first glimpse of the bride and groom. On entering the parlor where the ceremoney took place, the bride leaning on the grooms arm, they were accompanied by the bride's mother and brother, Mr. and Mrs. Wm Fox, Mr. and Mrs. Louis Fox and Mr. and Mrs. M. Shiretzki, and took their proper positions under a very pretty canopy, specially provided for the occasion, where the Rabbi, Dr. Mendes, of Savannah, performed the marriage ceremony according to the Jewish rites. The ceremony was very impressive and beautiful, and created a deep feeling among all present. At its conclusion Mrs. Benjamin showed deep emotion and was the first to tender her congratulations to the newly married couple, and was followed by other relatives and friends in turn

The bride wore an enchanting wedding dress of ivory satin, the entire front of lace embroidery with pearl seed. An orange blossom garniture commencing on the veil in a superb coronet was continued throughout the costume. Her veil was of silk tulle three yards in length, completely enveloping her and extending the entire length of her court train. The waist cut with square neck; Mary Antoinette collar edge with pearl seed, pearl neck lace, corsage boquet of the traditional orange blossoms, white satin fan with mother of pearl handle, and duchess lace handkerchief. She carried no flowers and wore no jewelry except a necklace and a gold wedding ring.

Mrs. H. Benjamin, mother of bride, wore a handsome black silk with jet trimmings.

Miss Rosalie Wish, niece of groom, a cream albatross trimmed with Egyptian lace and ottoman ribbons, ornaments natural flowers.

Mrs. Wm. Fox wore a handsome black silk, with cut jet trimmings.

Mrs. Louis Fox wore a garnet silk trimmed with garnet and gold embossed silk.

Mrs M. Shiretzki wore a black cashimere with passamentarie trimmings.

Miss Jennie Brown wore a pale pink nuns-veiling, with flounces of real lace ornaments of natural flowers and ribbons.

Mrs. D. Nathan wore a black silk.

Miss Gussie Nathan wore a white mull with front of Oriental lace.

Miss Lillie Nathan wore a white Persian lawn. The entire over-suit was of hand-worked lace.

... decorated and loaded down with the choicest viands, which were greatly relished by the assembled hosts. Among the drinkables were champagne, Rhine, Hungarian and sweet wines. During the repast twenty-five telegrams of congratulations were read, from many of the leading cities of the South and East, which added an additional evidence of the great popularity of the bride and groom. Pleasing toasts were responded to by Messrs. Simon and Morris Benjamin, of Atlanta, L. Fox and I. Schwerin, of Ocala, Revs. Turner and Bailey, Rabbi Mendes, Gus. Roth, Joe Manassee, and Dr. Montgomery.

After an hour's further pleasant social conversation the bride and groom made preparations for their departure. The bride's travelling dress consisted of very handsome steel gray cashimere, with trimmings to match. The special train arrived at 2:15 p. m., when the bride and groom took their deporture for an extended wedding trip. It is expected they will visit Atlanta, Cincinnati, St. Louis, Chicago, New York, and many other leading cities. They will be absent about two months. They were followed by the best wishes and benedictions of hosts of friends for their future happiness and prosperity which now seems so well assured.

THE PRESENTS.

Elegant plush case of solid silver table ware, Benjamin Bros., of Atlanta; silver cake basket, Mrs. L. Montgomery; silver fruit and flower stand, Mr. and Mrs. M. Shiretzki; carving sett, Mr. Herrman Benjamin; silver lemonade sett, R. I. Kohn, N. Y.; silver cake basket, Misses Edwards and Marshall; silver butter dish, I. H. Levine, Hawley, Pa; silver butter dish, Schwerin Bros., Ocala; silver syrup pitcher, Miss Endel, Gainesville; ½ dozen silver tablespoons, Mr. and Mrs. Wellman, Brooklyn, N. Y.; silver fish carving sett, Mr. and Miss Brown, Ocala; silver sugar spoon, Mr. and Mrs Cohn, Chester, S. C.; one plush case of ½ dozen silver teaspoons, butter knife and sugar spoon, Mr. and Mrs. Kamluskie, N. J.; ½ dozen teaspoons, Mr. and Mrs. I. Heyman, Chester, S. C.; silver fish knife, T. Brown, Gainesville; ½ dozen silver teaspoons and sugar spoon, Mr. and Mrs. H. Beck, N. J.; plush case with silver soup ladel, S. H. Benjamin; silver cake basket, Isidor Bladey, Patterson, N. J.; silver swinging water pitcher goblets and tray, Messrs. Roth and Manassee; two hands bust figure, Mr. and Mrs. W. Fox, Ocala; photograph album, Alber Fox, Ocala; crochet tidy, Miss Annie Heyman, Chester; crochet tidy, Miss Ida Cohen, Chester; pillow shams, Misses Nathans; hand embroidery sofa pillow, Miss Tillie Brown, Gainesville; hand embroidered chenille photograph case Mrs. R. B. Taylor; hand embroidered plush tidy, Miss Baskett; bronze Plaque, Mr. and Mrs. M. Bauer, N. J.; 2 steel engravings, Mr. and Mrs. L. Fox, Ocala; 2 oil paintings, Mr. Ottensoser, Eufala; 1 oil painting, Mr. and Mrs. Nathan; silver gravy spoon, Mr. and Mrs. S. M. Rosenberger, Camden, S. C.

Micanopy Gazette **article "Benjamin-Katz. The Marriage of Miss Rosa Benjamin and Mr. J. (Jacob) Katz," 1886.**

When S. H. Benjamin's twenty-five-year-old sister, Rosa, married his business partner, Jacob Katz, a rabbi came from Savannah to perform the ceremony, and eighty guests came from as far away as Charleston and Atlanta. Probably Micanopy's first Jewish wedding, the occasion prompted major coverage written in the meticulous descriptive style of those times and included what the guests wore and a listing of the presents.

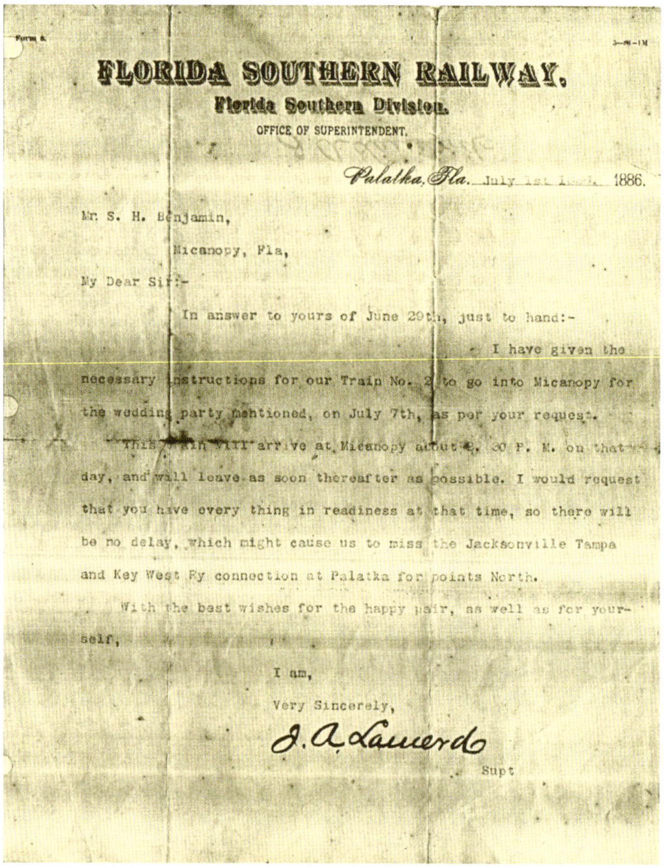

FLORIDA SOUTHERN RAILWAY.
Florida Southern Division.
OFFICE OF SUPERINTENDENT.

Palatka, Fla. July 1st 1886.

Mr. S. H. Benjamin,
Micanopy, Fla,

My Dear Sir:-

In answer to yours of June 29th, just to hand:-

I have given the necessary instructions for our Train No. 2 to go into Micanopy for the wedding party mentioned, on July 7th, as per your request.

This train will arrive at Micanopy about 8. 30 P. M. on that day, and will leave as soon thereafter as possible. I would request that you have every thing in readiness at that time, so there will be no delay, which might cause us to miss the Jacksonville Tampa and Key West Ry connection at Palatka for points North.

With the best wishes for the happy pair, as well as for yourself,

I am,
Very Sincerely,
J. A. [illegible]
Supt

Letter from the superintendent of the Florida Southern Railway to S. H. Benjamin regarding stopping the train to pick up wedding guests, Micanopy, 1886.

S. H. commissioned the Florida Southern Railway to stop in Micanopy to take the wedding party and guests to Jacksonville as part of the festivities and honeymoon.

Rosa Benjamin Katz and Jacob Katz wedding portraits, Micanopy, 1886.

CHAPTER 2

Mid-nineteenth Century Immigration: Prussian, Polish, and Germanic

Problems for Jews who lived in Germany began with the first crusade in 1096, and persecution continued when Jews were blamed for the onset of the plagues of the fourteenth and fifteenth centuries. Segregation of the Jews rose throughout Europe, and civil rights, occupations, and mobility were limited. As the situation became more chaotic, more Jews left. The 1848 wave of revolutions in the German states was accompanied by anti-Jewish riots in many places. Larger armed forces loomed with universal conscription. Future prospects for young, bright Jews were dim, and many looked to emigrate seeking freedom of choice.

Florida was a good choice for Jews. One German immigrant, Julius Potsdamer, settled in Lake City by 1873, likely the only Jew there, and he faced many obstacles. Reports show that he married Miss Medora Hausman of Madison in 1876. In 1891 the records of Florida's Department of Agriculture reflect they allocated $150 to Potsdamer, who they appointed as a special immigration agent to work "in the interest of immigration to Florida from Germany." The funds, paid by warrant No. 2197 of May 7, 1891, were spent for Potsdamer's trip to Europe to distribute printed matter about Florida in the German language. His report to the bureau states that he first met with Mr. Reinberg, a representative of the United Hebrew Charities at Castle Garden and, in Germany, visited the large cities and small towns in the province of Posen and convinced four young men to go to Ocala.

Gundersheimer-Barker Family

Children born in Milton to Fannie Mayer and Joseph Gundersheimer, circa 1883.

In the front row from left to right are David (1879) and Gustave Gus (1876). In the second row from left to right are Ralph Rafe (1875), Jeannette (1864) [Barker], Dorah (1870) [Barnette], Abraham L. (1865), Bernhardt Leon (1874). In the back row from left to right are Carrie (1862) [Metzger], Emma (1868) [Barnett], and Max (1871).

One of the oldest continuing Florida Jewish families was led by Joseph Gundersheimer when he emigrated from Lower Franconia, Bavaria, Germany, in the 1850s and settled in Milton. During the Civil War, Joseph accepted Confederate scrip in his dry goods store. After his death in 1879, his widow, Fannie Mayer

Gundersheimer (1841–1903), also from Bavaria, moved the children to Pensacola, where there was more family. There are descendants living in Pensacola and Sarasota. Ann Schops of Pensacola, granddaughter of David, gave me this photograph. In the 1980s, as I traveled around the state with my slideshow and projector (prior to the digital age!) to promote the MOSAIC project, I gathered photographs and stories from my audiences. One day in Sarasota, when I showed this photo, two women from opposite sides of the room ran up to tell me that the same woman was their ancestor—and they did not know they were related until that moment!

Watergate break-in "plumber" Bernard Leon Barker Jr. (center) on the way to prison, Miami, 1973. *Miami Herald.*

Sarasota is also where I discovered the story of Jeannette Gundersheimer in the family photograph. In 1885 she married a Russian Jew, Jacob Ralph Barker. In 1890 they had a son, Bernard Leon Barker, who lived in Cuba where he married Alicia Terry. In 1917 they had a son, Bernard Leon Barker Jr. That name haunted me until I realized who he was—the "plumber" (preventing information leaks) in the June 17, 1972, Washington Watergate break-in of the Democratic National Committee headquarters. The five burglars, recruited by Central Intelligence Agency (CIA) officer E. Howard Hunt, were trying to plant a wiretap to gather information on George McGovern, Richard Nixon's Democratic opponent in the upcoming presidential election. Barker was sentenced to federal prison in Pensacola, and one Friday night when Ann Schops was at Temple Beth El, some prisoners marched in, and she saw her cousin Bernard among them! Born in Cuba, he had moved to Miami in 1960 and first been recruited by E. Howard Hunt as an undercover operative in CIA-directed plots to overthrow Cuban leader Fidel Castro at the Bay of Pigs in 1961. After prison, he worked as a building inspector for the City of Miami; he died in 2009. "I think it's time that people forget the whole damn thing," he said in a 1997 interview with the Associated Press. "That was a sad time." So among Floridian Jews and their descendants, some are famous and some infamous!

Brash Family

German immigrant Henry Brash, Apalachicola, 1870s.

Henry Brash arrived in Florida just in time for the Civil War. Following his service, he mustered out in Apalachicola and had numerous businesses, including a retail store, a lumberyard, and a sponge fishing endeavor. He was also the developer of Brash block.

The Porches, one of nine hundred historic homes listed in Apalachicola's National Register District, 1878.

ABSTRACT OF TITLE

ROBERT MYERS & LOUISA P. MYERS, his wife,

To — Grantor

HENRY BRASH. — Grantee

Kind of Instrument WARRANTY DEED
Dated March 2, 1878 Sealed Yes.
Consideration $300.00.
Granting Clause Do grant,bargain,sell & convey.
Habendum Clause His heirs and assigns forever.
Warranty Clause Yes.
Witnesses William H.Clarkson & Charles Nettlet
Date of Acknowledgement March 2, 1878
Separate Examination wife Yes.
Dower and Homestead released No.
Before whom Acknowledged Charles Nettleton,Commi sioner for Fla.
Official seal affixed Yes.
Recorded June 12, 1879.
In Deed Book "A" Page 538-539.
Public record Franklin County, Florida
Limitation

DESCRIPTION OF LAND CONVEYED

All that certain piece or parcel of land, situate and being in the City of Apalachicola County and State aforesaid and known upon the Map and Plan of said City of Apalachicola, as lot number (1) One, in Block (16) Sixteen, fronting sixty feet in width on Live Oak Street, running back one hundred feet to an alley, in center of said Block, and fronting sixty feet on said alley, (or City Square) and one hundred feet on Center Street, together with all and singular the rights and appurtenances thereto belonging, or in anywise appertaining

Abstract of the title from the Brash home, the Porches, Apalachicola, March 2, 1878.

Henry Brash brought his wife, Henrietta, from Germany and built their home called the Porches, where they had eleven children. All the children married Jews, and descendants still live in Florida.

Porcelain plate, floral pattern with gilt border, one of a set, Apalachicola, 1880s.

The family was observant. They brought their dishes from Germany and *kashered* them in the Gulf of Mexico where they often had Shabbat dinners and *seders* on the beach.

Bear-Kahn Family

Bear-Kahn Family, Pensacola, 1892.

The families represented here have been in Pensacola for more than a century, and their relationships have been consolidated through many family marriages. Sitting left to right are Sallye Bear Kahn; her husband, Harry Kahn; and her sister Bertha Bear Rosenau. Standing and wearing a straw hat is Jacob Kahn, Pensacola.

Four generations of the Sidonia and Lewis Kahn family, Pensacola, circa 1890.

Front left to right are Amaleigh Bloom Simon, wife of Elias Simon and mother of Sidonia; Renie Cahn, daughter of Nettie (born 1867); and Sidonia Simon Kahn, who married Lewis Kahn. Standing we have Nettie Kahn Cahn. Widowed at a young age, Sidonia had a shoe store on Palafox Street.

Most families who settled in Pensacola during the mid-nineteenth century came from Bavaria, such as the Gundersheimers (whom you already met), the Bears, the Kahns, the Forcheimers, and the Dannheissers. Many eighth-generation descendants live in Pensacola.

The Bear family story reaches back to the 1830 marriage in Bavaria of Moses Bar and Esther Bademan, who produced five children. Lewis, Nathan, and David left around 1850, and somehow during the immigration process, the name became Bear. They settled in Greenville, Alabama, and were successful in the Lewis Bear Store, selling dry goods and spirits. The 1866 tax rolls list Lewis's net income as $115.00 and his personal local tax paid as $0.75. Lewis and David served in the Confederate army and then married sisters from Prussia (Henrietta and Julia Kugelman). Lewis and Henrietta had five children: Morris, Sallye, Max Lee, Bertha, and Jacob (Jake). With the 1875 vote to become a "dry county," the business suffered, and Lewis relocated his family by train to Pensacola in 1876.

Lumbering was helping the city prosper as the demand for Florida's pine boomed, mills expanded, and the city's port mushroomed. Sailing vessels arrived from Europe to pick up lumber cargoes, each needing sustenance for their crews in port and provisioning for the return voyage. Lewis Bear understood the opportunity and the need for a wholesale operation—and so the Lewis Bear Company was founded in 1876 and evolved into a wholesale distributor, selling groceries, hardware, and liquor. Max Lee Bear joined his family's business in 1888 and served in the Spanish-American War. This company readily employed early Jewish arrivals and was responsible for many future successful merchants whose careers began there.

Jacob Kahn had migrated to Pensacola with his wife, Caroline, in 1866. Jacob, a founder of the temple, had a men's clothing business. Their son, Harry Kahn, born in 1870, married Sallye Bear, a daughter of Lewis Bear. In 1896 Harry Kahn was one of the founders of the Welles-Kahn Co., which later became the Kahn Grocery Co. His son, grandson, and great-grandson carried on the business until 1982.

Forcheimer Family

Three generations of Forcheimers, Pensacola, 1921.

From left to right are Gerson Forcheimer, daughter Frances Forcheimer Lischkoff, Mozart, and baby Blanche Lischkoff. Abraham and Gerson Forcheimer of Bavaria settled in Milton by 1860. They had a general store that issued scrip to be used by workers of the lumber mill. Several years later, Gerson Forcheimer moved into Pensacola, where he became a leader in the Jewish community. He received the deed for the Jewish cemetery in 1869 from S. M. Goldbach, who in 1874 was a founding member of B'nai B'rith and served as first president of Temple Beth El when it was founded in 1876.

Dannheisser Family

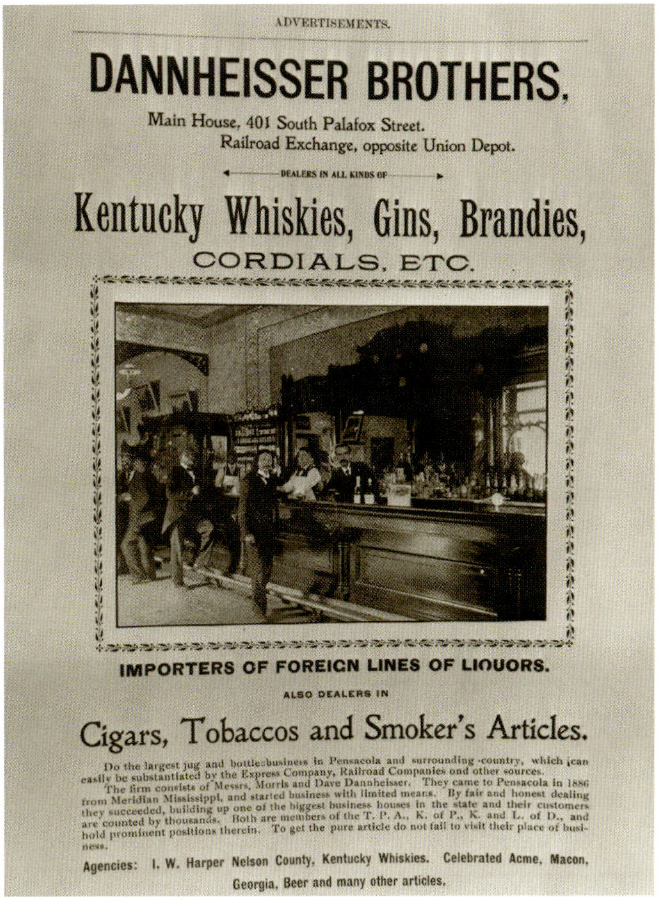

Dannheisser Brothers ad, Pensacola, 1893.

In 1869 Bavarian Marx Dannheisser arrived in Pensacola with wife, Jeannette Loeb, and his sister-in-law, Amelia Loeb Fries Myerson. Marx was a founder of Temple Beth El. Estelle Forcheimer, born in Pensacola in 1869, married David Dannheisser circa 1886. David had a wholesale liquor business with his brother Morris.

Polish Jews

Jews have lived in Poland for more than one thousand years. About 80 percent of the American Jewish community has origins in Poland. That is not surprising, as we know that this was the center of the European Jewish world with more than three million Jews before the Holocaust. Many Floridian Jews have a family history from Polish *shtetls*.

Jews lived in the territory that later became Poland as early as the eighth century when Jewish merchants were part of the trade routes across the continent, and by the tenth century, they were turning to agriculture and handicrafts. Then during the Crusades, more immigrants came and some became moneylenders. During the thirteenth and fourteenth centuries, intense urbanization and rising persecution of Jews in western Europe encouraged even more Jewish immigration to Poland, where they were welcomed. The period from 1580 to 1648 has been called the Golden Age of Jews in Poland. Then in the seventeenth and eighteenth centuries, Jews were expelled from a number of Polish towns and victimized by pogroms. After the Partitions of Poland in 1795 and the destruction of Poland as a sovereign state, Polish Jews were subject to the laws of the partitioning powers, the increasingly Russian Empire, and Austria, Hungary (the Austro-Hungarian Empire in 1867) and the Kingdom of Prussia (later a part of the German Empire). Antisemitism was a growing problem throughout Europe in the years prior to World War II, from both the political establishment and the general population. Even with the density of Poland's Jewish population, prescient ones who had the capability left for America.

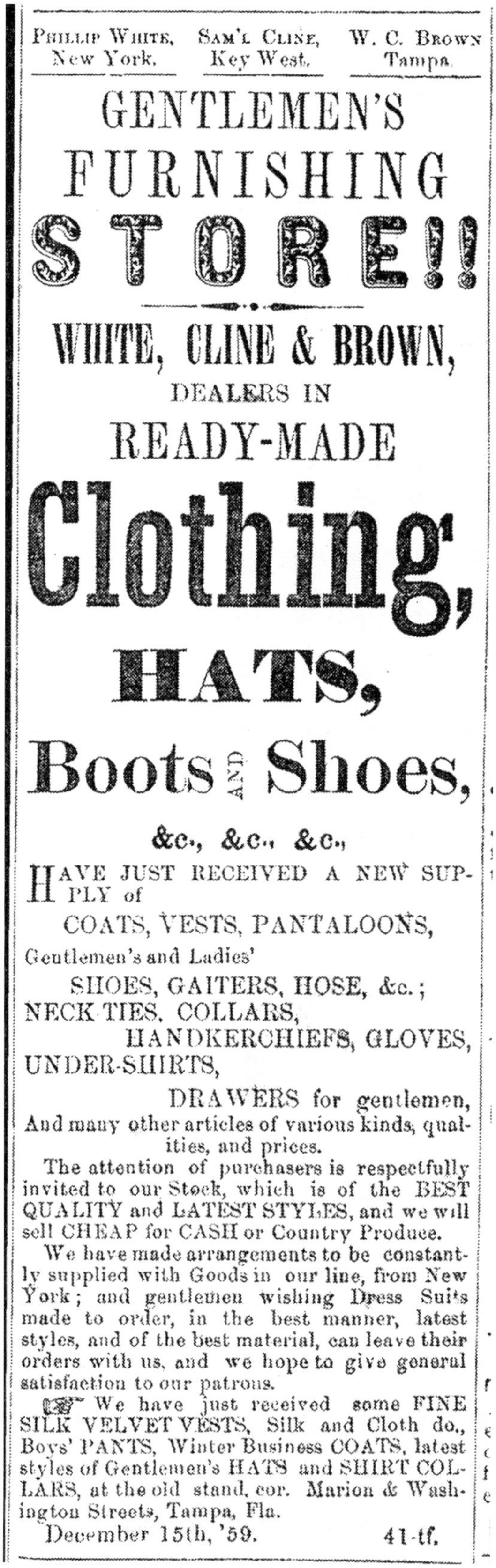

Phillip White, New York. Sam'l Cline, Key West. W. C. Brown Tampa.

GENTLEMEN'S FURNISHING STORE!!

WHITE, CLINE & BROWN,

DEALERS IN

READY-MADE

Clothing,

HATS,

Boots and Shoes,

&c., &c., &c.,

HAVE JUST RECEIVED A NEW SUPPLY of

COATS, VESTS, PANTALOONS,

Gentlemen's and Ladies'

SHOES, GAITERS, HOSE, &c.;

NECK-TIES, COLLARS,

HANDKERCHIEFS, GLOVES,

UNDER-SHIRTS,

DRAWERS for gentlemen,

And many other articles of various kinds, qualities, and prices.

The attention of purchasers is respectfully invited to our Stock, which is of the BEST QUALITY and LATEST STYLES, and we will sell CHEAP for CASH or Country Produce.

We have made arrangements to be constantly supplied with Goods in our line, from New York; and gentlemen wishing Dress Suits made to order, in the best manner, latest styles, and of the best material, can leave their orders with us, and we hope to give general satisfaction to our patrons.

☞ We have just received some FINE SILK VELVET VESTS, Silk and Cloth do., Boys' PANTS, Winter Business COATS, latest styles of Gentlemen's HATS and SHIRT COLLARS, at the old stand, cor. Marion & Washington Streets, Tampa, Fla.

December 15th, '59. 41-tf.

Gentlemen's Furnishing Store ad, Tampa, 1859.

One of the store owners, Phillip White, was an uncle of Max White, born Avraham Mordecai Weiss in Poland. Samuel Cline was a cousin. In the store, Max White was a tailor and made custom suits.

Jews have always sought religious freedom and economic opportunity. Even though Florida was not hospitable in the mid-nineteenth century, some Jews came as it was still better than being in Europe. Max White (1835–1919) wrote his memoirs recording his observations when he arrived in Key West in 1857 and then in Tampa in 1858 to work for his family's business. Excerpts of those memoirs were edited for publication in *Southern Jewish History* (2001) by his great-great-nephew Richard E. Sapon-White. Following the Third Seminole Indian War, Tampa was "gloom of glooms," a lawless town with sand streets. Max became part of a vigilante group, even though he'd never held a gun. Then yellow fever drove him back to Key West via a schooner where "men dressed mostly in white suits," and when yellow fever attacked him again, he retreated to New York. When I write about moving from town to town in these pioneer days before roads and cars, it is difficult to comprehend how challenging these trips were. Sapon-White showed up at my lecture for the American Library Association in Orlando in 2016 and shared family lore. For example, one of Max's granddaughters was Margaret Bourke-White, famed in later years as a photographer for *Life* and *Fortune* magazines.

Mack Brameister family getting off the boat in Havana, Cuba, 1924.

After America closed its doors to immigrants in 1924, many families escaping eastern Europe were welcomed in Cuba. This family migrated from Poland and six years later moved again from Cuba to Florida.

Frank Brameister, Palmetto, 1920.

Polish immigrant Frank Brameister came to Florida from New Jersey in 1923 because of his health. When he couldn't find any property in Miami that was within his budget, he went to Palmetto and opened a small department store in a converted feed store. Several years later, he built his own store and went north to find a wife, Rose Meltzer. When their first child was due, Rose went home to Coney Island where she had family. They raised their children, Marilyn and Herbert, in Palmetto. In 1930 Frank brought his brother and his brother's family over from Cuba. Mack; his wife, Eva; and their children, Sarah [Nelson], Nathan, and Herman, spoke only Yiddish and Spanish when they arrived in Florida. The families attended High Holiday services in Sarasota. Cousins Sarah and Marilyn moved to Miami as young adults for a more established Jewish community.

Polish Wooden Synagogues as Jewish Folk Art

Collage of Polish wooden synagogues with two Polish families who immigrated to Florida.

The Jews of Poland lived in concentrated areas of their towns, the "Jewish quarter," and the center of their lives was the synagogue. For four hundred years prior to World War II, the Jews of the *shtetls* built approximately one thousand wooden synagogues because lumber was plentiful. The architects and craftsmen were skilled at elaborate designs that followed the rules for the layout of the synagogue.

According to some art historians, the wooden synagogues of Poland with their painted and carved interiors were a truly original and organic manifestation of artistic expression—the only real Jewish folk art in history. The wooden synagogues were memorable because, unlike all previous synagogues, they were not built in the architectural style of their region and era but in a newly evolved and uniquely Jewish style. Moreover, while in many parts of the world Jews were proscribed from entering the building trades and even from practicing the decorative arts of painting and woodcarving, the wooden synagogues were actually built by Jewish craftsmen. To many people, the Polish wooden synagogue represents the only indigenous Jewish architecture, that is, a style of folk architecture that is both unique to the Jews and not primarily adapted from something else.

These beautiful and unique seventeenth- and eighteenth-century Polish wooden synagogues no longer exist. The Germans burned those still standing to the ground by 1939. (Some synagogues built in the nineteenth and twentieth centuries have been found in Poland and what is now Lithuania and are in deteriorated conditions.)

In 2005 I had a visit at the JMOF from Peter Maurice, who was seeking a permanent home for his ten Polish wooden synagogue models. These detailed models, at an average scale of 1/40, depict seventeenth- and eighteenth-century synagogues from the villages of Przedborz, Gombin, Zabludow, Gwozdziec, Wysoke Mazowieckie, Lutomiersk, Kornik, Narowla, Glinne, and Pilic. They all have distinct architectural elements that reflect the time and place in which they were created.

Englishman Peter Maurice (1937–2007) qualified with an aeronautical engineering degree to become a flight engineer in 1960. He qualified as a pilot in 1968 and flew a DC-6, Britannia, and later 707 aircraft for airlines such as Lloyd International, Anset, Monarch, Transglobe, and Swissair. He also flew missions for the Red Cross in the early 1970s. During time off in his flying career, Maurice made bronze and metal sculptures and was interested in photography. He had exhibitions of his work and sold many of his travel pictures to magazines and picture agencies, some of which are still in use today in postcards.

In 1973 he wanted to spend more time with his family and started a lighting company in London, specializing in making replicas of early nineteenth- and twentieth-century lighting. This has been a successful business that is now being carried on by his son Elliott. Peter and his wife, Wendy, retired to Spain in 2001.

Unfortunately, in 2003, he was diagnosed with an aggressive cancer. He consulted with his friend Rabbi Dr. Jeremy Collick in England for advice and guidance on how he should cope with the prognosis. Rabbi Collick knew of Peter's artistic talents and gave him a rare illustrated book on Polish wooden synagogues, written by Maria Piechotka, Kazimierz Piechotka, and Stephen Kayser.

After researching and studying, Peter realized he could make accurate models of some of these synagogues. He worked on them for nearly four years, often well into the night, finding relief from the pain he constantly suffered. He planned to make more, but time was not on his side.

The models convey the enormity of what was lost during World War II. Poland was the place where the Germans built all the death camps. This is the place where most of Europe's Jews perished. After he visited the JMOF and saw that we were housed in a synagogue representing continuity, preserving stories of immigrants' contributions to Jewish life in Florida, his dying wish was "to assure himself that this was the appropriate home for his artworks." According to his wife, Wendy, "Peter donated the models to the JMOF so that they could be seen and enjoyed in the hope that they would bring to life a heritage that was destroyed through hate and antisemitism."

The JMOF used items from its Collections and put out a call for more photographs, documents, and artifacts to tell the story of Jews in Florida who came (or whose ancestors came) from Poland and then in 2011 created an exhibit with the models and the Florida connection. This was one of my last exhibits before I retired and will always remain powerful in my memory for the story it portrayed.

CHAPTER 3

Romanian Immigration

By the late nineteenth century, the fate of the Jews in Romania was precarious. The government launched a series of anti-Jewish legal restrictions. Jews lived in ghettos, eventually could not attend schools, and faced expulsions and physical assaults. It was challenging to make a living. Some families who came to America settled in Florida. Key West was a popular destination as it was a direct port of entry and the Romanian language has many similarities to Spanish, which was spoken by the Cuban immigrants there.

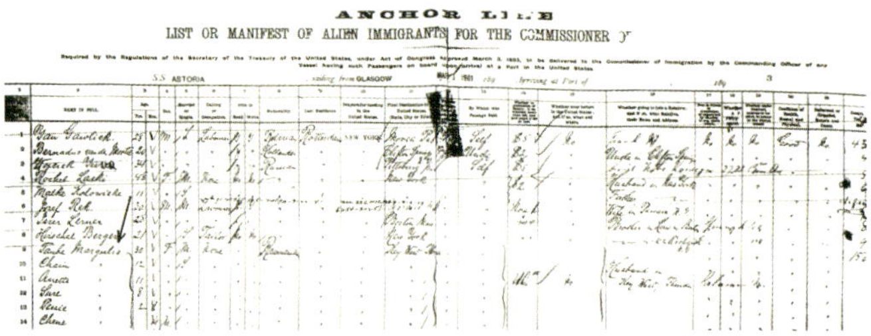

The Margulis (Margolis) family is listed on this Manifest of Alien Immigrants for the SS *Astoria*. They had traveled to meet Solomon Margolis, already in Key West, 1901.

Solomon Margolis, born in Husi, Romania, made at least three trips to America, bringing groups of young men. He settled in Key West in 1900, joining his brother-in-law, Ben Haimowitz. His wife, Toba, and the children came the next year. In 1923 they relocated to Tampa. Solomon served as a teacher, cantor, and *shochet*. For the High Holy Days, he traveled to Gainesville to conduct services. The large family in Florida gathers for reunions.

Samuel Rosenthal family, Romania, 1890.

In the front from left to right are Pepi, Louis, unknown, Edward, and unknown; in the back from left to right are Clara, Sipora, unknown, Katie, and Samuel.

In Romania in 1882, there was a blood libel, and in 1884 restrictive measures against the Jewish merchants were instituted. This prompted an emigration wave. Samuel and Sipora Rosenthal left for better opportunities and came to Key West from Husi, Romania, to find spouses for two of their daughters, Pepi and Katie. The girls married Charles and Herman Markowitz, sons of Jacob Markowitz. A third Rosenthal daughter, Bertha, married Herman Wolkowsky.

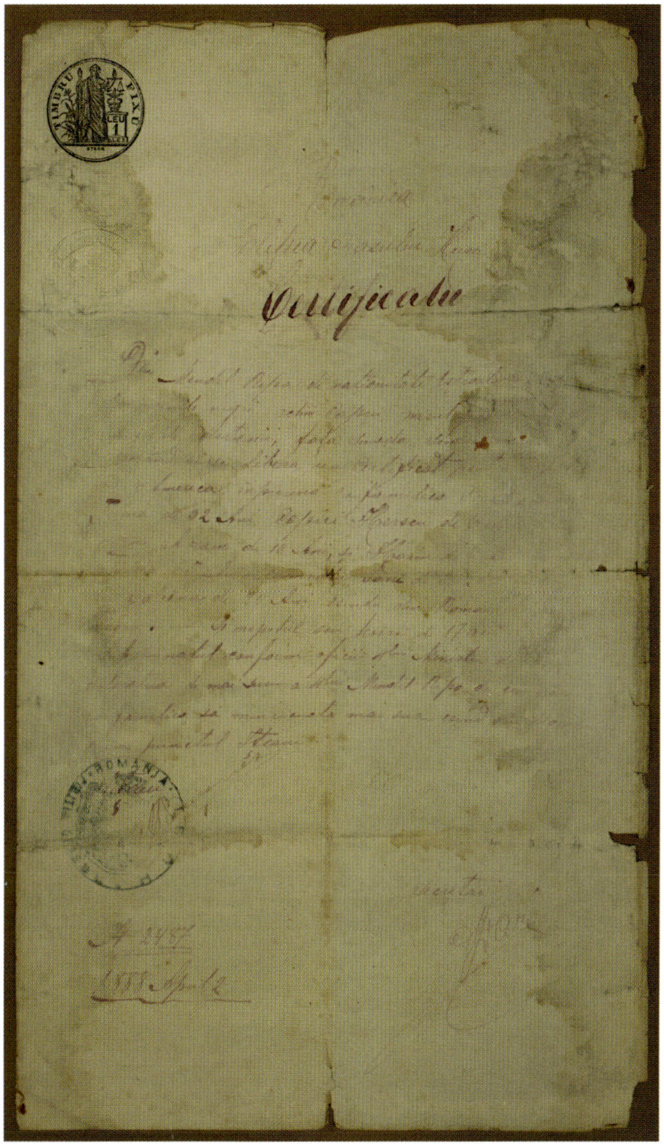

Family of Mendel Rippa, Romanian emigration certificate, April 2, 1888.

At age thirty-eight, Mendel Rippa came with his entire family from Husi, Romania, to Key West, which he called the new *medinat Yisroel*. This Romanian document refers to Rippa as being of Jewish nationality and lists each member of his family: his wife, Frima; children, Herscu (Harry), Avram, and Haim; brother-in-law, Sane; sister-in-law, Sabina; and nephew, Misu. Mendel started as a peddler, became a successful merchant in Key West, and in 1893 opened the Last Chance Saloon, which was close to the port. When Harry was seventeen, he served in the US Army in the Spanish-American War as a member of the Hospital Corp, stationed in the Philippines. When the cigar industry declined in Key West in 1891, some of the Rippas moved to Tampa (and are still there), and some remain in south Florida.

Kanner Family

Early in the MOSAIC project, Sam Proctor encouraged me to call Marcia and Lewis Kanner in Miami. They enthusiastically became part of my team and helped with more contacts around Miami and the state, even being one of my hosts providing bed and breakfast when I trekked to Miami for research. As I moved around Florida, I found numerous Kanners who did not know of their relatives in other communities. I eventually created a family tree that made all the connections and is now treasured by the descendants.

Not all Romanian Jews settled in Key West. Some, like the Kanner family, went to north and central Florida. In the 1880s the eldest, Zella (short for Gisella) Kanner, and her husband, Frank Seligman, were the first from the family to emigrate from Jassy, Romania. There the Kanner family of eleven lived in a mountainous, agricultural region in a five-room farmhouse made of clay covered with straw. It had yellow clay floors and a ceiling of wood joists painted red and was heated by wood and kerosene lamps.

Zella and Frank settled in Quincy. Seven Kanner brothers and sisters (Charles, Morris, Harry, Asher, Rose [Daniels], Pauline [Hershcovitz], and Kalman) followed to live and open retail stores in different small Florida towns so they would not compete (Palatka, Mulberry, Sanford, Orlando, and Ybor City). Their Orthodox parents, Esther and Samuel, joined the children in Sanford soon after the turn of the twentieth century. Emanuel, already in the army, was the only family member to stay in Romania, and he was killed in World War I.

Kanner-Salomon family, Orlando, 1905.

Sisters Pauline Abrams Kanner and Minnie Abrams Salomon with their mother (center); their husbands, Charles Kanner and Ben Salomon (standing in the back); and their children. In the front row from left to right are Herman Kanner, Ruth Kanner [Sandler], and Celia Salomon. In the second row from left to right are Harry Kanner, Pauline Kanner, Grandmother Abrams, Minnie Salomon with Blanche Salomon [Boolos] on her lap, and Abram Otto "A. O." Kanner. Descendants of both families live in Florida.

Charles Kanner arrived in Sanford in 1892 and brought from Romania his sweetheart, Pauline Abrams. Their marriage in 1893 was the area's first-known Jewish wedding. Ben and Minnie Abrams Salomon arrived in Orlando in 1903, settling down with no inside plumbing. The Salomons opened a store. Ben was a founder and president of Congregation Ohev Shalom. Minnie was the first president of the Ladies Auxiliary.

Wedding of Romanian immigrants and cousins Rachel Loben and Harry Kanner, Sanford, 1902.

Harry Kanner, born in Jassy, Romania, in 1875 is another example of an immigrant with strong initiative, character, and Jewish commitment. In Romania, his occupation was to purchase horses for royalty. At age twenty-five, he left because of the Jewish persecution. He came to Orlando in 1900 as he already had family there. He spoke Romanian, Russian, and Yiddish—no English. Like other immigrants, he acculturated and quickly learned English, which he spoke with a heavy accent. In 1902 a rabbi from Jacksonville married Harry and Rachel in Sanford in the home of his brother Charles. Rachel and Harry had three children: Rose in 1904, the first-known Jewish child born in Orlando; Aaron in 1905; and Samuel. Aaron grew up to attend the University of Florida, where he was a founder of the Tau Epsilon Phi (TEP) fraternity. Then he headed a prestigious law firm in Miami, where he was active in the Jewish community. His granddaughter Ellen Kanner lives in Miami.

Harry Kanner shows off his orange crop in grove, Orlando, 1910.

Harry Kanner represented both retail and citrus as he had stores and also owned groves. The meeting to organize Orlando's first Jewish congregation was at Harry's home in 1917, and he was president of that congregation, Ohev Shalom, in 1928. Five members of the Kanner family signed the congregation's charter. In 1953 Harry was buried in Ohev Shalom's cemetery.

Harry Kanner rides with son Aaron in a parade, Orlando, 1912.

With his knowledge and love of horses from Romania, Harry had trotters "Dan Patch" and "Melon Patch." The family used the horse and buggy for Sunday outings to the springs for swimming, and Harry participated in parades.

Descendants continue to live in Florida—and are still Jewish 118 years later. Harry Kanner is symbolic of our story!

CHAPTER 4

Russian Immigration

At one time, the vast territories of the Russian empire hosted the largest population of Jews in the world. During the reign of Catherine II in the eighteenth century, the Jewish people were restricted to the Pale of Settlement within Russia. Beginning in 1825 with Czar Nicholas I, the most dreaded thing for Russian Jews was to be called to serve in the army—which was antisemitic —and meant severe, remote, harsh duty that could last twenty-five years and often lasted until death. Because boys could be drafted at the age of twelve, most Jewish families sent their sons to America at an early age. In 1881 Alexander III instituted pogroms (organized massacres) that swept across different regions of the empire for several decades. The May Laws prohibited Jews from buying rural land, freely attending universities, or changing their names. Czar Nicholas II, who reigned from 1894 to 1917, intensified the pogroms and initiated a policy of marking Jewish identity passes with the word *Jew*.

More than two million Jews fled Russia between 1880 and 1920, mostly to the United States and what is today the State of Israel. Seeking better lives for their families and lured by tales from cousins of the *goldene medina*, Jews began to emigrate to Florida. My own maternal family came from Grodno, Lithuania, at the turn of the twentieth century. Lithuania was part of the Russian empire from 1795 to 1918. You will meet many Jews who came to Florida from Grodno, a town of about forty thousand in the late nineteenth century. Nearly 70 percent were Jews who spoke Yiddish, and Grodno supported more than forty synagogues, a Jewish orphanage, a poorhouse, a theater, and a hospital.

Pinsk

Pinsk was first mentioned in 1097, incorporated into the Grand Duchy of Lithuania in 1320, and the first Jewish settlers arrived in 1503. After 1569 the city was part of the Polish-Lithuanian Commonwealth. The Cossacks (military warriors) captured Pinsk in 1640 and carried out a pogrom against the city's Jewish population. The Poles retook it, killing 24,000 people and burning 5,000 houses. Eight years later, Russians burned the town. Pinsk was burned several more times over the next 100 years and fell to the Russian Empire in 1793 in the Second Partition of Poland. Up until World War II, Pinsk had a significant Jewish population. The 1897 census counted 21,100 Jews (74 percent) among the city's population. At the start of World War II in 1939, the Jewish population of Pinsk was 27,000 (90 percent). Pinsk is now in Belarus.

Shepard Broad: A Horatio Alger Story from a Russian Ghetto to Miami

Shepard Broad was born Szmuel Bobrowice in Pinsk in 1906 to Naum and Chana Rose Bobrowice. His mother and father died before he was ten.

Shepard Broad's family, Pinsk, circa 1900.
Ann Broad Bussel, Bay Harbor Islands.

In the front from left to right are David Skudin (maternal grandfather), unknown, Sarah Leighman Skudin (maternal grandmother), unknown, and unknown. In the back row from left to right are unknown, unknown, Naum Bobrowice (father), Chana Rose Skudin Bobrowice (mother), unknown, and Dinah Skudin Hart.

Shepard Broad (far right) with stepmother, Shosha Kosowsky, and half brothers David and Israel, Pinsk, circa 1918.

Following the death of Shepard's mother, his father remarried Shosha, and then he died.

Shepard Broad with Adolph Stark, his benefactor when he arrived in Montreal, Canada, from Pinsk, 1920.

When Shepard was thirteen, his uncle Daniel Broad sent him a ticket for boat passage from Antwerp, Belgium, to New York. On foot, by boxcar and cart, Broad got to the dock, but he missed that boat. So he was sent to Montreal, Canada, and was nearly returned to Pinsk. Adolph Stark rescued him and soon sent him on to New York, where his uncle adopted him. He was put in the third grade in school as he only spoke Yiddish. Seven years later, at the age of twenty, he graduated from New York Law School. Broad said, "When you have no money and nothing except a rather decent head on your shoulders, the thing to do is to use your head."

As an attorney in New York, Broad visited south Florida on a fishing trip with clients. Seeing a good life for his family and business opportunities where he could make his mark, he moved to Miami Beach in 1940 with his wife, Ruth, and their two children, Ann [Bussel] and Morris. Shepard Broad was the developer of Bay Harbor Islands and served as its mayor (1947–73). In 1951 he built the Broad Causeway, connecting Bay Harbor Islands with mainland Miami. Broad, an avid Zionist and giant in the Greater Miami community, was the founder of the American Savings and Loan Association and other banks and the law firm Broad and Cassel. In 1979 Dr. Norman Vincent Peale presented the Horatio Alger Award to him. Asked about his success, Broad said, "You have to be giving to achieve your desires." He died at the age of ninety-five in his Bay Harbor Islands home, having lived the American dream. His grandson John Bussel resides in that home with his family.

Pushalotes and Panevezy, Lithuania

Some of the Jewish immigration into Florida was called "chain migration." This term refers to the social process by which migrants from a particular town hear of opportunities and follow others from that town to a particular destination where they are given accommodations and employment. For example, many Jews who settled in Jacksonville in the late nineteenth century were from a primitive *shtetl*, Pushalotes, Lithuania, with a wooden synagogue; it was located in part of the Russian empire. Among the many immigrants to Jacksonville were descendants of Macy Meisel Slott. His son Herschel settled in 1887 and changed his name to Harry Goldman. The Goldman and Finkelstein families formed the nucleus of the city's Pushalotes contingent, comprised of thirty families by the 1920s and 1930s.

Sarah and Ethel Cohen saying goodbye at their mother's grave before leaving for America, Pushalotes, Lithuania, 1920.

The gravestone reads, "Here lies Chai, daughter of Reb Katz, who died three days earlier. October 21, 1914." It was a tradition for Lithuanian children to visit the graves of their parents to say goodbye before leaving for America.

The Pushalotes Ladies Society Auxiliary, Jacksonville, 1946.

Included left to right are Celia Schemer, Sarah Krulevitz, Mary Cohen, Annie Margol, Rose Sloat, Ida Cohen, Bessie Rose, Sarah Goldie Schemer, Minnie Schemer, and Molly Kroser. In 1946 this organization became the Ladies Hebrew Sheltering Aide Society and the River Garden Auxiliary. Many of the descendants of these women continue to live in Jacksonville.

David Ben Zion Dibobes and his mother, Hinda Reiza, at the grave of his father, scholar and scribe Joseph Schraga Dibobes, Panevezys, Lithuania, 1914.

Dr. Edwin Safer of Jacksonville, the family historian, says this is the only existing photograph taken in Lithuania of the huge Dibobes family.

Reverend Benjamin Safer at thirty-four years old, Jacksonville, 1905. *Dr. Edwin Safer.*

The first of the Dibobes to arrive in Florida from Panevezys was Reverend Benjamin Safer in 1902—and he changed the family name to Safer. After completing Yeshiva studies in Lithuania, Benjamin was certified as a *shochet*, *mohel*, *chazzan*, and *sofer*. From 1898–1902, he served the Pakroujis wooden synagogue in Lithuania. In 1902 Benjamin was offered a rabbinic position for the newly formed Congregation B'nai Israel in Jacksonville. He also served as the community cantor, *shochet*, and *mohel*. A group of Orthodox Jews of Jacksonville came from the same region of Lithuania as the Dibobes family—and so they knew him!

Fiftieth anniversary of Reverend Benjamin and Freida Leah Safer with their twelve children, Jacksonville, 1946.

In the front row from left to right are Edward Safer, Bluma Safer Haimwitz, Reverend Benjamin Safer, Frieda Leah Safer, Dr. Jacob V. Safer, and Max J. Safer. In the middle row from left to right are Israel Safer and Abraham "Abba" Safer. In the back row from left to right are David Safer, Ethel "Doll" Safer Davis, Perry Safer, Pearl Safer Kramer, Joseph Safer, and Ida Safer Goldberg.

Benjamin and Freida Leah Ziv married in Panevezys in 1896. Their first child, Bluma, was born in 1897 and then three more born in Lithuania; eight were born in Jacksonville. Reverend Benjamin Safer (1874–1959) was the oldest of the six children of Hinda and Joseph who came to Florida. With their spouses, Benjamin, Ida, Sarah, Jacob, Harry, and Max had forty-two offspring, which today has led to nearly one thousand descendants. Most of them—and their spouses—have served as leaders in their Jewish and civic communities for more than one hundred years in Florida.

Wolfson Family

Rosa Gruner and Louis Wolfson married in Russia in 1887, Key West, 1912.

The first Wolfson to land in Florida was Joseph, who came into the port of Key West around 1884 in the aftermath of a shipwreck. Key West was, at that time, the largest (population of 18,000) and richest city in Florida, but there were continuous threats of yellow fever, malaria, and typhoid fever. Nonetheless, he found Key West more desirable than his hometown, Botka, Russia, due to the harsh conditions for Jews in the latter.

So Joseph sent for his brothers to join him in 1887. First came Adam, who by 1920 had moved to Tampa with his sons, Abraham and William, and built a brick structure in Ybor City for his stores. "Wolfson 1922" remains engraved into the top of the building that survives.

Later in 1887, Louis and Rosa joined them in Key West. Louis learned English; began as a peddler, like many other Jewish immigrants; and then opened a large, successful dry goods business. The Wolfsons had four children in Key West: William (1888), O. Phillip (1891), Mitchell (1900), and Zenia [Meyer] (1902). William married Gertrude Quitman (1917), O. Phillip married Nora Pred (1922), Zenia married Sidney Meyer (1922), and Mitchell married Frances Cohen of Pensacola (1925).

Louis Wolfson was prominent in Key West, operating the House of Fashion and even becoming the first-known Jew elected to the city commission around 1910. Machine-made cigars and the military withdrawal took their toll on the economy of Key West. Louis and Rosa moved the family to Miami in 1915 because Rosa felt the future was better there for her children. And she was right as her family prospered and became major personalities. Descendants continue to live in Florida.

Wolkowsky Family

Abraham (Abram) Wolkowsky, Key West, circa 1900.

Russian immigrant Wolkowsky (1862–1932), settled in Key West in 1885. He began as a peddler, mostly of jewelry, but then expanded his inventory. Four years later, he married Rebecca Lewinsky. Abram nearly succumbed to typhoid fever but survived and became one of the town's most successful businessmen as the owner of prominent clothing stores, saloons, and eventually land. Saloons that were started by the Wolkowsky-Lewinsky families continue today as some of the most popular ones in Key West. One, Sloppy Joe's, was made famous by writer Ernest Hemingway.

Isaac "Ike" and Frank were two sons of Rebecca and Abraham Wolkowsky, Key West, 1898.

The third son was Joseph. A son of Isaac, David Wolkowsky (1919–2018), became an important developer who started the rejuvenation of Society Hill and Rittenhouse Square in Philadelphia. After Isaac died in 1962, David visited his hometown of Key West and ignited major renovation projects there, beginning with family properties.

Florida Keys Star
VOL. 28 NO. 5

A block from the southernmost point in the United States is the former home of Abraham Wolkowsky, who came to Key West many years ago and was in the clothing business. His grandson, David Wolkowsky, built Pirates Alley, Key West's tourist shopping center, and the Pier House, the beautiful low profile Key Westey type house at the north end of Duval Street. Also Tony's Fish Market, built above the old pier in the same area. David Wolkowsky is also known as a restorer of old sections of other American cities.

Abraham Wolkowsky's home, Key West.
Florida Keys Star, 1974.

Wolkowsky was one of the few Key West Jews who did not live in an apartment above the store. He built this "showplace" for his family next to his dry goods store.

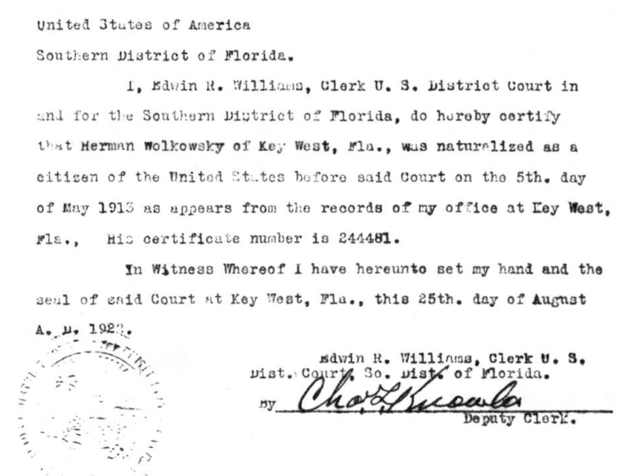
United States of America

Southern District of Florida.

I, Edwin R. Williams, Clerk U. S. District Court in and for the Southern District of Florida, do hereby certify that Herman Wolkowsky of Key West, Fla., was naturalized as a citizen of the United States before said Court on the 5th. day of May 1913 as appears from the records of my office at Key West, Fla., His certificate number is 244481.

In Witness Whereof I have hereunto set my hand and the seal of said Court at Key West, Fla., this 25th. day of August A. D. 192[illegible].

Edwin R. Williams, Clerk U. S. Dist. Court, So. Dist. of Florida.
By [signature]
Deputy Clerk.

Certificate of Naturalization of Herman Wolkowsky, May 5, 1913.

Herman Wolkowsky left Russia at the age of fourteen to avoid conscription into the Czar's army even after shooting off his trigger finger (which was not an uncommon act in order to be disqualified for army service). Herman came to Key West in 1913, knowing his uncle Abraham Wolkowsky could give him work. He was a liquor peddler in the beginning, selling to labor camps that housed the workers of Henry Flagler's railroad. Herman married, opened a furniture store, raised his family, and took a turn as president of Congregation B'nai Zion in Key West until moving to Miami in 1923.

More Russian Families

Louis Fine (standing front row, third from the left with a bow tie) sailing from Russia to Key West, 1896.

Fine (1866–1923) was an Orthodox Jew from Vilna who became a US citizen the year he arrived. He was one of a number of Jewish merchants in Key West who actively supported Cuba in 1898 in its fight for independence. They remembered the Jewish expulsion from Spain in 1492 and donated money and supplies to the cause. By 1908 he had moved to Miami, where he owned a saloon with his son Isador. Louis was a prime mover in founding the first Jewish congregation in Miami and served as its president.

Isidor Cohen arrived in Miami in 1896 and was the first permanent Jewish resident there, 1904.

Isidor Cohen (1870–1951) emigrated from Russia to New York. Then with the news of Henry Flagler's railroad coming into Florida, he ventured south. He had retail stores in Titusville, Fort Pierce, Cocoa, Bartow, and then West Palm Beach as the railroad arrived there in 1894. He moved to Miami the year the railroad extended there (1896), opened a store on the south side of the Miami River, and brought his customers across in a rowboat. A true pioneer in Miami, Isidor Cohen was a signatory of the city charter in 1896. He self-published a book, *Sketches of Miami*, which is the story of the city's early development told in his humorous style.

Pioneer merchants, left to right: Jacob Schneidman, Isidor Cohen, and Marcus Frank, Miami, 1898.

When the city of Miami was founded in 1896, of the sixteen merchants involved, twelve were Jews, mostly from Russia. Along with Schneidman and Cohen, opening stores was Julius Frank, who died in an 1896 fire. Marcus Frank was his son. By 1900 Schneidman, with his wife, Ida, and Cohen, were the only three Jews in the city.

Ida Schneidman Cohen, Miami, 1904.

Soon after, Jacob Schneidman died. Ida left Miami with her son Murray and moved to New York. On a buying trip there in 1904 Isidor Cohen convinced Ida to marry him and return to Miami. She did—and became a tireless leader who was dubbed "Mother of Miami's Jewish community." She was founder of the Miami Jewish Home for the Aged and served as president of most Jewish women's organizations.

Frank Family

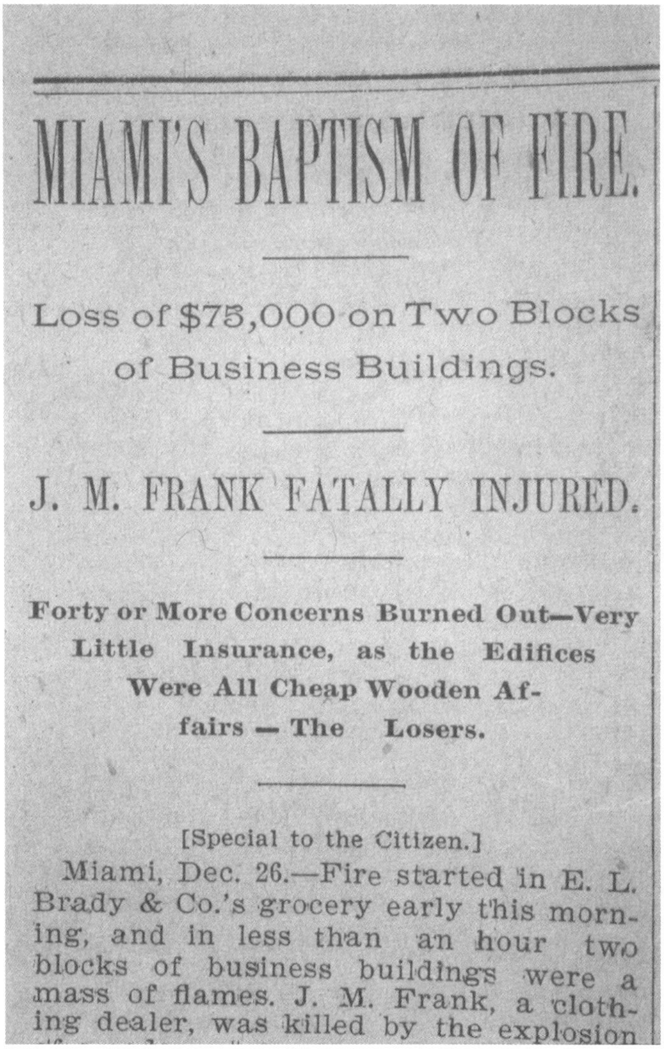

MIAMI'S BAPTISM OF FIRE.

Loss of $75,000 on Two Blocks of Business Buildings.

J. M. FRANK FATALLY INJURED.

Forty or More Concerns Burned Out—Very Little Insurance, as the Edifices Were All Cheap Wooden Affairs — The Losers.

[Special to the Citizen.]

Miami, Dec. 26.—Fire started in E. L. Brady & Co.'s grocery early this morning, and in less than an hour two blocks of business buildings were a mass of flames. J. M. Frank, a clothing dealer, was killed by the explosion

Obituary of Julius Frank, Miami, 1896.

Julius Frank, born in Russia in 1853, emigrated to New York in the 1870s. Later, his Russian cousin Julia Segal joined him. They married in 1881 and lived in New York and Augusta, Georgia, until 1894. Hearing of Flagler's railroad to West Palm Beach and the opportunities it opened up, they moved there and operated a store. When the railroad was extended to Miami in 1896, they moved there. Some say he built the first brick building in Miami for his clothing store, but it was not to last. On December 26 of that year, Frank was killed in an explosion caused by a fire that destroyed most of the stores.

Julia Segal Frank, Miami, 1898.

Marcus Frank, West Palm Beach, 1899.

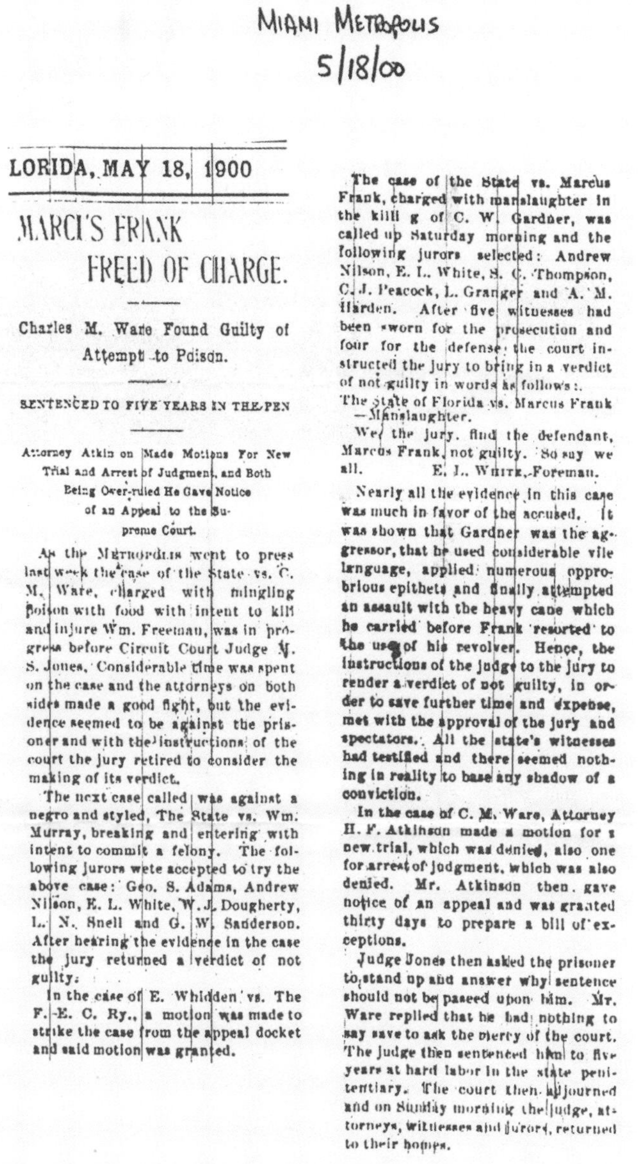

LORIDA, MAY 18, 1900

MARCUS FRANK FREED OF CHARGE.

Charles M. Ware Found Guilty of Attempt to Poison.

SENTENCED TO FIVE YEARS IN THE PEN

Attorney Atkinson Made Motions For New Trial and Arrest of Judgment, and Both Being Over-ruled He Gave Notice of an Appeal to the Supreme Court.

As the METROPOLIS went to press last week the case of the State vs. C. M. Ware, charged with mingling poison with food with intent to kill and injure Wm. Freeman, was in progress before Circuit Court Judge M. S. Jones. Considerable time was spent on the case and the attorneys on both sides made a good fight, but the evidence seemed to be against the prisoner and with the instructions of the court the jury retired to consider the making of its verdict.

The next case called was against a negro and styled, The State vs. Wm. Murray, breaking and entering with intent to commit a felony. The following jurors were accepted to try the above case: Geo. S. Adams, Andrew Nilson, E. L. White, W. J. Dougherty, L. N. Snell and G. W. Sanderson. After hearing the evidence in the case the jury returned a verdict of not guilty.

In the case of E. Whidden vs. The F. E. C. Ry., a motion was made to strike the case from the appeal docket and said motion was granted.

The case of the State vs. Marcus Frank, charged with manslaughter in the killi g of C. W. Gardner, was called up Saturday morning and the following jurors selected: Andrew Nilson, E. L. White, S. C. Thompson, C. J. Peacock, L. Granger and A. M. Harden. After five witnesses had been sworn for the prosecution and four for the defense the court instructed the jury to bring in a verdict of not guilty in words as follows:

The State of Florida vs. Marcus Frank —Manslaughter.

We the jury, find the defendant, Marcus Frank, not guilty. So say we all. E. L. WHITE, Foreman.

Nearly all the evidence in this case was much in favor of the accused. It was shown that Gardner was the aggressor, that he used considerable vile language, applied numerous opprobrious epithets and finally attempted an assault with the heavy cane which he carried before Frank resorted to the use of his revolver. Hence, the instructions of the judge to the jury to render a verdict of not guilty, in order to save further time and expense, met with the approval of the jury and spectators. All the state's witnesses had testified and there seemed nothing in reality to base any shadow of a conviction.

In the case of C. M. Ware, Attorney H. F. Atkinson made a motion for a new trial, which was denied, also one for arrest of judgment, which was also denied. Mr. Atkinson then gave notice of an appeal and was granted thirty days to prepare a bill of exceptions.

Judge Jones then asked the prisoner to stand up and answer why sentence should not be passed upon him. Mr. Ware replied that he had nothing to say save to ask the mercy of the court. The judge then sentenced him to five years at hard labor in the state penitentiary. The court then adjourned and on Sunday morning the judge, attorneys, witnesses and jurors, returned to their homes.

***Miami Metropolis* article about Marcus Frank's manslaughter acquittal, 1900.**

Miami's first store for women's apparel was owned by Julia Frank (1865–1934), who survived the fire and became a widow. Her children were Marcus (1883–1966), Asher (1885), Pauline (1886), Meyer (1887–98), Sara [Israelson] (1890), Nell (1891), Fannie (1895), and then Simmie Handelsman [Levy] (1899), fathered by Julia's second husband. Asher was taken with the Spanish-American War soldiers as a mascot when they were shipped to Cuba. Julia wrote to US President William McKinley appealing for her son's return. He was released, but another tragedy followed. Meyer, awaiting the arrival of his brother's ship, died when he fell out of a palm tree. Family members would later serve in the US military. In 1916–17, Asher fought during the Mexican Border campaign. Julia and Julius's great-great-grandson, US Army Specialist Jeffrey Wershow of Gainesville, served and died in the Operation Iraqi Freedom campaign in 2003.

After Julia Frank's family heartbreaks, she moved her family back to West Palm Beach and reopened a store. In 1899 an antisemitic newspaper editor accused Julia Frank of illegally shipping goods from Miami during a yellow fever quarantine. Editor C. M. Gardner visited the Frank store apparently to harass Mrs. Frank in person and was confronted by Julia's teenage son Marcus. Words were exchanged, Gardner raised his heavy cane to hit Marcus, and Marcus pulled out a pistol and fatally shot Gardner in the chest. Frank was charged with manslaughter and tried in Miami. The jury found the shooting justified because of Gardner's verbal and written harassment and because he had used his cane. Marcus received a directed verdict of acquittal.

In 1900, after the trial, the family started over in Ocala, where the shooting was unknown. Julia, now married to Morris Handelsman, opened a store there with her son Marcus. Marcus became a prominent businessman, an outspoken civic leader who served two four-year terms on the city council and also represented Marion County in the state legislature (1939 and 1949). Family lore reports he was so popular that even after he died in 1966, he got eight hundred votes!

Here I want to tell you a story that will illustrate my process to retrieve the Jewish history of Florida and piece it together—like a MOSAIC.

Marcus Frank's store, Ocala, 1900.

Throughout the 1980s, I gathered photographs and assembled a slideshow to tell the story as it was developing from our grassroots research. I took my show to Jewish organizations in communities throughout Florida. I had gotten this store photograph from Stanley Malaver in Ocala, who said this was his grandfather Joseph Malaver's store.

I was speaking to the board of the Tampa Jewish Federation. When I showed the 1900 photograph of Malaver's Ocala store, Nellye Israelson Friedman, sitting in the front row, stood up and emphatically said, "You are wrong. This was my uncle Marcus Frank's store. Go find his daughter, my cousin Ruth Frank Gross in Fort Lauderdale, and she will validate this!"

The very next day, I was meeting with my MOSAIC task force at the Soref Jewish Community Center in Fort Lauderdale, and there was one woman at the table who I had not met—Ruth Frank Gross! I showed her the photograph in question and she said that Nellye was correct: the photo was indeed of her father's store.

And there was even more! She told me to wait, that she was going home to bring me her family photo album. Going through her album, she showed me the photo (you saw on page 53) of Isidor Cohen. I was astounded because I had been asking for several years for an early photograph of Miami's first permanent Jewish settler, and no one in Miami had one. Why did she? Because as you just learned, Julius Frank was killed in 1896. So when his son Marcus married Annie Marcus, Isidor was the best man, standing in for his friend Julius, the father of the groom!

Now I had the photograph of Isidor Cohen that I had sought for so long. And I learned the early Jewish history of Miami. And so importantly, I learned that both Stanley Malaver and Nellye Friedman were correct. Marcus Frank had sold his store to Joseph Malaver in 1905, the Frank's sign had not yet been changed, and Frank had opened a larger store up the street.

This is part of the validation process and demonstrates that the statewide collecting was so important for the crossover resulting from the migration of Jews around Florida. And it was such fun! Thanks to Carol Gross Clarkson, granddaughter of Marcus Frank, and Mary Friedman Kramer, Nellye's daughter and granddaughter of Sara Israelson, for sharing family photographs and stories.

More Russian Immigrants

Morris Zion, Miami, circa 1919.

Morris Zion, born in 1862 in Kiev, Russia, came to Key West in the 1880s where he founded Congregation B'nai Zion in 1887. He moved around the US, married, divorced, and then married his second wife, Clara, in New York. They had two children: Ruth Belle (1908) and Jack (1910). The family settled in Miami in 1911 where he founded Miami's first Jewish congregation that was also named for him, but the name changed to Beth David in 1917 when merchant David Afremow contributed $5,000. Zion, who was in the dry goods business, also served as founding president of the United Jewish Aid Association in 1920.

Ruth Belle Zion and Leo Benjamin with alligators (yes, stuffed!), Miami, 1911.

I loved this photograph so much I used it for the cover of my book *Jews of Greater Miami*. Benjamin worked for Morris Zion. The alligator is a symbol of Florida, found in all sixty-seven counties. Ruth Belle, daughter of Morris and Clara Zion, grew up in Miami and in 1927 married Albert Dubbin, who also grew up in Miami. Ruth and Albert had four children: Murray, Sandra [Kohlenberg], Bonnie [Askowitz], and Robin [Yablonsky]. In 1963 Murray Dubbin was one of the first two Jews elected to the Florida House of Representatives from Dade County; he served for twelve years. In 1977 Dubbin served on the Florida Board of Regents, becoming its chairman in 1983. In 1995 he was appointed as Miami Beach's city attorney.

Felix Glickstein on alligator, Jacksonville, 1916.

As I mentioned earlier, I traveled around the state to find the material evidence of Jewish life in Florida and stayed in private homes. In Jacksonville, I sometimes stayed with Natalie "Pat" Glickstein Haas, the mother of an Orlando friend, Marty Glickstein. On my first visit, Pat went to the back of her large closet and dragged out this image that had been enlarged to a poster. She said, "Would you like this adorable photo of my former husband, a dentist here in Jacksonville?"

This was the first photograph I had seen of a Jewish child on an alligator, and I immediately recognized that this represented our story—a Jewish boy, native to Florida, perched on the back of a stuffed alligator, native to Florida! This was the same year, 1987, that the Florida Legislature designated the American alligator, originally a symbol of Florida's extensive untamed wilderness and swamps, as the official state reptile. This image became the catalog cover and icon of the *MOSAIC: Jewish Life in Florida* traveling exhibit.

As I was outlining this book, I remembered that the family had donated Felix's *tallit* and *tefillin* from his 1926 *bar mitzvah* at St. Augustine's Sons of Israel Congregation. I asked the family why the ceremony was in St. Augustine if Felix was identified with Jacksonville. The answer to that question resulted in the following story, which is a good example of movement around Florida for economic fluctuations.

Morris, Sarah, and Felix Glickstein, St. Augustine, circa 1917.

Felix's father, Morris Glickstein, was born in Russia in 1878 and arrived in the US in 1890. By 1899 he had settled in Jacksonville because it had increasing employment opportunities and a growing Jewish community. Sarah Goldie Peltz was born in Russia in 1884 and arrived in Savannah in 1890. By 1902 her family had settled in Jacksonville where she met and married Morris Glickstein. Morris was a tailor and then a store manager in Jacksonville. They had three sons: Max (1903); Irving, originally Isadore (1905); and Felix (1913). In 1916 the family moved from Jacksonville to St. Augustine. Then around 1919 they moved back to Jacksonville. They again moved to St. Augustine in the 1920s to more easily manage the Cut Price Store. After Morris died in 1929, Sarah ran the store there. By 1934 she had opened her own women's clothing store, Morry's. Sarah eventually bought the entire building. Her father, Aaron, lived with her in St. Augustine for several years until his death in 1941. Sarah's store was open until at least 1945, and then she was back in Jacksonville by 1947, where she died in 1968.

Felix (the little guy on the alligator) went from St. Augustine to the University of Florida in 1931 and then to dental school, moving to Jacksonville by 1938 to open his dental practice. He married Natalie "Pat" Hackel in 1941, just at the time he was called to active duty in the US Army. After World War II, he returned to Jacksonville to resume his profession. They had two children: Martin "Marty" (1946) and Paul (1949). Marty has two children: Rachel (1978) and David (1983). Felix died in 1987. Pat died in 2014.

Cecelia Tarapani and Philip Levy, Sarasota, circa 1915.

Philip Levy fled Lithuania in fear of losing his life in a pogrom and immigrated to New York in 1905. Working as a sales agent for a pant-manufacturing firm, he traveled to St. Petersburg in 1909 where he met and married Cecelia Tarapani. In 1913 Philip and Cecelia Levy settled in Sarasota and opened a women's store on Main Street. They were the only Jews in their town until 1925 and conducted services in their home as Jews began to trickle into Sarasota.

Jennie and Henry Seitlin, Miami, 1915.

Henry and Louis Seitlin, ardent Zionists, escaped from Russia in 1910 and were sent by the Hebrew Immigration Aid Society to Florida to join a Zionist farm settlement in Homestead. The settlement soon folded, so Henry peddled stockings and sundries. In 1912 he opened Boston Shoe Store in Miami and then brought over his wife, Jennie; son, Sam; and brother Harry. The Seitlin family members were among the founders of the Jewish organizations in Miami.

Vinikowsky (Weinkle) Family

During my trek around Florida in the 1980s lecturing for Jewish organizations and congregations, I spoke several times in Sarasota. Charlotte Weinkle Chazin approached me to relate the story of how her father Marcus Joseph Weinkle got to nearby Moffitt. Also contributing to this story were family members James Weinkle of Miami (who has possession of Marcus Weinkle's invaluable journal), Joseph Weinkle, and Romelle Tarler.

From Charlotte, I got the photographs and phenomenal immigration saga of her family. She told me they had donated some ritual items to the Ellis Island Museum, but the Torah that her father brought from Russia was "in one of the synagogues in Jacksonville." She described the personal-size Torah with a broken finial. With this clue, I began my treasure hunt. All the rabbis were most helpful. When I got to the Jacksonville Jewish Center, the leadership said they had a Weinkle Torah, but never knew the significance. I related the story and asked if the MOSAIC project could borrow it for the traveling exhibit, and then when I started the JMOF, I went to the board of directors again and asked them to gift the Torah to the museum—and they did. **That Torah is in the "Building Community" section of the core exhibit at the JMOF-FIU.** It is loaned for family *simchas*. (See Torah in part 4, page 288).

Vinikowsky (Weinkle) family in Russia, 1885.

From left to right are Yehuda Hirsch Vinikowsky (1855–1918); Rosa Manchman Vinikowsky (Louis's wife); Yehuda's wife, Nechamo Frieda Mazursky Vinikowsky; Dora (their daughter); and Louis Vinikowsky (their oldest son). The family lived in Sokolka, a province of Grodno, Lithuania. The father of Yehuda Hirsch was a baker. Yehuda was sent to the Yeshiva in Grodno. He was first a teacher, then a bookbinder. He married Nechamo Frieda in 1861 and became a farmer and merchant for the village of about five thousand. Marcus Joseph was born in 1866 and was a good student. At the age of fourteen, school was completed, and he was helping to manage the family business.

In his journal, Marcus writes, "On May 6, 1881, a wave of pogroms was perpetrated upon the Jews of Czarist Empire, and the peasants, deciding that we were also Jews, did not miss us. In a few hours, there was left not even a nail in the wall, and it was the same on our farm that was 15 miles from the village. Twenty years of hard work of my father, mother and children—gone. We had no means at all to start up again and there were eight children in the family. It was the only time in my life that I saw my father in tears, and I'll never forget it."

Photograph of cotton handmade pants worn by Marcus Joseph Vinikowsky when he escaped Russia from his grave in 1887.

In 1887 Marcus was drafted into the Russian army for five years. To avoid service, the family faked his death "from a high fever." They held a funeral and actually buried him alive. After dark, Marcus crept out of his grave, retrieved a bundle of clothing, a Torah, and money that was hidden for him. Then he smuggled himself out of the country.

Marcus Joseph Vinikowsky, Jaffa, Palestine, circa 1888.

Marcus (1866–1933) made his way to Palestine, via Germany, Austria, and Egypt, as it was determined "that was the only safe haven for Jews" and had this photograph taken of himself in Jaffa to send to his family to inform them he had arrived. With a portion of the 5,000 rubles that his father had deposited in a banking brokerage house in Jaffa, he chose to stay in the nearby colony of Rishon Lezion. He purchased sheep as his father had been successful with them, but over time they were all stolen. When his health and the family's reserves in the bank failed, he decided to leave Palestine.

After various plans, he chose America as his destination. In 1890 Marcus made his way back to Russia to convince the family to join him—and there in his house, a neighbor lady came to bring some sewing and almost fainted when she saw Marcus as she had been at his funeral! When she returned for compensation to keep the secret from the Russian authorities, she was told "she had been mistaken." Marcus had made a clean getaway through the three-mile-long village in broad daylight!

Yehuda Hirsch Vinikowsky gave his son Marcus sufficient funds to go to America and invest in a business. Marcus sailed on the SS *Augusta Victoria*, Hamburg-American Line, which took seven days for the crossing, and landed at Castle Garden at the age of twenty-four, speaking Russian, Slavish, Polish, and German and with the name and address of another "greener" (a recently arrived immigrant). He was given a one-dollar derby hat, his introduction to the *goldene medina*. He prayed each morning with his *tefillin*, became a peddler, and soon learned of another Vinikowsky who had poor credit—so he changed his name to Winkle/Weinkle, a Dutch name, as Holland had been good to the Jews. And he "threw in the *e* so all the family could identify each other." (Note: the story and quotes are from Marcus Weinkle's journal.)

Hannah Rosa Ratkowsky Weinkle with her children, Charlotte [Chazin] and Abraham Moses, Moffitt, circa 1910.

Marcus learned that the American South would be a desirable place to live. He went to South Carolina, where he opened a store. Eventually, probably around 1902, he made his way to Moffitt, "a wide place in the road near Zolfo Springs," purchased forty thousand acres of pine trees, and opened a lumber mill for telephone poles and railroad ties. He was lonely, and in 1904, on one of his buying trips back to New York City, he was matched with Hannah Rosa Ratkowsky, a daughter of Rabbi Elihu Baer Ratkowsky, a founder of what is now Yeshiva University. The couple had two children in Moffitt: Charlotte (1905) and Abraham Moses (1907). The family kept kosher.

The Marcus Weinkle family lived in Moffitt until 1916. Charlotte tells a story about her mother, who was deeply religious, stepping on a rusty nail in the mill yard. One of the workers rushed to wrap salt pork (the "forbidden meat") around her foot to draw out any infection—and that was it for Hannah. She had wanted to move to Jacksonville where Marcus's siblings Dora and Louis and "all the Jews lived" so her family could experience Jewish community life—and the fact that *treif* was wrapped around her foot was the impetus! Nearly all the pine trees had been cut down, and Moffitt became a ghost town. The post office that opened in 1908 closed in 1916. According to Charlotte, Marcus sold the mill and land for one dollar an acre. In Jacksonville, Hannah and Marcus became leaders in the Jewish community and benefactors of both religious and secular causes. After the death of Marcus in 1933, the family moved away.

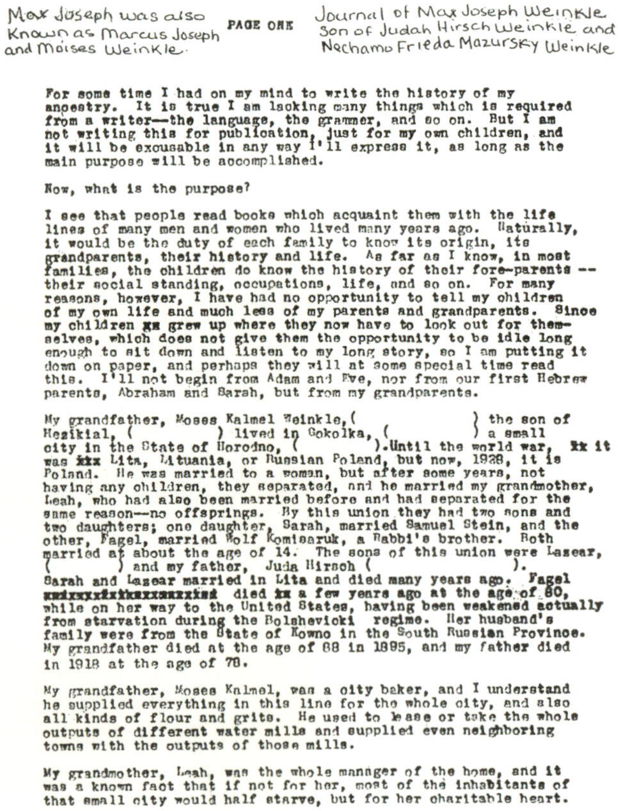

Max Joseph was also Known as Marcus Joseph and Moises Weinkle.

PAGE ONE

Journal of Max Joseph Weinkle Son of Judah Hirsch Weinkle and Nechamo Frieda Mazursky Weinkle

For some time I had on my mind to write the history of my ancestry. It is true I am lacking many things which is required from a writer—the language, the grammer, and so on. But I am not writing this for publication, just for my own children, and it will be excusable in any way I'll express it, as long as the main purpose will be accomplished.

Now, what is the purpose?

I see that people read books which acquaint them with the life lines of many men and women who lived many years ago. Naturally, it would be the duty of each family to know its origin, its grandparents, their history and life. As far as I know, in most families, the children do know the history of their fore-parents -- their social standing, occupations, life, and so on. For many reasons, however, I have had no opportunity to tell my children of my own life and much less of my parents and grandparents. Since my children grew up where they now have to look out for themselves, which does not give them the opportunity to be idle long enough to sit down and listen to my long story, so I am putting it down on paper, and perhaps they will at some special time read this. I'll not begin from Adam and Eve, nor from our first Hebrew parents, Abraham and Sarah, but from my grandparents.

My grandfather, Moses Kalmel Weinkle, ( ) the son of Hezikial, ( ) lived in Sokolka, ( ) a small city in the State of Horodno, ( ). Until the world war, it was Lita, Lituania, or Russian Poland, but now, 1928, it is Poland. He was married to a woman, but after some years, not having any children, they separated, and he married my grandmother, Leah, who had also been married before and had separated for the same reason—no offsprings. By this union they had two sons and two daughters; one daughter, Sarah, married Samuel Stein, and the other, Fagel, married Wolf Komisaruk, a Rabbi's brother. Both married at about the age of 14. The sons of this union were Lazear, ( ) and my father, Juda Hirsch ( ). Sarah and Lazear married in Lita and died many years ago. Fagel died a few years ago at the age of 80, while on her way to the United States, having been weakened actually from starvation during the Bolshevicki regime. Her husband's family were from the State of Kowno in the South Russian Province. My grandfather died at the age of 88 in 1895, and my father died in 1918 at the age of 78.

My grandfather, Moses Kalmel, was a city baker, and I understand he supplied everything in this line for the whole city, and also all kinds of flour and grits. He used to lease or take the whole outputs of different water mills and supplied even neighboring towns with the outputs of those mills.

My grandmother, Leah, was the whole manager of the home, and it was a known fact that if not for her, most of the inhabitants of that small city would half starve, but for her charitable heart.

First page of the journal of Marcus Joseph Weinkle, Jacksonville, 1928.

Marcus had been the first of his family to come to America. His parents and siblings followed in 1897. His father, Yehuda Vinikowsky, now Weinkle, came with a considerable sum of money. He bought land in Georgia and opened a large lumber mill, called J. H. Weinkle & Sons, which was bombed—perhaps by the Ku Klux Klan (KKK).

CHAPTER 5

Americans

In addition to the Jews who migrated directly into Florida from out of the country, some came from various states within the US—and Canada. Most were immigrants or their parents had been immigrants during the nineteenth century who had first settled in New York and then looked for better opportunities in Florida. Some of the migrants were aided by organizations, some were part of chain migration, some more adventurous ones just struck out on their own—all enticed by the pioneering economic opportunities and the climate.

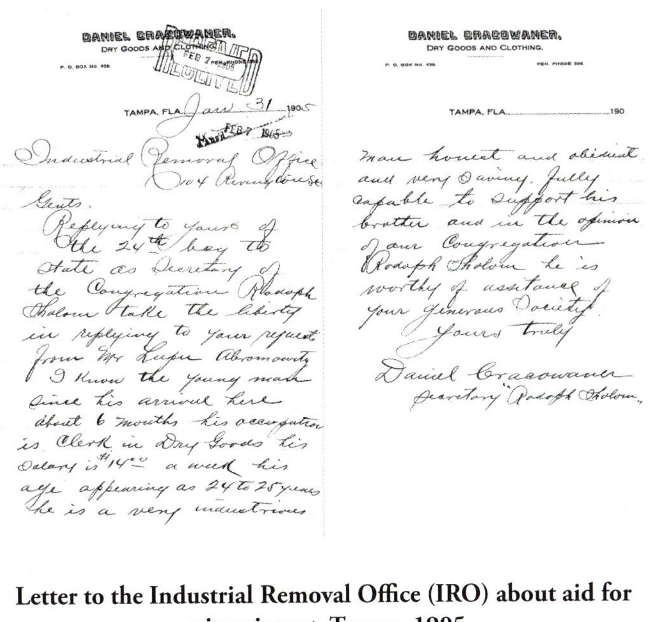

DANIEL CRACOWANER,
DRY GOODS AND CLOTHING.
P. O. BOX No. 436

RECEIVED FEB 7 1905

TAMPA, FLA. Jan 31 1905

Industrial Removal Office
104 Rivington St

Gents.
Replying to yours of the 24th beg to state as Secretary of the Congregation Rodoph Sholom I take the liberty in replying to your request from Mr Lupu Abromowitz. I know the young man since his arrival here about 6 months his occupation is Clerk in Dry Goods his Salary is $14.00 a week his age appearing as 24 to 25 years he is a very industrious

DANIEL CRACOWANER,
DRY GOODS AND CLOTHING.
P. O. BOX No. 436 PEN. PHONE 396

TAMPA, FLA. ________ 190

man honest and obedient and very saving. fully capable to support his brother and in the opinion of our Congregation Rodoph Sholom he is worthy of assistance of your generous Society.
Yours truly
Daniel Cracowaner
Secretary "Rodoph Sholom"

Letter to the Industrial Removal Office (IRO) about aid for an immigrant, Tampa, 1905.

In 1901 some Romanian Jews fled antisemitic decrees to New York. The Romanian Committee organized to help relocate the immigrants to other cities and help find homes and employment—sometimes in Florida. This committee rapidly evolved into the Industrial Removal Office (IRO) as part of the Jewish Agricultural Society, which took over the work on a much larger scale and opened its availability to any unemployed Jewish immigrant, regardless of their origin. The philosophy behind the IRO was to help the immigrants adapt to American society, both economically and culturally. Daniel Cracowaner wrote this letter to the IRO in support of assistance for a recent immigrant.

In 1896 Hyman Roth went from New York to Daytona Beach, 1926.

Celia and Hyman Roth with their sons, Mack (1894–1993), Nat, Alan, Dan, and Burnett (1912–2008), and Hyman's sisters, May Feldman, Sylvia Krugman, and Rae Frisco. There were also four daughters: May, Anna, Sylvia, and Sophie. Austrian immigrants Celia Zeiger and Hyman Roth each came to New York by 1890, met, and married. Some children were born there, and by 1896 Hyman had seized an opportunity in Daytona Beach to open straw hats and ladies' ready-to-wear shops. He went back and forth until the family moved to Florida with him in 1910. The oldest son, Mack, was a founder of Temple Israel and cemetery in Daytona Beach. Family members also lived in Orlando, Miami, and Miami Beach where they were all deeply involved in their communities.

Rebecca Silverman Rosin with son, Marcus Aurel Rosin, in 1908 and Arcadia mayor Simon Rosin, 1919.

Simon Rosin came from Chicago first to Ocala, then settled in Arcadia in 1905 where he opened the Boston Store. In 1906 he married Rebecca Silverman of Baltimore, and they had one son, Aurel, in 1907. In 1927 he built an arcade in Florida-Mediterranean style that housed the US Post Office. The name Rosin is faintly visible on the facade. Aurel married Elsie Paderewski of Savannah in 1928. They raised four sons in Arcadia, where he was a lawyer and cattle rancher. They had 4,500 acres and struggled to keep the alligators from eating their cows. In 1951 the family moved to Sarasota to get a better Jewish education for the boys. Aurel was elected state president of the Elks (1949) and served as city attorney for Sarasota. He was 45 when he was killed in a car crash on his way to argue at the Florida Supreme Court. There is a fifth generation in Sarasota today.

Lithuanian Louis Frank, first-known Jew in Clearwater in 1912, and Darwin and Hannah Frank, Clearwater, 1919.

Louis Frank (1873–1964) literally traveled the world before he settled in Florida. In 1901 he was a soldier in the Second Boer War in Southern Rhodesia and then served in the Colonial Defense Force of Canada. From there, he settled in Clearwater with $500 to open the New York Department Store (later Frank's Department Store), a twenty-by-thirty-foot building in a town with no paved streets or sidewalks. Six months after his arrival, the lonely merchant contacted a matchmaker in New York, who arranged for him to meet Hannah "Annie" Levy.. Hannah had been sent to America because her family had opposed the czar in Lithuania, and soldiers had taken her sister and brother-in-law. Louis proposed with a diamond he had from Rhodesia, and they married that same year, 1912, in Tampa. Then they went to Clearwater in a horse and wagon over a dirt road. Their son David was born in 1913 and then Darwin (1919–94). Darwin, who contributed the history of his family to MOSAIC, managed his father's store from 1948 to 1975 and expanded it to a two-level store with ten thousand feet of floor space.

Jacobs (Probolsky) family from Lithuania to Wales to Milwaukee to Chicago to St. Petersburg in 1920.

Included in this photograph are, in the front row from left to right, Celia Jacobs [Sweet] and Bessie Jacobs [Silverman]. In the back row from left to right are Harry Jacobs, Ethel Jacobs [Rothblatt], and Hyman Jacobs. Due to Bessie's influenza, Lithuanians Bessie and Hyman Jacobs left Chicago with their daughters, Goldie [Schuster], Jean [Miller], and Annabel [Carson], and Hyman's father, Isaac. They turned right instead of left on a highway to Florida and settled in St. Petersburg, where they became the tenth Jewish family. Renee [Silverstein] and Arnold were born later. In St. Petersburg, they opened O. K. Markets, and Hyman, a Hebrew teacher, became the first president of Congregation B'nai Israel in 1923. Hyman was the first Jew to be a member of the St. Petersburg Chamber of Commerce. He was killed in an automobile accident in 1938 while he was congregation president. Many stores—owned by both Jews and non-Jews—closed for the funeral that was held in the synagogue. Goldie (1906–87), who married Harry Schuster in 1930 and had Phyllis and Irwin, began to write a Jewish history of St. Petersburg in 1969. I was fortunate to meet with her and get copies of her documents that are now in the Collections of JMOF-FIU. She and Harry were pioneer merchants, first on Treasure Island in 1934, then on Corey Avenue on St. Pete Beach—where I live today.

Amputee David Rothblatt, owner of Southern Grocery, driving his delivery truck with hand controls, St. Petersburg, circa 1930.

Another example of chain migration, David (1895–1958), with his wife, Ethel, moved from Milwaukee to St. Petersburg in 1922. He became a partner with his brother-in-law, Hyman Jacobs. The partnership eventually dissolved, and then each had his own business. David, with a sixth-grade education, had served in the Mexican conflict during World War I and suffered from the freezing of his feet, resulting in amputations of both legs above the knees. He had his car outfitted with hand controls for the clutch and brake so he could drive his grocery delivery truck. Their three daughters were Tobias [Snyder], Audrey [Chenkin], and Bernice "Bunnie" [Katz], who served on my MOSAIC task force, helping to document the Jewish history of St. Petersburg. The family was deeply involved in the Jewish community.

Galbut Family, New York to Miami Beach, 1926

Abraham "Al" and Bessie D. Galbut, Miami Beach, 1934.

Abraham "Al" and Bessie Galbut came from Monticello, New York, with their family to Miami Beach after the 1926 hurricane and rented an apartment for $300 a year. Al sold newspapers before entering the restaurant business and was a founder of Congregation Beth Jacob, which now houses the JMOF-FIU. Bessie worked closely with him while raising their family: Paul, Hyman, and Miriam.

Second-generation Galbuts, Miami Beach, 1954.

Hyman, a US Navy captain during World War II and Miami Beach City Council member, also married a Bessie, the same name as his mother. This family portrait includes (seated) Hyman and Bessie, with their children (left to right): Robert, Abraham, Russell, and David. Standing is Grandmother Bessie Galbut. The third generation of the Galbut Family became professionals and developers. Now into the sixth generation (as of 2019), the family has a total of more than one hundred Galbuts living in Florida today. They are a major charitable force in the Jewish community as well as in Israel.

CHAPTER 6

Post–World War II

Before 1945 Florida had the smallest population in the South with about 2.3 million people. Migration helped swell the numbers—particularly senior migration, many known as "condo commandos," because of their political involvement. Despite a severe recession in 2008, people continued to arrive. The state's population barreled past 20 million people in 2018, when it overtook New York and became the nation's third largest population (after California and Texas). At the time of this writing, people were arriving in Florida at an average of 1,000 a day.

The largest number of Jews began to settle in Florida after World War II, and many are from out of the country. Dr. Ira M. Sheskin, director of the Jewish Demography Project at the Sue and Leonard Miller Center for Contemporary Judaic Studies at the University of Miami, reports in his 2014 Miami Jewish population study that 33 percent of Miami's adult population are foreign born—the highest in the nation and up 10 percent since 1994.

Jewish children who arrive from different countries can acclimate easily as all Florida counties have student populations that are hugely diverse. For example, Miami-Dade County's school district student population is 92 percent minorities, coming from 155 nations. Miami Beach Senior High School has students from more than 50 nations who speak 29 languages.

Florida's Jews currently include Holocaust survivors, snowbirds (living up to six months) and snowflakes (who take many short trips during the winter season), the elderly, Jews from other places in North America, Jews from Cuba and other Latin American countries, and Jews from Israel, Russia, France, England, and other countries around the globe. They joined the earlier Jewish immigrants and native-born Jews who made Florida home.

Holocaust Survivors

The Holocaust was the systematic, bureaucratic, state-sponsored persecution and murder of six million Jews by the Nazi regime and its collaborators during 1941–45. *Holocaust* is a word of Greek origin meaning "sacrifice by fire." It ended a long and remarkable Jewish presence in Europe, in some countries, of more than two thousand years. The Nazis, who came to power in Germany in January 1933, believed that Germans were racially superior and that the Jews, deemed inferior, were an alien threat to the so-called German racial community. There were seventeen million victims overall at thousands of concentration and extermination camps—including the mentally and physically disabled, gypsies, homosexuals, political opponents, and religious dissidents.

As observed by Nobel Peace Prize Laureate Elie Wiesel, "Although not all victims of the Holocaust were Jewish, all Jews were victims." The American Jewish Yearbook estimates that there were about 15,750,000 Jews worldwide before World War II. Around 9 million lived in Europe, of which 6 million perished (two-thirds of European Jewry) in the Holocaust. Despite losing almost 40 percent of the world Jewish population, the Jewish people rebounded.

Since 1945 several thousand Holocaust survivors have come to Florida. Most settled in south Florida, but there are some in nearly every Florida community. They built new lives in peace and freedom, yet many struggled daily. Samuel J. Dubbin of Miami is a Florida lawyer and Holocaust Survivors' rights advocate who works to help them. They continue to bear witness as they help others to remember.

Here are a few stories of Holocaust survivors in Florida. You will meet others within the chapters depicting what they accomplished.

Passengers on the German ocean liner *St. Louis* denied entry to the United States, June 3, 1939. *Miami Herald.*

American hostility to Jewish immigration was expressed most powerfully with the incident of the *St. Louis*. On May 13, 1939, four months before Germany invaded Poland, this passenger vessel left Hamburg, Germany, carrying 937 passengers, nearly all Jewish refugees fleeing the Nazis. These Jews had paid the Cuban consulate in Germany for visas and landing permits for Cuba with hopes to then apply for entry into the US. Antisemitic reaction and political pressure blocked their admission to Cuba two weeks later. The ship, under threats of military action, sailed north, following the Florida coastline, and then anchored off Miami Beach—awaiting the decision by US President Franklin Roosevelt to take in the Jews even though immigration quotas were filled. Florida residents and visitors waited in hopeful anticipation. On June 4, a much larger ship joined the *St. Louis*. It was US Coast Guard *Cutter 244*, from the US Coast Guard Base Six in Fort Lauderdale. The cutter was sent to thwart the movements of the *St. Louis* so that it would not make landfall. On June 5, Fort Lauderdale protestors massed along the beaches south of Las Olas Boulevard near the Coast Guard base. The cutter stayed by the *St. Louis* as it moved slowly down the coast and prevented any possible attempts by refugees to jump off and swim ashore. On June 7, a mass protest took place in Miami's Bayfront Park—but the voices of the protesters went unheeded. Later that day, the *St. Louis*, with a low reserve of food and water, left on its return trip. About 287 passengers were allowed to enter Great Britain. Those remaining were returned to the continent. When Germany conquered western Europe, 254 *St. Louis* passengers in Belgium, Holland, and France died in the Holocaust. The story of the *St. Louis* was portrayed in the 1976 movie *Voyage of the Damned.*

Karliner family on the deck of the *St. Louis*, June 4, 1939.

Herbert Karliner was a boy traveling with his family on the *St. Louis* while it was looking for a Florida port to accept its passengers. After seeing the palm trees and hotels off the Miami Beach coastline, Herbert promised himself that if he survived, he would return there someday. He did, in 1954—and got a job at the Fontainebleau Hotel. He lives on Miami Beach today. His parents and sister perished in the Holocaust; one brother survived with him.

Allan Hall with his parents, Maria and Edmund Horowitz Hall, Cracow, Poland, 1937.

Allan Hall says, "I strongly suspect that my brother Andy and I are the only Holocaust survivors who went to Miami Beach High and perhaps to the University of Florida." Born in Cracow in 1935, Hall led a charmed life until September 1939 when the Nazis marched into Poland. Seeking safety, the family walked 212 miles to Lvov, where they were ordered into the ghetto. With false identity papers, the family fled to Warsaw where Allan and his mother were arrested and taken to the train station to be sent to Treblinka. When the trains briefly stopped running, Allan was marched to an orphanage in the Warsaw ghetto. Allan's father, passing as Aryan, rented an office in a high-rise building that housed German Air Force headquarters. For two years, Allan and his mother hid in the closet in that office. "My mother and I were in the dark, day and night. The closet was maybe 30 inches deep and five feet across. We had two pillows—not for comfort, but to muffle a sneeze or cough or any other noise." During the Warsaw ghetto uprising, the family crawled under sniper fire to a bomb shelter where Allan's mother gave birth to Andy.

When the war ended, Allan's father was arrested. Knowing the children would be used as hostages, Allan's mother instructed Allan to take his baby brother, Andy, and make his way to Palestine. For months, hunted by the Soviets, eleven-year-old Allan carried Andy across Europe trying to get to Italy and a ship to Palestine. Miraculously, the family reunited and, in 1947, emigrated to the US and settled on Miami Beach. Twelve-year-old Allan began school, unable to read or write and not speaking a word of English. He went on to graduate from Miami Beach High School, the University of Florida, and its School of Law. He lives on Miami Beach.

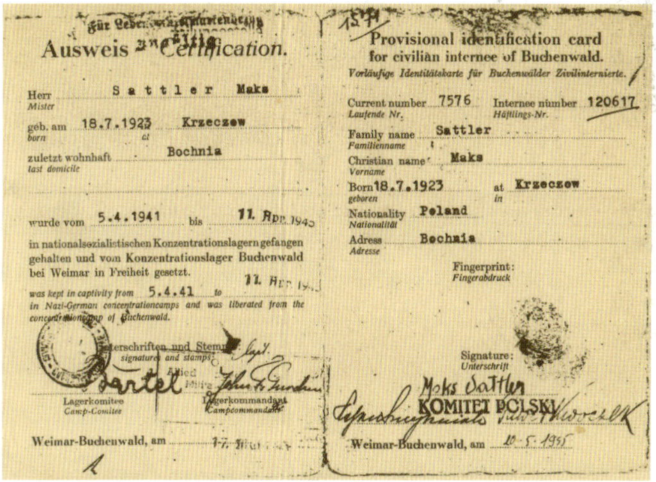

Ausweis Certification.

Herr / Mister: Sattler Maks
geb. am / born: 18.7.1923 at Krzeczow
zuletzt wohnhaft / last domicile: Bochnia

wurde vom 5.4.1941 bis 11. Apr. 1945 in nationalsozialistischen Konzentrationslagern gefangen gehalten und vom Konzentrationslager Buchenwald bei Weimar in Freiheit gesetzt.
was kept in captivity from 5.4.41 to 11. Apr. 1945 in Nazi-German concentrationcamps and was liberated from the concentrationcamp of Buchenwald.

Unterschriften und Stempel: / signatures and stamps:
Lagerkomitee / Camp-Comitee
Lagerkommandant / Campcommandant

Weimar-Buchenwald, am

Provisional identification card for civilian internee of Buchenwald.
Vorläufige Identitätskarte für Buchenwälder Zivilinternierte.

Current number / Laufende Nr.: 7576
Internee number / Häftlings-Nr.: 120617
Family name / Familienname: Sattler
Christian name / Vorname: Maks
Born / geboren: 18.7.1923 at / in: Krzeczow
Nationality / Nationalität: Poland
Adress / Adresse: Bochnia
Fingerprint: / Fingerabdruck
Signature: / Unterschrift: Maks Sattler
KOMITET POLSKI
Weimar-Buchenwald, am 10.5.1945

Max Sattler's death camps liberation papers, 1945.

These identification papers were granted to Max Sattler upon his liberation from Auschwitz and Buchenwald concentration camps in Poland. Max lives in Melbourne, and to this day, he feels guilty that he survived and asks why. He performs Jewish rituals and continues to tell his story in hopes that the horror can be prevented from ever happening again.

Stained glass window depicting fractured lives from the Holocaust by Vera Sattler, Melbourne, 1990.

Vera Sattler, artist and wife of Max Sattler, designed, painted, and constructed this original work of art for the original MOSAIC exhibit that traveled to thirteen cities from 1990 to 1994. The artwork is part of the core exhibit in the JMOF-FIU.

This twenty-four-by-forty-inch stained glass window tells of the transition from the hell of the Holocaust to recovery and the survival of Judaism. The panel starts at the bottom with a collage of hand-painted and kiln-fired reproductions of twelve (the number of tribes of Israel) black-and-white photographs depicting scenes from Hitler's concentration camps during World War II. American soldiers who liberated the camps took some of these photographs that Sattler painted on the glass; others are well-known illustrations.

The ball of orange in the center represents the crematoria. Out of the crematoria come flames, bright in wonderful colors in the shape of the Hebrew letter *shin*, to represent the Hebrew word *shaddai* (*God Almighty*). At the top is another *shin* and a Torah scroll representing the survival of Judaism, and the blue background represents the Israeli flag. Superimposed on the entire window is entwined barbed wire and the *yizkor* prayer, "a memorial to the generations who sacrificed their lives to sanctify thy name."

Vera Sattler, born in Germany, began her art career there in 1946. She started her new life in America in 1951, working at Detroit Stained Glass Works. Sattler has done work for many synagogues, churches, private collectors, and interior decorators, primarily in stained glass and also in acrylics, collages, and copper enameling. She has taught and exhibited extensively. When asked about her favorite part of her work, she said, "Picking glass—the colors!" Vera Sattler has lived in Melbourne since 1983.

Survivor of Nazi Horror Camps Awaits Husband Stranded in Paris by Red Tape

By TOM LOGUE

Mrs. Julian Herzfeld, 1006 Holly lane, is thrilled at the prospect of getting her final naturalization papers and becoming an American citizen. Somehow she can't take it as calmly as her black-thatched daughter of three months, who is a citizen already. But after all, Margaret Dorothy did it the easy way—by being born here.

With Mrs. Herzfeld it has been different. Behind her on the road to citizenship are the ghetto of Zawiercie, in Upper Silesia; a job in the morgue of the notorious Nazi concentration camp at Auschwitz; imprisonment in and escape from the equally ill-famed camp at Ravensbrueck. In 1946, after years of this, she wrote to her uncle, Harry Wyman, retired Jacksonville jeweller, and he helped arrange her admission into the United States.

* * *

But the real story—told in the Saturday Evening Post which is on the newsstands today—is not so much that of Francesca Herzfeld as it is of her husband, who is still in Paris waiting for an opportunity to enter the United States and join his family. He's not waiting too patiently, it's true, but after nearly three years of battling red tape and regulations and policy barriers that's understandable. There's still no one who can tell him when he'll be able to come to Florida.

At 41, Julian Herzfeld has a lot

At the home of her uncle, Harry Wyman, 1006 Holly lane, Mrs. Julian Herzfeld and daughter, Margaret Dorothy, await the arrival of the baby's father from Paris, where he is bogged down in immigration rules. Tattooed number on arm is memento of Ravensbrueck concentration camp. (Journal photo.)

Holocaust survivor Francesca Herzfeld with her daughter, Jacksonville, 1948.

Francesca Herzfeld tells of ghetto life, a job in the morgue at Auschwitz, and finally escape from Ravensbrück concentration camp for women in northern Germany. This was followed by travel, marriage, and separation from her Parisian husband, Julien, who had an equal tale of horror. Their daughter, Margaret Dorothy, was born in Jacksonville in 1948 because Francesca came to live with her uncle Harry Wyman while she awaited her husband's arrival.

Holocaust survivor and philanthropist Henri Landwirth (right) displays the Give Kids the World building plan at groundbreaking, Kissimmee, 1989.

To Henri Landwirth (1927–2018), Florida in America was the land of the free. "I never thought I would come out alive," he said, referring to his time in the concentration camps, "and so I am here on borrowed time." To make good use of it, Landwirth devoted his resources, gained from owning Holiday Inns since his settling in Florida, to Give Kids the World. In 1986 he created the 79-acre resort with 144 villas to bring children with life-threatening illnesses to dream vacations in Disney World. Landwirth has hosted more than 160,000 of them and their families from every state and all over the world.

Born in Belgium, Henri and his twin sister, Margot [Glazer], were prisoners in Auschwitz and Mauthausen Nazi camps from ages thirteen to eighteen during World War II. Both of their parents were killed, but miraculously the twins survived and were reunited. In 1949 Landwirth worked his way to America on a freight ship, arriving with twenty dollars.

After serving in the US Army, he used his GI benefits to learn hotel management, toiling and excelling at every menial task. In 1954 he became manager of the Starlight Motel in Cocoa Beach, near Cape Canaveral, where he became friends with the first astronauts and news reporter Walter Cronkite. Former astronaut and senator John Glenn (D-OH), a partner in several hotel ventures, said, "With his background, it would have been easy for Henri to be bitter. But he's an American success story. Out of his successes, he gave back."

He and Margot settled in Orlando. Landwirth formed the Astronaut Scholarship Foundation in 1984 with the survivors and widow of the original Mercury project. In 2000 Landwirth founded Dignity U Wear, which provides new clothing to homeless, abused, or abandoned children nationwide. He started Hate Hurts, a program that teaches forgiveness to end hatred. Landwirth was named "Most Caring Individual in America" by the Caring Institute (1988) and in 1994 "Humanitarian of the Year" by *Parents Magazine* and "Floridian of the Year" by the *Orlando Sentinel*, among many other honors.

Groundbreaking for the Holocaust Memorial Resource and Education Center of Florida, Orlando, 1986.

In the front row from left to right are the Rev. Dr. Earl Scarbeary (first president), Tess Wise, Henrietta Katzen, Helen Greenspun, Susan Arkin, Marilyn Goldman, and Eddie Titen. In the back row from left to right are unknown, Marc Katzen, Eva Ritt, Stanley Creel, and Abe Wise.

In 1980 Polish Holocaust survivor Tess Wise approached the Jewish Federation of Greater Orlando and Valencia Community College to develop a Holocaust educational center. They began with a major Holocaust conference in 1981 that brought in nationally known scholars. The following year they sponsored a conference on terrorism. In 1986 the Holocaust Center was constructed on the Jewish Federation campus that included a permanent exhibit and a library with documentary and archival collections. The center received national and international recognition as a unique resource, the only one of its kind in the Southeast until 1996. The building expanded in 1994 to have space for temporary exhibits and programs and again in 2005.

Most of the visitors who come to the Holocaust Center are students who learn the lessons of hate. As they observe the exhibits and discuss the history, students develop insight into what it means to be a good person and good citizen. From the stories of rescuers, they see the importance of standing up for the rights and safety of others. From stories of resistance, they learn about courage and community. The center's exhibits contain very few graphic images. Instead, they identify the experiences of the people whose lives were interrupted by hate.

The freshly named Holocaust Museum for Hope & Humanity, in partnership with the City of Orlando, will be a new museum that will allow them to build upon the legacy started by Tess and Abe Wise more than three decades ago. It will stand as a beacon of light and a reflection of the city's values and culture of inclusiveness; its respect for people of all backgrounds, faiths, and cultures; and a community that celebrates differences of all kinds. Maurizio Maso, design principal with HuntonBrady Architects, is designing the new museum, anticipated to open in 2023.

Holocaust Memorial, Miami Beach, 1990.

The founding group (inset) (left to right) includes Jack Chester, Helen Fagin, Abe Resnick, Kenneth Treister, chairman Norman Braman, Harry Smith, George Goldblum, and David Schaecter.

In 1984 a small group of Holocaust survivors joined together to develop a permanent memorial to the six million Jews who perished at the hands of the Nazis. A year later, the Holocaust Memorial Committee was formally established. The committee decided that Miami Beach was the perfect location as south Florida has one of the highest populations (twenty to twenty-five thousand) of Holocaust survivors in the US, with many of them residing within the city limits.

As preparations were being made to build the memorial, there were those who objected, arguing that Miami Beach was a place for "sun and fun" and the memorial would be too somber for the vacation destination. Others said the memorial's presence on city-owned land violated the separation of church and state, arguing it was a religious monument. While the memorial is in memory of the six million Jews who died during the Holocaust, it is a patently historical monument, and religious symbols were removed.

On November 27, 1984, approximately five hundred people packed a meeting of the Miami Beach Planning Board. Dozens of Holocaust survivors from across south Florida arrived, many making emotional pleas to the board. "I lost five sisters and five brothers," seventy-nine-year-old Clara Linder said in Yiddish through a translator. "They were all killed." Machela Oksenhenbler, eighty, pulled up her sleeve to show a grainy tattoo on her forearm bearing the numbers 54092, put there by the Nazis. The Planning Board unanimously approved the memorial, and eight days later, the City Commission approved the plans. The proposed location spanned several city blocks with a physical address of 1933–1945 Meridian Avenue—street numbers that exactly match the years of the Nazi regime and its war against the Jews. This fact helped convince several city legislators that the memorial belonged in that specific spot.

Miami architect Kenneth Treister was selected to design and build the memorial. "Imagine you're in a concentration camp in Poland surrounded by the Nazis, no communication with the outside world and you're suffering and you're giving up your life," Treister said, discussing how he thought about memorializing the Holocaust victims. "Each one probably died thinking that no one would ever care, no one would ever know, no one would ever remember." The centerpiece is a 50-foot-high bronze sculpture of a hand with numbers, surrounded by 130 bronze figures that cry out in anguish. Treister had the sculpture cast in Mexico City foundry Fundiciòn Artística between 1987 and 1989. Giant blocks of pink-hued Jerusalem stone were brought in from Israel and set as the memorial's foundation and watched diligently by Abe Resnick, who guarded the memorial overnight, afraid thieves would steal the pricey materials not yet secured to the ground.

The memorial took more than four years to build, and on February 4, 1990, a dedication ceremony was held with Nobel Laureate Elie Wiesel as guest speaker. "One day, a man or a woman will enter this sanctuary of remembrance and wonder: Was it all true? Were the killers really that cruel? And the victims that helpless? That lonely? That abandoned?" Wiesel said. "Will this museum, or any other, bigger or smaller, make a difference? I hope that visitors will bring their children. I hope they will look at the pictures. Pictures: Old emaciated grandparents lying in the street. Naked mothers shielding their children. A group of SS men enjoying themselves while tormenting an old man, who looks like my grandfather, and everyone else's. Look at his face. Look at all the faces. Look and you will realize that there existed a suffering that transcended suffering. Woe unto us, for the tragedy which this museum is trying to integrate is beyond words, and beyond imagination, but not beyond memory. And only those who were there know, will know, what it meant being there."

Florida Holocaust Museum, St. Petersburg, 2018.

Founder Walter Loebenberg (left) greets Helen Fagin of Sarasota, sitting next to Sidney Fagin's sculpture *Butterfly Boy*, which his widow donated to the museum. Standing to the left is Loebenberg's daughter Sandy Mermelstein, museum senior educator, and to his right is Fagin's sister Terrie. The sculpture was inspired by a poem written by twenty-one-year-old Pavel Friedman in 1942 when he was at Terezin ghetto and concludes: "That butterfly was the last one. Butterflies don't live here, in the ghetto." And neither did he. A larger version of the sculpture is at the Fagin Holocaust Collection at New College in Sarasota. A building contractor in Miami after the Holocaust, Sidney Fagin created a nine-foot benediction that is in the courtyard of the Kendall Jewish Community Center in Miami.

Helen and Terrie Fagin were born in Poland and forced into a ghetto where Helen ran a clandestine school for Jewish children. When their parents were taken away in a raid, they managed to hide. The underground provided false papers, and after the war, they immigrated to the US. Helen taught herself English, earned a PhD (philosophiae doctor) from the University of Miami and became a professor of English and director of Judaic studies there. She has received many honors and was an advisor in the development of the US Holocaust Memorial Museum in Washington, DC. In 2019 New College of Florida in Sarasota honored her with the Dr. Helen Fagin Holocaust, Genocide, and Human Rights Collection in their library.

On November 10, 1938, Walter Loebenberg (1924–2019) witnessed as *Kristallnacht*, the "night of broken glass," swept through Frankfurt, Germany, and destroyed the Jewish community. Hoping to escape Nazi persecution, he, with his mother and father, sailed on the American ship *Manhattan* from Germany to Cuba in 1939 with a stop in New York. The passengers were not allowed to disembark in Cuba. The *St. Louis* and the *Manhattan* shared that night in Havana before the *Manhattan* set off to return to New York and the *St. Louis* was sent back to Europe.

Walter remembers watching a man jump from the rim of the *St. Louis* and into the Atlantic Ocean. That sail to New York saved the Loebenbergs from returning to Europe. But the family could not disembark because they had no visas. They stayed in Ellis Island for four months, and the government released them as "enemy aliens." The family moved to Chicago, where Walter graduated from high school and joined the military, which granted him citizenship. While overseas, General Dwight D. Eisenhower presented Walter the Bronze Star Medal for his involvement with an interrogation that led to information that saved the lives of many American soldiers. After he returned to Chicago, he married Holocaust survivor Edith Lowengard, and they had three children: Michael, David, and Sandy. In Chicago, with no college education, Walter took any job to support his family.

In 1969 the family settled in St. Petersburg for Walter's business opportunity with his brother-in-law to own and operate hospitals and nursing homes. With money loaned by banker Hubert Rutland, the first facility was acquired in the early 1970s in Leesburg. The facility in St. Petersburg was called Rutland Hospital, now Humana Northside.

The Florida Holocaust Museum (FHM) is dedicated to advancing public awareness, education, and understanding. Accredited by the American Alliance of Museums and one of the largest Holocaust museums in the country, FHM is the result of Walter Loebenberg's vision. Together, with a group of local businessmen and community leaders, the concept of a living memorial to those who suffered and perished was conceived. FHM began in 1992 as a small (four-thousand-square-foot) endeavor in Madeira Beach. The first exhibition was *Anne Frank—in the World*, which attracted more than twenty-four thousand visitors in the first month. The first major acquisition for the museum was a boxcar from Poland that had carried Jews to concentration camps.

It was *beshert* that when the FHM was seeking a larger building in 1996, the former Hubert Rutland Bank building was available in downtown St. Petersburg! In a major move in 1998, FHM bought the twenty-seven-thousand-square-foot building to house its core exhibit, collections, and traveling and special exhibitions and expanded its mission to include other recent examples of genocide. They promote the concept that all the suffering and loss is meaningless if the public does not understand what took place in the past and act to ensure that it will never happen again. They strive to challenge and educate those who promote hatred and intolerance. The vision of FHM is a future in which peace and harmony are a reality in our neighborhoods, nation, and world.

In south Florida, the Holocaust Documentation & Education Center was founded in 1980 and in 2016 moved into their new site at 303 North Federal Highway, Dania Beach. The Holocaust Museum and Cohen Education Center was created in 2001 in Naples. The newest one of which I am aware is the Al Katz Center for Holocaust Survivors and Jewish Learning in Bradenton, founded in 2012 by Katz's daughter Beverly Newman and focused on elder guardianship abuse.

In 2018 there was an article in the *Tampa Bay Times* about Salomon Pila, a former Oscar Schindler factory worker, who came to Brooksville after surviving the Holocaust and operated the 440-acre Milk-A-Way Farm. There are so many haunting stories in most Florida communities, and soon the survivors will be gone—making Holocaust education even more critical in a time where Holocaust deniers still lurk.

Florida was one of the first states in the nation to mandate Holocaust education in public schools. In 1994 Governor Lawton Chiles signed Florida Statute 1003.42, mandating that Holocaust education be implemented from kindergarten through twelfth grade.

> The history of the Holocaust (1933–45), the systematic, planned annihilation of European Jews and other groups by Nazi Germany, a watershed event in the history of humanity, should be taught in a manner that leads to an investigation of human behavior; an understanding of the ramifications of prejudice, racism, and stereotyping; and an examination of what it means to be a responsible and respectful person for the purposes of encouraging tolerance of diversity in a pluralistic society and for nurturing and protecting democratic values and institutions.

Guidelines include grade-appropriate instructional goals and a bibliography for teaching the Holocaust. These guidelines are used by teachers throughout the nation as well as in Florida. Miriam Klein Kassenoff, who fled Nazi Europe as a child with her family, became a teachers' teacher for Holocaust education. As the education specialist for Holocaust studies for Miami-Dade County Public Schools, she is responsible for all staff development/teacher training on teaching the Holocaust. Linda Medvin was the Holocaust specialist for Broward County Public Schools for twenty-seven years and now directs Florida Atlantic University's Center for Holocaust and Human Rights Education.

Rositta Kenigsberg, a daughter of a Holocaust survivor, was born in a displaced persons (DP) camp in Austria. Recipient of dozens of awards and honors for her leadership and contributions to Holocaust education, she is president of the Holocaust Documentation & Education Center in Dania Beach and authored the Florida teaching mandate. Kenigsberg was appointed (1995) the founding chair of the Florida education commissioner's Task Force on Holocaust Education, where she continues to serve, along with Kassenoff and Medvin, among others.

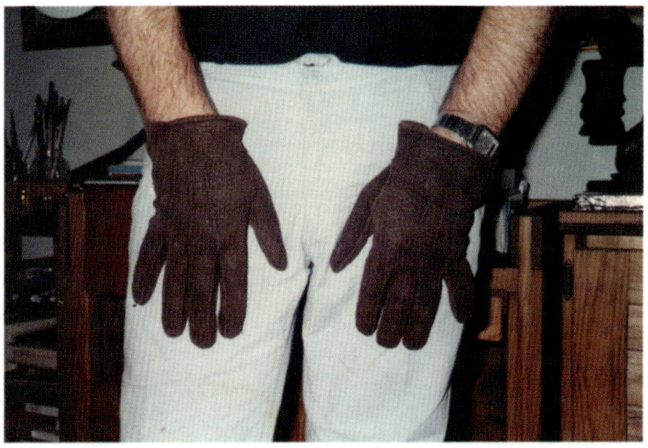

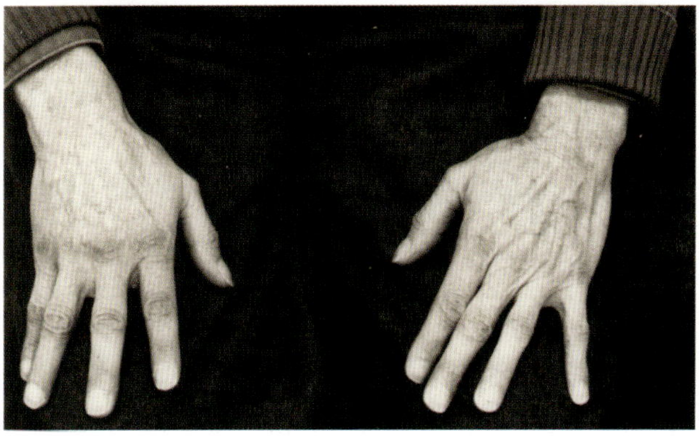

Top, Israel's Mossad agent Peter Zvi Malkin's hands with the gloves he wore to capture Adolf Eichmann. Malkin's hands were used for morality and justice, New York, 1989. Bottom, Adolf Eichmann's hands. Eichmann's hands were used to commit genocide, Israel, n.d.

Patti Ambinder with Peter Zvi Malkin, Orlando, 1996.

As a curator, it is usually pure joy and exhilaration to select the photographs and tell the stories. Occasionally, I've had to make difficult decisions of what and how much to reveal in telling a story—always focusing on what I want the audience to remember. Sometimes an artifact can evoke such deep emotion that it will overwhelm the story—of Florida Jewish history.

An example is the pair of gloves used by Israel's Mossad (secret service) agent Peter Zvi Malkin in his capture of Nazi war criminal Adolf Eichmann in Argentina. Malkin explained that on May 11, 1960, he awoke realizing that he could not touch Eichmann with his bare hands. This was the man who had sent millions of people to their deaths in the concentration camps, including Malkin's sister Fruma and her three children. He went out to buy gloves. Malkin said, "Then, at 8:20 p.m., when Eichmann was walking towards me in the street, I was ready. These are the gloves that seized and held Eichmann. To me these gloves are a symbol of morality and justice." Malkin guarded Eichmann in Buenos Aires as part of the team that brought him to trial in Israel for war crimes against the Jewish people during the Holocaust. In June 1962 Eichmann was found guilty and hanged in Israel.

A legendary spy-catcher, Malkin was born in Poland in 1927 and, after a 1933 bloody pogrom, immigrated with his family to Palestine (which became Israel in 1948), where he grew up and spent twenty-seven years in the Mossad.

Patti Ambinder, who has lived in Winter Park for forty years, was Malkin's executive assistant, editor, and cowriter. In 1996 two strangers sat together on a plane; this meeting led to a ten-year working relationship between the two. Painting was one of Malkin's covers during his years in the Mossad. For example, to maintain his cover while in Argentina, he drew stained glass windows for churches. Malkin lived in Celebration (near Orlando) from 1998–2000, where he continued his artistic pursuits. Before his 2005 death, in tribute to their partnership in sharing Malkin's story as a memoir with his paintings and personal narratives in the *Argentina Journal*, Malkin presented Ambinder a bronze mold of those Eichmann gloves.

Snowbirds

An important segment of Florida's Jewish population are the snowbirds, who are actually people—not birds at all—who have come south to escape the harsh winters in the north since the 1950s. The movement fits between tourists and permanent residents. Snowbirds tend to be younger retirees who can't quite cut their ties with the north and are still sufficiently mobile to travel back and forth. They are found all over Florida in high-rise condos or gated communities. They like walks on the beach or at the mall; a round of golf, canasta, or mah-jongg; and welcome visits from their grandchildren. Snowbirds flock to restaurants that feel like home.

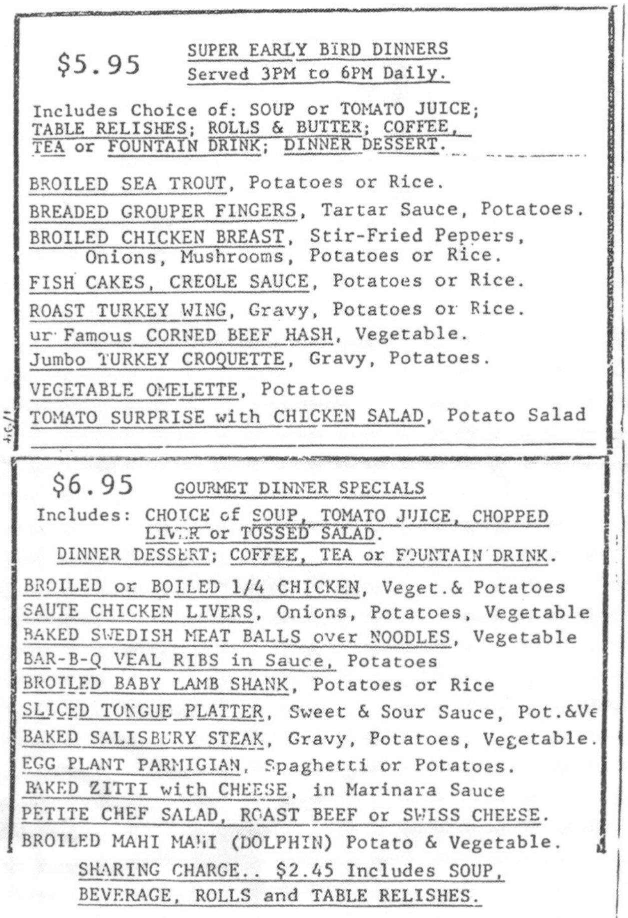
$5.95 SUPER EARLY BIRD DINNERS
Served 3PM to 6PM Daily.
Includes Choice of: SOUP or TOMATO JUICE; TABLE RELISHES; ROLLS & BUTTER; COFFEE, TEA or FOUNTAIN DRINK; DINNER DESSERT.
BROILED SEA TROUT, Potatoes or Rice.
BREADED GROUPER FINGERS, Tartar Sauce, Potatoes.
BROILED CHICKEN BREAST, Stir-Fried Peppers, Onions, Mushrooms, Potatoes or Rice.
FISH CAKES, CREOLE SAUCE, Potatoes or Rice.
ROAST TURKEY WING, Gravy, Potatoes or Rice.
ur Famous CORNED BEEF HASH, Vegetable.
Jumbo TURKEY CROQUETTE, Gravy, Potatoes.
VEGETABLE OMELETTE, Potatoes
TOMATO SURPRISE with CHICKEN SALAD, Potato Salad

$6.95 GOURMET DINNER SPECIALS
Includes: CHOICE of SOUP, TOMATO JUICE, CHOPPED LIVER or TOSSED SALAD.
DINNER DESSERT; COFFEE, TEA or FOUNTAIN DRINK.
BROILED or BOILED 1/4 CHICKEN, Veget.& Potatoes
SAUTE CHICKEN LIVERS, Onions, Potatoes, Vegetable
BAKED SWEDISH MEAT BALLS over NOODLES, Vegetable
BAR-B-Q VEAL RIBS in Sauce, Potatoes
BROILED BABY LAMB SHANK, Potatoes or Rice
SLICED TONGUE PLATTER, Sweet & Sour Sauce, Pot.&Ve
BAKED SALISBURY STEAK, Gravy, Potatoes, Vegetable.
EGG PLANT PARMIGIAN, Spaghetti or Potatoes.
BAKED ZITTI with CHEESE, in Marinara Sauce
PETITE CHEF SALAD, ROAST BEEF or SWISS CHEESE.
BROILED MAHI MAHI (DOLPHIN) Potato & Vegetable.
SHARING CHARGE.. $2.45 Includes SOUP, BEVERAGE, ROLLS and TABLE RELISHES.

Early bird menu for Wolfie's Restaurant, "Eat Early, Eat Cheap," Miami Beach, 1996.

Florida restaurants are well known for serving early bird dinners at a reduced price. For decades, Wolfie's on South Beach catered to long lines of retirees and snowbirds. The original Wolfie's opened in 1947 at Collins Avenue and Twenty-First Street.

The Elderly

The myth of South Beach—the last *minyan* in 1986. When I opened the JMOF in 1995, I got many phone calls from filmmakers, photographers, and writers saying that they were coming to report on the community of elderly Jews of South Beach. I would respond regrettably, "Sorry, you are too late."

During the 1970s, South Beach was the last leg of a historic migration from the Old World—the *shtetls* of eastern Europe, Czarist pogroms, and Holocaust—to this country, to the formidable years primarily as teachers and garment workers in the Northeast, and at last to the summer-in-winter climate. Some elderly Jews made South Beach their last resort: the last vestige of mores and traditions that testified to their perseverance, faith, and resolve. This was a community of about twenty thousand people packed into a two-square-mile area that comprised a subculture—a vibrant ingathering of free spirits who had already suffered losses and chose to live out their lives by living it up. They dressed in colorful clothes; lounged on the front porches of Art Deco buildings in decline; created *shuls* in the lobbies of those buildings; congregated on the beach, in delis, and parks; loved music; and partied hard. It was a modern-day, safe *shtetl*. But the culture was fragile.

In the 1980s they were dying off. The ethnic community was out of touch and out of time. Crime soared with the 1980 Mariel boatlift, and they felt unsafe. Sunrise swims came to an abrupt end. Then came the popular TV series *Miami Vice*. The Art Deco preservation movement that propelled the restoration of the Deco buildings also propelled a real estate boom *and* the movement *out* for the elderly. In a rush to redevelop the southern shore, Holocaust survivors were told that they would be *relocated*! Their plight was also one of aging in America. The precious legacy of the culture they had established in South Beach came to the end of the line. The average age of trendy South Beach's population dropped by about fifty years within a decade.

Today's Jewish population on the beach is Americanized, and the non-Jewish population is largely Hispanic and European. It is a different world. For every twenty-year-old today who cruises Ocean Drive, imagine an eighty-year-old back in the day, pulling a shopping cart. Where the clubs are today, imagine a makeshift synagogue. On the beach, for every "hard" body today, imagine an elderly person—and no traffic!

Miami natives Gary Monroe and Andy Sweet recorded through poignant photographs how those "front porches, where the elderly used to sit and talk about their grandchildren and Israel, became restaurants. Old ladies who had protected their lower lips from the blistering sun with sea grape leaves gave way to super models who posed for international ads. Roller blades replaced mandolin bands along Lummus Park. Kosher signs yielded to designer labels."

More currently, of elderly Jews who move, about 60 percent have moved to Florida. With more than 350,000 people, Florida has one of the nation's largest elderly Jewish populations. Jewish tradition respects age and the support that each generation can bring to one another. There are many facilities, food programs, and social activities for the Jewish elderly.

Madison Apartment: Memories on a bureau top, Miami Beach, 1979. *Photo by Gary Monroe.*

This apartment building that had housed Jewish elderly has been restored at Third Street and Washington Avenue, across the street from the JMOF-FIU.

Exercising on the beach on Ocean Drive, Miami Beach, 1978. *Photo by Gary Monroe.*

The ocean air was therapeutic, and the group activity was social bonding.

Elderly musicians entertaining friends in Lummus Park on South Beach, circa 1980. *Photo by Gary Monroe.*

Many of them were musicians in Europe, then in the Northeast, before migrating to South Beach to live out their lives.

Generation to generation, Miami, 1981.

Lee Streicher escorts Ida Kutcher to a play staged by Jewish high school students at the Miami Jewish Home and Hospital for the Aged at Douglas Gardens.

Century Village residents getting fit with Richard Simmons in their clubhouse, West Palm Beach, 1979.

Century Villages, "a Club Med for middle-income retirees," are home to more than 60,000 senior adults, mostly from the urban Northeast. Bob Rapaport, Aaron Schecter, and Irwin Levy created four large, innovative, lifestyle villages in Broward and Palm Beach Counties. The construction of the first of the villages in West Palm Beach began in 1968, offering thousands of highly affordable housing units spread over huge acreage. In 1970, for example, many of the units were selling for just $9,000. After the last of more than 7,850 units was sold in 1974, the group went on to build three other Century Villages—Deerfield Beach in 1978, Boca Raton in 1985, and Pembroke Pines completed in 1998, totaling more than 20,000 units. Century Villages offer golf, lakes, and clubhouses with amenities. Their successful formula was to sell condos at low prices and make money by charging for the use of recreation facilities and services. Most of the residents are unattached to any local family and make new friendships there.

Americans

In October 2004 former New York City mayor Ed Koch visited the JMOF, and the first words out of his mouth were, "I bring *all* of you greetings from your relatives in New York!" I had to give him a quick overview of the Jewish history of Florida to make the point that not *all* Jews in Florida are from New York! Some were actually born in Florida!

Of those Jews who live in Florida today, approximately 50 percent do have roots in the New York metro area, according to Ira M. Sheskin. His 2016 Broward study reflects how 37 percent came from a combination of New York and New Jersey, down from the 53 percent in the 1997 study. Jews on the west coast of Florida tend to arrive from the Midwest.

Of all those who have come to Florida from other places in America, what could be more American than a connection to the sixteenth US president, Abraham Lincoln! Lincoln was the first president to make it possible for rabbis to serve as military chaplains by signing the 1862 Act of Congress, which changed the law that had barred all but Christian clergy. He was the first president to revoke an official act of antisemitism by the US government also in 1862 when he canceled Ulysses S. Grant's Order No. 11, which had expelled all Jews from Tennessee. (Jews had been allowed to live in Florida one hundred years before.) He worked with Jewish financiers on innovative ways to fund the Civil War. Lincoln's protection of the growing Jewish community in the border states and his outreach to Jews in the metropolitan areas are among the more interesting facets of lesser known but significant Lincoln lore.

On January 13, 2008, the JMOF hosted the nation's first observance of Lincoln's 200th birthday with the largest audience ever for a public program—432 people seated in the historic *shul* plus 100 outside listening on speakers. A panel discussion, "Lincoln and the Jews," included Harold Holzer, noted Lincoln scholar and then vice president of the Metropolitan Museum of Art, New York; Rabbi Gary P. Zola, executive director of the Jacob Rader Marcus Center of the American Jewish Archives in Cincinnati, Ohio; and Jean Soman, Miami historian and author, who coedited the book, *A Jewish Colonel in the Civil War.*

Jean Soman served on the original advisory committee of the Abraham Lincoln Bicentennial Commission created by Congress and on the board as interim chair of its foundation. Her maternal great-great-grandfather was Marcus Spiegel, a Jewish colonel in the Union Army. Her great-grandfather (through her mother's father) was famed Lincoln photographer Samuel G. Alschuler.

Portrait of Abraham Lincoln by Samuel G. Alschuler, April 25, 1858.

Samuel Alschuler came to America from Bavaria in the 1840s and settled in Urbana, Illinois, where he established a photography studio. When Abraham Lincoln was riding the circuit in his campaign for US Senator from Illinois in 1858, he came to Alschuler's studio in a shabby linen duster. Alschuler removed his velvet-collared black coat and lent it to then beardless Lincoln for the photograph. By the time Lincoln campaigned for US president in 1860, Alschuler also had a studio in Chicago. His portrait on November 25 was Lincoln's first with a beard—a short one. Alschuler also photographed Lincoln in his coffin during the Chicago funeral procession in 1865.

Jean and William Soman family, Miami, 2014.
Photo by Roy Llera.

In the front row from left to right are Jill Soman Reiter, Joseph Reiter, and Jean Soman holding Sarah Caroline Dereser Soman. In the back row from left to right are Gabriel Reiter, Jack Reiter, Noah Reiter, William Soman, Jennifer Soman, and Andres Dereser.

Jean's father, Gabriel Powers (the family's original name was Opoznauer from Austria), was born in New York, went to law school, and was inducted into the US Army Air Corps in 1941. He became the inspector general for the US Central District, stationed in Chicago; was promoted to major, and met Caroline Alschuler who he married in 1947. After the war, he practiced law in New York and became a successful businessman. Their daughters, Jean and Susan, were born there. In 1958 the Powers family moved to Miami, following his parents who had moved to Miami Beach in 1955. Gabriel began investing in real estate. A history major in college, Jean married William Soman, an attorney. Their daughter Jill married Jack Reiter, and they have three sons. Their daughter Jennifer and Andres Dereser have a daughter Sarah. There is a fifth generation in Miami!

Cubans

Prior to 1959 Cuba had received Jews for one hundred years. Some American Jews helped support José Marti and the efforts for Cuban Independence beginning in 1892. Some settled in Cuba seeking economic opportunities. Sephardim arrived in 1902 and started a congregation in 1906. Escaping antisemitism, Ashkenazim went to Cuba in the 1920s, some because the airfare was less than going to Mexico or Argentina but mostly as a result of the US Johnson–Reed Act or Immigration Act of 1924. This xenophobic US federal law limited the number of immigrants through a national origin's quota, issuing visas to 2 percent of the total number of people of each nationality in the US as of the 1890 national census. So, for example, when Polish Jews tried to enter the country after World War I, they could not—and most went to Cuba, which was welcoming. That is why most Cuban Jews are Ashkenazic.

After World War II, German-speaking refugees and Holocaust survivors found a safe haven there. Jews in Cuba founded institutions, educated their children in Jewish schools, supported Zionism, and contributed economically and culturally. Cuba at first was reluctant to grant Jews nationalized status; the US State Department pressured Havana not to change its policies lest the Jewish immigrants seek entry into the US. By the 1930s Cubans Jews were permitted to become citizens in Cuba and did not experience antisemitism. Most lived comfortable lives until Fidel Castro seized power from Fulgencio Batista on January 1, 1959.

By 1960 many private holdings in Cuba were expropriated. As most of the island's Jews were engaged in business and had gained a secure place in the middle class, many became disenchanted with the revolution, which was beginning to show communist tendencies—and left. Today, Miami-Dade County hosts approximately 15,000 people of Cuban Jewish heritage. As the Cuban society living on the island disintegrates, the world's last Jewish community under communist rule (about 1,200 people) is having somewhat of a resurgence.

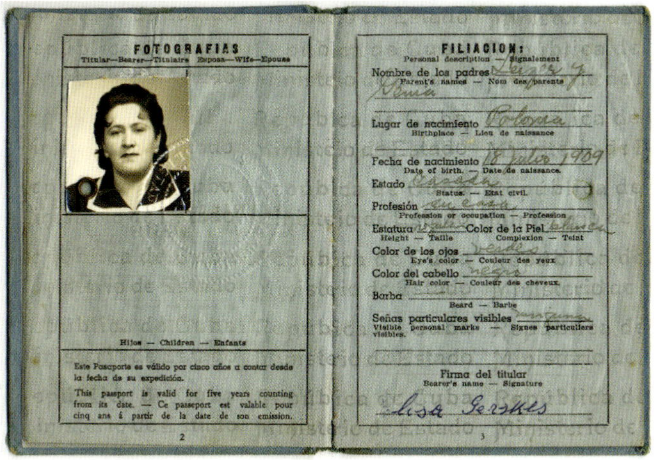

Cuban passport of Elisa Gerskes-Feldenkreis, 1955.

When Fidel Castro came to power in Cuba in 1959, about 3,500 Jews fled to south Florida. Gerskes-Feldenkreis had immigrated to Cuba from Poland in 1917 and then to Miami in 1962 to join her daughter Eva [Feig] and son George Feldenkreis, who were both already there. In the early days of MOSAIC, when I was collecting the history, Eva Feig was very generous with her time and introduced me around the Cuban community.

George Feldenkreis (second from left) with his family, Miami, 1962.

Barred from taking much out of Cuba, Jews began new businesses and professional careers in Miami. Feldenkreis, born in Cuba in 1935, received his doctorate in law, was a Zionist youth leader, and learned English there. In Miami, he started as a small importer of guayaberas. Having the feeling of insecurity passed down to him by his family's flights from both Poland and Cuba, he diversified into several other businesses and employed more than two thousand people. He established Carfel Incorporated, an import and export company for motorcycle and automobile parts, then Supreme International in 1967 to import and wholesale apparel. In 1999 this became Perry Ellis International Inc., which now includes women's lines. George evolved into one of south Florida's leading businessmen and civic leaders, and his companies are among America's largest and fastest growing. He brought his daughter and son into his businesses. He assumed major leadership roles in the Miami Jewish community and founded the Judaic Studies program at the University of Miami. The success of Feldenkreis epitomizes the American dream. He says, "If you make money, you should give money back." When I was creating the JMOF, he organized the Cuban Jewish community to be a part of it. He conducted the 1993 meeting in the museum (before it was restored) in Spanish, so I'm not sure what he told them—but they joined us!

Isaac (third from left) and Nieves (fourth from left) Olemberg's Olem Shoe Company with their employees, Miami, 1986.

When he was born in Cuba to Polish immigrants, his parents said, "Es un toro." "It's a bull" seemed apt. Olemberg weighed thirteen pounds at birth. Following their 1960 arrival from Cuba, the Olembergs started their Miami company in 1964. A giant of a man with a soft heart, Isaac with Nieves endowed the Olemberg

Family Chair in Neurological Disorders at the Miller School of Medicine at the University of Miami and supported many charities, including in Israel. Their son, Roberto, runs the shoe company today.

Welcome station, Miami, 1965.

When US President Lyndon Johnson began Freedom Flights from Cuba in 1965, groups, including the Cuban Hebrew Congregation of Miami, welcomed the immigrants. Serving at the welcome station are Estela Egozi, Esther Egozi Garazi, Alegra Barrocas, and Raquel Egozi Silverstein.

Left to right: Jack Chester, Rabbi Mayer Abramowitz, and Rafael Kravec of the Greater Miami Jewish Federation Cuban Division, 1978.

Rabbi Abramowitz, born in Israel and ordained in 1944, went to Europe in 1945 as a US Army lieutenant and military chaplain. Because of his experience with helping close displaced persons camps and getting Holocaust survivors out of Europe, he was sensitive and responsive to resettling refugees such as the Cuban Jews. He moved to Miami Beach in 1951 with his wife, Rachel, who he met in a DP camp. When the Cuban Jews arrived in Miami, the organized Jewish community (with the noted exception of the National Council of Jewish Women) ignored them. No help was offered, as they were thought to be wealthy, when in reality, they had had to leave Cuba with practically nothing.

Rabbi Abramowitz opened the doors of Temple Menorah to them with no payment for five years, and many stayed as congregants. Some Cubans organized their own congregations: Cuban Hebrew (Ashkenazic) and Torat Moshe (Sephardic). The Jewish organizations had Cuban divisions. By 1996 Cuban Jew Isaac Zelcer ascended to the presidency of the Greater Miami Jewish Federation. By that time, this group had become American Jews.

Employees of National Brush Company, Cuba, 1959.

This was a forebear of today's Corona Brushes in Ybor City. Jude Waksman is seen here wearing a tie. Gregory and David Waksman are pictured in the center. The story of Corona Brushes Inc. spans thousands of miles and nearly a century. In a small village amid the turmoil of post–World War I Russia, Jude Waksman learned the trade of processing hog bristles for paintbrush manufacturing. After the Bolsheviks seized power, Jude left Russia. Immigration quotas prohibited him from coming to America. He settled in Havana, Cuba; found work as a laborer; and sent for his wife and daughter back in Russia.

After the family reunited in Cuba, two boys and another daughter were born. World War II disrupted the supply of Chinese and Russian bristles to US paintbrush manufacturers, so Jude Waksman seized the opportunity and built a processing facility outside Havana to supply bristle from Cuban hogs. When the communist regime took over in 1959, the family left behind a thriving business and fled to Miami—and then to Tampa to start another paintbrush factory.

Jude and his sons David and Gregory adapted their paintbrushes and began again. Gregory's sons, Benjamin and Albert, have continued the family business and have now taken over the leadership of Corona Brushes, which is celebrating nearly sixty years of business in Florida.

Other Latin American Countries

These are Jews in flight. Today the greatest global movement of Jews is from Latin America due to the economic and political shifts within the continent to the south of us. Sephardic Jews (Sephardim) have been migrating to Latin America since 1492 to escape the Inquisition, and some went as *conversos* with the earliest discoverers. Most arrived in the 1800s and 1900s. Ashkenazic Jews left to flee the pogroms in eastern Europe and then the Holocaust.

These pioneers brought their culture, language, and customs to the New World. They remained a religious minority, marginalized in countries that also welcomed Nazi refugees. They made lives for their families, created Jewish institutions, and contributed greatly to their adopted lands. Propelled by revolutions, coups, economic turbulence, and antisemitism, some eventually made the next leg of their journey to the US, and many settled in Florida. As in the other sections, I have chosen sample stories to represent the large number of Jewish families who emigrated from Latin America to Florida.

Gaucho in Moisesville, Argentina, circa 1892. *Composed photography from* Pioneers in Argentina: The Jewish Immigrants. *Edited by Manrique Zago. Argentina, 1982.*

The first Jews in Argentina were *conversos* in the late sixteenth century who quickly assimilated. In the nineteenth century, Jewish immigrants fleeing Russian pogroms settled mostly in large towns, but some became gauchos (cowboys and farmers). Jewish gauchos were immigrants who settled in the fertile regions of Argentina in agricultural colonies established by the Jewish Colonization Association in 1889. The association was established by Baron Maurice de Hirsch, a French Jewish industrialist who amassed a fortune building railroads in Russia and bought more than eighty thousand hectares of land in Argentina.

Imagine Orthodox Jews leaving a cold land where everyone spoke Yiddish to go to a hot, humid place where everyone spoke Spanish! Upon arrival, each family was leased a 123-acre plot, given bricks to build a home and a set of tools, and told to dig a well. Ninety percent of the immigrants knew nothing about working the land. Each family began to farm and raise cattle and started to pay off the land. They built synagogues, Jewish schools, and Jewish communities there.

The last group came in 1936; they were German Jewish families narrowly escaping extermination to start a sort of Argentine Borscht Belt. This included sixteen colonies where residents spoke Yiddish, introduced eastern European–style agricultural cooperatives, and laid out hamlets not unlike the *shtetls* that the immigrants had called home back in Russia.

Today, isolated buildings adorned with Jewish stars and fading scribbles of Yiddish can be seen from main roads connecting the colonies. Train stations that were built and tracks laid to accommodate the transport of goods produced by each farm have shuttered—empty silos sit along hundreds of miles of track overgrown with weeds. With the political situation and antisemitism in Argentina, the Jewish population has declined drastically. About eight thousand Argentinean Jews live in Florida.

Trilnik Family from Russia to Argentina to Florida

Tenth anniversary of Cora and José Trilnik, Buenos Aires, Argentina, 1948.

Sitting in front is Marcello. In the front row from left to right are nine-year-old Eleonora Trilnik, Rosa Schilman Staravolsky, Berta Epstein Schilman, Adriana Schilman, Mauricio Schilman, the baby Mariana Trilnik, and Cora Schilman Trilnik. In the back row from left to right are Bernardo Staravolsky, Elena Schilman, Luis Bacciadonne, and José Trilnik.

Eleanora Trilnik, a dentist who migrated from Argentina to Broward County, is a descendent of Orthodox Jewish grandparents who left Grodno, Lithuania, in 1889 for Moisesville, Argentina. Their goal was to settle in the US, but they could not because of immigration quotas. Her father, José Trilnik, was born in a house his parents built in Moiseville. He grew up to be a dentist and, in 1938, married Cora Shilman, born in 1919 to Mauricio and Berta Shilman, who also came from Russia—near Odessa. Eleanora, born in 1939, started studying English when she was seven years old with a goal of coming to America. Under Argentina's president Juan Peron, the situation for Jews became very stressful. Jews were accused of being communists and singled out if they belonged to or contributed to Jewish organizations or to Israel. Then, in 1960, a Nazi gang shot her cousin. She and all seventeen of her cousins got phone calls, "You know what we did to your cousin? We are going to make soap from you, so you'd better get out of this country."

Always fearful to identify as a Jew in Argentina, Eleanora's dream was realized when she was invited to come to the US as a professor of pediatric dentistry at the University of Pittsburgh. As a result of a serious eye problem, she had to quit dentistry. Eleanora moved to Florida in 2000 to become a dental office manager in Plantation, eventually specializing in management and marketing for the health professions.

Tania and Israel Lapciuc Family, Moldova to Colombia to Florida, 1976

Lapciuc family, Miami Beach, 2001.

The Lapciuc family originated in Beltz, Moldova, where Israel was born. In the 1940s Israel escaped the Romanian death camp of Transnistria with his parents, Samuel Lapciuc and Perla Kleiman. After the war, the entire family migrated to Medellin, Colombia, where Samuel founded a textile company in 1952. Israel ran his father's company in Medellin.

Tania's family also came from Moldova. Tania's father, Jacobo Fraiman, immigrated to Lima in 1927, where he became a wholesaler and importer. Jacobo married Sara Zaidman in 1929. Soon after, they moved to Arequipa, Peru, where Tania Fraiman was born. Tania was raised in Arequipa, but due to the antisemitic conditions and lack of a Jewish community, they moved back to Lima where Tania completed high school and became an active member of the Zionist Organization of Peru.

In 1961 Tania and Israel met in Colombia and married. They lived in Medellin where they raised three children: Marcos, Isaac, and Yair. Israel volunteered in the Jewish community, serving as president of the Jewish Federation of Colombia. Here he also penned *No Olvidaras* (Thou Shalt Not Forget), chronicling his family's survival in Transnistria. Due to the unstable political situation in Colombia and the kidnapping of his father, Samuel, in 1976, the Lapciucs moved to Miami Beach, where the family is deeply involved in the Jewish community. Israel is an exporter to Latin American countries.

Mario Kreutzberger Family, Germany to Chile to Miami, 1986

***Don Francisco Quién Soy? Telebiografia de Mario Kreutzberger*: Autobiography by Mario Kreutzberger (from Chile) about his television career as Don Francisco, 1980s.**

Mario Kreutzberger spent more than fifty years entertaining a worldwide audience. Known as Don Francisco, he hosted the television series *Sabado Gigante* (*Giant Saturday*), which holds the Guinness Book record for the longest-running television variety series in history (1962–2015). It was also Univision's longest-running program. *Sabado Gigante*, transmitted to forty-two countries, ran for five hours each Saturday. Kreutzberger has interviewed more than fifty thousand people throughout the world.

Mario Kreutzberger's parents, Anni Blumenfeld and Erik Kreutzberger, married in 1937 in Germany. During Kristallnacht, Erik was sent to a concentration camp. Anni escaped and then got a visa to Chile. Erik went to a refugee camp in England and from there took a ship to Valparaiso, Chile. In 1940 Erik and Anni were reunited and settled in Talca, south of Santiago, where they had two sons, Mario and Rene. Mario started his TV show in 1962, the same year he married Temi Muchnick; they raised three children: Patricio, Vivian, and Francisco. Inspired by Jerry Lewis's telethon in the US, in 1978 Kreutzberger founded a telethon in Chile that resulted in the opening of eight hospitals for handicapped children that have helped more than five hundred thousand patients.

In 1986 the Kreutzbergers moved to Miami to do his show from there. *Sabado Gigante* is the most famous Hispanic program in the US, spanning five decades. In 2016 Don Francisco returned to television and signed a multiyear deal with Telemundo.

Kreutzberger has received numerous awards and the 2,179th star on the Hollywood Walk of Fame. In 2012 he was inducted into the Television Academy Hall of Fame. In 2015 the city of New York named a street in the Washington Heights district in his honor, named "Don Francisco Boulevard." He says, "I'm always trying to give the best service I can, the best values, so that people can have a better life. You might ask, 'How is that possible by being a television host?' I believe that even entertainment is a service, that people need it, like any other service, like food or transportation."

Lapco Family from Russia to Venezuela to Florida

***Bar mitzvah* of Paul Lapco (second row center in suit), son of Anita Lapco, Latin Division director, Jewish Federation of Broward County, Caracas, Venezuela, 1978.**

To the left of Paul is an aunt, and behind her is Anita Lapco. Natalio Glijansky (with glasses) stands behind Paul. To the right of Paul is a sister-in-law, and behind her to the right is Leon Lapco (with glasses) next to the wall.

Anita Lapco was born in Caracas, Venezuela, to parents who had fled Russia because of antisemitism. In 1929, after his military service, Natalio Glijansky left his family and *shtetl* to go to Venezuela. Eight years later, he asked Ghenea Rechtman to join him. They married in Caracas and had three children: Judith, Alex, and Anita. Natalio brought the rest of his relatives to Venezuela. They were all leaders in the Jewish community and dedicated to Jewish education, where every child went to the Jewish school. Anita studied education at university, returned to her childhood school as a counselor, was a principal for sixteen years, and then became director of ORT Venezuela, part of World ORT, a global Jewish educational network. Lapco said, "In Venezuela we taught trades to the disadvantaged so they could join the job market and improve their quality of life. We were hired by the oil, electric, and telephone companies to train their human resources, but when the government changed, they did not want to hire ORT anymore, as they said to me they did not know what else we were teaching them besides a trade." Lapco continues, "In 1998 Hugo Chavez was elected president of Venezuela. The minute my husband, Leon, heard his populist speech, he said, 'This will become another Cuba. We must leave.'"

Leon Lapco founded and was the president of a youth group called "Jovenes Hebreos" that grew to have one thousand members. He was a physician but had to change his occupation when they immigrated to Florida in 2004. Anita was fortunate, through her connections, to get a position as Latin Division director of the Jewish Federation of Broward County where she is educating Latin Jews about the federation and the importance of giving back to the community. The Lapcos chose to live in Aventura, where many former Jews from Venezuela settled. "One of the things that shocked me here in Florida was that not all Jewish children could receive a formal Jewish education due to the cost. Nevertheless, as a newcomer, you have to adapt to your new community," said Anita.

Hebraica Center dance group, Miami Beach, 1995.

A group of Jews from five Latin American countries formed a Hebraica Center in 1983, which then affiliated with the Michael Anne Russell Jewish Community Center (JCC) in North Miami Beach in 1991.

Israelis

In Florida, there are more than one hundred thousand Israelis, who contribute in every way to their communities. Most are in business or Jewish education. Sometimes called *yordim*, a Hebrew term that means those who "go down," they are the opposite of making *aliyah*, which means "go up." Organizations attempt to maintain a connection between them and Israel with lectures and gatherings. The most challenging part of settling here is separating from family and friends, so Florida's Israelis tend to congregate among themselves. The Israeli American Council was founded in 2007 to conduct programs that strengthen the identity of the next generations of Israelis here and the bond between Americans and the State of Israel.

American Marrying Israeli: Goldstein–Zadok

Left to right: Shai, Ofer, and Adi Zadok and Jacqueline Goldstein, Miami, 2014.

Ofer and Itamar are brothers, and Boaz and Erez Zadok are their cousins.

Left to right: Boaz Zadok, Ofer Zadok, Erez Zadok, and Itamar Zadok, Tel Aviv, circa 1974.

Ofer Zadok, born in 1968 in Holon, Israel, is the son of Yaffa Tanami and Avner Zadok, whose parents were born in Yemen and went to Israel in the 1930s on one of the first flights to transport the Yemenite Jews there. Ofer grew up between Israel, New York, and Los Angeles, shuttling back and forth over the years. After graduating from Boston University in 1996, Ofer returned to New York and enrolled in a landscape design certificate program at the New York Botanical Gardens.

He met American Jacqueline Goldstein in 1998; they married in 2000. In 2004 Ofer and Jacqueline moved to Miami, where Ofer did landscape design throughout south Florida until they moved to Israel in 2011 for one year. Upon their return to Miami, Ofer began working with manufacturers to produce and sell organic linens. This was a result of searching for sheets and towels without any chemical dyes for their two sons, Shai (born 2006) and Adi (born 2011).

Today, Ofer, Jacqueline, Shai, and Adi live on Miami Beach. Ofer has developed his own company, Fine Linen Organics. Art historian Jacqueline is the curator at the JMOF-FIU. Yaffa Tanami's business is manufacturing and selling custom wigs in Miami, New York, and Tel Aviv.

According to *Florida Trend* magazine (January 26, 2017), Zev Bufman is a Florida icon.

When the Russian Revolution was taking hold, bringing with it antisemitic pogroms, Zev Bufman's family fled to Palestine, where he was born in Tel Aviv in 1930. Zev's father owned movie theaters, and he grew up in the back of the projection room. He began his career in the performing arts by entertaining troops during Israel's 1948 War of Independence and returned for the Six-Day War and Yom Kippur War.

Bufman went to Hollywood, California, in 1951 to be a star; did about eight movies, including Cecil B. DeMille's *Ten Commandments*, and then realized he was not that good. He went to Miami in 1962 to purchase and renovate the historic Coconut Grove Playhouse; was a founding partner in 1988 of the National Basketball Association (NBA) Miami Heat; produced forty-one Broadway shows with major stars, mostly during the 1970s and 1980s; has run fourteen performing arts centers, mostly in Florida; and partnered to build four twenty-thousand-seat amphitheaters in the 1990s.

From 2011–18, he made huge improvements to Ruth Eckerd Hall in Clearwater as its president and CEO. Bufman, a giant in the industry with so many awards, is writing a memoir and producing a Broadway play. He died in 2020.

Israeli teachers at the David Posnack Hebrew Day School, Plantation, 1996.

Bringing the Israeli culture, history, and Hebrew language to students in Jewish schools enhances the quality of education and appreciation for 1,800 years of Jewish migrations up until the modern State of Israel was founded in 1948. The personal stories of the Israelis bring into focus the realities in our spiritual homeland.

Other Middle Eastern Countries

After thirty-five years of research, I have come to the conclusion that Jews have lived in every nook and cranny of the world! The adrenaline that kept thrusting me forward in my position at the JMOF was meeting people and learning their stories. These people became my friends, and one is Lina Zargar Samimy, who came to Miami in 1973.

Dr. Samimy walked into my office after the September 11 attacks and said, "I think the history of my family moving between Persia (Iran) and Turkmenistan according to the treatment of Jews by the ruling regimes is unique, and I have dozens of fabulous artifacts to tell the story." Of course, everyone thinks her or his family's story is unique—but this one was—and I created an entire exhibit around it!

Here was an immigration story of secrecy and success that takes you to the land of Queen Esther (500 BCE), where Jews have lived and also been persecuted for more than 2,600 years. The country was known as Persia until 1935, when the name changed to Iran. Jews endured 450 years of hardship under Muslim rule from 1501 until Shah Pahlevi's reign began in 1941. From 1941 to 1979, it was a golden age for Jews as the shah showed them great respect. Since the Islamic Revolution of 1979, Jews have only been allowed limited freedoms. There are approximately 18,000 Jews living in Iran today (mainly in Tehran, Shiraz, and Isfahan), down from 80,000 before the 1979 revolution.

Turkmenistan has been a migratory state for the past 1,500 years. Because of its diversity, it accepted Jews, who were originally traders. In the eleventh century, Islam took over, and although interrupted, it returned in the 1700s. Turkmenistan was annexed by Russia in 1881 when Jews were expected to adopt Islam or flee. Pogroms began. From 1890 to 1917, Turkmenistan was ruled as a Russian military colony but with a level of neglect that allowed a tolerance for Jews. After Lenin overthrew the Russian government in 1917, things got worse for the Jews. The early 1920s was their last opportunity to escape (many Jews went to Palestine) before the Soviets closed the doors. By 1924 Turkmenistan was part of the Soviet Union. Turkmenistan declared independence in 1991. There are only about 1,000 Jews living in Turkmenistan today.

Zargar Family from Persia to Turkmenistan to Persia to New York to Florida

Zargar family, Tagtabazar, Turkmenistan, circa 1908.

Seated in the center is Shahverdi Zargar, Lina Zargar Samimy's great-grandfather. Standing in the back left is Lina's grandfather Haci Ibrahim Zargar, holding her father Parviz in his arms, and Golandam is standing in front of him. The other boys are all cousins of Parviz.

Photograph of a painting by Lina Zargar Samimy of her father, Parviz Zargar, Turkmenistan, circa 1919.

Parviz is wearing a jacket of purple velvet with gold embroidery and a black cap of Persian lamb, made by his mother for his *bar mitzvah*. The name Zargar means "goldsmith" in Farsi, the language of Persia. Lina Zargar Samimy's great-grandfather Shahverdi Zargar had been a jeweler for the king in Persia in the 1800s. In 1908 as a result of antisemitism, the Zargars moved to Turkmenistan and raised Persian lambs for the fur business. Because this prosperous Jewish family was a target during the Bolshevik Revolution, they decided to flee from Turkmenistan back to Persia in 1920.

Since they were not allowed to leave Turkmenistan with valuables, a box containing jewelry made by Shahverdi was buried under a stone in the backyard of their home. Lina's grandfather showed his fourteen-year-old son, Parviz, the spot so that he could return when the political situation eased. Haci Ibrahim Zargar died in Persia soon after their return. In 1926, when Parviz was selected to study electrical engineering in Paris, he realized that the jewels would help support his mother and sister in his absence. He traveled back across the border in his father's fur coat with hidden pockets created in the lining by his seamstress mother. Parviz returned to his former home in Turkmenistan and found the jewels under the stone. Trembling from fear, he crossed the border, the jewelry undetected.

Parviz and Ita Zargar with their daughter, Lina, Tehran, Iran, 1938.

In Paris, Parviz met his wife, Ita, a Romanian Jew who had come to Paris to escape the pogroms. In 1937 to welcome her to the family, Sultan Zargar (mother of Parviz) gave the jewelry to Ita. The intricate earrings, brooches, and necklaces made from gold and precious stones reflect the flavor of the region and remain in the family's collection.

Parviz and Ita moved to Tehran and had two children: Lina and Dara. Lina was born in 1938 in Tehran and raised there. In the image, notice the samovar on the table. Tea became a cultural staple in Central Asia after its introduction from China. One of the ways to prepare tea that has been most associated with Russia and Persia is the samovar, using water heated with charcoal. *Samovar* is a Russian word that means "self-burning." To symbolize our friendship, Lina gave me a teapot for the samovar that my great-grandmother brought from Russia to America in 1915.

Zargar-Samimy family, Miami, 2009.

In the first row from left to right are Darius Drier-Zargar, Gabriel Krantz, Layla Krantz, Perry Samimy, and Eve Drier-Zargar in a stroller. In the back row from left to right are Dr. Jean Samimy, Ellen Samimy, Luka Krantz (being held), Annabel Samimy-Krantz, Jay Krantz, Roland Samimy, Dr. Lina Samimy, Yasmine Samimy, and Alexandra Zargar.

Antisemitism caused the family to live in constant fear in Iran and to suppress their Jewish identity. Lina did not even know she was Jewish until she was eight years old, even though her grandmother raised chickens and bought kosher meat. Her family celebrated Passover with a *seder* at relatives' homes, never their own.

At the age of fifteen, Lina was sent to the Alliance Israelite Oriental School in Paris, where she learned Hebrew. She continued her studies at Paris Medical School, where she met her husband, Jean Samimy. Lina Zargar was one of the first Iranian Jewish women to earn a medical degree there. Lina and Jean came to New York in 1965 to continue their medical studies; she became a tumor pathologist at Memorial Sloan-Kettering Hospital. Lina visited Miami in 1966, which motivated the family to move there in 1973.

Lina's brother, Dara, born in 1941, became a civil engineer. He has residences in Manhattan and Miami, is a software architect in the film industry; and collects Iranian artifacts and books. Lina's daughter Yasmine Samimy is a graphics artist in Miami.

The Exhibit

Along with the Zargars' amazing journey to Florida came the remainder of those retrieved family jewels that were not sold to support the family in Iran. The jewelry looks like it was made for a king—because it was! Intricate earrings, brooches, and necklaces made from gold and precious stones reflect the flavor of the region. Other equally interesting heirlooms that Lina Zargar Samimy has include Persian rugs and silver, a gold brocade caftan given to her great-grandfather by the king of Persia, the purple velvet jacket made for the *bar mitzvah* of Lina's father in Turkmenistan, coins from the Russian Czar, a Persian *ketubah*, Persian and Russian samovars, and dozens of family photographs.

Former Soviet Union

About 6,000 Jews are in Miami-Dade County from the former Soviet Union and probably about 8,500 throughout Florida. After the Holocaust, American and Floridian Jews were sensitized to responding to the plight of Jews imposed with restrictions. During the 1960s and 1970s, Jews here protested the Soviet Union's attempts to destroy their Jewish communities by closing down synagogues and denying permissions to emigrate. The Soviets often imprisoned leaders of the Jewish movement, and then these prisoners of conscience became the new focus of the international Soviet Jewish protest movement. Jewish communities in Florida joined others in staging demonstrations and rallies, lobbying in Washington, and then sponsoring Soviet Jewish families to resettle in our communities. The most prominent legislative victory was the 1974 congressionally sponsored Jackson-Vanik amendment that linked trade with Russia to freedom of emigration for Soviet Jews. The Soviet Jewry organizations also encouraged tens of thousands of American and Western Jews to visit Russia as tourists and to spend time with Jewish dissidents to express support.

Eva Trakhter–Shvedova Family

The last photograph of the Trakhter family together in the small *shtetl* Stepan in Poland that became Russian land, 1936.

The family's mother, Chava, and father, Chaim, are surrounded by their four children: Shlomo (sixteen), Rachel (twelve), Abram (seven), and Pearl (four). In 1939 Stepan became part of the Soviet Union, and Shlomo was drafted into the Russian Army. When the Nazis seized Stepan in 1941, all the family were taken to the Jewish ghetto. Chava, Chaim, Rachel, and Pearl were killed in the fall of 1942; the two boys survived. Abram lived because when the Nazis captured them on a bridge, Shlomo pushed him from the horse-pulled wagon, and he fell into the river. He then walked in the forest until he found partisans and joined them to fight the Nazis from December 1942 through July 1944.

At age twelve, Anna Leibovich from *shtetl* Berdichev (Ukraine) worked in a military plant in Siberia making bullets for the rifles of Russian soldiers fighting the Nazis. After the war, Anna came to Pinsk, the Soviet Union; completed medical school; and was a doctor's assistant. There she met and married Abram Trakhter in 1948. They had three children: Eva, Efim, and Polina. Abram worked for fifty years as a director of the Food Distribution Center in Pinsk.

When World War II was over, Shlomo became a leader in a displaced persons camp in France, where he married Raqil and assisted in getting many DPs to Israel. During Israel's War of Independence (1948), he fought with Menachem Begin in the Irgun and helped deliver weapons in sugar sacks. After the war, he and Raqil moved to Cuba, where he had relatives. After the revolution in Cuba, they moved to Miami in 1960, where Shlomo had a successful shoe business. Abram and Anna moved to Miami in 1993 from Russia—and at last, the Trakhter brothers were united!

The oldest daughter of Anna and Abram, Eva Trakhter [Shvedova], was an electrical engineer working in St. Petersburg, Russia, as a designer of navigation devices for submarines for the Military Research Institute. In 1994 she moved to Miami with her sons, Maksim and Oleg, and I hired her at the JMOF as the admissions and store manager.

France and Other European Countries

After the US, France has the second largest Jewish population outside of Israel—even after the long history of expulsions and exclusions and barely being tolerated. As I write this, the Cathedral of Notre Dame de Paris is burning, and I think of the *Ecclesia and Synagoga* statues I saw on each side of the main entrance that capture the French feeling about Jews. Ecclesia is a dignified, finely dressed woman standing upright, wearing a crown, carrying a chalice and a staff with a cross at its peak. She is seemingly triumphant and represents the victorious Catholic Church. Synagoga is a ragged woman, defeated. Her eyes have been blinded by a snake, and her head is bowed. She holds a broken scepter, and the tablets of Jewish law are slipping from her grasp. Under her feet lies a crown trodden into the dust. She represents the synagogue and the Jews. The Catholic Church wanted those entering Notre Dame to believe that Judaism was finished, downcast and humiliated.

Following World War II and the experience of selective persecutions and murders during the Holocaust, Jews were leaving as soon as possible, primarily for either Palestine (which became Israel in 1948) or the US—and some came to Florida.

Dr. Leon Weissberg was a new immigrant from France who came through the Port of Miami, 1952.

After the Holocaust and following Leon's birth in a DP camp in Landsburg, Germany, his mother, Eva, died there. Leon and his father, Sam, went to Paris to be with family. They lived on Rue de Pressoir in the IX arrondissement in a building with one bathroom per floor. Sam remarried an Auschwitz survivor and became a shoe cobbler with his brother. With a cousin in New York, the family was able to arrange with the Hebrew Immigration Aid Society to emigrate to America—specifically Florida. Leon Weissberg grew up to become executive director of the Jewish Education

Commission for South Palm Beach County. He said, "I thoroughly enjoyed being immersed in the Jewish world…I devoured it in every sense."

In the last twenty years, more than 20 percent of Jews have left France, and about half who remain have considered emigrating because of antisemitism and the lack of freedom to express their traditions, such as wearing a *kippah* on the streets. Unlike the state-sponsored antisemitism in Europe of the nineteenth and twentieth centuries that was focused on hatred for Jews as a people, today the threats for Jews are coming from hatred for their nation—Israel. Israel continues to be challenged for its existence as are the Jews of Europe.

Most are considering whether they can remain as Jews in France and the rest of Europe, and the population that is leaving increases annually with the increasing hateful rhetoric, racist attacks, and murders coming from the citizens there, not the government. European Jews cannot relax and enjoy their lives—they feel fear and no sense of safety. So they are fleeing.

America and Florida offer a stable, safe environment with a broad-based economy and welcoming Jewish community. Those who come to America largely settle in New York, Los Angeles, and the Miami area, and the latter appears to be the most organized in accepting the French Jews.

LA COMMUNAUTE JUIVE FRANCOPHONE DE MIAMI

Son pilier : le Rav Israël Frankforter, un homme toujours attentif aux besoins des autres

Depuis le début des années 2000, on estime qu'environ cinq mille Juifs français sont partis s'installer dans le sud de la Floride. Des familles souvent séduites au cours de vacances par le paysage grandiose et le mode de vie américain, ont décidé de quitter l'Hexagone afin de tenter de se faire une place sous le soleil de Miami. Mais, en temps de crise le rêve américain est parfois devenu un mythe lointain et les difficultés peuvent être à la mesure du gigantisme du pays. Le Rav Frankforter le sait, et depuis vingt ans il n'a de cesse d'aider les membres de la communauté juive française à trouver leurs repères.

Rav Israel and Louiza Frankforter, Miami Beach, 2012. *Israel Magazine.*

Rabbi Yisroel Frankforter came from Paris in 1986 to study for the rabbinate in New York and settled in Miami in 1991 with his wife, Louiza, and one young daughter; they now have five children and are grandparents.

Once a trickle, the number of French Jews in Florida has swelled into an unmistakable wave. Rabbi Frankforter says the number (2019) in south Florida is about ten thousand. Most identify as Jewish, and he helps them to acclimate. Several years ago, Rabbi Frankforter could complete his scheduled visits to French Jews in the Miami area in two hours. Now his regular routine of teaching and counseling takes the entire week.

Today, most who arrive are young families with children who see no future as Jews in France and have come to ensure a Jewish life for the next generation. A big challenge for them is that there are no state subsidies for religious education, as in France, so Chabad here allows them to pay the same as they did in France for up to two years, even though the tuition here is about four times higher.

"The American dream under the sun and palm trees sounded very attractive to them. However, not everything is always rosy, and my wife and I are here providing all sorts of support. Many French Jews can get along with some English. They can ask directions to the post office, but they cannot have a deep discussion in English," said Rabbi Frankforter. "An interesting new experience for these French Jews is hurricane planning!"

Jonathan Symons is the largest private JMOF-FIU donor and his primary residence is London, England, 2018.

The historic *shul* that was restored in 2007 to be part of the museum is named the Jonathan Symons Building. Born in London, Jonathan first came to Miami Beach in 1985 as his father, Cyril Symons, had purchased a condo for retirement there in 1979. Father and son were in commercial real estate in England. Raised in a kosher home and having attended an Orthodox *shul* since childhood, Jonathan has been deeply involved in the English Jewish community. There are about 270,000 Jews there, which is less than one-half a percent of the general population, most living in Greater London.

Symons, now retired, spends the Jewish holidays and much of the winters on Miami Beach. Coming from a country with an expulsion history and increasing antisemitism where Jews think each day about whether to stay or leave, he says, "I support the JMOF-FIU because 'History is our rearview mirror.' This is such an important time in Jewish history to get involved and ensure the support of our museum that strengthens Jewish identity and tells our story to the public. I enjoy being a docent because I want to convey to others what Jews have accomplished in Florida, and it makes me proud to be Jewish."

PART 3

Land of Opportunity

The Land of Opportunity lies under your hat.
—Unknown

Most Jews who came from Europe arrived penniless, with only their adroit minds. Some Jews who came from other places in America transferred their traditional businesses to the Florida setting. Many have used the state's unique resources to develop or expand bases in and for Florida. They became farmers, ranchers, cigar makers, retailers, restaurateurs, hoteliers, corporate CEOs, scientists, doctors, engineers, architects, developers, politicians, attorneys, musicians, artists, writers, athletes, educators, and more. Many of their names have become household words for all Floridians.

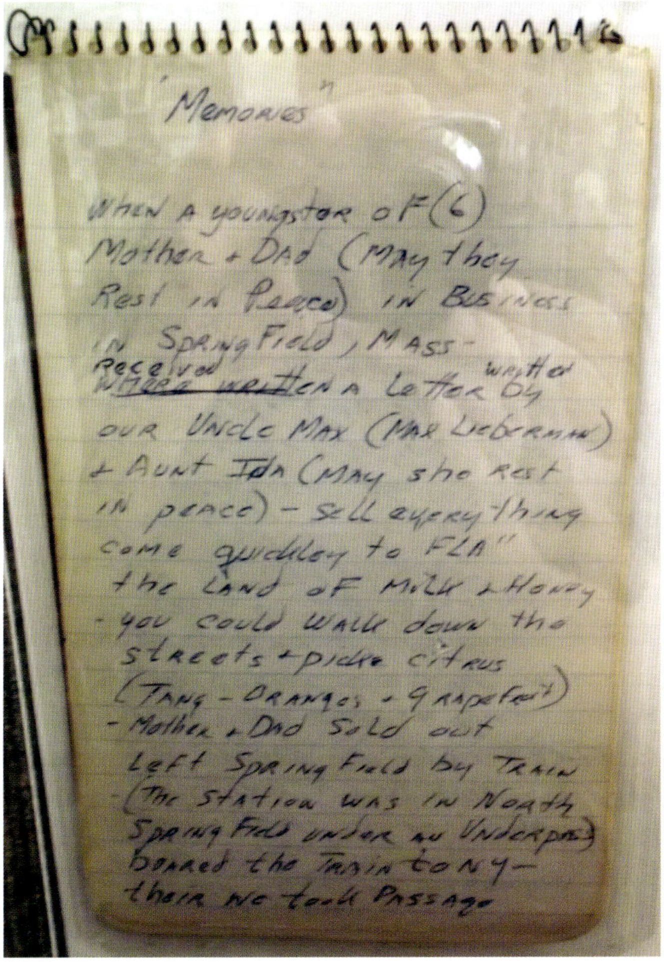

"Memories"
When a youngster of (6)
Mother + Dad (May they
Rest in Peace) in Business
in Springfield, Mass-
Received ~~Where written~~ a letter written by
our Uncle Max (Max Lieberman)
+ Aunt Ida (May she rest
in peace) - sell everything
come quickly to FLA"
the land of Milk + Honey
- you could walk down the
streets + pick citrus
(Tang - Oranges + grapefruit)
- Mother + Dad sold out
Left Springfield by Train
- (The station was in North
Springfield under an Underpass)
boarded the Train to NY -
there we took Passage

"Memories" notebook, 1915.

Ben (left) and Abe Chepenik, Jacksonville, 1929.

"Sell everything—come quickly to Florida, the land of milk and honey—you could walk down the streets and pick citrus." These words were part of a letter received by the Massachusetts branch of the Chepenik family from an uncle in Jacksonville in 1915 who had discovered the business potential of growing oranges. Brothers Ben and Abe Chepenik left quickly with their parents via train to New York City, where they boarded the Clyde Line Steamship the *Lenape* for the three-day sail to Florida. Upon arrival, the brothers were very surprised as they had never seen an orange tree or used an outhouse!

CHAPTER 1

Lure of the Land: Citrus, Agriculture, Ranching, and Tobacco

Jews are usually perceived to be an urban people, but in Florida they have engaged in producing every kind of farm crop and livestock animal. From the Middle Ages, European countries barred Jews from owning land, which prevented Jews from making their living from agriculture. This is one reason Florida attracted Jews as they had an opportunity to own land and work it. Jews were also attracted to farming in Florida because of the climate, excellent markets, and the diversity of agricultural opportunities. Some even got loans from the Jewish Agricultural Society, an organization chartered in New York City in 1900 to provide east European immigrants with placement, advice, training, and loans with generous terms to become self-supporting farmers.

You already met Moses Levy, who brought citrus fruits, sugar, roots, and seeds to his Pilgrimage Plantation in Micanopy in 1822. Here you will find stories of more Jews who have contributed much to the state's farming economy—in citrus, produce, dairy, poultry, cattle, and tobacco. Their beneficiaries are worldwide, wherever Florida's agricultural products are consumed.

Citrus

According to Florida Citrus Mutual, Christopher Columbus brought the first citrus to the New World in 1493. The early Spanish explorers, probably Juan Ponce de León, planted the first orange trees around St. Augustine sometime between 1513 and 1565. Grapefruit was a relative latecomer, arriving in Florida in 1806 courtesy of the French Count, Odet Philippe, who planted the first grove of grapefruit near Tampa in 1823. Around that time, Florida had established a citrus business in the north, with growers packing the fruit in barrels for boat trips to market. By the nineteenth century, citrus trees could be found growing wild throughout Florida, and cultivated orange groves could be found along the St. Johns River and around Tampa. Florida's unique sandy soil and sub-tropical climate were ideal for growing the seeds that early settlers planted. It took nearly 400 years from the time citrus was first introduced to Florida until enough was grown in the state to turn it into a profitable business venture. Although Florida's citrus industry has encountered freezing temperatures and diseases, the industry has continued to thrive as new groves are planted farther south after each freeze. Today, there are nearly 4,000 citrus growers cultivating almost 437,000 acres of land in Florida. More than 45,000 other people also work in the citrus industry or in related businesses. The state produces more oranges than any other region of the world, except Brazil, and leads the world in grapefruit production. The citrus industry generates more than $8.6 billion in economic activity in Florida. As such, the citrus industry plays an important role in the life of every Floridian.

And Jews have played a major role in Florida's citrus industry!

Martin Miley with a Major Dade orange tree, Thonotosassa, 1927.

I wrote earlier about Emaline and William Miley in Thonotosassa in 1844. Their son Martin stands in their grove with an orange tree that has a most interesting history. During the Second Seminole War in December 1835, when Major Francis Dade and his company started on their famous march toward Fort King, they rested and ate their lunch on the first day at a point about three miles southwest of Lake Thontosassa. They had some sweet oranges that had just been brought to Fort Brooke (Tampa) from Cuba, a rare treat in those days. They ate the oranges and dropped the peel and seeds on the ground. The seeds sprouted, took root, and grew into trees. By 1850 they were regularly bearing fine, sweet oranges. William Miley transplanted several of them to his farm. Over time, all but one died, and this one stands twisted and broken by wind storms. It had survived the hard freezes of 1886 and 1895 and continued to bear fruit. More than a half-century later, Martin picked nearly ten thousand oranges and sold them for a penny each in Tampa.

Dr. Philip P. Phillips settled in Orlando in 1897, becoming the king of citrus with an empire of five thousand acres and two packinghouses, circa 1926.

Dr. Phillips (1874–1959) earned a medical degree at Columbia University. Migrating from Tennessee, he purchased a grove in Orlando in 1894, but within a year his new holdings were wiped out in a devastating freeze. He returned to settle in 1897 and purchased more land for groves. Phillips and his wife, Della Wolf Phillips, hosted concerts in their home and contributed greatly to the cultural development of the city. As his business grew, he built housing, a US post office, and even a cemetery for his employees. In the 1950s, recognizing that proper local health care for black citizens was almost nonexistent. Dr. Phillips helped establish the Dr. Phillips Memorial Hospital. His son Howard was also dedicated to this project and encouraged two black doctors to relocate to Orlando to establish their practice. A second son, Walter, was born in Kissimmee.

***The Doc Knows*, Orlando, circa 1937.**

Dr. Philip Phillips introduced pasteurized citrus juices to the industry. His patented innovation called flash pasteurization was the first to successfully can juice without the metallic taste, a hallmark of earlier canning processes. His company was the first to market its citrus nationally and the first to secure certification from the American Medical Association to advertise the health benefits of its juice products. Dr. Phillips established a fertilizer manufacturing plant and also used the airstrip on his property to conduct the first aerial spraying of citrus. He achieved great success with promotional films, using what was then the new, stunning Technicolor.

Dr. P. Phillips Company: "Head 'em up! Move 'em out!," Orlando, circa 1938.

With extensive citrus holdings in Orange and Osceola Counties, Dr. Phillips had a fleet of trucks to nationally deliver fresh citrus fruit, canned citrus fruit sections, and pasteurized citrus juice.

Many places in Central Florida are named in honor of Dr. Philip Phillips, whose legacy impacted local agriculture, health care, education, and the cultural arts.

In 1954 Dr. Phillips sold his citrus business to Granada Groves, a partnership between Investors Diversified Services and Minute Maid. His legacy continues to fund many charitable community projects. The accomplishments of Dr. Phillips were recognized in 1986 when he was inducted into the Florida Citrus Hall of Fame.

Engraved on the tombstone of Dr. Philip Phillips (center photo) are the words, "Under His Hand the Wilderness Bore Fruit." And indeed, citrus greatly improved the quality of life for Central Florida residents. Clockwise starting at the top left are places named after him: the **Dr. Phillips House**, where Dr. Phillips lived downtown, is now a restored historic bed-and-breakfast. **Dr. Phillips** is a suburb in unincorporated Orange County. **Dr. Phillips Elementary School** opened in 1979 in Bay Hill. The **Dr. Phillips Center for the Performing Arts** opened in 2015. The 80-acre **Dr. Phillips Community Park** opened in 2007. **Dr. Phillips High School** opened in 1987 for approximately 2,500 students. **Dr. P. Phillips Hospital** serves southwest Orange County. Not shown are the **Dr. P. Phillips Baby Place** at Winter Park Memorial Hospital and the **Opera House** he built downtown in 1916 (now an Arts Factory and comedy club).

Palm Beach Shores citrus label, Palm Beach, 1930s.

In 1915, after Nathan and Harry Cohen had brokered fruit and produce "up north," they drove thirty days to Florida. In Arcadia, Fort Pierce, and Palm Beach, they brokered produce. They opened the Cohen Brothers Tropical Fruit Shop near the Breakers Hotel in Palm Beach and then started a citrus grove. In the 1930s they founded Riviera Groves and became packers and shippers. Larry and Patricia Cohen and Frank and Barbara Cohen Thrasher bought the business in 1962 and ran it until 1987 when they sold it to Cushmore Fruit Co.

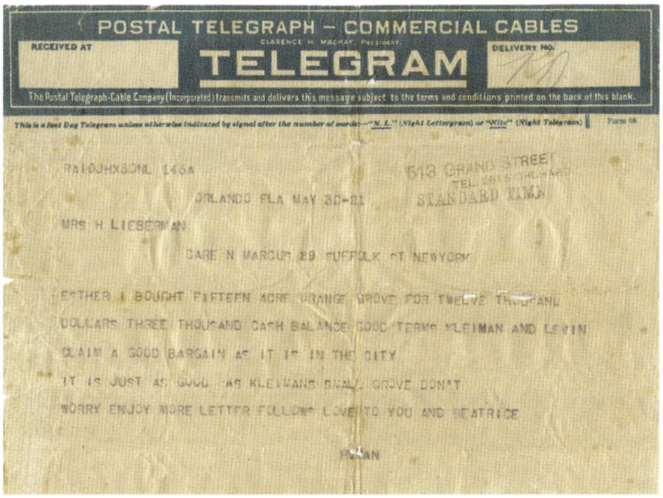
POSTAL TELEGRAPH – COMMERCIAL CABLES

CLARENCE H. MACKAY, PRESIDENT

RECEIVED AT | TELEGRAM | DELIVERY NO.

The Postal Telegraph-Cable Company (Incorporated) transmits and delivers this message subject to the terms and conditions printed on the back of this blank.

This is a fast Day Telegram unless otherwise indicated by signal after the number of words—"N. L." (Night Lettergram) or "Nite" (Night Telegram) Form 16

RA[illegible] 146A

613 GRAND STREET

STANDARD TIME

ORLANDO FLA MAY 30-21

MRS H LIEBERMAN

CARE N MARCUS 29 SUFFOLK ST NEWYORK

ESTHER I BOUGHT FIFTEEN ACRE ORANGE GROVE FOR TWELVE THOUSAND DOLLARS THREE THOUSAND CASH BALANCE GOOD TERMS KLEIMAN AND LEVIN CLAIM A GOOD BARGAIN AS IT IS IN THE CITY IT IS JUST AS GOOD AS KLEIMANS [illegible] GROVE DON'T WORRY ENJOY MORE LETTER FOLLOWS LOVE TO YOU AND BEATRICE

[illegible]AN

Esther, "I Bought A Grove!," Orlando, 1921.

With this telegram, Hyman Lieberman announced to his wife, still living in New York, that he had just purchased a fifteen-acre citrus grove for $12,000 with a $3,000 down payment. Like many, the Lieberman family moved to Florida and invested in citrus groves. The land boom was on. His daughter Bea told me that it was not such a bargain after he found that others had paid as little as $2.50 an acre!

Citrus crate label of David Bilgore, who established David Bilgore & Co. in Clearwater in 1924 to grow, pack, and ship citrus, 1940. *Florida Southern College, McKay Archives.*

Russian immigrant David Bilgore (1874–1948) first came to New York where he was a wholesaler and on the fruit auction markets. His three children were Morris, Aaron, and Molly [Bragin]. David settled in Pinellas County, became a leader in the industry, and was active in promoting the shipping of citrus by refrigerated steamer. He branched out to canning for national companies such as Libby and A&P. A community mentor and humanitarian, he was known to buy fruit with just a shake of the hand. His son Morris handled the New York end of the shipping business, then moved to Clearwater in 1951 after his father's death. He was joined by Aaron; his brother-in-law, Jules Bragin; and eventually Steve Bragin. Encroaching development ended the business in 1981, when they sold the groves.

Following the coldest temperature since 1899, prominent citrus grower Albert Morrell inspects a freeze-damaged tree, 1941.

Arriving in Clermont in 1935 with his wife, Dorothy Bornstein, Albert Morrell began a new career in citrus production. He attended citrus classes at the University of Florida and numerous citrus production seminars. He became a charter member of the Florida Citrus Growers Organization, a lifelong member of the Florida State Horticultural Society, and a consultant. Known globally as a progressive citriculturist, he traveled to practically all the citrus-producing areas of the world. In the early days of Israeli statehood, citrus production was considered a valuable industry. In 1951 Morrell took a two-month trip to Israel to study citrus conditions and evaluate a new test designed by Israelis to help diagnose tree disease. Israel presented him the Negev Award in 1962 for spearheading the exchange of technology between Israel and Florida citrus growers. During his lifetime, he owned and managed his own citrus holdings of 550 acres. Morrell died in 1964, leaving his son Laurence to take over the family business. Other members of the Bornstein family became involved in the citrus industry.

Brothers Jack and Jules Freeman planted probably the largest orange grove in the world, Arcadia, 1971.
National Geographic magazine, front cover.

This aerial photograph of Florida was taken from the National Aeronautics and Space Administration's (NASA's) first manned satellite in orbit. It shows the thirty-seven square miles of American Agronomics Corporation's Joshua Grove. After seeing this photograph of three million trees newly planted trees, Federal Bureau of Investigation (FBI) agents came to visit the Freemans as it looked to them like martians had landed in Florida! To develop the grove, the Freemans built two hundred miles of graded roads and two hundred miles of drainage canals, cleared and graded every inch of the land, and built an air strip, office buildings, a machinery depot, and a facility to repair engines. Then they had to buy the trees, which saved many Florida nurserymen from bankruptcy.

Jack and Jules Freeman's parents came from Poland to New York in 1905. The brothers grew up during the Depression and, by 1946, had an accounting firm. After being charmed by a visit to Florida, they settled in 1953 with $10,000 and began new careers in land and agricultural development.

Ralph Meitin's one-year-old daughter, Judy [Toll Cope], was the model for this Zellwood Fruit Distributors label, Orlando, 1944.

For marketing purposes, many fruit shippers designed colorful and distinctive crate labels, some with their children's faces, as a method of product identification.

Zellwood Fruit Distributors packinghouse employees, Orlando, 1952.

Ralph Meitin and Myer Shader (back row, fifth and sixth from the left) started Zellwood Fruit Distributors in 1943. The company was involved in fruit harvesting, packing, and caretaking and was often ranked in the top ten packinghouses in Florida. In 1954 Zellwood Fruit Distributors became a partial owner in the Winter Garden Citrus Product Cooperative, a citrus juice concentrate plant. In 1963 Julian Meitin joined his father in the business. Then in 1988, one year before a final devastating freeze, the family sold their share in the cooperative.

Founded in 1911 by brothers Isidore and Murray, Heller Bros. Co. continues today under third-and fourth-generation leadership, Orlando, 2016. *Harry Falk.*

From left to right are great-grandsons Alex Heller and Harry Heller Falk and grandson Harvey Heller. For more than eighty years, Heller Bros. has been a major force in Florida's citrus industry. When Murray Heller moved to Orlando in 1936, Heller Bros. added a citrus operation to their New York produce company. Isidore's son James joined his uncle in Orlando two years later. In 1940 Heller Bros. formed Heller Bros. Packing Co. (HBPC), and they started buying groves to meet packing demands, growing to five thousand acres. Isidore's grandson Harvey joined the Orlando

Company after college in 1964. HBPC grows and sells ten varieties of Florida citrus. The oranges are grown, picked, packed, and shipped from Florida, then sent all over the world, where the brand is synonymous with quality and freshness. While most of the citrus business has moved further south since the freezes of the 1980s, HBPC has stayed loyal to Central Florida. It is still operating from its original packinghouse in Winter Garden and has other facilities around the state, extending as far south as Immokalee in Collier County.

Harvey Heller's father, Seymour, lived in Miami and focused on tomato farming in south and east Florida. Seymour was a principal of Pacific Tomato Growers of Palmetto, along with the brothers Nathan and Joseph Esformes, a partnership that lasted nearly sixty years. The company now produces in numerous areas of the country and in Mexico and is recognized as a major year-round supplier of tomatoes.

Babijuice is a product from Albertson Citrus Inc., a family business, Orlando, 1970s.

Of the seven siblings in the Albertson family from Boston, Charles came to Orlando. He arrived after World War II and started a fruit packinghouse. A brother-in-law, Sidney Brown, came in 1946 and led the diversification into juice. The next generation infused their ingenuity when Paul arrived in 1954. His brother Harvey came in 1956, and David came in 1964. Later, Paul's son Brian joined. Babijuice and Southern Gold fruit and juice products became recognized throughout North America and Europe during this period. David Albertson continues to be involved in agribusiness and, with his wife, Judy, is deeply involved in education and cultural organizations in Orlando.

Top down: Al, Bob, and David Roth at New River Groves, Davie, 1989.

Opened as a family business in 1964, New River Groves is one of the largest and better-known growers, packers, and shippers based in western Broward County. Area residents visited to "pick a peck" of fresh fruit right off the trees for only one dollar. In the early days, the entire family lived in a small apartment above the retail store where the operations focused on fruit deliveries and Florida gift fruit shipping. They added Terry's homemade key lime pie, homemade fudge, and a fruit-of-the-month club—perhaps you've received some of these Florida delights! In 2006 the State of

Florida named key lime pie as the official state pie of Florida, and New River Groves proudly took part in the ceremony at Florida's capital. Today, operations have expanded, and Bob Roth's New River Grove ships thousands of pounds of citrus fruit and sends its fruit creations and Florida-inspired gourmet treats throughout the US and Canada.

Cobbs Fruit & Preserving Company, Miami, 1947.

You might have received a box from Henry Cobbs, the "king of packaged fruit." Brooklyn native Cobbs even sent one to Buckingham Palace for Princess Elizabeth on the occasion of her marriage to Philip Mountbatten in November 1947—and received a thank-you letter, which is in the Collections of the JMOF-FIU.

In the early 1930s, Henry Cobbs quit his job as a chemist in Brooklyn and moved to Florida due to his wife's health. He got a job picking oranges and then made marmalade from surplus oranges. He sold his product to local Miami residents and then to hotel guests. His hotel customers liked it so much, they asked Henry to continue to send them the marmalade by mail. Before long, Cobbs was also selling fresh fruit by mail. He packed it artistically and shipped it in colorful cartons. By the 1940s, Cobbs had become one of the nation's biggest promoters of Florida citrus. He diversified into candied citron, brandied figs, and tropical cakes. During World War II, Cobbs was appointed to the National Food Advisory Committee.

By 1947 Cobbs was taking in more than $3 million a year. His business had expanded to more than four hundred employees, and he had purchased the building in Miami's Little River district, where he was manufacturing his products. In addition, he had more than fifteen showrooms and retail outlets around Florida, covering most of the major resort hotels throughout the state through the 1960s.

Agriculture

Both immigrants from Europe and migrants from around the US arrived in Florida for the opportunity to "live off the land." Jews have produced, packed, and distributed numerous types of farm crops throughout the state—from Key West to Pensacola and Tallahassee and all communities in between. I've mentioned Moses Levy, who introduced farming at his Pilgrimage Plantation in the early 1820s. Robert S. Williams, who married into the Dzialynski family, grew cotton in Tallahassee in the 1880s. Among the early Jewish dairy farmers were Polish brothers Benjamin and Nathan Bear in Pensacola in 1911. Other crops and products produced by Jews in Florida include pineapples, celery, tomatoes, cucumbers, pineapples, strawberries, blueberries, watermelons, trees and plants, and poultry.

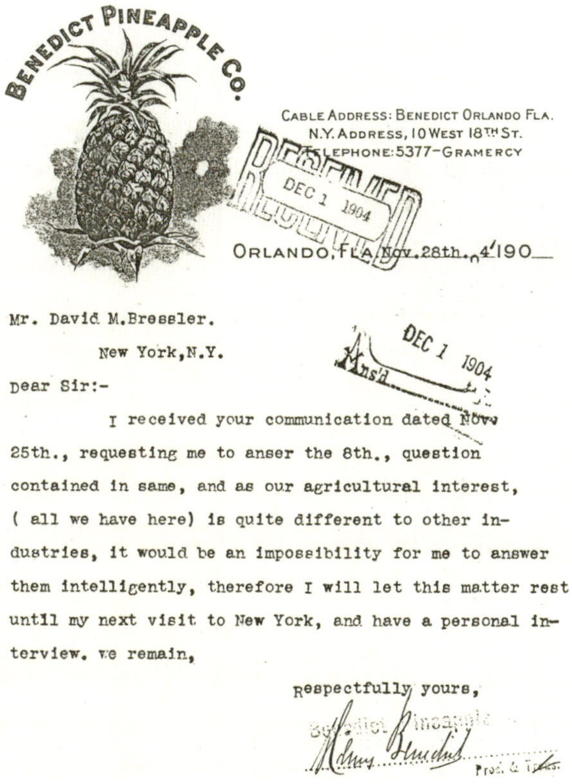

BENEDICT PINEAPPLE CO.

CABLE ADDRESS: BENEDICT ORLANDO FLA.
N.Y. ADDRESS, 10 WEST 18TH ST.
TELEPHONE: 5377-GRAMERCY

DEC 1 1904

ORLANDO, FLA. Nov. 28th. 1904

Mr. David M. Bressler.

New York, N.Y.

DEC 1 1904

Dear Sir:-

I received your communication dated Nov 25th., requesting me to anser the 8th., question contained in same, and as our agricultural interest, (all we have here) is quite different to other industries, it would be an impossibility for me to answer them intelligently, therefore I will let this matter rest until my next visit to New York, and have a personal interview. we remain,

Respectfully yours,

Benedict Pineapple Co.
Henry Benedict
Prest. & Treas.

Letter from Henry Benedict's Pineapple Company, Orlando, 1904.

German Jews Henry and Sylvia Benedict settled in Orlando around 1890. Henry went into the pineapple packing business and was also a downtown developer. This letter was in response to a communication from the Industrial Removal Office (IRO) in New York, questioning him about the chances of harmonious relations between present employees and new Jewish employees before they would send him immigrants for employment. It was reported in the 1903 *Fruit Trade Journal and Produce Record* that Benedict sued the Atlantic Coast Line Railway Company for $10,000 because their train caused a fire that burned the cover off his pineapples, resulting in damages.

Samuel Delmar Adelson, the "Cucumber King," Plant City, 1930s.

A son of German immigrants escaping persecution, Adelson was born in New York. On his way to Cuba in 1901, he stopped in Plant City. There he was attracted to Pearl Alderman, whom he married, and to the produce business. First, he became a buyer and shipper of fresh fruits and vegetables, and then he opened his own business to ship fresh strawberries and cucumbers throughout the eastern US. Involved in the produce business in Plant City for forty years, he was, at one time, the largest buyer in the state. Adelson Field is named to honor his efforts to bring sports to his community, including baseball spring training. His daughter Dorothy was queen of the Strawberry Festival in 1934.

Left to right: Aaron Harry, Saul, and Eddy Levy, sons of Moses Levy (inset), savor their watermelon that won first prize as the largest at the state fair, Orlando, circa 1915. *Dan Levy.*

Beginning in 1912, several families started a migration from Pittsburgh, Pennsylvania, to Orlando. Moses and Sarah Levy were among the first to arrive. They purchased twenty-four acres in today's College Park for their farm. Regular Sabbath and High Holiday services were observed there, which filled both the religious and social needs of the early residents. The Jews in the area arrived by foot and horseback, and after Yom Kippur eve prayers, they slept in the rooms and on the veranda of the Levy house.

Morris Moses inspects a shipment of celery heading north, Sanford, 1926.

The Sanford area was major for the production of produce. Several Jewish growers, packers, shippers, and brokers, such as Morris Moses of Moses and Son, were actively involved. Today, the production of vegetables in the Sanford area is almost nonexistent.

Strawberry carton of Wishnatzki and Nathel with Star of David, Plant City, 1990s.

Russian immigrants Harris and Yetta Wishnatzki came to Plant City in 1931 after Harris had been a produce peddler and then wholesaler in New York beginning in 1900. A committed Jew, Harris designed his label with a Magen David or Star of David, in spite of threats from his competition. His son Lester used this identifying label until 2011, when it was replaced by "Wish." These strawberries, along with their other berries, are found in most Florida supermarkets today. Third-generation owner Gary Wishnatzki continues the family legacy.

When celery was supreme, Sanford was the celery capital of the world, and C. I. & M. Dingfelder was an industry leader, 1935.

Julius Dingfelder came to America from Bavaria in 1922 and became involved with his family's produce business in New York. At his uncle's request, Julius and his bride, Gertrude Bauer, moved to Plant City. There they had two children Margaret [Corey] and Simon. Julius was responsible for the purchase and shipping of strawberries, tomatoes, and other produce to the northern market. Shortly after that, they moved to Sanford where he became involved in growing, buying, and shipping celery. The company shipped thousands of crates to northern markets each year. The Golden Cockerel label was their top-of-the-line product. Gert and Julius were actively involved in their community, including as founders of Congregation Beth Israel in Sanford. In Orlando, Margaret married Dr. Arthur Corey, who delivered most of the Jewish babies there from the 1960s through the 1980s. After Cornell and Army service, Simon settled in Tampa, where he was president of Congregation Schaarai Zedek. Julius's grandson, Simon and Adele Brawer's son, attorney John Dingfelder, married County Democratic Chair Lynn Marvin and served on Tampa's City Council from 2003 to 2010 and from 2019 to the present.

Left to right: Hope, Alan, and Marsha Levy in eight-hundred-acre cucumber field at Great American Farms, Wauchula, 1982.

The Levy family migrated to Florida from Chicago in 1942. Richard Levy, the father of Alan and Pat, started his produce business in 1920. He relocated this enterprise to Fort Lauderdale and later Pompano, which was already the seat of a large produce economy, especially winter vegetables. Richard became a produce distributor. After college, Alan Levy returned to Broward County and followed his father into the agricultural business and his deep involvement in the area's Jewish and civic community.

David Posnack surrounded by children at the David Posnack Jewish Community Center, Hollywood, 1980.

David Posnack was one of the most important figures in the development of Broward County's Jewish community. Born in New York's Lower East Side, he left school in the ninth grade when his vegetable seller father died. He began his work life as a peddler, then a porter and buyer at the markets in New York, before moving with his mother, Leah, and sisters, Rhea and Sadie, to Hollywood around 1944. Posnack became a partner in Pompano State Farmer's Market, then left to form his own business, David Posnack Produce, and prospered. He quickly immersed himself in philanthropic pursuits and was especially devoted to assisting children in education and health. This singular man died in 1984 in Hollywood. The David Posnack Jewish Community Center and David Posnack Hebrew Day School ensure his legacy.

Logo for Carnival Fruit Co. owned by Ruth and Irving Karp, Miami, 1960.

Ruth and Irving Karp honeymooned on South Beach in 1946, fell in love with the area, came back to settle, and by 1960 had opened their own fruit business. Irving's father had taught him the trade in New York before he served in World War II. He fought in the Invasion of Normandy and the Battle of the Bulge, earned a Purple Heart, and was a translator for British intelligence. What started as a retail produce store on Miami Beach with a single pickup truck grew to a fleet of more than seventy trucks that distributed produce wholesale mostly across south Florida and the Caribbean until 1984. Their son Martin Karp remembers that the colorful trucks could be seen in the background scenes of the *Miami Vice* TV series. Martin became a public school teacher and, since 2004, has served on the Miami-Dade County Public School Board, now as vice chair. Dr. Karp says that his parents taught him devotion to work and that Ruth and Irving were involved in reviving the basketball program at the University of Miami. Ruth is an award-winning artist whose works are in collections around the world. Both their daughter Janice and Martin are graduates of Miami Beach Senior High School.

Peckett's Nursery keeps growing, Apopka, 2016.

Started in 1978 by Chet Peckett with a greenhouse of only 10,000 square feet, this nursery expanded to 750,000 square feet using 50 acres for foliage production. As the former chairman of the Tropical Plant Industry Exhibition, Peckett has been a leader in his industry. He expanded his operation to include a state-of-the-art tissue culture lab for plant propagation. He also introduced new varieties of both holiday cactus plants and peace lily plants. After close to 40 years in foliage, he has divested his foliage business and has ventured into a new area of agribusiness—blueberries.

Betty and Ed Rosenthal (right), founders of Florikan Fertilizer Corp., and Dr. Gioia Massa (left), NASA payload scientist for "Veggie," observe ground control experiments, Kennedy Space Center, Cape Canaveral, 2017. *NASA/Bill White.*

Florikan Fertilizer produced this outredgeous red romaine lettuce (note the feet in photograph for proportion) grown in space in thirty-three days from seed, 2017.

Florikan was selected as a collaborator when NASA started its "Veggie" program to grow sustainable food in a spaceship for long-duration voyages to and from the International Space Station (ISS), which is envisioned for the next decades, and one day on another planet. Using the Rosenthals' Florikan Controlled Release Fertilizer, the red romaine lettuce was the first crop of lettuce grown in space and consumed by the astronauts. A porous, baked-clay substrate is used instead of soil. The veggie nutrition comes from the fertilizer, coated with patented polymers, that controls when and how much of each nutrient—nitrogen, phosphate, potassium, magnesium, and zinc—is released.

Betty and Ed Rosenthal moved from Montreal to Sarasota and founded Florikan in 1982. They formulated their fertilizer, recognized by the State of Florida and the National Society of Professional Engineers as one of the most innovative new products. Then they connected with NASA's Space Alliance Technology Outreach Program. Florikan developed new products with patents to sell to agribusiness giants with the benefit of using less fertilizer with the potential to not run off into groundwater. Sales growth prompted the need for an eighty-five-thousand-square-foot plant in Hardee County, managed by their son Eric, that created eighty new jobs. In 2017 Ed and Eric Rosenthal and the company Florikan were inducted—along with NASA's Kennedy Space Center—into the Space Technology Hall of Fame for the development of the controlled release fertilizer and its successful use in space. Their son Jonathan manages the patents.

Brothers Benjamin S. and Nathan Bear's Dairy Bar (and milk bottle), Pensacola, 1950s.

The Polish immigrant brothers came to the US in 1905 and founded Pensacola Dairy Company in 1911. At first, they delivered milk by bicycle, then bought a horse and wagon within a year. In 1922 they began producing butter. The family, who have continued to run the business, says they were among the earliest to produce pasteurized milk and ice cream in Florida. The building was a city landmark until it was demolished in 1976 to make room for the construction of an overpass for Interstate 10.

Israel Shader (center) with his sons Myer (left) and Isadore at Shader Dairy Farm, Fairvilla, 1916.

Israel Shader, born in Russia, immigrated to Pittsburgh, Pennsylvania. In 1912 he and his wife, Rose, followed their daughter Esther [Wittenstein] to Orlando with their sons Isadore, Myer, and Ben. Their daughters Fannie [Meitin] and Sarah [Miller] arrived several years later. Israel started a grove and a fifteen Jersey cow dairy farm that was operated by the family until 1949. The Shader farm grew to eighty acres and one hundred head of cattle. Eighty of the cows were milked, another twenty were heifers. Gentile neighbors milked the cows on the Sabbath and Jewish holidays. Thirty-eight acres were set aside for citrus.

Israel came seeking a place where he could follow tradition. He brought the first Torah to Orlando that was used for services in the Levy grove. Prior to Saturdays (the Jewish Sabbath), a large oven was filled with food so that no cooking was done on the holy day.

Milk bottle from Morris Wittenstein's College Park Dairy, 1927.

In 1912 Morris married his former Pittsburgh neighbor Esther Shader. They purchased property where Morris operated the College Park Dairy with sixty cows. He served milk products to schools and hospitals and processed milk from other dairies. As a founder of the Orlando Chevra Kadisha, Morris contributed much to the Jewish community. Morris and Esther had four children: Joseph, Florence [Tobias], Neil, and Tybe [Kahn].

Of historical interest, Harry and Minerva Nirenberg arrived in Orlando in 1937, and Harry bought this dairy. Their son Marshall was awarded the Nobel Prize in Physiology or Medicine in 1968.

Theodore and Ann Berman at their first dairy farm soon after their marriage, Miami Springs, 1942.

The Berman family represents one of the more interesting migratory business stories in the history of Broward Jewry. The family members have been farmers for six generations. In the 1930s the family patriarch, Bernard Berman, migrated from Germany to England. His son Theodore went to Cuba and then to Miami. Theodore Berman created the dairy in Miami Springs in 1939 and later moved to Carol City. By the 1960s Theodore and Ann and their son Bill had relocated the dairy, now known as the Davie Dairy Inc., to Davie, in west Broward, which, at the time, was almost exclusively farmland.

Later, the dairy moved again to Okeechobee County where Bill Berman operates it today. The flourishing dairy spreads across 960 acres, and its two milking facilities can accommodate 90 cows each, enabling the dairy to produce 15,000 gallons of milk daily. The dairy was the first in the cattle-rich Okeechobee County watershed to construct a total confinement system for housing milk cows. Environmentally conscious, Davie Dairy uses a system called "edge of farm phosphorous treatment" to filter out phosphorous before it reaches the creeks that drain into Lake Okeechobee. In addition, dairy cow waste is recycled into fertilizer that is reused in pastures and fields for various crops.

Gross Farm chicken coop carrier invented by Ralph Gross, Fort Lauderdale, 1950.

Ruth Frank and Ralph Gross came to Broward County in 1939 to operate a poultry farm west of today's I-95 on West Broward Boulevard. They purchased ten acres of property for $500 and then purchased thirty acres more over the years and operated Gross Farms, selling eggs. One of their customers was the US Government for the Naval Air Station in Fort Lauderdale. When the bills were not paid, the egg deliveries ceased. Then the pilots collected cash among themselves to buy fresh eggs! Their daughters, Carol [Clarkson] and Pat [Bergman], grew up on the farm. In 1955 the city ordered them to close. (Note: in the Russian immigration section, you met Ruth's father, Marcus Frank, and her grandfather, Julius Frank, when I told the story of his being killed in an explosion at his store in the new city of Miami in 1896.)

Before settling in Sanford, Frederick Stein received awards from Adolph Hitler in Essen, Germany, for raising his prize black Langschan chickens, 1935.

Stein was rounded up with German Jews during the Holocaust and sent to a concentration camp, from which he escaped. When he immigrated to America in 1940, the Jewish Agricultural Society resettled him in Sanford and loaned him $700 to start a chicken farm. With that, and an additional $3,000 in support from the Sanford community, he purchased fifty-seven acres to begin his business. During World War II, he was drafted to fight against Hitler! Stein married German Doris Lowenberg in 1945, and she joined him in Sanford, where they got involved with the Jewish community. The family still lives in Florida.

Shrimp fishing boat, *Sheila L*, of Charles Ludwig, Fernandina, 1930s.

CHAS. LUDWIG
WHOLESALE SHRIMP — FRESH AND FROZEN
Phones FRanklin 9-9743 - 9-0518
1901 So. Miami Ave. MIAMI, FLORIDA

Charles Ludwig wholesale shrimp advertisement, Miami, 1957.

Jews in the shrimping industry? Yes, Charles Ludwig came from Romania to Fernandina in 1920, purchased three shrimp boats in a bankruptcy sale, and sold shrimp for five cents a pound. In 1929 he married Anna Kronberg who had settled in Miami in 1921. They moved to Miami in 1947 where he founded Ludwig Shrimp Company to supply local stores and restaurants.

Cattle Ranching

When Juan Ponce de León discovered Florida in 1513, it was mostly wide, green spaces. In 1521, when he returned and landed near Fort Myers, he brought horses and seven Andalusian cattle, the ancestors of the Texas Longhorns. He knew he'd found pastureland. Spanish explorers turned Florida into America's first cattle-raising state. Some of the abandoned Spanish cows roamed free, while others were bred and domesticated by Native Americans in Florida. As pioneer settlers came to Florida in the mid-1800s, establishing a cattle industry seemed prudent. During the Civil War, Florida became the primary supplier of beef to the Confederate Army. The cattle industry has had an important economic impact on the economy of the Sunshine State—and Florida Jewish cowboys have been part of it!

Saul Snyder on his cattle ranch, "The Pasture," St. Augustine, 1950.

Solomon Schneidermann completed his duty as a Russian soldier at the turn of the twentieth century, then emigrated to America. The Jewish Agricultural Society sent him to Fernandina where he packed oysters for $2.50 a day—not very kosher! To acculturate, he changed his name to Saul Snyder. In 1906 Saul brought his wife, Sarah, to Florida; they had four children. In 1907 the Jews in St. Augustine gave him work in a grocery store there to entice him to move to make the tenth man for a *minyan*. From there, he journeyed to Jacksonville to buy a horse and wagon and paid off the debt at $1.00 a week. His family had raised cattle in Russia, so he rode his horse back to Jacksonville and bought a cow—and subsequently more cows until he developed a big spread.

He became a very successful rancher, a founder of the Cattlemen's Association in 1916, and then a charter director of the state group when it was organized in 1934. He was instrumental in the formation of the St. Johns County Livestock Association, which honored him in 1968.

When I visited Snyder's daughter and son-in-law, Rita and Jerry Kass, in St. Augustine during my research in the 1980s, they showed me his branding iron—a Magen David or Star of David! When I formed the JMOF in the 1990s, I assembled a humanities advisory panel of notable scholars, including prominent American sociologist Marshall Sklare of Brandeis University. During my slide presentation of research findings, when I got to Saul Snyder, Sklare scoffed, "He was a social deviant—an immigrant Jew who was not in the dry goods business!"

Immigrant to cattle baron George Terry (fourth from the left) showing off his field of clover to Orange County Agriculture agents, Orlando, 1953.

George (Tichler) Terry (1895–1982) had a full life before he arrived in the US in 1920 with forty dollars. He had served in the Austro-Hungarian army, was captured twice by the Russians during World War I, and had escaped Siberian concentration camps and gone to Japan. The advent of World War II brought him to Orlando, where he bought six hundred acres of citrus groves. By the late 1940s, he had expanded to seventy thousand acres to raise cattle on his Magnolia Ranch, where he was the first in Florida to introduce clover feed to fatten cattle and seepage irrigation. He built a ranching empire that, by 1955, grew south to Palm Beach County to one hundred thousand acres with fifty thousand head of cattle and included timber, sod farming, a large citrus grove, and even oil wells. Terry served as president of the Orange County Cattlemen's Association (1949). The ranch was sold in 1979 and became part of Deseret Ranch. He and his wife, Betty, had four children in Orlando.

Leonard Wolf on his cattle ranch, Lakeland, 1987.

Nathan Wolf was fourteen years old in 1910 when he left his native Poland with the family to settle in Paterson, New Jersey. In 1936 he came to Florida with his wife, Mollie Opper, and bought his first citrus grove in Lake Garfield (between Bartow and Lake Wales). His son Leonard (1918–2006) married Rhoda Bernard in 1947, settled in Lakeland, and expanded the business to thirty-four thousand acres on six ranches. They had four children: Susan [Scheinberg], Robert, Michael, and Laurie [Altshuler]. The Nat Wolf Corporation included citrus, cattle, hay, grass seed, and shells. Leonard Wolf attended the University of Florida in the 1930s where he was number 124 in Tau Epsilon Phi (TEP) fraternity. In 1991 he received the national TEP Man of the Year Award—the same year I visited to conduct his oral history, when he bragged that he even wore his TEP pin (Tau Alpha Chapter) on his pajamas!

Nathan Rosenblatt (right) with his cattle, Tampa, 1942.

Children of Nathan and Bess Rosenblatt, Tampa, 1925. *Dolly Williams.*

From left to right are Pauline, Nathan Jr. (Sonny), Isabel, Charlie, Eddie, and Frank. Nathan and his Russian-born wife, Bess Stolberg, came to Tampa after their wedding in 1912. For many years, Rosenblatt was in the wholesale and retail grocery business, which included fifty stores of United Markets. In 1939 he began National Meat Packers Inc.

After Frank returned from World War II, he married Doris Chaite in 1947 and joined his father in the meat packing business (along with Pauline, Sonny, and other family members) where he was in charge of the seven-hundred-acre ranch with about seventy-five heads of cattle to feed and a meat packing plant with forty-seven employees. He traveled to markets in Tampa, Gainesville, Ocala, and Arcadia to buy livestock and helped the Cattlemen's Association pass legislation to improve the industry. "What I loved most," said Frank, "was being able to look at a cow and know its dress out (usable weight)." The meat was sold to hotels and restaurants and the crews of banana boats going to Central America. Doris and Frank had Nancy Linsky, Beverly Levinson, and Robert. The family now represents five generations in Tampa—four who have already been proven leaders in every aspect of the Tampa Jewish community.

Tobacco and Cigars

When Christopher Columbus landed in the Bahamas in 1492, he was met by Indians who offered him dried leaves as a token of friendship. Those leaves were tobacco, which was and still is a controversial crop. For more than 175 years, Florida has a history of growing some of the world's finest cigar tobacco. At the turn of the twentieth century, many farmers attempted to diversify crops and end their reliance on cotton, which had become less profitable following the Civil War. By 1910, from Key West to Tampa to Quincy to Tallahassee, Florida Jews engaged in growing tobacco as a cash crop, especially shade (wrapper) tobacco, and manufacturing cigars. Among the most prominent was the company owned by Alfred Wahnish. As I write, the cigar industry, specifically premium handmade cigars, is facing new regulations by the Food and Drug Administration, and Congress has gotten involved in the health issue.

Alfred Wahnish, Morocco to Florida, 1890s

Alfred Wahnish, Tallahassee, circa 1898.

Interior of Wahnish cigar factory, Tallahassee, circa 1905.

Wahnish shade tobacco plantation, Tallahassee, 1920.

As a youth in Casablanca, Morocco, in 1884 Alfred Wahnish accidentally hit a teacher, became frightened that he had killed her, ran to the docks, and stowed away on a ship that was leaving for Boston. In the US, he sold cigars as a traveling salesman. Along his route, in Louisville, Kentucky, Alfred met and married Carrie Metzner. They moved to Pensacola and then settled in Tallahassee where Alfred started a tobacco plantation in the late 1890s. Lured by the reports of favorable soil and climate conditions, Wahnish planted shade tobacco on 3,600 acres. By 1907, employing 150 people, he opened a large, two-story brick cigar-packing warehouse on a road that was named "Wahnish Way" in 1966. He erected two more buildings. By 1915 the factory was producing about 10,000 hand-rolled cigars a day, and the workers were paid on a "piece work" basis. By 1922 the tobacco industry in Leon County had declined considerably due to conflicts with organized labor and the arrival of machines. The structure remains and is an important link with the area's agricultural past. One of the six children, Sam, worked with Alfred in the tobacco business, became the first Jewish mayor of Tallahassee (1938–1941) and was involved in state government for 35 years, introducing the Florida sales tax as a source of revenue. Descendants still live in Florida.

Charles Peyser and his son, Nathan, in their cigar store, Ocala, 1900.

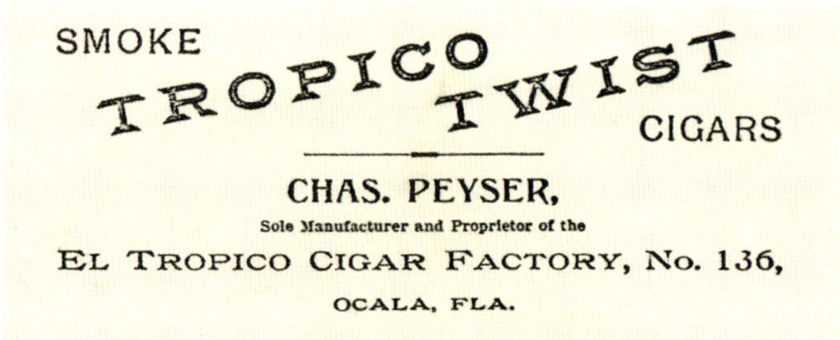

El Tropico cigar ad, Ocala, 1891.

German immigrants Charles and Hannah Peyser settled in Ocala around 1860, when Charles began manufacturing and marketing El Tropico cigars. By 1891, Peyser claimed El Tropico was turning out nearly fifty thousand cigars weekly and having trouble keeping up with orders from all over the country. Peyser was using imported Cuban tobacco as well as locally produced tobacco in his product. Their son, Nathan, was a salesman for the company until he died at age thirty-one. They also had a daughter Gertrude. The store was open until 1920. When I was researching in Ocala, I found an interesting article about Peyser in the 1905 *Ocala Evening Star*. Peyser had received a late order for his celebrated "Grand Royal" smokers to be distributed at a banquet for Florida physicians—but not in time for him to imprint on each cigar the date and name of the association as part of his normal marketing plan. But as the physicians opened their boxes for a fragrant smoke, they saw that he had placed a card printed with the date and occasion. That would have been a great artifact—smokes for physicians! But it was 1905.

Wedeles Tobacco Company building, Quincy, circa 1905.

The first and longest-lasting name in the Gadsden County tobacco industry was Wedeles. In 1896 Max Wedeles with his family and cousins, Emil and Joe Wedeles, came from Chicago, Illinois, to Quincy as growers and packers of shade tobacco. Their label was Browns Dot because Brown was the family name of the wife of Max Wedeles. The family still resides in Quincy in the home Max Wedeles built in 1891. Miles Kenan Womack Jr. wrote *Gadsden: A Florida County in Word and Picture* in 1976, and it includes photographs and text about many Jews in the tobacco industry there.

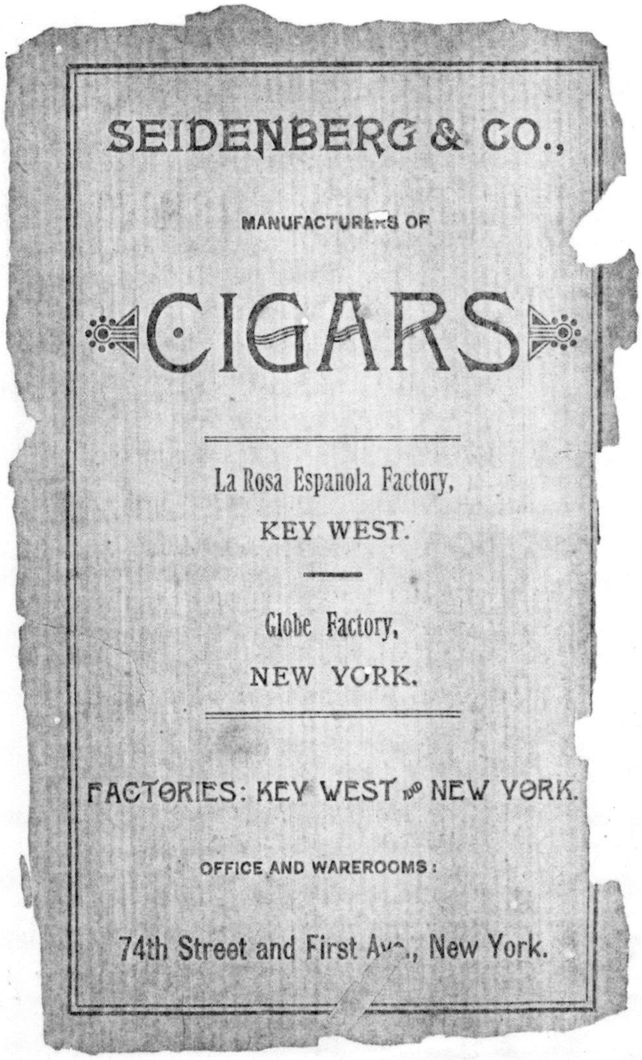

Seidenberg and Co. cigars ad, Key West, 1893.

The story of the Key West cigar industry is very much a Jewish story. German immigrant Samuel Seidenberg was a wholesaler of Cuban tobacco in New York soon after he arrived around 1855. When the US government introduced tariffs that raised the cost on imported Cuban cigars but not on the unprocessed tobacco leaves, he realized that Key West had the optimum warm and humid climate to roll cigars like Cuba. In 1868 Seidenberg built a huge factory in the southernmost US continental city. La Rosa Espanola employed six hundred people, including many Cubans arriving when the Cuban rebellion began. In spite of fires and strikes, bankruptcy, and an eventual factory move to Tampa, Seidenberg was one of the most influential in the US cigar industry.

Why the Move of Cigar Factories from Key West to Ybor City?

There are several reasons that many Jewish cigar manufacturers and merchants moved from Key West to Ybor City at the turn of the twentieth century. In 1886 Don Vincent Martinez-Ybor (not Jewish) purchased forty acres to establish Ybor City northeast of downtown Tampa. Tampa offered real estate advantages to lure the factories to this new city. Henry Plant completed his railroad, which provided transportation to northern markets. There were two major fires in Key West that impacted the factories in 1886 and 1896.

Many of the pioneer Jewish settlers in Key West worked as peddlers. In 1891 the Key West City Council passed an anti-immigrant, anti-peddler annual license tax of $1,000 for each peddler. This was to protect the gentile merchants. After the city attorney argued that the tax was illegal, the council ignored him and even increased the tax to $1,000 each day (the equivalent to more than $25,000 in today's currency). This resulted in their relocating to Ybor City where they were welcomed with other immigrants.

In Ybor City, just before the Great Depression, there were nearly 13,000 workers in nearly 150 factories who rolled nearly 600 million cigars annually—and all these people needed clothes and groceries and other services that the Jews could provide there. For the MOSAIC project, Irving Weissman created a walking tour of Ybor City Jewish businesses (from the 1920s through the 1970s) that includes 84 listings. Some storefronts remain, primarily on Seventh Avenue or La Setima.

Cigar factory of Max Marx and Company, Key West, 1889.

Max Marx is another name among the Jews in the Key West cigar industry. In this factory during the 1880s, he produced the equivalent of $5 million in annual cigar sales. He moved his factory to Tampa.

Left to right: Rippa Brothers Cigars owners, David and Toba Rippa, with Della, Louis, and Jack Rippa, Tampa, 1904.

In 1888, due to the persecution of Jews in Romania, the large Rippa Family became part of a chain migration to Key West. From there, in 1904, they—like other Key West Jewish cigar factory owners—moved their cigar factory to Ybor City to produce their own brand. In 1910 Della married William Friedman who was twice mayor of Dade City.

Three generations of the Newman family in front of their historic cigar factory, Ybor City, circa 2002. *Newman family.*

From left to right are Drew; his brothers, Eric and Bobby; and Stanford, the son of founder Julius Caesar Newman. Cigars were to Tampa what Mickey Mouse is to Orlando. As I write, J. C. Newman is the only surviving cigar factory operating in Ybor City. One hundred years after its peak in the 1920s, following the Depression, two world wars, the Cuban embargo, taxes, smoking bans, and government regulations, the others have since closed.

Tampa's celebrated heritage as the Fine Cigar Capital of the World lives on at J. C. Newman Cigar Company. America's oldest family owned and operated premium cigar maker began with twenty-year-old Hungarian immigrant and founder Julius Caesar Newman. He started in Cleveland in 1895 and moved to Ybor City in 1954 to be closer to Cuba, the primary source of tobacco. The company moved into the 1910 landmark Regensburg factory with the clock tower. For generations, the clock chimed hourly—and it still chimes—after a 2002 restoration. They use the same 1895 machines, producing fifteen cigars a minute made only of fermented tobacco, water, and vegetable glue.

On May 31, 2019, J. C. Newman Cigar Co. announced the debut of "The American," the only commercially hand-rolled premium cigar that is fully US made. Some tobacco is grown in Florida, something that hasn't happened since 1977. The boxes are made in Miami, the labels in Sanford, and the cigar molds in Dade City. Even the ink on the band and the cellophane are made in America. Newman will offer tours of their hand-rolled operation, complete with a lector who reads for the factory workers in the tradition of the cigar city's heyday of the early 1900s.

Notice the Magen David or Star of David necklace on the woman in the J. C. Newman Cigar Co.'s Cuesta-Rey cigar box label, Ybor City, 1884.

The handmade Cuesta-Rey brand, sold in 61 countries, was purchased by the Newmans in 1959. "This is currently one of 128 unique boxes offered by the Newman Company with our 135 employees that crank out 60,000 cigars a day," says J. C.'s grandson Eric Newman who runs the company with his brother Bobby. They hope to pass the business on to the next generation.

I was in Prague in 2015 and went into a tiny shop to buy tickets to visit the Prague castle. As I entered, I was astounded to see a cigarillo tin with the so-familiar-to-me Cuesta-Rey label on the top shelf in the window. When I shared with the clerk my interest in the tin label, he gave it to me—Florida Jewish history encountered in Czechoslovakia!

DAVID BERGMAN/HERALD STAFF

TEAM ROSENBLATT: Smokers' attorney Stanley Rosenblatt grabs wife Susan's hand after leaving the courthouse following their landmark legal victory Friday.

The headline of the *Miami Herald* from July 15, 2000, reads, "$145 billion Tobacco Verdict," with a subhead, "No-name lawyers make history."

Those no-names were Susan and Stanley Rosenblatt. It was the biggest civil damage award in US history. When the judge read the verdict, the mom-and-pop attorneys lowered their heads and sighed, "Six years of work!" While that figure was immediately appealed and would later be set aside, and while class members seeking compensation would be instructed to file separate lawsuits, the verdict was nonetheless a breakthrough in holding Big Tobacco accountable for diseases developed and health risks acquired through smoking. Additionally, the jury found that the companies had committed fraud and had conspired to hide evidence that their products were dangerous. These findings paved the way for how smoking is viewed in the world today. Stanley Rosenblatt said about the case, "It was good against evil."

An Orthodox couple with nine children (at that time), they are Shabbat observant. Susan was born in Brooklyn, her family moved to Miami Beach, and then she went to the University of Miami and the law school—which mirrors Stanley's background. A *shadkhan* matched them at Susan's father's funeral, and they have been a strong team since.

CHAPTER 2

Retail

From Peddlers to Shopping Malls

In the nineteenth and early twentieth centuries, it was not unusual to find Jewish merchants on main streets and country crossroads, in cities and towns throughout Florida. Many arrived as peddlers who soon set down their packs and opened small stores. They sold fish, groceries, clothing, footwear, cigars, dry goods, and furniture. In some cases, they also manufactured what they sold. These small-scale merchants arrived in search of economic opportunity. Often, they organized or joined local fraternal and commercial organizations and rose to leadership in their business communities.

Some Jewish merchants were mobile, moving from place to place in response to climate, disease, and economic disasters. In 1858 on the heels of a financial panic, Samuel Cline and Max White closed their Key West clothing store and moved to Tampa. Some, like the Cohen Brothers in Jacksonville and the Frank family in Clearwater, remained in one place. And still others, such as the Maas Brothers in Tampa and the Rheinhauers in Ocala, expanded to other cities, and their department store chains grew over several generations.

Some were immigrants who paved the way for their *landsmen* to join them, offering jobs and monetary help to the newer arrivals. Romanian immigrant Berman Weintraub settled in Key West in the 1890s where his store was a magnet for other Jews from his country.

Some communities, such as Live Oak, were stop-off points for Jewish newcomers heading into Florida from Georgia. Russian immigrants Sarah and Jacob Fleet settled in Live Oak in 1903 with their eight children. Within a generation, each of the six sons and one of the daughters had stores—two in Live Oak and also in Winter Haven, Perry, Fort Walton Beach, Tallahassee, and Haines City.

Retailing was undeniably a family business. Another example is the Gussie and Ben Gibbs family who settled in Live Oak in 1913. The Gibbs's sons, David, Sam, Lew, and Irving, branched out to Deland, Jacksonville, Tallahassee, and Orlando. Brothers Morris, Louis, and C. Davis Turner came to Florida in the 1920s and operated a large chain of clothing stores. C. Davis was headquartered in Marianna and Louis in Perry and Tallahassee. There were also Turner stores in Live Oak, Madison, Monticello, Quincy, and DeFuniak Springs. During World War II, they supplied uniforms to officers and enlisted men and women stationed on nearby bases.

The city-block Cohen Brothers Department Store was founded in Jacksonville in 1867. In 1896 twelve of Miami's first sixteen merchants were Jewish. Hartman's grocery store opened in Fort Myers in 1898. Zundel Kessler settled in Leesburg at the turn of the century and opened a dry goods business. P. G. Blanck moved his department store from Key West to Miami in about 1910, and at the same time, Morris Piekansky moved his clothing store from St. Augustine to Miami. Abe Tarapani and Sam Lovitz opened a department store in Tarpon Springs in 1913—that one is still in existence. Cecelia Tarapani Levy and her husband, Philip, arrived in Sarasota in 1913, where they opened a women's clothing store.

Through the 1950s, shopping in downtown communities all over Florida, you could find hundreds of mom-and-pop Jewish retail businesses. In a 1980 column in the *Tallahassee Democrat*, Howard Jay Friedman reminisced about the changes in retailing. "You were allowed to browse and handle the merchandise, yet spending nothing. When you went shopping, in those days, you really went 'visiting.' And the difference made all the difference."

This small sampling of stories that follows reflects those who pioneered as Jewish retailers in Florida's frontier communities. Through their courage, perseverance, and civic contributions, they established the roots and credibility that enabled others to follow.

Jewish developers were very much a part of the shopping center and mall phase of retailing that began in the 1950s. Many of the largest shopping centers in Florida today are a result of Jewish visionaries and risk-takers. From 1968 to 1987, Mel Sembler of St. Petersburg served as president of the forty-thousand-member International Council of Shopping Centers.

William Schemer was a fish peddler, Jacksonville, 1906.

During my oral history phase in the 1980s, when I asked second-generation Floridian Jews what their parents did for a living in the beginning, many responded "peddlers." When I asked if they had a photograph, the typical response was "They were too poor to have a camera!"

Indeed, this is a rare photograph—the only one of a Florida Jewish peddler I have found in thirty-five years of research. So poor he did not even have his name on the cart, William Schemer was robbed and murdered in the 1930s. As the MOSAIC exhibit traveled around Florida, I conducted docent training in each city. When in Jacksonville in 1992, I was showing slides from the exhibit to a large crowd at the Jacksonville Community Alliance. As I put Mr. Schemer on the screen, a woman in the last row got up from her chair, shrieked, and collapsed. This was her father, and she had never seen a photo of him!

New Store! New Goods.

The undersigned calls attention of the public to the fact that he has opened in BISHOP'S BLOCK, First Street, Sanford, Fla., an entirely new stock, consisting of the following lines of goods, to-wit:

Dry goods, fancy goods, notions, ladies' underwear, sheeting, shirting, checks, ginghams,

AND OTHER GOODS TOO NUMEROUS TO MENTION.

Also a full line of GENTS', BOYS' and YOUTHS' CLOTHING and HATS, &c., which he proposes to sell at prices to suit the times.

Call before making your selections elsewhere, and see for yourself that you can do as well OR BETTER with me.

Remembr the Place

T. Cohen, Bishop 's Block, First Street,

Sanford, Florida.

Mr. T. Cohen's store ad in the *Sanford Journal*, Sanford, November 15, 1883.

On the same date, in the same newspaper, there was a story about the circumcision ceremony for the infant Louis Henry, son of Mr. and Mrs. T. Cohen (see part 4, page 285).

Makinson-Katz Hardware, founded in 1884 by W. B. Makinson and J. Moses Katz, Kissimmee.

This is the oldest-known retail hardware store still in operation in Florida.

Schutz Bros. billboard is slightly visible in the center background of this image of Orange Avenue on market day, Orlando, circa 1884. *Orange County Regional History Center.*

208 Schutz Bros. ad, Orlando, 1886. *Webb's City Directory.*

This dry goods and clothing store was owned by German immigrants Nathan, Max, and Henry Schutz. They lived at the Windsor Hotel where the rates were "$2.50 per day and upward." Nathan was secretary of the fire department, serving with another Jew, A. H. Birnbaum. By 1901 Henry was settled in St. Petersburg, where he was the first-known Jew, president of the first congregation, and a longtime, respected merchant.

Marcus Loeb's store, Palatka, 1891.

Marcus Loeb came from Germany in 1870 at the age of eighteen. He stands in front of his store with two cousins. His Sample Room Saloon is next door. Enterprising Marcus also operated orange groves; built homes; founded a clothing manufacturing company, Marcus Loeb & Co.; and was an alderman, president of Palatka's first telephone company (1894), and active in the Democratic Party.

Brash Family Bargain Store interior, Apalachicola, 1895.

You met German immigrant Henry Brash earlier. In 1865, after serving in the Civil War, he opened this store. Very industrious, he was also in the lumber, real estate, and sponge-fishing businesses—with so many storefronts, the block was named "Brash Row."

K. Kanner Dry Goods interior, left to right: Sophie, Samuel, and Kalman Kanner, Orlando, 1905.

These store interior photographs are typical of stores owned by myriads of Jewish merchants throughout Florida in the late nineteenth and early twentieth centuries. For example, from that period through the 1960s, there were at least 200 Jewish merchants with 340 stores in Orlando and 30 more in the surrounding area. The concentration of downtown Jewish merchants disbanded and shifted to the suburban malls in the 1960s.

Tailors

On record in the Collections of JMOF-FIU is an ad from an 1844 Jacksonville newspaper for Morris Keil's tailor shop. Most of the early retailers were tailors as well to meet the needs of their customers. There is an old joke: "What's the difference between a tailor and a doctor?" Answer: "A generation." Throughout Jewish history, most Jewish communities had at least one tailor—think Motel Kamzoil in *Fiddler on the Roof.* Economic factors often led to the large numbers of Jews in garment-related fields. The role of Jews in the trading of secondhand goods required some knowledge of tailoring. Eventually, Jews went from selling old clothes to becoming retailers, manufacturers, and wholesalers—and then by the 1970s, Jews no longer were major in the clothing industry—many became doctors!

Zelda Berman [Gross] models suit tailored by her father, Nat Berman, in 1909, Orlando, 1927.

After Pauline Klein and Russian immigrant Nat Berman married in Jacksonville in 1908, they settled in Orlando, joining four other Jewish families there. Berman started as a tailor before he and Pauline opened four businesses. Both were deeply involved in civic and Jewish activities. They had two daughters: Sylvia [Prince] and Zelda [Gross], who remained in Orlando. Zelda's son Raymond Gross served as a judge of the Sixth Judicial Circuit Court (1995–2014).

Key West Stores

As antisemitism was heating up in Russia and Romania, Jews began to hear enchanting stories about Key West as a paradise and economic boomtown following the Civil War. The population included many political exiles and was multiethnic and multilingual—a perfect place to flee to freedom and start all over again. And so they came, some as peddlers, more as merchants, and some in the cigar business. These are just a few of the retail stores in Key West at the turn of the twentieth century.

Over Sea Dry Goods Store owned by the Davis family, Romanian immigrants who lived over the store, Key West, circa 1900.

Aron and Sarah Davis settled in Key West around 1893 and raised their children there: Ida, Charlie, Annie, Marcus, Max, and Isadore. They dispersed to Ybor City, Jacksonville, and St. Petersburg to open retail shops, and there are descendants around Florida today. St. Petersburg pioneers told of having *minyans* in the back of Max Davis's store in the early 1920s before the congregation was formed. As soon as the tenth man arrived, a curtain was drawn, business was put on hold, and prayers began.

Uncle Doodle's Dry Goods Store of Dave Aronovitz, Key West, circa 1900.

Romanian immigrant Aronovitz arrived in Key West in 1889 with his wife, Kate, and remained, capitalizing on the American way of doing business. Kate and Dave had ten sons; one, Abe, became Miami's mayor.

The Store of Fashion owned by Rosa and Louis Wolfson on Duval Street, Key West, circa 1900.

You met the Wolfson family in part 2, chapter 4 ("Russian Immigration"). Louis and Rosa Gruner Wolfson married in Bodka, Russia, in 1887 and came to Key West that year at the urging of Louis's brother Joseph Wolfson who had been shipwrecked there in 1884 and stayed. The young couple opened this grand Key West store and were respected civic leaders. In 1915 they moved with their four children to Miami and opened East Coast Wholesale Dry Goods Co. They are the parents of Mitchell Wolfson.

Harry, Rose, and Jack Rippa in their store, Key West, 1903.

This Romanian family moved to Ybor City when the economy declined in Key West. Eventually they settled in Miami, where Jack had a store on Miami Avenue. He was born in Key West in 1889.

Other Stores around the State

Isidor Kaunitz was known for the white hat he habitually wore, Ybor City, 1891.

Romanian Isidor Kaunitz was attracted to Ybor City when it became a center of growth with Henry Plant's South Florida Railroad (1884). He was the first Jewish merchant in multiethnic Ybor City. He named his store Sombrero Blanco (Spanish for "white hat") for all the Cubans there. As other Jewish immigrants arrived, they knew they could get employment from Kaunitz, who empathized with their plight of antisemitism and knew many of their families from the old country.

First brick building in Ybor City, 1903.

Needing more space for his growing clientele propelled by a bustling city and regular paychecks, Isidor Kaunitz constructed a new store on Seventh Ave in Ybor City. Records indicate that Isidor and his wife, Rebecca, had three children: Elizabeth, Julius, and Ernestine; they lived above the store.

Max Argintar (center) in his store, Ybor City, 1908.

In 1904 Max Argintar was the first in his family to arrive in Tampa. He first got a job with Isidor Kaunitz, who had met him at his home in Romania. Four years later, he opened his own store in Ybor City. In 1910 he visited *landsmen* in Key West where a *shidduch* was made with Annie Davis. Patriotic and civic minded, they raised six children in Tampa: Sammie, Arnold, Rachael, Lena, Esther, and Florence. Max had a pawnshop portion in this store that included cases with jewelry and walls with musical instruments. After a fire, he moved the shop and featured quality menswear.

Second Argintar store exterior, Ybor City, 1937.

The Argintar son, Sammie (at right in the inset), began working full time in 1937. In 1964 he and his wife, Dorothy, took over the business until it closed in 2004 after ninety-six years of a continuous, family-run operation. The mostly Latin and black customer base remained loyal during urban renewal. Even after closing, the building with the family name remains in Ybor City. Arnold opened the first fine menswear store in St. Petersburg in 1935 and ran it for seventy-two years. The family said he allowed customers to buy on layaway long after others had stopped the practice and accepted returns without a receipt.

Tarapani's New York Department Store, Tarpon Springs, circa 1914.

From left to right are clerk A. Loescher, Abe L. Tarapani, and Benny Lovitz. Russian immigrant Abe L. Tarapani (1892–1960) opened this business in 1911 with Sam Lovitz, who he met on a train as they both headed to Florida. Abe's sister Olga had been in St. Petersburg since 1908. In 1936 the store was moved to another location. Tarapani's featured clothing for women, men, and children and fabric in bulk if you preferred to sew your own.

In 2000 the third generation converted the store into an antique mall. Tarapani's has been operated by the family for more than one hundred years. The tile nameplate remains in the sidewalk. Abe served in the US Army in France during World War I. When he returned, he purchased Sam's interest in the store. Abe married Margaret Mizell, a native of St. Petersburg, and they had two children: Helen and Abe Jr. Abe was extremely civic minded and served as city commissioner for four terms. He said he was able to accomplish so much for his community because Jews did not face discrimination in Tarpon Springs. There was a Jewish postmaster Edward Blum in 1887.

Louis Brown, first-known Jewish settler in Broward County, owned this store in Dania, 1912.

An immigrant from Grodno, Lithuania, Louis (1886–1952) arrived from Jacksonville by train and by 1912 had opened Brown's Department Store on Main Street, which is now US 1. He married Sarah Sokolow, also from Grodno, and they had a son, Earl, in 1924. Louis and his brother-in-law David Sokolow had three department stores in Hollywood, Dania, and Pompano. Earl attended Riverside Military School in Hollywood, served in the Army Air Corp in 1944, and that year married Helen Sarah Seigel.

Joseph Behr Schupler and his wife, Maryetta Schutzer Schupler, in their Hat Store with a clerk, West Palm Beach, 1925.

Austrian-born Joseph opened this store in 1912. He was a 32nd degree Mason and founder of Temple Israel in West Palm Beach. Maryetta's brother Sam was a newspaper publisher there. Their son Moe served in World War II, then became an attorney in West Palm Beach.

Russian immigrant Ben Gibbs (right) in front of his country store, Live Oak, 1914.

Gibbs family, Live Oak, 1925.

From left to right are Ben (father), David, Louis, Samuel, Irving, and Gussie (mother). Gussie Gibbs's brother Walter Turner had settled in Perry in 1895 and convinced Ben and Gussie to move from New York to Live Oak in 1913 when a retail business was for sale—and join several Jewish retailers there. Being in a remote community away from any center of Jewish life, the Gibbs family, along with the Rubenstein, Weiss, Mendelson, and Fleet families managed to keep kosher. They got their meat from Jacksonville and had to bury it in the ground to keep it cold as this was before dry ice. But the meat would still spoil, so the families hired a *shochet* to live in Live Oak to produce kosher chickens and meat. This man was also the Hebrew and religion teacher for the children. Religious holiday services were held at the Masonic Temple. Another merchant, Ben Gilmore, moved there and became the city manager.

Second-generation Florida Jewish retailer: Gibbs-Louis clothing label, Orlando, circa 1955.

Irving Gibbs was nine years old when the family settled in Live Oak and remembers falling asleep on the bolts of fabric in the store, singing "Way Down Upon the Suwanee River" in school, and being accepted as a Jewish Yankee in the town of about three thousand people. Irving graduated from the University of Florida in 1935 with a bachelor's degree in business and served in World War II. He settled in Orlando in 1945 and bought an existing store, Louis. Gibbs-Louis was one of the most popular women's retail stores, first in downtown Orlando during the 1950s and the 1960s, and then he branched out to malls with four stores. In 1991 Gibbs retired and sold the company.

Leon Haliczer's first store, St. Petersburg, 1923.

Haliczer family, Tampa and St. Petersburg, 1961.

In the front row from left to right are Nathan Gordon (Nettie's husband) and Lilyan Haliczer Schonbrun. In the second row from left to right are Charlotte Haliczer (Sol's wife), Nettie Haliczer Gordon (sister), and Anna Haliczer Shonbrun. In the third row from left to right are (three brothers and their wives) Morris Haliczer, Molly Haliczer, Leon Haliczer, Lilly Haliczer, and Sol Haliczer.

Leon Haliczer (1897–1987), a native of Austria, spoke five languages by the age of six, learned watch repairing at age twelve, and fought with the Austrian army in 1916. His brothers Sol and Morris, who came to Tampa around 1907, encouraged him to join them where they had a pawnshop. Leon did, and using his skills, opened a watch repair and jewelry store in St. Petersburg in 1921 that he operated for forty-three years. He married Russian immigrant Lilly Rubin in 1926, and they had two daughters: Sonya [Miller] and Marilyn [Benjamin]. This family remains in St. Petersburg. In 1923, when Congregation B'nai Israel was formed by twelve families, Leon wrote the charter by hand.

Fort Lauderdale's first women's clothing store, Mack's Ladies Shop, opened 1924, Fort Lauderdale, 1939.

This is the Katz family in front of their store (left to right): Moe; Mack; Mack's wife, Sadye; and Abe. Among the most remarkable of the early Jewish settlers of Broward County were the Moe and Mack Katz family. Two days after his first visit to Fort Lauderdale in 1923, Moe Katz purchased a building on Brickell Avenue. Moe's excitement over his impending move led his brother Mack to open a dress shop with Sadye in

Moe's building, which also contained Moe's real estate office. The brothers and Sadye succeeded in their businesses and became involved in community affairs. Moe Katz ranked his 1937 founding of Broward County's first Jewish congregation, Temple Emanu-El in Fort Lauderdale, as his supreme accomplishment in a lifetime of achievement.

Benjamin and Sarah Wengrow's Department Store ad with daughter Marcia Wengrow [Weil] striking a pose, Panama City, 1938.

The Turner family, who had stores throughout Florida, set up their Wengrow relatives in business in Panama City in 1935. They joined three other Jewish families there, all in the clothing business: Schneider, Zivitz, and Wakestein. Daughters Marcia and Maxine were born there. The town was so small that Marcia recalls picking up the phone and saying to the operator, "I want to speak to my daddy," and then she was connected based on voice recognition! The Wengrow name is still visible on the building on Harrison Avenue.

Brown family (inset left), first-known Jews to settle in Boca Raton in 1931, with their diner, 1940s.

Originally from St. Louis, Missouri, with the name Boguslavsky, Russian immigrants Harry and Florence changed their name to Brown before they came to Boca Raton. Harry's sister Nettie and her Polish husband, Max Hutkin, joined them in 1936. The Browns opened Brown's Sundries on Federal Highway; it later became a diner. After Harry passed away, their sons George and Herb ran the place with Florence.

Boca Raton was founded in 1924, and the two couples were probably the only Jews there until after World War II. They recalled that there were so few people in Boca that they could have played cards in the middle of the main highway on Saturday night and not been disturbed by cars. The Boca Raton Historical Society records that by 2015 almost half the population of their city was Jewish.

Department Stores and Chains

Cohen's Department Store, built by the Cohen brothers and now the Jacksonville City Hall, 1930s. *Hazel Mack, archivist, Congregation Ahavath Chesed.*

Samuel and Morris Cohen arrived from Ireland in 1867 when Jacksonville was still under military occupation from the Civil War and established the Cohen Bros. Store on Bay Street. Brother Jacob Elias Cohen joined them in 1875. They instituted fixed pricing, rather than the typical bargaining, and money-back guarantees. Starting as a dry goods store, they moved several times due to fires. In 1912 they hired architect Henry John Klutho and built a mammoth department store on the site of the St. James Hotel that had been destroyed in the big 1901 fire. Cohen's was the largest structure in the city, occupying a city block. It featured a large glass dome as a skylight, and the elevators were open cages. At one time, this was the ninth-largest department store in the US. It became May-Cohens in 1958 and then closed in 1987. On the National Register of Historic Places, the building reopened as the city hall in 1997 after remodeling.

Kohn–Furchgott Company on Bay Street, Jacksonville, 1880.

Hungarian-born Leopold Furchgott, Charles Benedict, and Morris Kohn opened their department store in 1868, and it had several locations. By the 1960s the stores had transitioned to specialty stores of fashion and accessories in two malls. Furchgott's history was intertwined with Jacksonville's for more than one hundred years.

Rheinauer's Department Store, Ocala, 1880s.

The sons of a cantor in Germany, brothers Charles and Morritz Rheinauer came to the US in 1871. They arrived in Ocala in 1880 and opened a general store on the west side of the public square. Benjamin, a third brother, arrived in 1885 and was surprised by the wooden sidewalks and sand streets where livestock roamed free. Morritz left in 1895. Benjamin and Charles continued to operate their store, becoming prosperous by selling groceries, clothing, and dry goods and evolving into a department store. Rheinauer's remained at their location for more than fifty years before relocating to the Ocala Shopping Center.

The store continued in business until 1997, when Rheinauer and Co. ended their 117-year history of doing business in Ocala—and then it became a chain of stores throughout Florida. The brothers also took an active part in the cigar business in the 1880s and 1890s, and Benjamin was cofounder of the first bank in Ocala, the Bank of Ocala, later the Merchant's National Bank. Benjamin will be remembered best, perhaps, as the father of what is now Munroe Regional

Medical Center. He witnessed a bloody accident in front of his store where a pedestrian lost a leg, and he helped carry the man to an upstairs doctor's office. That marked the beginning of his long struggle to organize a hospital in Ocala.

Maas family in front of Dry Goods Palace, Tampa, 1896.

Abe Maas is at the far right, leaning against a column, and his cousin Ernest Maas is to his left. Maas, Glogowski, Kaunitz, Brash, Oppenheimer, Wolf, and Wohl are some of the Jewish families that settled in Tampa during the boom period of the late twentieth century and were active in commerce. This was the first store of Abe Maas that he opened with his wife, Bena Wolf, in a 23-by-90-foot space in 1886 when there were 720 residents in Tampa. His brother Isaac joined him the following year to form Maas Brothers, which grew to be Tampa's leading department store with a chain of 39 stores throughout Florida over 105 years.

Abe and Philabena (Bena) Wolf Maas with their children Sol (left) and Jessie, Tampa, 1895.

Bena Wolf (1863–1947) and Abe Maas (1855–1941) were childhood sweethearts in their native Germany. They married in 1883 before emigrating, moving first to Georgia and then to Florida (Tampa). The Maas were founding members of many Jewish, charitable, and civic groups in Tampa. Abe Maas was a longtime leader of the Tampa Board of Trade. As the founder of the Tampa Elks Lodge #708 in 1902, he was known as the father of the lodge. A founder of Congregation Schaarai Zedek, Abe was president for twenty-nine years. Bena worked alongside Abe until the business stabilized. As a pioneer for women's rights and involvement, she was president of the Children's Home for twenty-five years and was engaged in many other charitable and welfare projects, especially for orphans. Bena Maas was the last surviving charter member of the Order of the Eastern Star in Tampa.

Maas Brothers Department Store, Tampa, 1925.

In 1921 Abe and Isaac Maas built this eight-story, twenty-five-thousand-square-foot building. The sales force had grown from three employees to more than one hundred, and capital had expanded from $625 to $250,000. The growth of Maas Brothers was fueled by the growth of Tampa, which by 1900 had grown to nearly 16,000 people, due mostly to the railroad, tourism, the cigar industry, and the military. In 1929 Abe and Isaac sold their interests to Hahn Department Stores but continued as president and chairman of the board, respectively.

In 1935 Isaac died, and Hahn changed the name to Allied Stores Corp. Despite being owned by a national company, Maas was still operated by the Maas family. Abe died in 1941. By that time, the population had grown to 500,000, and the west coast was greatly expanding. The first branch for Maas Brothers was in St. Petersburg (1948), then Lakeland (1954), Sarasota (1956), Clearwater (1961), and Fort Myers. In 1987 the Maas Brothers chain absorbed the Jordan Marsh stores, and by 1991 Maas was closed. When Maas was merged with Burdine's (now Macy's) in 1991, all 39 stores were renamed, the doors to the central office closed, and the Maas building sat abandoned until it was demolished in 2006.

The New York Department Store, Miami, 1921.

This popular site was first David Afremow's New York Bargain Store in 1909. He generously donated $5,000 several years after the founding of Miami's first congregation, which now bears his name, Beth David. In 1913 Afremow sold the store to Daniel Cromer, who was joined by Irwin Cassel. They had unbounded faith in the future of Miami and in 1926 opened a nine-story, $5 million department store, the most modern in the South. It was severely damaged four months later in the hurricane that swept through the city just as the Kol Nidre service was ending on Yom Kippur—and this store and so many others never recovered.

Jay Stein in Stein Mart, a third-generation retail story, Jacksonville, 2017.

Stein Mart is a discount department store chain based in Jacksonville that carries clothing for men and women, home decor, accessories, and shoes. Stein Mart did not originate in Florida. It was founded in 1908 by Sam Stein, a Russian Jewish immigrant who arrived in America in 1905 with $43, was first a peddler, married a Jewish immigrant, and then opened his first store in Greenville, Mississippi. He sold general merchandise until his death in 1933, when his son Jake took over. Eventually the town expanded, and a better location opened up down the street. Jake Stein told his brother and sister to open up the new store, and he would take care of selling out the merchandise in their old space. That going-out-of-business sale did so well that he told his siblings to keep running the new store, and he would make the old space a promotional store. He had stumbled onto the off-price model that would make a hit—selling merchandise at deep discounted prices.

In the late 1950s and early 1960s, Jake continued to expand and renamed his store Stein Mart, mimicking Walmart. Jake's son Jay (born 1945) became the chairman/CEO of Stein Mart and moved the corporate headquarters to Jacksonville in 1984—perhaps because he'd gone to school there. I recall being in Jay Stein's home around 1989 and was bedazzled with the plethora of silver picture frames throughout—something I mimicked on a smaller scale (from the Stein Mart, of course, that was very near my house in Altamonte Springs). Stein Mart went public in 1992 with about forty-six stores and in 2017 had eleven thousand employees. As Stein says, "Stein Mart does best where the sun shines."

Shopping Centers and Malls

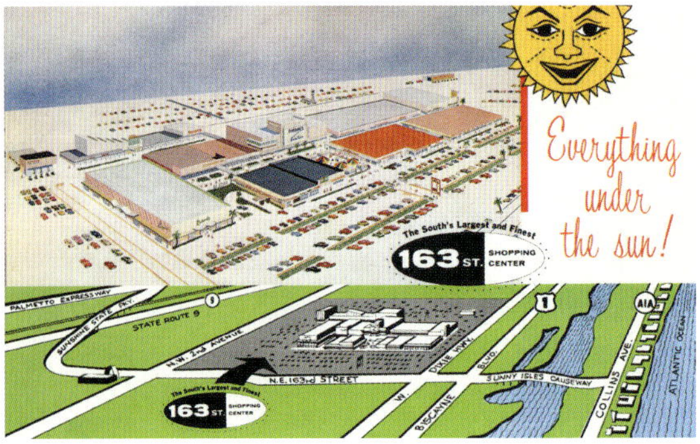

Samuel Friedland's shopping center at 163rd Street, one of the earliest in the US, North Miami Beach, 1956.

Developed by Food Fair Properties and owned by visionary Samuel Friedland, this was first an open-air shopping center and then converted in 1980 to a climate-controlled enclosed mall. Over the years, this nearly 350,000 square feet property has gone through many reconfigurations of tenants as the retail market has changed, and it is currently in decline.

Stuart Golding developed shopping centers, Tampa, 1981.

Stuart Golding moved to Tampa from Boston in the late 1950s. His projects included Seminole, Park Plaza, Sunset Square, Gateway, Brandon, Town and Country, and Twelve Oaks Plaza. In 1971 he merged his business into US Homes Corp. and became president. His development activities reached a new plateau in the mid-1970s when he oversaw construction of the one-million-square-foot Countryside Mall in Clearwater. His obsession, however, was the restoration of the fabled Willard Hotel in Washington, DC, to its former elegance and prestige. From the late 1960s until the mid-1980s, the Willard, the hotel of presidents and political bosses, had been derelict. Golding reached that restoration goal in 1986.

His wife, Roberta, an artist and philanthropist, was a daughter of Simon and Fannie Marks who immigrated from Romania to Tampa in 1921. They moved to Clearwater in 1936. This family has had reunions for seventy-five-plus years, and they include Marks, Markowitz, Golding, Scher, Peckett, Herris, Gettis, Salz, Jenkins, Brenning, and Losner relatives.

Leonard Farber's The Galleria, the signature Broward County mall, Fort Lauderdale, 1990.

The son of Russian immigrants, Leonard Farber hailed from New York City. As a kid, this son of a tailor hawked peanuts and hot dogs at Yankee Stadium. Later, he became a decorated soldier in World War II. After the war, Farber was an early builder of suburban shopping centers, developing dozens of them throughout the country. The Galleria, transformed in 1980 from an earlier open-air shopping center, remains the largest and most popular upscale regional shopping center in Broward County. He also built the Pompano Fashion Square Mall. Since arriving in Broward in 1969, Farber evidenced a deep commitment to his adopted community. He served on the board of directors of the Boys' Club, the Jewish Community Center, Holy Cross Hospital, and the Performing Arts Center. Farber also served as chairman of the board of trustees of Brandeis University. Reflecting on his success as the son of immigrants, Farber modestly maintained, "It's a fairly common situation in this country, and a wonderful thing, that someone from a very poor background can go almost anywhere he or she wants, if that individual is willing to fight for it."

The Soffer family's Aventura Mall attracts twenty-eight million annual visitors, Aventura, 2016.

In 1983 the Soffers of Turnberry Associates opened Florida's largest mall. In 2014 it was ranked the second-largest shopping center in the US with 2.7 million square feet after they added 4.2 more football fields' worth of shopping spaces and 300 retailers with an extensive food court. Then in 2017 they added a 315,000-square-foot luxury wing accentuated by artworks and lush landscaping.

Nathan Benderson developed one of the nation's newest shopping centers, The Mall at University Town Center, Sarasota, 2014.

This mall on the Manatee-Sarasota county line is 880,000 square feet, with more than 140 stores and restaurants. Benderson Development Company, with more than 8,000 employees, is a national commercial real estate powerhouse that moved to Sarasota County in 2003. Benderson (1917–2012) helped create one of the first outlet malls and was one of the first developers to venture into suburbia. The company has a portfolio that includes 30 million square feet of office buildings, industrial parks, residential communities, and hotels. Three grandsons work for Benderson and one of them, Shaun Benderson, is an executive in the Florida operations. According to Sarasota's Herald-Tribune, Benderson started his development career in Buffalo, New York, by picking up shards of glass as a child. He quit school at age sixteen to haul bottles, started a factory to make root beer, served in World War II, opened a brewery, and then got into building. "He's remarkable," said an attorney quoted by the *Herald-Tribune*. "He knows every tenant, every lease, the terms, the rents, and he knows the vacancy rates at each of his shopping centers."

Benderson responded, "Everything is hard work and common sense. If you don't have common sense, you don't have anything." Right up until his death, he exercised daily and was very frugal, although also very charitable, and asked probing questions before he gave.

Adjacent to the shopping center is Nathan Benderson Park, originally pastureland that was excavated to provide fill for the construction of Interstate 75. It is now a six-hundred-acre public park with a four-hundred-acre lake where world rowing regattas are held. It was named for Benderson, who donated $1 million to Sarasota County to enhance the park.

Some other shopping malls developed by Jews in Florida include Tibor Hollo's Omni Mall in Miami in 1977, Schmier & Feurring's Mission Bay Plaza in Boca Raton in 1991, and Schmier & Feurring's Wellington Green Regional Mall in western Palm Beach County in 2001.

Drugstores

Wedding portrait of Selma Minden and pharmacist Ben Grenald in Congregation Beth Jacob (now the JMOF-FIU), Miami Beach, 1943.

Ben Grenald credits all his success to his wife. He moved to Florida from Kentucky after he served in World War II and owned and operated 38 retail drugstores, Moderne Pharmacy, in Miami Beach and Miami. While in college in 1938, he had developed the formula for a medicated sunburn, Shuttle Lotion, which he sold and distributed. Then he developed more skin care products named D'Lanerg (Grenald spelled backward) under his company's name, American Hygienic Laboratories Inc. He continued to create new formulations and owns more than 150 patents, trademarks, and copyrights. Grenald is very proud that in 63 years, none of his ingredients have needed to be replaced due to government regulations. When I went to interview Ben at his Miami Beach condo in 1998, every wall and surface was filled with mementos, including 24 jumbo-size scrapbooks, too heavy for me to lift, about his family. He remembered the phone numbers from all his stores. Grenald served as a Miami Beach city commissioner in the 1980s.

Sheldon's Drugs, where Isaac Bashevis Singer learned he had won the Nobel Prize, Surfside, 1961.

When she was nineteen in 1948, Ethyl Cohen left the cold of New York to soak up the sun on Miami Beach for the winter season. But she sunbathed too much, netting a bronze burn that called for a trip to the local pharmacy for ointment. The pharmacist who sold her homemade cream at Sheldon's Drugs was its owner, Sheldon Spector. He took her to dinner, and seven months later, Ethyl and Sheldon were married co-owners of the drugstore with a food counter. At one time, there were seven Sheldon's Drugs locations on Miami Beach. The family remembers the Rat Pack popped in, as well as newspaper magnates James L. and John S. Knight, shoe designer Donald Pliner, politicians, and celebrity newsmen.

The couple's children are Toby, Becky [Herrup], and Stacey [Hipsman]. Herrup remembers the time her creative mother and her friend Charles Revson, the founder of the New York–based Revlon Cosmetics, met for dinner at the Fontainebleau Hotel. Spector made sure the drugstore carried the largest line of Revlon products in the city. "Charles was looking at her and said, 'How is it you're not wearing one of my lipstick colors?'

"'Oh, Charles, I'm absolutely using Revlon—a combination of colors.' That was the inspiration for the lustrous color Pink Cloud," her daughter said.

Author Isaac Bashevis Singer learned he had won the 1978 Nobel Prize in Literature while sitting at a back table at Sheldon's. The 2002 movie *All About the Benjamins* filmed scenes at Sheldon's with rapper Ice Cube. The store closed in 2004.

Targeted for seniors, Fedco Discount Drugs sold health and beauty aids, Miami, n.d.

Joseph Herzel Davidson came to Florida to retire from his family's chain of stores in the Midwest. He changed his mind in 1962 when he opened his first Fedco store on Miami Beach. That same year he began opening additional stores and offering private label generics. As the chain continued to expand to twenty-five stores, it became the largest independently owned and operated drugstore chain in Florida. Joseph and his wife, Isabel, had two daughters: Jo Ellen [Multack] and Candace [Ruskin]. The entire family, including sons-in-law, William Multack and Lloyd Ruskin, and eventually the grandchildren, were involved in every aspect of its development and operations. Known as "Mr. D," Joseph was kind and generous to his employees, who often went into the next generations at the stores. He remained chairman of Fedco until the family sold the business in 1999.

In 1962 Miami Beach High graduate Alex Grass founded the Rite Aid health and beauty aids discount drugstore chain, circa 1970.

During the Depression, Alex Grass's father died. Grass (1927–2009) moved from Scranton, Pennsylvania, to Miami Beach in 1940 with his mother and brother after his *bar mitzvah*. He graduated from the University of Florida Law School in 1949. Grass founded Rite Aid after fair trade was overturned. He took his company public in 1968 with more than fifty stores, and by 1995, he had retired as chairman and CEO. That year, Rite Aid had the largest number of drugstores in the country (3,000) and was the nation's number two drugstore in terms of revenue. He served as the longtime director of the National Association of Chain Drug Stores.

Grass donated money to the University of Florida to establish a chair for its Center for Jewish Studies and construct a new law school building. He said that law school helped him think in a logical fashion. Grass was a national chairman of the United Jewish Appeal campaign and a leader with Hebrew University. His grandson Harrison Grass was injured fighting for the Golani Brigade of the Israel Defense Forces in Gaza in 2014.

CHAPTER 3

Other Businesses and Industries

Food and Beverage

With a history of wars, revolutions, depressions, relocating, and not having control of their own destinies, many Jews, both immigrants and native born, sought a business that would give them control. When all else is in peril, people always have to eat! The food industry involves agriculture (which I covered in chapter 1, "Lure of the Land"), wholesale groceries and suppliers, mom-and-pop grocery stores or retail markets to grocery chains, and restaurants. The beverage industry includes wholesalers and retailers.

Group of men in the Lewis Bear Company warehouse, Pensacola, n.d.

Wholesale

Lewis Bear Company (LBC) Wholesale Grocers has continued in business since 1876, Pensacola, 1916.

I wrote about the Lewis Bear Company (LBC) earlier (part 2, chapter 2), but I need to include it here under food and beverage as this Pensacola company remains in business today—nearly 150 years and 5 generations later! This is the oldest privately held corporation in Florida (1876) and Anheuser-Busch's oldest continuous distributor—since 1892. Lewis Bear handles more than 300 different brands, from iconic global labels to local craft beers. In the Collections of the JMOF-FIU, there are early twentieth century bottles marked "Lewis Bear Co. Bottlers of Fine Whiskeys, Pensacola, Fla."

Morris and Max Bear took over the company after Lewis's death in 1895 and expanded with new facilities and transportation capabilities, delivering goods to the small lumber towns sprouting up along the Gulf of Mexico. Morris Bear served as president from 1901 until his death in 1928 when Lewis Bear was in charge. He served until 1973, followed by his nephew Robert

Kahn. Kahn served as president for 15 years until his cousin Lewis Bear Pollak took over in 1988, and he was followed in 1990 by Lewis Bear Jr. And currently, there is David Morris Bear. Generation by generation, LBC has evolved and adapted to changing markets and innovations. In 1995 LBC was sold, and the immediate family bought out all the other (54) stockholders. Today, LBC has two warehouse facilities, employs a team of 225 professionals, and handles the distribution and merchandising for more than 2,500 accounts.

Samuel Blank's beer distribution trucks, Miami, 1936.

Most of the early residents of Miami were devout churchgoers who voted "dry" in 1913. When the Prohibition law was repealed in 1933, Samuel Blank quickly saw an opportunity and started his beer distributorship, which included Anheuser-Busch and Michelob. Blank was a president of the Greater Miami Jewish Federation, founded in his home in 1938, and a member of the Miami Group that helped develop Israel.

Left to right: Mel Dick, Harvey Chaplin, and Jay Weiss of Southern Wine and Spirits, Miami, 1971.

Chaplin started in the industry in New York, working in the mailroom for Schenley. In 1968, in Miami, Harvey Chaplin, Jay Weiss, and Howard Preuss founded Southern and hired Mel Dick to head their wine division. Southern was probably the first to provide statewide distribution and promotion of leading wine and spirits brands. Today, they are the largest wine and spirits distributor in the US with operations in 35 states and 22,000 employees. The company represents more than 1,600 different suppliers and 5,000 brands. They service more than 200,000 individual retailers, including restaurants and hotels.

In 2000 President Jacques Chirac of France presented Mel Dick with the country's highest medal, the Legion of Honor, for his work in promoting French wines across the globe. Since its founding, Southern Wine and Spirits has given its support throughout the community. Weiss, who passed away in 2004, and Chaplin were instrumental in founding FIU's Chaplin School of Hospitality and Tourism Management. Wayne Chaplin, Harvey's son, is (at the time of this writing) the president of Southern Glazer's.

Among other Florida liquor distributors were Ben Stein in Jacksonville and Gene Davis in Tampa.

Retail Mom-and-Pop Grocers

Engler's Grocery Company's horse-drawn wagon, Jacksonville, 1910.

Romanian immigrants Harry and Sarah Engler settled first in Key West in 1890, where Harry bought Rippa's Last Chance Saloon. With earnings, in 1907, he and Sarah helped purchase Dr. John Maloney's office, a wooden structure that was used as the first synagogue in Key West. The couple moved to Jacksonville and opened a grocery store. It was very entrepreneurial to have a delivery service!

Proctor Grocery Store, Jacksonville, 1924.

The little guy is Samuel Proctor (1919–2005), oldest of the six sons of Celia Schneider and Polish immigrant Jack Proctor, who came to Jacksonville in 1917 as single people, married, started a family, and operated this store. Referencing this photo, Sam said his mother was "always behind the cash register!" Sam Proctor grew up to become a professor of history at the University of Florida, known as "Mr. Florida History." He and his wife, Bessie, were beloved mentors to the TEP fraternity and AEPhi (Alpha Epsilon Phi) sorority over their fifty years in Gainesville. Celia and Jack Proctor's other sons were Meyer, David, George, Sol, and Irving.

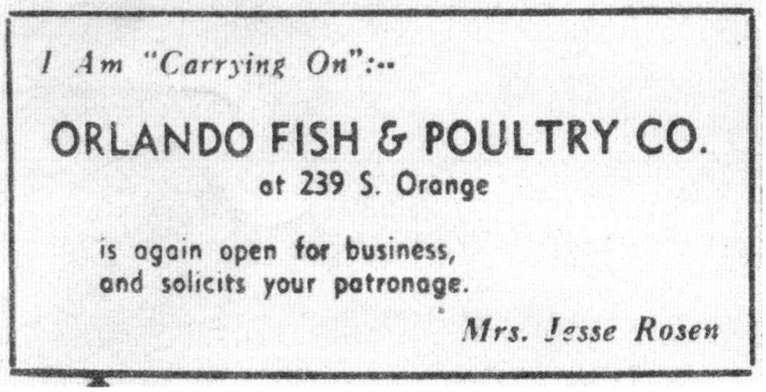

I Am "Carrying On":--

ORLANDO FISH & POULTRY CO.
at 239 S. Orange

is again open for business,
and solicits your patronage.

Mrs. Jesse Rosen

When Jesse Rosen died, widow Mollie took out this advertisement for Orlando Fish and Poultry Co., 1934.

Arriving in Orlando in 1924 with their daughter, Ruth Esther, Jesse and Mollie Rosen opened their establishment. This ad makes it clear, even though unusual for the times, that Mrs. Jesse (Mollie) Rosen would continue the business after her husband's sudden death. The *Orlando Evening Reporter-Star* wrote an editorial in tribute to the "courageous woman who was confident of the future." Her daughter, Ruth Esther, married Joe Wittenstein in 1938; they remained in Orlando and were deeply involved in the community.

Nettie Brown Hutkin and "Mr. Boca Raton" Max Hutkin, Boca Raton, circa 1940.

The Hutkins, married in 1919, opened Hutkin's Food Market on Old Dixie Highway and Federal Highway (US 1) in 1936 in an old building they rented for five dollars a month. In 1940 they also opened a small motel. Max Hutkin (1895–1987) cofounded the Chamber of Commerce, organized the first Boy Scout Troop in 1937, founded the Boca Raton Lions Club, and helped found Florida Atlantic University. He was a volunteer firefighter for fourteen years, was a Red

Cross disaster chairman for twenty-five years, posed as Santa Claus, and paid for Christmas lights for the city.

In 1967 he was a founder of Boca Raton's first Jewish congregation, Boca Raton Hebrew Congregation (now Temple Beth El), and served as a president. Hutkin earned the sobriquet, "Mr. Boca Raton," for his many volunteer accomplishments. When I interviewed him in 1983, he said, "I stuck my finger into everything that needed it. I made Boca Raton my hobby." In the local library are copies of speeches that Max Hutkin delivered at nearly every civic event held in Boca Raton when he was alive.

Sam (left) and Eli Bobo, Blue Ribbon Market, Tampa, 1999.
Tampa Tribune *and Bobo family.*

These are two of Salha and Ralph Bobo's seven children. When Syrian immigrants Salha (1907–2001) and Ralph Bobo moved the family to Tampa in 1946, they bought the Blue Ribbon Market in Ybor City. Ralph died three years later, and then Salha ran the business. Later, she opened a second store and three minimarts, until the children took over and eventually sold them in 2000. Sam and Eli and their siblings had twenty-six children and more than fifty grandchildren—many live in Tampa.

Bakeries

Horovitz Vienna Bakery, Jacksonville, 1899.

Louis and Dora Horovitz ran their store while raising their daughters, Lillie and Fannye.

Model of Levitt Bakery, Lakeland, 1930s.

This model of the family bakery was made by the family's daughter Zena [Levin], who also made a model of the JMOF, and both are on display at the JMOF-FIU. Eastern European immigrants Eli and Yetta Levitt settled in Lakeland around 1929, where they ran a bakery until 1946. Their four children were born in Palmetto and Lakeland. Eli was also a *shochet* and a founder of Temple Emanuel in Lakeland. Their son Morris married Rhoda Berman, whose parents, Sylvia and Al, started Hi-Grade, a food distribution company in Miami focused mainly on cheese. Morris joined the business in 1958. By 1982 Hi-Grade had become a full-service distributor and an exclusive distributor of many kosher foods. Rhoda and Morris Levitt have been very active in the Jewish and cultural community in Miami. Rhoda is a former chair of the Florida Arts Council and, in 2001, received the Howard Kleinberg Award, a south Florida theater and arts honor.

Portion of a label from the August Bros. Bakery that opened in Miami in 1923 and became south Florida's largest specialty bakery. *HistoryMiami Museum.*

Russian immigrants Jack and Gershom August came to Miami around 1915 to start a small retail bakery. In 1923 Gershom bought out the bakery and with his sons, Sam, Louis, and Harry, expanded into wholesale, supplying bread and rolls throughout Florida and the Caribbean. Its true test came during the 1926 hurricane when the power failed. Dough was hand-mixed in the headlights of delivery trucks parked outside an open door. The Augusts removed the heating elements of their ovens and fired them up with wood. They were able to deliver the bread on schedule! The business continued under the leadership of grandsons Fred and Arnold August for about seventy years.

Butchers

Advertisement for P. Ullendorff Company, Miami, 1906.

German immigrant Phillip Ullendorff (1867–1923) came to the US in 1890. In 1892 he moved to Fort Pierce and then followed the railroad to Miami in 1897. He sold both salted and fresh meats, and his business was so successful that he expanded into a corporation in 1911. He formed a real estate company in Miami, bought and sold many lots and buildings, and became wealthy. He made a large contribution to Miami's first congregation, Beth David. When the Reform Jews left to form their own congregation in 1922, he contributed there as well and was given the privilege of naming it Temple Israel, his father's name.

Kosher butcher Sol Kahlenberg in his shop, Miami Beach, 1940.

Kahlenberg came to Miami Beach in 1939 with his wife, Pauline, and was first employed at Malters Market. He opened his own kosher meat department within another market in 1944. At that time, there was a Kosher Butchers Guild for the dozens of kosher markets in the South Beach neighborhood to accommodate the Jewish community there. Kosher butchers must slaughter animals to prevent undue suffering, and the meat must be devoid of disease and drained of any vestiges of blood. In 1949 Kahlenberg started his own kosher butcher shop on South Beach. He retired in 1969. His daughter, Lorraine [Feuer], was active in B'nai B'rith Young Women, and in 1948 his son, Arnold, became *bar mitzvah* at Congregation Beth Jacob, the synagogue that became the JMOF-FIU.

Markets That Became Chains

Before chains such as Winn-Dixie, Walmart, Publix, and Whole Foods dominated the grocery business, chain names now gone once anchored shopping centers and street corners throughout Florida cities.

Setzer's Food Store, inset Benjamin Setzer, Jacksonville, circa 1930.

Benjamin Setzer came from Pushalotes, Lithuania, and settled in Jacksonville around 1914 where he married Hannah Bloom. He first ran an ice business with his brother Abraham, then a lumber business. Then he became a butcher, and by 1925 he had opened his first Setzer's Supermarkets. By the end of the Depression, it was much larger than the mom-and-pop grocery stores around town as it grew to a forty-store chain across north and central Florida, creating the need for a distribution hub. In 1958 Mr. Setzer sold his grocery chain to Food Fair Stores.

Then Setzer focused on his other business, Pic 'n Save Drugs, designed to be the area's first self-service store, which was considered a new concept in retailing at the time. His motto was "Stack It High And Sell It Cheap."

At the time of Setzer's death in 1969, the chain had grown to twenty-five stores. The corporate entity was branded as the National Merchandise Company, with Pic 'n Save being a trademark name owned by the company. Under the leadership of Setzer's son Leonard, the chain peaked in the mid-1980s, employing more than three thousand people in forty stores throughout Florida and Georgia. Benjamin Setzer was also a partner in Arlington's Town and Country Shopping Center and served as the chairman of the board of trustees for the Jacksonville Jewish Center.

Samuel Friedland, founder of Food Fair, Miami, 1960.

You will read about Russian immigrant Samuel Friedland (1897–1985) in several sections in my book as he was a mover and shaker, both in several business and many Jewish organizations. Friedland founded Food Fair in Harrisburg, Pennsylvania, during the late 1920s. By 1957 the chain had expanded to 275 stores. A year later, it purchased the Jacksonville-based Setzer's Supermarket chain. Food Fair filed for chapter 11 bankruptcy protection in 1978, and the family gave up control of the company. In 1981 the company exited chapter 11 bankruptcy; reorganized with a new corporate name, Pantry Pride Stores Inc.; and moved the company headquarters to Fort Lauderdale. At its peak, there were more than five hundred stores in the chain. By 1986 only forty Florida locations remained. The last store opened in 1991 in Sunny Isles. By 2000 all remaining locations were closed.

Carl Weinkle's store, Miami, 1925.

Ernest Weinkle (left) behind the soda fountain and Louis Weinkle (right), are the uncle and father of Carl. Carl and his wife, Esther, opened Carl's Market in Miami in 1925. This became south Florida's first supermarket and grew to nineteen stores. Carl's merged with Food Fair in 1956. The family moved to Miami Beach in the 1930s and became very involved in the Greater Miami Jewish Federation and Mount Sinai Hospital. This is the family you met in part 2 (with Marcus Weinkle and his Torah).

Ernest Harris, owner of the Food Spot convenience store chain, Miami, 1952.

Ernest Harris (1926–2011) moved to Miami from Pennsylvania in 1947 as a veteran of World War II. He met his wife, Dolly Levick, when he was a student at University of Miami. They had four children: Larry, Mindy [Wilner], Andrea [Shosfy], and Stuart. A successful entrepreneur, in 1949, he opened the Red Road Food Market, which he ran until 1991. In 1963 he launched the Food Spot convenience store chain, which he expanded to fifty stores across south Florida with two hundred employees. Ernest and Dolly were very involved in the Jewish community. He also served as state president of the Florida Retail Grocers Association and served for thirteen years as board chairman of Associated Grocers of Florida.

Restaurants

Miscellaneous.

RIVERSIDE RESTAURANT

AND

OYSTER SALOON.

Mr. GUSTAVE OPPENHEIMER having purchased Mr. Johnson's interest in this Saloon and nicely refited the same, is now prepared to entertain customers in first class style. Will serve during the season, at all hours Oysters in Fulton Market style. Game, Fish and all the variety of a well selected bill of fare.— The prices for all dishes have been fixed at a moderate figure. Give me a call.

Tampa, Jan. 20, 1870. tm.

Riverside Restaurant and Oyster Saloon, Tampa, 1870.
University of Florida George Smathers Library & Digital Archives.

Arriving on a steamer from New York, Gustave Oppenheimer brought vitality and style to the local business environment. According to the *Florida Peninsular*, Tampa's weekly newspaper that was published from 1855–74, his restaurant was located near the Hillsborough River ferry and offered Fulton Market–style food.

Jennie and Joe Weiss, in front of their original Joe's Stone Crab Restaurant (same location as today), Miami Beach, circa 1917.

Doubtless the best-known Florida restaurant is Joe's. More than one hundred years ago, in 1913, Hungarian immigrants Jennie and Joe Weiss came from New York to Miami Beach with their son, Jesse, because of Joe's severe asthma problem. His doctor said, "Move to Florida." The first permanent Jewish residents of Miami Beach, they opened a small lunch counter at Smith's bathing casino in this quiet town that was founded two years later (1915), and they were an integral part of its growth.

In 1917 Jennie and Joe purchased a house on Biscayne Street on South Beach to open their own restaurant where the family lived in the back. To get there from mainland Miami, you had to take a ferry. The Weiss couple began selling stone crabs in 1921 when a Harvard ichthyologist asked them to cook them up as an experiment. They were not good hot, so Jennie suggested trying them chilled—"delectable"—and they charged seventy-five cents for four or five crabs! Their son, Jesse, came on the scene in 1930 with his wife, Grace, and knew how to draw celebrities from gangsters to presidents. Their famous key lime pie was introduced in the 1960s. The recipe is a family secret, and one man makes about one hundred pies a day, six days a week.

JoAnn Weiss [Sawitz-Bass] in the courtyard of her family's restaurant, Joe's, Miami Beach, 1938.

Named after her grandfather Joe, JoAnn has spent nearly every day of her life at the business. She ran Joe's with her first husband, Irwin Sawitz. By 1985 she was totally in charge (with Rose and Dick McDaniel at her side), with more than two hundred employees who she calls her family. And she busies herself with "mopping the floor and cleaning the bathrooms, if that needs to be done," says JoAnn. Today, there are nearly four hundred employees. She knows every inch of the operation and moves around the restaurant to greet all her guests. Today, her children Jodi Hershey Koganovsky and Steve Sawitz run Joe's and a fifth generation is being groomed.

The restaurant, in the original location, is open during stone crab season (October to May) and does not take reservations, so when you go, you have to be prepared for long lines. Customers wear bibs, which in the early days, Jennie handmade and hand-washed and ironed every night. Some of the more than 70 tuxedoed waiters with international backgrounds have been with Joe's for decades. They serve up to 2,000 pounds of claws daily that are harvested from their own fleet of boats in the Everglades and Florida Keys. In 1993 JoAnn Weiss Bass wrote a book (with Richard Sax) with stories and recipes called *Eat at Joe's*. There are now branches in Las Vegas, Chicago, and Washington, DC. In 2017 *Business Insider* reported that Joe's Miami Beach was the nation's second-highest-grossing restaurant, serving 316,000 meals a year.

The Famous Restaurant, Miami Beach, 1960s.

In 1945 Morris Lerner came from New York to Miami Beach. He and his wife, Ruth, opened the Famous Restaurant that same year. The restaurant became a Miami Beach landmark, with seating for 500 and up to 1,500 meals served in an evening. The long lines outside were an indication of the quality of the food served inside—and out! As people were waiting outside for their tables, the Lerners would serve them knishes to calm their appetites. The Famous closed its doors in 1981.

Bernard's Surf, Cocoa Beach, 1960.

Bernard's Surf holds a special place in the history of the Space Coast. As a rocket went up, anyone at the bar got a free drink! Bernard Fischer opened his restaurant on A1A in Cocoa Beach in 1948 when it was a beach hamlet of about three hundred people. Former patrons recall, "We hung out to see the astronauts between launches and the newsmen during the launches."

"In the 1960s, it had a 'class' other places did not."

"You could surf all day, then go to work there—nearly everyone who grew up in the town worked there at some time."

"When I left Cocoa Beach in 1965, I vowed to return because I loved it so much. Thirty years later I kept my vow to myself. The first place I went, the Surf. It was still a classy place."

Bernard's nephew Rusty Fischer took over the operation in 1965 and ran the restaurant until 2006.

Bern's Steak House, Bern Laxer, Tampa, 1990s.

Bern's is famous for its dry-aged steaks, for having the largest private wine collection in the world, and also for having organic foods. Bern (1923–2002) and Gert married in 1950 in New York and the next year came to Tampa to visit his aunt who was working really hard in her restaurant. He vowed not to go into "that business." But circumstances led them to purchase the Beer Haven Bar. When they started the steak house in 1956, they used letters they could salvage from their original sign and bought an *s* to create the name Berns. They gradually bought adjoining buildings for expansion from 40 seats to 350. The Harry Waugh Dessert Room was built in 1985, using redwood wine casks to create 48 private rooms. Their son David runs the business today with 300 employees, plus a sister restaurant, Haven. A family member said that Bern "made it on guts and [the] willingness to take chances."

These are just a tiny sample of restaurants owned by Jews in Florida. An iconic mostly outdoor restaurant on South Beach is News Café, opened on Ocean Drive in 1988 by Israeli Mark Soyka. This popular eatery played a major role in my obtaining City of Miami Beach support to convert the historic synagogue into the JMOF as I met the politicos and historic preservationists there in 1992–93. Many people remember the 1997 murder of fashion designer Gianni Versace who had just picked up his newspapers at the News Café and was shot on the steps of his home, one block away. Visionary Soyka has opened many restaurants in Miami.

Restaurant Chains

Larry Singer (left) with William "Bill" E. Singer (inset), founder of the Royal Castle hamburger chain, Miami, 1961.

Bill Singer (1900–88) was born in Russia, came to America at the age of six, married Esther Goldberg in 1922, and had three children: Lawrence (Larry), Marlene [Stone], and Dorothy. By 1938 he was in Miami with $1,000 to invest, looking for a Depression-proof business and a way to feed his children. He opened a five-cent hamburger stand, Royal Castle, and then opened many more. The burgers were thin, about two half-dollars wide, and often served with birch beer, which came in tall, frosty mugs. Singer's restaurants were painted orange and white on the outside and featured a crown logo and the motto, "Fit for a King." By 1960 Royal Castle was the third-largest short-order chain in the country. Their son, Larry, joined his dad in 1947 and propelled the business's expansion to 175 restaurants. It went public in 1965, was sold in 1969, and closed in 1975.

Bill Singer was deeply involved in all things Jewish and best known for his service on the Florida Road Board (1957–60), which was instrumental in developing the state's highway system. The portion of Interstate 95 going through Miami-Dade County is named for Singer. Their daughter Marlene married Richard Stone, who became a US Senator from Florida. When Senator Stone asked me to chair his reelection fundraising in Central Florida (1979), I had regular contact with both Marlene and Bill as he was the campaign treasurer. Marlene and Richard Stone shared a concern for improving quality of life and Jewish continuity—a trait inherited by their son Elliot Stone, who was the JMOF-FIU's board president during 2012–14.

Alex Schoenbaum, founder of Shoney's Big Boy restaurant chain, Sarasota, 1994.

When Alex Schoenbaum was a student at Ohio State University (OSU), he bought loaves of bread and cold cuts at the grocery store and sold sandwiches in the dorms. When he died in 1996, there were about 1,800 Shoney's restaurants in 36 states. In 1947 he started the business in Charleston, West Virginia, with the Parkette (Park and Eat) drive-in featuring fifteen-cent hamburgers that grew to include Big Boy restaurant franchises. In 1953 the name changed to Shoney's (from his name), and twenty years later, it was the nation's third-largest family-owned restaurant group and one of the first to use television for advertising. In the 1960s Shoney's was advertising in *Life* and *Look* magazines.

Alex was reared with three brothers during the Depression, setting pins at his father's bowling alleys in Huntington and then Charleston, West Virginia. In spite of being called "all kinds of names" as a Jew, Alex played football at Huntington High School, making West Virginia All-State and at Ohio State University, where he was named by Grantland Rice as an All-American tackle from 1936–38. Alex played in the 1939 College All-Star Game, in all-star games against the New York Giants and Cleveland Rams of the National Football League, and was inducted into the Jewish Sports Hall of Fame in 1990.

Alex met his wife, Betty Frank, on her first day at OSU. They raised their children (Raymond, Jeff, Joann [Miller], and Emily) in West Virginia and then moved to Sarasota in 1977. Alex was recognized as "Pioneer of the Year" by *Nation's Restaurant News* (1984), probably the restaurant industry's highest accolade. Betty and Alex were extremely active in civic and philanthropic activities in West Virginia, Sarasota, and Israel, especially through educational and sports facilities and scholarships. At OSU, the business school honors his name. Alex said he was inspired to participate in philanthropy by former Ohio State football coach Woody Hayes, who said, "You don't give back, you give forward." He attributed much of his entrepreneurial success to the name he made in football. (Note: Alex and my mother were first cousins.)

Rose and Israel Stein family (Ben, Lukie, Rose, Frank, and Joe) playing baseball, Lake City, 1909.

Rose Rosenthal Stein left Grodno, Lithuania, in 1892 and came to New York where she met and, in 1894, married peddler Israel Moses (Papilsky) Stein. They moved around until Rose decided she wanted to settle in Lake City where there were just a few Jewish families. The family moved to Jacksonville around 1920 as Rose felt that the youngest daughter, Jennie, should have a stronger Jewish environment.

Ben Stein, Duval County Burger King owner, Jacksonville, 1955.

David Stein (center), with Burger King cofounder ames McLamore (left) and Burger King Corporation founder David Edgerton, Jacksonville, 1967.
The David Stein Collection.

Ben Stein (1898–1984), a son of Rose and Israel, grew up in Jacksonville and had a liquor distributorship when Prohibition ended (1933). With the transition to fast food after World War II, Ben saw an opportunity and invested in Burger King of Miami in 1954. The restaurants to which he provided loans did so poorly that he assumed control of the Duval County operations and appropriated and registered two trade names: Whopper and Home of the Whopper. But his restaurants did not profit, so the Miami office bought out Stein's trademarks with an agreement for Stein to receive 15 percent of all royalties of the national operation. Stein retained the Duval County stores, which he turned over to his son David to manage, and he was successful. David had dropped out of college in 1955 to work for fifty cents an hour in his dad's first Burger King. Burger King Miami eventually bought out Ben's royalties arrangement, and David continued as a franchisee and supplier (King Provision Corp.) of thirty-three Burger Kings for four more decades.

In 1989 I asked David Stein to sponsor the MOSAIC exhibit in Jacksonville. He was generous, as were both Ben and David in the Jewish and civic communities. David Stein's extensive support in the community includes his founding of the Jewish Community Alliance, his support of the Greenwood School for students with learning differences, and his $2 million scholarship endowment at the University of North Florida. This high-energy entrepreneur also owns sixty Applebee restaurants.

Linda [Richards] and Joy Benjamin [Zerivitz] at a Burger King opening, Orlando, 1970.

You met Simon Benjamin in part 2, chapter 1. His grandson George M. Benjamin moved from Jacksonville to Orlando in 1962 with his wife, Winnie, to join his childhood friend Paul Nathan in up to ten restaurants from 1962–72 in central Florida. George's daughter Linda remembers making milk shakes in the College Park Burger King and her sister Joy remembers going with George on weekends to all the stores to pick up the receipts. Of course, all their birthday parties were Burger King events! For Shabbat dinners, they picked up tenderloins from the commissary. George and Paul sold most of the restaurants but kept several and renamed them Pages (short for Paul and George). George served as president and director of the Central Florida Restaurant Association.

Clifford Perlman with his father, Bernard, and brother Stuart at the original Lum's Restaurant, Miami Beach, 1956.

Feel like having a hot dog steamed in beer for thirty-five cents? If you were living in south Florida from 1956 through the 1970s, you'd know exactly where to go. The Perlman family founded Lum's on Miami Beach with $6,000 and aggressively expanded to 450 restaurants, going on the New York Stock Exchange in 1969. That year, they bought the premiere gaming enterprise Caesar's Palace in Las Vegas for $60 million. The original Lum's location closed in 1983. The last one closed in 2017.

Bob Yarmuth with the new logo for Sonny's BBQ, Orlando, 2015.

Yarmuth made Orlando his home in 1982. In 1991 he and his cousin Jeff Yarmuth bought the southern-style, slow-cooked barbeque restaurant chain, Sonny's Real Pit Bar-B-Q. The Sonny's Franchise Company, of which Bob is CEO, now has 129 restaurants across 9 southeastern states and more than 7,000 employees. In 2013 Sonny's announced a new branding initiative that included a new name, uniforms, logo, and prototype. The brand refresh is a return to Sonny's roots, with a tagline that reads, "Local Pitmasters Since '68"—when the business started in Gainesville.

Jeremy Litwack's motto is "Live life to the coolest," Orlando, 2016. *Photo by Roberto Gonzoles.*

Jeremiah's Italian Ices help keep everyone cool. Litwack opened his first shop in 1996 in Orlando and has grown his business to twenty-one locations around Florida, hoping to eventually make it a national franchise. This young entrepreneur's sweet delights have customers lining up outside his shop windows day and night, no matter the temperature, to select from a variety of more than forty flavors of ices, gelati, and ice creams.

Delis

When Jewish immigrants arrived in New York City, many were single males working hard and saving money to bring over their families from Europe. They were looking for inexpensive places to eat and were attracted to home kitchens and small stores, some called delicatessens. The meat was cured and sold on rye bread with a pickle on the side—simple and filling. The meal was also portable and could be taken home or to work. During the 1930s and 1940s, there were more than five thousand delis in metropolitan New York. The sandwiches got bigger and bigger, as did the matzo balls in the soup and the heapings of chopped liver.

The concept spread to other cities as the Jews spread out—even all the way to Florida—as the delis became gathering places. By the 1960s Jewish corned beef became mainstream American. In 1965 Orlando's NASA astronaut John Young (not Jewish) smuggled a corned beef sandwich from a Jewish deli near Cape Canaveral on a Gemini 3 flight to give to Gus Grissom, who did not want to eat NASA food. Because of the potential hazard of sandwich crumbs, there has been no more corned beef in space!

Delicatessens have lost their popularity. There is only one today on Miami Beach—shocking! Some say it was because of high rents, real estate costs, and the modification of dietary habits. Some say that delis are part of a wave of mom-and-pop restaurants that have closed in place of fast casual restaurants. Also, Jews no longer have to rely on the social and cultural support that delis provided. Things change, and we do have the mouthwatering memories!

Safer's Delicatessen, Jacksonville, 1921.

In 1911 Safer's Kosher Market and Deli on Broad Street was the first in Jacksonville. Rev. Benjamin Safer had the kosher meat department and his brother Jake Safer ran the deli. It was later joined by Becker's and Hammersmith's. The delis were meeting places that bordered the neighborhood of east European immigrants and their American-born offspring. Max Safer, born in 1900, was destined to work in the family business. He left school after the fourth grade and started cutting meat at Safer's. Later, Max moved to Miami and opened Max's Deli on Flagler Street. In 1926 he married Mary Friedman, and they moved to Orlando and opened a deli there. The Safers returned to Jacksonville in 1938, where Max joined his brother Abba in running Safer's.

Morris Worman and Pearl Worman Leibowitz at Worman's Bakery and Deli, Jacksonville, 1993.

These are children of the original owners, Polish immigrants Sam and Rosa Worman, who opened the business in 1923 with a $300 down payment. Their daughter Pearl met her husband, Sol, there when he was stationed in Jacksonville. In its own way, it was a unifying element for the community. Old-timers say they felt that they were all eating at the same table. The deli closed after eighty-five years in business, having served generations of customers.

Ronnie's Restaurant sign is an icon of its time, Orlando, 1956–95.

Owners Larry and Hap Leckart offered everything from breakfast to steaks to down-home stuffed cabbage. Desserts were outrageous, such as the Extravaganza—a foot and a half of different ice cream flavors, covered with nuts and fruits, topped with swirls of whipped cream and of course a cherry. Spoons were passed around, and everyone dived in. Their rigid rules (like only two pats of butter) and rude service didn't deter patrons, who would line up outside: three or less on the left—four or more on the right—and woe to those who were in the wrong line!

Milt Medine shows off his famous cheesecake, Orlando, 1956. *Louise and Dick Weiner.*

Samuel and Esther Medinkowitz settled in Orlando in 1935 and opened a popular deli and butcher shop. After World War II, their son Milton and his wife, Rae, moved to Orlando. They changed their name to Medine and opened the delicatessen restaurant Medine's. Milt, famous for his cheesecake, proudly sent one to President Dwight Eisenhower at the White House. The restaurant closed in the mid-1980s.

Saul Cohen opened Miami's first kosher deli, 1923.

At the age of nineteen in 1921, Saul Cohen traveled from Philadelphia to Miami on a freighter to bring fruits and vegetables. At first, he worked in a grocery store owned by the Abrahamson family with whom he lived. In 1923 Saul Cohen had a hankering for kosher corned beef sandwiches for his fishing trips. Since kosher meat had to be brought from Jacksonville, he opened his own delicatessen in Miami. He married Carolyn Simons of Ocala in 1924. They had two children: Nanette and Nathan. In 1930 Saul moved his family to South Beach when he opened the Clinton Hotel. In later years, he opened many more hotels, including the Miami International Airport Hotel.

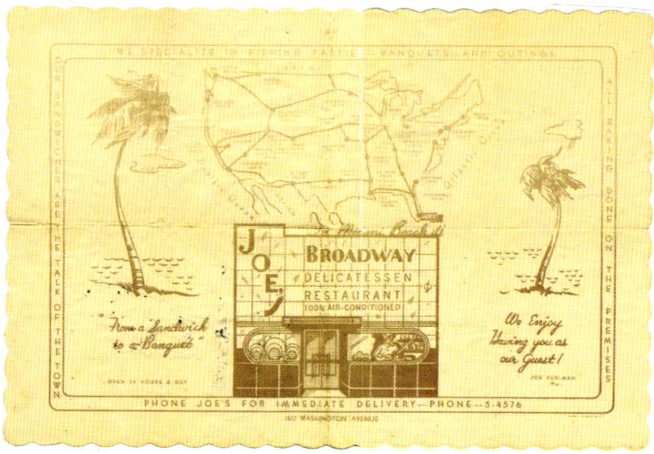

Joe's Broadway Deli placemat, Miami Beach, 1940s.

Joe Perlman opened his first deli in Miami in 1933, after Prohibition, so he added a bar. His daughter Sissi Perlman Feltman said, "Because it was in a rough neighborhood near the dock, in 1936, they made a courageous move [due to the known antisemitism] to Miami Beach. I remember seeing Al Jolson come in all the time." Joe's Broadway was the most popular spot to eat and meet, especially during the war period. In 1948 they offered "tender roast beef" for one dollar. Sunday was deli night for many Jews. Joe's had a bakery to make their own rye bread and cured their pickles in big wooden barrels.

Left to right: Raphil's founders Ray and Elsie Malschick and Miriam and Phil Seldin, Miami Beach, 1960.

Ray Malschick came to Miami Beach in 1939 and started working at Rosedale's Deli, which was owned by Dave and Mary Alper. This first job set the course for the rest of his life. At Rosedale's he met his future wife, Elsie Halpern, who worked there as a cashier. In 1948 Ray and his partner, Phil Seldin, combined their names and assets and opened Raphil's. Their wives, Elsie and Miriam, worked with them in the deli. Raphil's served meals to the famous and the infamous. One day, an FBI agent came in to ask Ray about a customer named Meyer Lansky, who had eaten at Raphil's that day. In 1973 Raphil's was sold and became Arnie and Ritchie's, which is now closed.

Restauranteur Wilfred "Wolfie" Cohen, Miami Beach, 1960.

Former Catskills busboy Wolfie Cohen (1912–86) came to Miami Beach and opened Wolfie's, Pumpernik's, and Rascal House. These restaurant names immediately conjure images of Miami Beach, chicken soup, chopped liver, rye bread, pastrami, pickles, and cheesecake.

Interior of Wolfie's restaurant (1947–2002) on Lincoln Road, Miami Beach, 1950.

Rascal House (1954–2008) general manager Arthur Goodman (left) checks on Chef Ozelle Johnson's preparation of matzo balls, Miami Beach, 1985.

In 1947 Wolfie Cohen and two business partners opened the original twenty-four-hours-a-day Wolfie's 21 at Collins Avenue and Twenty-First Street. This deli, a vestige of Miami Beach's Yiddish past, was the site of many political events. Wolfie's on Lincoln Road followed—and you dressed up to go there—and then one in North Miami Beach; these two closed around 1983. In 1953 Wolfie Cohen sold Wolfie's 21 to his partner, Ed Lassman. So closely was Wolfie's identified with Miami Beach that in 1959 Northeast Airlines chose it to cater meals for Miami-to-New York passengers; Lindy's in New York supplied delicacies to those flying south. At various times, there were Wolfie's branches or franchises in St. Petersburg, Boca Raton, Fort Lauderdale, Gainesville, Cocoa Beach, and Jacksonville.

Since the very first day that Wolfie's opened, Joe Nevel had been a regular customer. In 1984 he bought Wolfie's 21. Like its original owner, Joe Nevel knew the regulars and was involved in the community. He and his son David ran Wolfie's until it closed in 2002. The Rascal House was the last of the old-school New York Jewish–style delis on Miami Beach that survived until 2008. The population of Jewish retirees dropped dramatically due to natural causes as well as a flight northward to Broward and Palm Beach Counties to escape a perceived threat of crime and a cultural shift.

Wolfie Cohen was very active in civic and charitable organizations. From 1959–63, he served on the Miami Beach City Council, and during many of those meetings that ran through lunch or dinner, sandwiches and pickles were served—from Wolfie's!

Pumpernik's at 67th Street and Collins Avenue, Miami Beach, opened in 1954 and had branches that finally closed in 1993, n.d.

Sandee and Alvin Burger tasting Alvin's *latke*, Miami, 1981.

Roasters 'n Toasters founder Alvin "Bugs" Burger created cream cheese bagel sticks, Miami, circa 1989.

The only deli left on Miami Beach is Roasters 'n Toasters. Now in four locations, the deli was first founded as a coffee shop in Pinecrest by Sandee and Alvin Burger in 1989. Alvin had a hunger for a schmear of cream cheese on a toasted bagel, so he created cream cheese stuffed Bagel Sticks and Bagel Balls, patents he sold to Kraft in 2006. And this is a guy who was "Bugs Burger Bug Killer" since 1960, after he spotted roaches in a Miami restaurant. I worked with Sandee and Alvin in 1985 when I led a fundraising campaign for Hadassah's Camp Judaea in North Carolina, and he got right into the kitchen to cook for the campers. He'd been cooking since he was eight and was a cook in the Army. He was never shipped overseas during the Korean War because the commanding officer would not relinquish his cook!

TooJay's Gourmet Deli, Boca Raton, 2018.

In 1981 New Yorkers Jay Brown and Mark Jay Katzenberg combined their names to form the brand, the two "Jays," and opened this deli chain that now has about thirty restaurants throughout Florida. They are known for consistency, likely because of their central commissary in West Palm Beach. Customers tend to carry out fabulous bakery items, including their black-and-white cookies of which more than two million are sold annually.

In Hialeah's former Jewish-run garment district, Stephen's Deli has been churning out Bubbie's matzah ball soup and Reuben sandwiches since 1954. Matt Kuscher is the eighth owner of this last of the original delis in the Miami area.

Today, a new generation of delis is emerging, such as Josh's Deli in Surfside. Josh Marcus is offering Jewish techniques on typical Miami foods such as octopus in brine and kippered grouper.

I also want to mention, before we leave food, that Allen Susser, Mark Moyel, Art Ginsburg, and Michelle Bernstein are some of Florida's most famous chefs and cookbook authors, with their own restaurants at one time.

Boarding Houses and Hotels

As new immigrants arrived from Europe and North Americans came south in increasing numbers for the winter season, Jews saw the need for accommodations as an opportunity to make a living—and a place for their families to live. The facilities ranged from mom and pop (or sometimes just mom!) to major hotels—and even include a ghost story.

Simon Feinberg (inset) owned the Island Hotel in Cedar Key, a Florida heritage historical site listed on the National Register of Historic Places, 1915.

David Levy Yulee's railroad arrived in Cedar Key in 1861. Two years prior, a pioneer built a general store to last by mixing oyster shell, limestone, and sand to pour the walls ten inches thick. In 1914 Lithuanian immigrant Simon Feinberg bought the property and converted it into a hotel. Feinberg already had properties in Gainesville, Ocala, Lake Butler, and Dunnellon. In 1919 Feinberg traveled to Cedar Key to collect the rent and was distraught to find a whiskey still in the attic. After confronting the manager, Feinberg was persuaded to stay for dinner and the night. Feinberg never awoke—hotel lore claims friendly sightings of his ghost. No one was charged with his death. The copper pipe from the still was discovered during remodeling, and it was found that Feinberg died of food poisoning. The hotel, on the National Register of Historic Places, is open for business, and in 1999 the Fox Network television series *Haunted Inns & Mansions* filmed a segment there.

Finkelstein Boarding House, Jacksonville, 1910.

Finkelstein family at the boarding house for the wedding of their daughter Tillie to David Kaufman, Jacksonville, 1914.

Among the first to settle in Jacksonville from Pushalotes, Lithuania, were the Gabriel and Sarah

Finkelstein family who opened a kosher boarding house in 1905 and were founders of the Orthodox community. Many immigrants first stayed in this boarding house, and weddings and other family *simchas* were held here.

Gilmore sisters who fed the Jewish boys at the University of Florida in their boarding houses, Gainesville, 1939.

The photograph shows the house where Sadie Gilmore Singer (right) cooked kosher meals for the Phi Beta Delta fraternity (merged into Pi Lambda Phi in 1941). Rose Gilmore Rabinovitz (center) cooked kosher meals for Tau Epsilon Phi in her house and Anna Gilmore Mazo (left) cooked for the Jewish boys who weren't in either fraternity.

Rose and David Rabinowitz were the first in the family to settle in Gainesville (1912). Their children changed their name to Robbins. Leib Gilmofsky immigrated from Russia, changed his name to Leon Gilmore at Ellis Island, and brought over his wife and six children over. Their daughter Sadie met Sam Singer when she visited Rose. They married (1916) and moved between the college town and Lake Butler, settling in Gainesville in 1920. At that time, the Gainesville population was about ten thousand strong with seven Jewish families: Sadie's sisters' families, Fanny and Willie Sobol, the Abraham Buns, Moishe Edelsteins, and the Sternbergs.

The Singer children were Leon, Marvin, and David (Duddy). In 1918 for Leon's circumcision ceremony, he wore a beautiful *bris* suit, which has been worn by twenty-eight male descendants of Sadie and Sam Singer and was exhibited at the JMOF.

Miami was a segregated city when Ben Danbaum built the Lord Calvert Hotel for blacks, 1951.

The best customers were the black entertainers who performed at Miami Beach hotels but were not allowed to sleep there or use the beaches. The name came from the popular whiskey of that name as Danbaum owned a liquor distributorship. Ben's son-in-law Sam Rabin ran the Miami hotel until 1962.

Nemo Hotel, the first kosher hotel on Miami Beach, 1921.

Located at First Street and Collins Avenue, the hotel was built by Joseph Goodkowsky, Harry Goodkowsky, and Samuel M. Magid. The Nemo name was that of Samuel's costume jewelry manufacturing company when he made items for F. W. Woolworth. Today, this is the site of a fine restaurant of the same name.

Blackstone Hotel, at thirteen stories, was the tallest structure on Miami Beach at that time, 1929.

From Odessa to Belgium to New York, where he was a hotel contractor, Nathan Stone built the Mediterranean revival style Blackstone to accommodate his northern Jewish customers who came to Miami Beach and were turned away at other hotels. Assisted by his son Alfred with his wife, Lily, they opened the largest hotel on South Beach at the time at Eighth and Washington in less than one year after construction began. This was the first hotel on Miami Beach to welcome blacks in 1954. George Gershwin composed *Porgy and Bess* while reposing in the buff in the rooftop solarium. Blackstone was actually the Anglicized surname of Nathan "Schwartzstein." Alfred and Lily, deeply rooted in the Jewish community and in Israel, were the parents of Florida's US Senator Richard Stone. Richard grew up in the hotel handing out keys and carrying luggage for the guests. The building still exists. The building still exists.

Hoteliers at an Amit meeting, Miami Beach, 1940s.

"The best-known hotelkeeper in America," Jennie Grossinger (1892–1972; front, third from the left) and Lily Stone (front, fourth from the left) were leaders in the hotel industry. Both humanitarians, they were involved in dozens of Jewish organizations, such as Amit, and the development of the State of Israel, hosting meetings at their hotels.

Grossinger Pancoast Hotel, Miami Beach, 1945.

Partial view of stained glass window dedicated to Selig Grossinger at the JMOF-FIU.

Seeing the opportunity to market Miami Beach as a winter Catskills, some resort owners bought Miami Beach hotels. Jennie and Harry Grossinger founded their famous Catskill resort in 1914. During World War II, the Grossingers built the Ritz Plaza Hotel on Miami Beach. The US Army took it over for rest and recreation for the soldiers. After the property was returned in 1945, the family sold it and bought the previously restricted Pancoast Hotel. The former antisemitic owners had translated the slogan, "It is always June in Miami Beach" to "It's always Jew'n in Miami Beach." The Grossingers immediately advertised a kosher kitchen and Passover holiday packages!

I was eager to meet their daughter Elaine Grossinger Etess when I opened the JMOF. Elaine had been executive vice president of the American Hotel and Motel Association (and then its first woman president). She lived in Boca Raton and was serving as director of hospitality at the Forest Trace resort retirement community. Elaine visited to see one of the stained-glass windows in the JMOF building that is dedicated to Selig Grossinger, Jennie's father. My paternal great-grandfather, Abraham Yurmark, lived in the same village, Baligrod, Austria, as the Grossingers. Family lore is that in Selig's home, he tutored Jennie as a child in Hebrew and Talmud before the family came to America. Yurmark did not come to America, but when Jennie became successful in New York, his son-in-law, my paternal grandfather, sold her jewelry! Love these stories of connections!

Art Deco

Hotels were built all around Florida as vacationers discovered "summer in winter." Historically, the hotels built on Miami Beach between 1934 and 1940 have passed the test of time for popularity. Hundreds of hotels were designed and built by relatively unknown architects and contractors in zig zag, streamline modern, and Depression moderne styles. During their time, they were not held in high regard but were less expensive to crank out than the Spanish baroque style of earlier days. The Art Deco motif was colorful and whimsical, with features that looked like gaudy eyebrows over the windows. Then in the 1970s Jews were in the forefront in the development of this tourist mecca that is now the Art Deco District.

Architect Henry Hohauser with his wife, Grace Lehrer, Miami Beach, 1950.

Hohauser's parents, Esther and Herman, came from Hungary to New York, where Herman was a plumber. The building plans used by his father were Henry's inspiration to become an architect. After training and practicing in New York, Henry and Grace Hohauser started going to Miami Beach in 1932 and moved there in 1936 because of Grace's sinus condition.

I interviewed Grace in 1994, and she was proud to share the stories and renderings of Henry's long-lasting achievements. She told me, "I grew up Orthodox, so when we settled, we went to services at Congregation Beth Jacob (which became the second part of the JMOF) in their original 1929 building on Washington Avenue. The congregation had just purchased the lot next door to expand, and when they learned that Henry was an architect looking to establish himself, they asked him to design their new sanctuary—and he did, as his first project in his new city." (This building became the first part of the JMOF.) Grace continued, "It was a boom town and things got rolling fast. I worked as Henry's secretary and everything had to be typed 13 times!"

Hohauser (1895–1963) built a reputation for his streamline moderne designs. He created more than three hundred hotels and apartments on Miami Beach, including many of the jewels of the Art Deco District. In 1993 Henry Hohauser was ranked as one of the one hundred most influential people in south Florida history by the *Miami Herald*.

Cardozo Hotel, Miami Beach, 1939.

A totally Jewish project, this Art Deco jewel was named for US Supreme Court justice Benjamin Cardozo, designed by Henry Hohauser, and built by Irving Miller. The Cardozo was the first of the Art Deco hotels to undergo restoration after a large portion of South Beach won a place on the National Register of Historic Places as a historical district in 1979.

Park Central Hotel, Ocean Drive, Miami Beach, 1937.

Designed by Henry Hohauser and built by L & H Miller General Contractors in 1939, this was a favorite destination for Hollywood royalty. Louis and Harry Miller built more than thirty hotels on Miami Beach during the 1930s and 1940s. Tony Goldman, who bought this hotel in 1985, said, "I got out of my car, saw the Park Central, and felt like I had fallen upon King Solomon's mines." This Deco jewel was among the earliest to lure the nightlife set and fashion photographers after regentrification.

Lord Tarleton Hotel dedication, Miami Beach, 1940.

Arriving in 1924 and first operating a grocery store, Yugoslavians Samuel "Pop" and Rose Jacobs and their family were Miami Beach hoteliers for sixty-five years. The first of many hotels was the Alamac in 1930. In this photograph, Al Jacobs (left), Walter Jacobs, and Samuel Jacobs (right) dedicated this $600,000, eighteen-story, kosher hotel, which was the beach's first skyscraper. In 1947, the year that Jackie Robinson was the first black in the major leagues, the Brooklyn Dodgers (with Robinson) stayed at the Lord Tarleton—blacks and whites in one hotel.

Royal Palm Hotel, Miami Beach, 1939.

Russian immigrant Joseph Rose came to Florida with his wife, Sylvia, in 1924 for health reasons. Soon, he was building apartments on South Beach. Joe's noted accomplishment was the Art Deco styled Royal Palm Hotel he built in 1939 on Collins Avenue that stayed in the family until 1995. Its facade is now part of the convention center hotel complex. Rose was active in Democratic Party politics and many Jewish organizations.

Tudor Hotel, one of Leonard Wien's properties, Miami Beach, 1930s.

Leonard and Marjorie Wien came to Miami in 1935. Leonard started with Dade Millwork and Lumber Company, and then with his brothers, he began building hotels on South Beach. The 1100 block of Collins Avenue includes three of his hotels: Tudor, Palmer House, and Kent, all examples of the streamline moderne or Art Deco style of architecture. In 1948 Wien built the first airport hotel, called the Miami Airways Motel, which had 113 rooms. Marjorie and Leonard Wien were founders of Mount Sinai Hospital and major leaders in both the Jewish and civic communities. During the 1950s, Wien purchased 1,000 acres in the Kendall area for $500–$750 per acre, and the selling price on the last piece in 2005 was roughly $80,000 per acre.

Barbara Baer Capitman in front of 1936 Cavalier Hotel designed by Henry Hohauser in the Miami Beach Art Deco District, circa 1983. *Photo by Tom Hollyman.*

In the late 1970s Barbara Baer Capitman launched the campaign that established the square-mile Art Deco District, bounded by Fifth Street to Twenty-Third Street and Lenox Avenue to Ocean Drive. Comprised of more than eight hundred structures, the largest concentration of 1930s and 1940s resort architecture in the world, this was one of the earliest National Register listings to recognize the importance of the designs of this period. These vibrantly colored buildings represent an era when Miami Beach was developed as a tropical playground.

Russian-born architect, forerunner of post-modernism, Morris Lapidus designed 1,200 buildings (250 hotels), Miami Beach, 1960.

As the social and cultural fabric of Miami Beach changed following the end of World War II, so did Miami Beach's physical appearance. Hotels were built rapidly to satiate the desire of tourists for "the fanciest and newest." The hotel industry was greatly bolstered by Jews, including Ben Novack who built the Fontainebleau Hotel (1954). Designed by Morris Lapidus, the elegant hotel quickly became a trademark property. A year later, Harry Mufson commissioned Lapidus to design the equally grandiose Eden Roc Hotel next door.

When Morris Lapidus came to Miami Beach on his honeymoon in 1929, he fell in love with the city. In 1949 he designed his first Miami Beach hotel, Sans Souci, and moved there. Lapidus's architecture comes from an old school in which every element of a building's design must be in harmony. In addition to the hotels mentioned, he designed the Americana in Bal Harbor (1956), the Hebrew Academy on Miami Beach, Temple Menorah on Miami Beach, Temple Beth El in St. Petersburg, and Temple Judea in Coral Gables. As new shopping centers opened in the 1960s and Lincoln Road on Miami Beach had a downturn, Lapidus was asked how it could be saved. He designed an artistic open-air mall, closed to vehicles, the first in the US. His plans were controversial and radical. "Too much is never enough," propelled his success.

Fontainebleau Hotel and Eden Roc Hotel designed by Morris Lapidus, Miami Beach, circa 1960.

Lapidus designed the glamorous 1,200-room Fontainebleau with its "staircase to nowhere" on the former Firestone estate—perhaps the most famous hotel in the world. Its amenities and live entertainment lured tourists and the movie and television industries. Stephen Muss bought the hotel out of bankruptcy in 1978. In 2005 it was sold again. In 2008 it reopened after an extensive renovation and was listed on the National Register of Historic Places.

The Eden Roc was built on the Warner Brothers estate and has 631 guest rooms. There was a famous spat in 1961 when the Fontainebleau's owner Ben Novack retaliated for Mufson's building the Eden Roc next to his property. Novack built a blank 14-story North Tower as a "spite wall" on the Fontainebleau property to shade the Eden Roc's pool. In response, Mufson built an addition on the south side of the Eden Roc to cover the wall, and new pools were built in unshaded spots!

Rendering of the Diplomat Hotel designed by Norman M. Giller, Hollywood, built in 1958. *Artist J. M. Smith.*

The Diplomat on the Atlantic Ocean, Broward County's most important hotel to open since the 1920s, was designed to compete with Miami Beach. The masterpiece of Samuel Friedland's hotels, ground was broken on his 60th birthday in 1956. Its claim to fame was the parade of stars that entertained at the Café Crystal, Tack Room, and Regency Ballroom. During the high season, the Diplomat employed 1,400 people. Architect Norman M. Giller, who designed many Friedland supermarkets and shopping centers, considered this one of his finest "MiMo" or Miami moderne designs. In the late 1990s the hotel was replaced with the Westin Diplomat Resort and Spa.

Abraham "Sonny" Sonnabend of Sonesta Hotels, Palm Beach, 1950.

During World War I, Sonnabend (1896–1964) trained to become a naval aviator in Miami and Pensacola. He married Esther Lewitt in 1920 and built a multimillion-dollar fortune. One project was the Sonesta Hotels—combining the shortened names of its owners Sonny and Esther. This undertaking saw the operation of seventy hotels and resorts in seven countries, some in Orlando and Miami. He bought and operated facilities where Jewish families were welcome in contrast to the antisemitic practices of other hotels. In 1956 Sonnabend created the Hotel Corporation of America, one of the world's first major hotel companies. His sons, Roger, Paul, and Stephen, joined him in business and developed a hotel management company. Now a third generation has joined the ranks. Active in civil rights and detesting discrimination, Sonny was a president of the American Jewish Committee. Stephen told me that his dad had a rare knack of mixing red and black ink on corporation ledgers and producing pure black.

"Mr. Key West" David Wolkowsky in his 1926 Rolls Royce in front of the 1890 Cuban Ferry Dock that became Tony's Fish Market, circa 1964.

Born in Key West in 1919 to Freda and Isaac Wolkowsky, David Wolkowsky grew up in Key West and Miami, received his degree from the University of Pennsylvania, and began to restore buildings in the inner city of Philadelphia. He visited Key West in 1962 and decided to develop some of the family properties there, including the original home of Sloppy Joe's of Ernest Hemingway fame. For $106,000, he purchased the old Cuban Ferry Dock, lifted it off its foundation and moved it three hundred feet out, setting it on pilings in forty feet of water. He transformed it into Tony's Fish Market restaurant and cocktail lounge where guests could watch shrimp boats in the channel on their way into port. He is credited with putting Key West on the road to being a major tourist destination. In 1967 Wolkowsky added a motel around the restaurant, with fifty unique rooms, then added fifty more rooms that faced the ocean—to become Pier House Resort Motel. Both Jimmy Buffett and Bob Marley started their careers in the hotel's funky Chart Room Bar.

David Wolkowsky (left), with author Truman Capote at the Wolkowsky home on Ballast Key, donated his island as a legacy for wildlife preservation, Florida Keys, 1970.

In the photograph, notice Wolkowsky's trademarks—his white linen shirt and on the table, his Panama hat. In 1974 Wolkowsky bought Ballast Key from the US Navy for $160,000. It was an uninhabited, fourteen-acre private island, eight miles off Key West, the southernmost point of land in the contiguous US. He built a large stilt house jutting from coral rock and a guesthouse on the island and entertained many of his writer friends there, including Capote and Tennessee

Williams. He served hot dogs with potato chips, white wine, and chocolate soufflé to guests including Leonard Bernstein, Nancy Sinatra, prime ministers, the Rockefellers, the Mellons, and the Vanderbilts. The island was the site of the 1989 James Bond book and movie, *License to Kill*. In true celebrity style, 007 landed on the island and called Mr. Wolkowsky to say, "David, it's James, James Bond…I've broken into your island. I hope you don't mind."

In the Keys in 1908, President Theodore Roosevelt had established a 375-square-mile expanse as a preserve and breeding ground for nesting wading birds and other wildlife. Wolkowsky's island was the last remaining privately held part in this refuge. On August 16, 2018, one month before David died, the Monroe County Commission voted to change the name of Ballast Key to David Wolkowsky Key. About that time, Wolkowsky agreed to donate his gem of an island to the US Fish and Wildlife Service for marine and coastal research and education while preserving its natural resources. It is a critical habitat for sea turtles, birds, butterflies, and fish. This was his legacy to protect the place he loved for generations to come and let people see, appreciate, and learn from it.

Harris Rosen, owner and operator of seven Rosen Hotels & Resorts with more than six thousand rooms, Orlando, 2016.

Rosen began his hotel career as a file clerk at the Waldorf Astoria in New York. After moving to Orlando in 1970 as director of hotel planning for the Walt Disney Company, he fulfilled his dream of owning hotels. In 1974 Rosen purchased his first hotel in Orlando with a down payment of $20,000—all his savings. He took a risk when he hitchhiked to New York to meet with top motor coach companies that might use his hotel for bus tours. He later established the Rosen College of Hospitality Management at the University of Central Florida, which has grown to be the largest of its kind in North America and among the top five in the world.

In 1990 Rosen told himself, "Harris, it's time for you to start giving back to those who need a helping hand." Over the past two decades, Rosen has spent more than $11 million on preschool education, parenting programs, free day care, and mentoring and college scholarships for the residents of the Tangelo Park and Parramore neighborhoods. In Tangelo Park, the crime rate was cut in half, and the graduation rate went from 25 to 100 percent. Rosen says, "I just gave them hope." The *Orlando Sentinel* chose Rosen as the 2011 Central Floridian of the Year.

Jeff Adler (left) and his partner sell time-shares, Orlando, June 1998. *Premier magazine.*

Jonathan Tisch, Miami Beach, 1998.

Vistana was Orlando's first time-share company in the market in 1980. Jeff Adler and business partners, Art Zimand and Rip Gellein, were trailblazers, helping to legitimize the time-share business for resort destinations. The purchasers of a time-share unit received seven days of vacation time per year for a lifetime in exchange for a price of $5,000–$25,000 plus annual maintenance fees of $400 plus. Adler and Gellein took Vistana public in 1997 and then sold to Starwood Hotels in 1999. "I loved going to work every day," said Adler. "How can you not love it when you are selling happy vacation memories in resort destinations throughout the world!"

Loews Miami Beach Hotel built by the Tisch family in 1998.

Shortly after I opened the JMOF, the City of Miami Beach requested proposals to build a convention hotel. There had not been a major hotel built in that city for thirty-one years. Jonathan Tisch's father and uncle built the Americana hotel in Bal Harbour in 1957. The swanky Bal Harbour Shops are where the tennis courts used to be. Jonathan Tisch said that in the 1960s, he learned how to swim in the Americana pool and met President John Kennedy there. That hotel is now the St. Regis Bal Harbour.

In 1996 Tisch considered bringing his family name back to Florida. He donned a blond wig, dress, high heels, pearls and pressed-on nails and went into the South Beach streets to ask people what they thought. He used the video of his "act" to win the votes of the Miami Beach City Commission for the contract. The $135 million project involved renovating the St. Moritz Art Deco hotel and building 700 new rooms in a seventeen-story tower. Time flies, and they recently completed a $50 million renovation!

Entrepreneurs and CEOs

Meyer Lansky (1902–83), the "Chairman of the Board," with his sons Paul (left) and Buddy, Miami Beach, circa 1942.

The FBI called Meyer Lansky public enemy number one. Known as the architect and brains of the mob, Meyer Suchowljansky was born to Yetta and Max in Grodno, Lithuania, and came to New York with his mother and brother Jacob in 1911. Max had immigrated two years prior. Meyer's career in crime began when, before Shabbat on a Friday, his mother gave him her last five cents for a space on the baker's oven shelf for the *cholent*. He used the nickel for a street crap game—which he lost—and the family had a cold Shabbat meal. But he became a student of the system of winning, and soon he was delivering hot *cholent* to the family's table. This escapade expanded to bootlegging during Prohibition. From there, with "Lucky" Luciano, he was instrumental in developing the National Crime Syndicate. Lansky had met "Bugsy" Siegel when he was a teenager, and they became lifelong friends. In the 1930s he branched into gambling, establishing casinos in Saratoga Springs, Omaha, Chicago, Las Vegas, Havana, and Hollywood and Miami Beach in Florida. Lansky was one of the few non-Sicilian mafia.

In 1951 Senator Estes Kefauver named Lansky as one of the principal partners in the crime syndicate dominating New York and the eastern US. The hearings started the nation's fascination with organized crime. From then on, Lansky was the target of the law, but his only jail term was two months in 1953 for gambling. His business boomed. He is reported to have said in 1962, "The American Mafia is bigger than US Steel."

In 1972, when Lansky was indicted on income tax evasion, he attempted *aliyah* to Israel. He was denied entry as a threat to the people there and returned to Miami. Soon after I opened the JMOF in 1995, I was in my North Miami condo pool with neighbor Kenneth Whittaker, former head of the Miami FBI. During our conversation, he revealed that he was the FBI agent who had gone onto the plane to arrest Lansky upon his landing at Miami International Airport when he returned from Israel. Whittaker shared remarkable Lansky stories with me. I already knew Lansky's accountant and one of his lawyers and put together a program at the JMOF about Lansky's world—it was a huge success!

Lansky's last years were spent quietly at his condo on Collins Avenue on Miami Beach. He lived a low-profile existence, making life difficult for the FBI. Lansky's associates usually met him in malls and other crowded locations. His chauffeur drove him around town to look for new pay phones almost every day. Lansky was so elusive that the FBI essentially gave up monitoring him by the mid-1970s. He was one of the few gangsters who died of natural causes (lung cancer), and the government was never able to convict him. His death was front-page news when he left a widow and three children. On paper, Lansky was worth almost nothing. At the time, the FBI believed he left behind money in hidden bank accounts, but they never found anything.

When I interviewed his second wife, Teddy, in their Miami Beach condo, she shared warm stories of his attentiveness to his children; that he regularly walked their dog, Bruzzer; was an avid reader of challenging books; broke up 1930s meetings of Nazi sympathizers; and generously supported orphans, Israel, and many Jewish causes. She told me of his work for the US government during World War II when he helped protect the docks in New York City from traitors who destroyed ships. She also shared details of their ordeal of being deported from Israel, their rejections by other countries, and their eventual return in defeat to Miami. They tried again to go to Israel in 1977 and were again denied, even after Rabbi S. Swirsky of Congregation Beth Jacob (which became the second part of JMOF) asked on their behalf, "Why can't one Jew forgive another Jew?"

The sons in the photograph were with his first wife, Anne Citron. Bernard "Buddy" Irving was born in 1930 with cerebral palsy and declined rapidly after his father's death. US Air Force Captain Paul Lansky attended West Point (class of 1954). In 1962 the Kennedy Administration sent Captain Lansky to Vietnam as one of the first American advisors. Paul retired in 1963 and went to work for Boeing in Seattle, Washington, eventually working on NASA's Apollo space program that landed the first humans on the Moon. Their daughter Sandra said he was a loving father. She thought he was a businessman, an owner of casinos and nightclubs, until her "uncles" were being murdered. In 2014 she wrote *Daughter of the King: Growing Up in Gangsterland*.

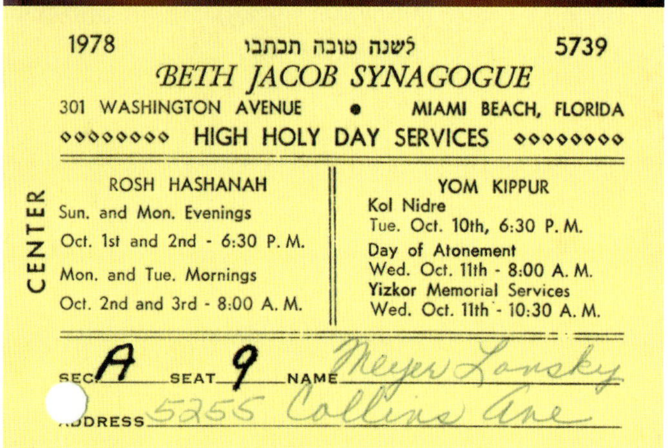
1978 לשנה טובה תכתבו 5739

BETH JACOB SYNAGOGUE

301 WASHINGTON AVENUE • MIAMI BEACH, FLORIDA

HIGH HOLY DAY SERVICES

CENTER

ROSH HASHANAH	YOM KIPPUR
Sun. and Mon. Evenings Oct. 1st and 2nd - 6:30 P. M. Mon. and Tue. Mornings Oct. 2nd and 3rd - 8:00 A. M.	Kol Nidre Tue. Oct. 10th, 6:30 P. M. Day of Atonement Wed. Oct. 11th - 8:00 A. M. Yizkor Memorial Services Wed. Oct. 11th - 10:30 A. M.

SEC A SEAT 9 NAME Meyer Lansky

ADDRESS 5255 Collins Ave

Stained glass window at Beth Jacob Synagogue (the building that became the JMOF) and High Holy Days ticket issued to Meyer Lansky, Miami Beach, 1978.

When I opened the JMOF, there was a large amount of media coverage. A Jewish newspaper in Montreal referred to our museum as the "Museum of the Mob" because of the affiliation of Meyer Lansky to the building. The stained-glass window honors his philanthropy and is visible at the museum.

Auto tycoon Norman Braman, Miami, 1990s.

Born in 1932 to immigrant parents, young Norman Braman was taking a walk with his dad one day in Philadelphia when they saw a Cadillac on the street. Norman was told that if he worked really, really hard, he might own one of those one day! He made his first fortune selling vitamins and drugs, then moved to Florida in the early 1970s and bought a Cadillac dealership in Tampa. In 1975 he bought another in Miami. Today his dealership is one of Florida's largest with six locations and more than $2 billion in annual revenue.

Once a water boy for his hometown football team, he bought the Philadelphia Eagles in 1985 and sold it in 1994. Braman and his wife, Irma, are avid art collectors with their own museum. They helped bring the Art Basel art fair to Miami Beach in 2002; it is now an annual event. Civic activist Norman is one of the founders of the Holocaust Memorial on Miami Beach and served as a president of the Greater Miami Jewish Federation. Self-made Braman is on the Forbes 400 list (2017).

Sanford Ziff (right) holding gold Ray-Ban sunglasses when Sunglass Hut sponsored the Lipton Tennis Tournament, Biscayne Bay, 1988.

Ziff (1925–2017) opened his optometry practice in Miami in 1950, developing new techniques in orthokeratology. One of his patients in 1971 was the owner of the Dadeland Mall. He pitched the idea of selling nonprescription sunglasses in a mall kiosk to make them a year-round fashion statement in addition to easy protection from the sun's rays. Sanford and wife, Helene, expanded Sunglass Hut to a chain of 550 boutiques in malls throughout the US and Canada. After becoming the world's largest retailer of Bausch and Lomb sunglasses, Ziff sold the company in 1991.

Monroe Milstein and Burlington Coat Factory personnel closing the stock market at the New York Stock Exchange, 2005.

Since 1946 Milstein had worked with his Russian father, Abe, in the wholesale women's coat business. In 1972 he bought a factory and outlet store in Burlington, New Jersey, for $75,000 down and started Burlington Coat Factory as a single store. The cash came from Monroe's wife, Henrietta, who was a school librarian. She suggested he add other women's clothing, accessories, shoes, a baby department, and gift items to his inventory. Their son Lazer opened a second store in 1975, but it remained closed on Saturdays as he was religious. Milstein grew the business to a multidepartment retail chain with 367 stores in 42 states, bringing in his sons Stephen and Andrew. In 2006 he sold his chain to Bain Capital for more than $2 billion and, 10 years later, it was a Fortune 500 company. When I asked Milstein in his Bal Harbour home what made him a success, he said, "I worked hard and listened to my customers."

Helene Gralnick, cofounder of Chicos, Sanibel Island, 2017.

Helene and Marvin Gralnick met in Mexico in 1971. They settled in Sanibel Island in 1983 and opened a shop to sell folk art. They found a uni-family, one-size sweater that propelled them into the clothing and accessories business, selling to women older than forty. Chico's FAS Inc. also has subsidiaries, White House Black Market and Soma Intimates. Chico's, named for a friend's parrot, began with one eight-hundred-square-foot store and grew to more than nine hundred boutiques nationwide, with international (franchise) partners and internet shopping. Chico's went public on NASDAQ in 1993 and in 2001 moved to the New York Stock Exchange. The Gralnicks started a foundation, which in 2002 won the Clara Barton Humanitarian Award from the American Red Cross of Lee County. They retired in 2006. Helene says, "Style is ageless because it comes from within…It's who you are."

Sara Blakely's creation and marketing of Spanx made her the youngest self-made billionaire in the world (at that time), *Forbes* magazine, 2012.

Blakely was born in Clearwater in 1971. She was raised there, attended Florida State University, and then sold fax machines, among other brief pursuits. At twenty-five, she was getting dressed for a party when she realized she did not have the appropriate undergarment for the white slacks she planned to wear with open-toe shoes. Armed with ingenuity and a pair of scissors, she cut off the feet of her tummy-control pantyhose—and Spanx was born within two years with a $5,000 investment. She had to overcome the reality that the hosiery industry was run by men (who did not use their products!) and successfully pitched her idea to Neiman Marcus by personally taking the buyer to the ladies restroom to show her the benefits of Spanx. Bloomingdales, Saks, and Bergdorf Goodman followed. She handled all aspects of the business from marketing to logistics and product positioning.

In 2000 Oprah Winfrey named Spanx her favorite product of the year, and sales took off, reaching $1 million in sales in its first year and $10 million in sales its second year. In 2001 Blakely signed a contract with QVC, the home shopping channel, where she sold eight thousand pairs in the first six minutes. Spanx is now available in fifty countries. Having struggled to learn on her own how to launch a successful business, in 2006, she created the Sara Blakely Foundation to provide female entrepreneurs with mentorship and training. In 2012 she was named one of *Time* magazine's 100 most influential people.

Chuck Steinmetz (with scissors), founder of Middleton's Pest Control, Orlando, 1992.

Miamian Steinmetz built upon his knowledge of farming and friendship with farmers from working with his father, a wholesale produce broker. An agriculture major at the University of Florida, he took entomology classes. A mentor at Orkin pest control suggested he also take business classes. With degrees in entomology and business, Steinmetz worked with Orkin, which relocated him to Orlando in 1970. He began Middleton Pest Control in 1977 with 3 employees and had 2,500 when he sold it in 2005. He began All America Termite and Pest Control in 1982 and sold it to Sears in 1997.

Alvin Burger founded Bugs Burger Bug Killers (BBBK), Miami, 1984. *Photo by Nubar Alexanian for* Inc. *magazine.*

BBBK (Bugs Burger Bug Killers) is an industry leader because it guarantees the elimination of bugs, not just control. A fourth-generation exterminator, Alvin "Bugs" Burger started BBBK with his wife, Sandee, in 1960 out of a bedroom at Sandee's mom's Miami home. BBBK was the first company to offer guaranteed pest elimination services to the hospitality industry. The initial charge is not paid until every infestation is gone. If a guest sees a pest, the company pays their bill and invites them back to the business as their guest. For example, in 1986 it paid out only $120,000 on sales of $33 million. Harvard Business School uses BBBK as a model for one of its courses. When the Burgers sold to S. C. Johnson Wax in 1986, they gave a portion of their proceeds back to their employees according to years served. Their son Andy Burger bought back the company name from S. C. Johnson Wax in 2001—fifth generation—and continues to run BBBK today!

Truly Nolen shows his pest control car with mouse ears and tail and an antique car, Naples, 2015.

Founded by Truly Wheatfield Nolen in Miami in 1938, Truly Nolen is probably the nation's largest family-run pest control company with about 320 offices in 63 countries. Second generation Truly David Nolen, a graduate of Miami Beach High School in the early 1940s, was a marketing genius, creating in 1961 the fleet of yellow mouse cars you may have spotted on a highway. He was very active in Jewish Federation and Temple Shalom in Naples, where he was presented the Jewish National Fund Tree of Life award for his outstanding community involvement.

S. Daniel Abraham, founder of SlimFast, Palm Beach, 2018.

In 1976 Abraham founded Thompson Medical and introduced the line of diet products SlimFast. Sales exploded in the late 1980s when former LA Dodgers manager Tommy Lasorda became its spokesman. He sold to Unilever in 2000 for $2.3 billion. Abraham is a major philanthropist to the Democratic Party, Jewish causes, and Israel. He believes in working for a peace process and created a Healthy Living Center at the Mayo Clinic.

Adolph Levis who created Slim Jim with his wife, Rose, Boca Raton, 1970s.

Levis (1913–2001) had to drop out of high school in Philadelphia, Pennsylvania, during the Depression. Operating out of his garage, he sold spices, pickles, and condiments and then started selling pickled pigs' feet, tomatoes, and cabbages to bars and delicatessens. In the 1940s he worked with his partner, Joseph Cherry, to have a local meatpacker concoct a small, easy-to-eat dried beef stick for snacking—Slim Jim. Originally, they were stored in jars of vinegar and served at bars, but by the 1950s Cherry-Levis Food Products began wrapping the Slim Jim in cellophane. Levis sold the company to General Mills in 1967 for about $20 million. He moved to Florida with his wife, Rose, in 1972 and became a philanthropist, donating funds to the Jewish Federation of South Palm Beach County and the Boca Raton Jewish Community Center, which was renamed the Levis Jewish Community Center.

A conference room at the Tupperware Worldwide Conference Center was named in Joe Hara's honor for his being the "heart of Tupperware," Kissimmee, 1985.
Heritage Florida Jewish News.

Joe Hara (1925–2017) grew up in Chicago, Illinois, and started working for Tupperware in 1953. He and his wife, Anita, moved to Orlando in 1966 where Joe was president of Tupperware International for twenty years. Under Hara, Tupperware grew an American plasticware company into an international sales phenomenon. He presided over Tupperware's elaborate annual Orlando gatherings of saleswomen called Jubilees, handing out advice and stoking enthusiasm for the home goods brand that flourished in nuclear family America. "When he spoke with you, he would gently touch your arm and look into your eyes—his approach to people and the value of relationships is at the core of Tupperware's success today," said CEO Rick Goings. Generous to his core, Hara was deeply involved as a community leader.

Ervin Shames, CEO of Borden, General Foods, Kraft USA, and Stride Rite and chairman of Select Comfort Corporation, Orlando, 2010.

Who could have predicted that Ervin Shames, 1958 graduate of Edgewater High School in Orlando and past president of Florida Aleph Zadik Aleph (an AZA Zionist teen organization), would become the head of major American companies! He graduated from the University of Florida and Harvard (master of business administration). Ervin Shames received the National Leadership Award from A Better Chance, the nation's leading organization for identifying and placing talented minority youth in exceptional education environments. Shames is an independent management consultant.

Fashion

Jews have played a dominant role in the American fashion industry from the late 1800s, when waves of European immigrants fled persecution and pogroms, often bringing with them only the clothes on their backs and their skills of the trades. Many became known for shaping the New York garment industry. Floridian Jews have also left an indelible footprint in this business. They span the spectrum from designing and manufacturing to dressing and influencing the local and international scenes in all types of clothing from beachwear to ball gowns, furs, shoes, and handbags. One example: for the past thirty years, couture designer Vicky Tiel splits her time between a studio and boutique in Paris, France, that she's had since the 1960s and a farmhouse near Pensacola. Tiel, who created the minidress, the wrap dress, and Julia Roberts's red dress in *Pretty Women*, has been selling her line of fragrances and apparel through St. Petersburg's HSN. She says, "Spend your whole day working on doing what you want to accomplish and being happy."

Rosengarten fur stole, Miami, 1957.

Fur stoles became very popular in the 1950s when most film stars and celebrities were spotted with them. Isaac and Dora Rosengarten arrived in Miami in 1929. By 1933 they began refrigerated storage and were the exclusive fur storage for Burdines department store (now owned by Macy's). That year *Ripley's Believe It or Not!* had an entry "Can you believe there is a furrier in Miami, Florida!" In 1934 they expanded to making fur coats. When Isaac died in 1947, Henry Rosengarten took over the business until he died in 1976.

Another furrier was Adrian Thal, who had a fur shop on Lincoln Road on Miami Beach in the 1960s. Thal was president of the Lincoln Road Association.

La Belle Furs, Orlando, 1957.

Like countless others escaping pogroms, Ben and Sarah Labellman fled on foot from Ukraine to Paris, then sailed to Montreal. They settled in Orlando in 1919 with their sons, Morris and Meyer, and five daughters. In 1929, suffering hard times, Ben deserted the family. Morris left school after the sixth grade to help his mother in her tailor shop. There she sewed coats, some trimmed with fur, for the wealthy residents of Winter Park. After World War II, Morris Labellman traveled home to Orlando by train. To pass time while waiting for a connecting train in Dallas, he took a walk and passed a window at a Neiman Marcus department store where furs were on display. Morris figured if they could sell furs in 100 degrees in Dallas, he could sell them in Orlando. He built his downtown store in 1956, offering cold storage where more than four thousand fur coats were stored at 44 degrees and low humidity. His son Arthur next ran the business at this same location. Third-generation Alex Labellman and his wife, Santa, have initiated an additional service of reinventing family-heritage fur pieces—turning coats into teddy bears or vests.

Left to right: Walter Raymond "Ret" Turner with his parents, Gene and C. Davis Turner, Marianna, circa 1950.

Ret Turner with Cher on the set of the movie *The Player*, Hollywood, California, 1992.

Arguably, the most recognized fashion designer to come out of Florida was Ret Turner (1929–2016), who was born in Marianna to parents who owned Turner's Your Store. He was introduced to fashion from the age of seven when he worked in the family's store after school. In 1950 he went to Hollywood to become an actor. When he realized that wasn't going to happen, he got a job in the wardrobe department at NBC and headed it for twenty years. He became a legendary wardrobe and costume designer who won five Emmy Awards and dressed glamorous stars such as Cher, Dinah Shore, Dolly Parton, Diana Ross, and Mitzi Gaynor. He also worked on the opening of Disneyland in 1955, Disney World in 1971, and Epcot in 1982. With partners, Turner opened a design and costume rental company, Ret Turner Costume Rentals.

Industrials

Jews in Florida have been involved in countless other diverse enterprises from laundries to scrap to steel production. Actually, the scrap metal, junk, or salvage business—collecting and selling rusty pipes and auto parts and reselling them, now called recycling—has often been thought of as a Jewish business.

Originally driven by the land boom of the 1920s, some went into banking. Those names include Leonard Abess, Shepard Broad, Arthur and Jack Courshon, Abe Mailman, Baron de Hirsch Meyer, Milton Gaynor, Ben Giller, Norman M. Giller, Bart Goldberg, Jack Gordon, Jay Kislak, Philip Liberman, Harry Lipton, E. Albert Pallot, Leo Robinson, Ben Tobin, and Carl Weinkle.

These are a few unique examples of other industries in which Jews have been involved in.

The Orlando Steam Laundry Company

THE Orlando Steam Laundry which was established in 1900, is one of the real industrial show places of Central Florida and has no rival for size, completeness and efficiency in the entire state.

It is a fascinating story to follow a bundle of laundry, from the time it enters the receiving door, through the marking and sorting rooms, where every modern device is used for proper identification and where the various items are sorted for fabric and color, so that they may be given the proper treatment. Now it comes to the battery of washers, where by the use of nets and compartments, each customers goods are kept by themselves. Here the finest of soaps are used to accomplish the proper cleansing action and each batch of clothes is soaped and rinsed in from 8 to 12 different waters. Now to the great centrifugal extractors, where practically all the water is taken from the clothes in such a gentle manner, that no buttons are broken nor any damage results. Now part of the bundle goes through to flat work ironer, where the great rollers finish the work perfectly even and flat and sterilize thoroughly. The balance goes to the various finishing machines, of which there are between 35 and 40, not including the 10 hand finishing boards. Such items as socks, stockings, collars, skirts, handkerchiefs, etc., each have their special finishing units. Now all the finished items are bundled or boxed and are ready to go out on one of the service cars, of which this company maintains the largest fleet in Central Florida.

The item of service trucks alone, shows how we are ever mindful of your wants and needs in gathering your clothes and quick delivery of them.

One of the most interesting places in the plant, is the dry cleaning department. In this branch of the work, a special non-explosive, dry liquid is used to clean garments that will not withstand the action of water. One of the most modern of systems, keeps this cleaning fluid pure and sweet, no matter how many garments are cleaned. Here the finest of fabrics and the most delicately colored garments are brought back to their original cleanliness and lustre. The finest automatic pleating machine that can be purchased, is just being installed in this department for the benefit of the host of patrons.

Mr. I. N. Burman is president and Mr. J. N. Wigfall, Jr., is in active charge.

Oldest Customer of FLORIDA PRESS, Inc.

In 1919 the Orlando Steam Laundry was purchased by I. N. Burman and a partner, 1929. *Orlando Memory, Orange County Public Library System.*

This business was operational from 1900–75. For more than 50 years, it had Jewish ownership. When airmail began in 1929 and one of the mail pouches fell into the Halifax River on a flight from Daytona Beach, the wet letters were brought here to be dried out! In the late 1950s, with 110 employees, the name changed to Orlando Cleaners and Laundry.

Harry Pepper in junkyard with his son, Leonard, (left) on running board, Daytona Beach, 1916.

Harry and Bella Pepper settled in Daytona Beach around 1912. In this junkyard behind his home, recycling entrepreneur Harry bought and sold automobile parts and metals. Instrumental in establishing all the Jewish organizations in the area, the Peppers had religious services in their home until Temple Israel was founded in 1925. Leonard Pepper was Florida assistant attorney general where he fostered legislation designed to strengthen civil liberties for protected classes and to disrupt violence and hate crime activity.

Bob Gamson in his scrapyard, Orlando, 1980.

Gamson's parents moved to Orlando in 1953, but college, the army, and marriage in Atlanta to Elaine Gaeser delayed Bob's permanent move. In 1967 Bob established Aaron Scrap Metals, and in 1980, with his partner, S. Goldman, he founded Surplus Steel and Supplies, a scrap metal business. A division of Surplus Steel, Iron Age, is the largest distributor of ornamental iron in Central Florida. The business meets the construction needs for theme parks, the government, developers, and others. Both Elaine and Bob have served in leadership positions in their congregation, community agencies, and the Jewish Federation.

Louis Kamenoff (seated), shown with his sons, Jack (left) and Abe, started Central Florida Bag Exchange (CFBE), a family business for more than fifty years, Orlando, 1960.

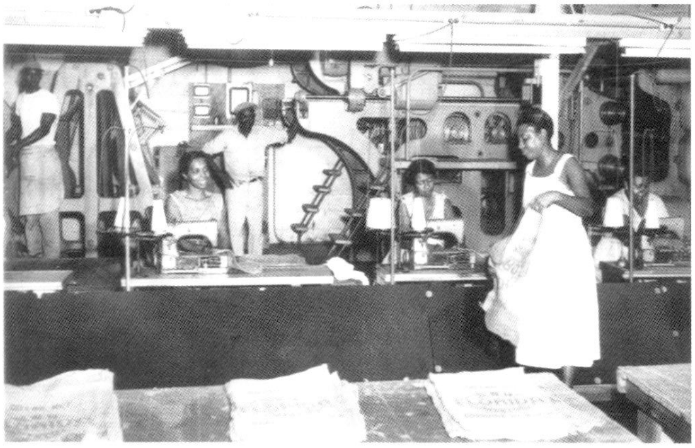

Interior of CFBE, where employees were treated like family and most worked for the business for forty to fifty years, Orlando, circa 1950.

Louis and Sophie Kamenoff settled in Orlando with their two sons where Louis began the bag business in 1926. He purchased burlap bags that had contained feed for horses and cows from ranches and dairies around central Florida. The bags were brought back to the warehouse and reprocessed, which entailed patching holes, vacuuming, and baling to sell them to the feed companies. After World War II, their sons, Abe and Jack, joined Louis in the business and then married the sisters Phyllis and Madaleen Schulman from Coral Gables. The couples met when the sisters sang at the Flamingo Club in Orlando. In the 1950s Central Florida Bag Exchange (CFBE) began manufacturing new bags. In the 1960s rip-rap bags became a very popular product. The surrounding municipalities purchased the bags to fill with a sand cement mix and place along expressways to keep soils from eroding. The bag rotted and a concrete bulkhead remained. As technology advanced, trucks delivered feed, making bags superfluous. Likewise, the municipalities began using poured concrete, and the brothers retired in the 1970s.

Jacksonville's Wolfson family—from junk to ships. The children of Sarah and Morris Wolfson are from left to right: Irene, Sam, Louis E., Edith, Saul, and Cecil, 1921.

Lithuanian Morris Wolfson (1879–1947) came to the US in 1896, married Sarah Goldberg in 1905, and settled in Jacksonville around 1913. Morris collected junk and peddled from a horse-drawn cart. As each child entered the family, they became part of the business, which evolved into Florida Pipe and Supply Co. during the Depression.

With the proceeds, their son Louis E. Wolfson (1912–2007) acquired shipyards in Jacksonville and Tampa, took over the DC transit system, battled for control of mail order giant Montgomery Ward, and by 1951 became head of the country's first corporate conglomerate, Merritt Chapman and Scott, a Fortune 500 company. He was listed in a 1955 *New York Times* article, "Today's Giants in Finance." In 1969, in a controversial Securities and Exchange Commission (SEC) case, Louis E. Wolfson served nine months in a federal prison near Pensacola for selling unregistered stock, the first criminal prosecution of its kind at that time.

The Wolfson family has been one of Jacksonville's most charitable in areas of health care, poverty, civil rights, education, and athletics.

Samuel Louis Flom (right) and then his son Edward headed Florida Steel, Tampa, 1975.

Samuel Flom came to Tampa in 1926 to work for Truscon Steel. In 1937 he and D. F. Taylor opened Florida Steel. The nation's largest producer of reinforcing steel (rebar) had 2,300 employees in five electric steel mills, two transportation divisions, a rail products division, a steel and wire division, and 17 fabrication plants to produce rebar for projects ranging from homes and businesses to the Sunshine Skyway and stadiums. Samuel was chairman of the board until his death in 1980. Then Edward held the position until 1993. Both were very active in community affairs, including as presidents of Congregation Schaarai Zedek .

Transportation: Land, Sea, and Air

Jews in Florida have made meaningful contributions to the transportation industry, primarily dealing with passengers but also with goods. You learned about David Yulee's Florida Railroad in part 1 and the involvement of the Dzialynski and Benjamin families in forming railroads in part 2—all during the nineteenth century. In addition to some jitney services, one the earliest taxicab services was started on Miami Beach in the 1920s by Morris "Pop" Segal. Segal Safety Cab business evolved into a bus company, American Sightseeing, headed by his son, Norton Segal. The cruise industry contributes about $8 billion annually to Florida's economy. Today there are three major public cruise lines that dominate 80 percent of the industry that drew 30 million Americans in 2019. All three are chaired by Floridian Jews: Micky Arison at Carnival, Richard Fain at Royal Caribbean, and Russell Galbut at Norwegian.

Sidney Alterman (inset) founded Alterman Transport Lines (ATL) when he settled a debt at his gas station with a trucker in exchange for his truck, Miami, circa 1955.

Alterman Transport Lines (ATL), begun in 1938, is an example of goods transportation. Sidney Alterman (1912–2001), a son of Latvian immigrants, came to Miami in 1936 and had a 63-year career in the trucking industry where he was a pioneer. He drove the truck, found the loads, and even built his own trailers. Eventually, with a fleet of 600 tractors and 1,000 trailers, 17 terminals, and 1,400 employees, his was the nation's second largest LTL (less than truckload) refrigerated trucking company for perishable foods. ATL transported many national brands and became the only carrier of Godiva Chocolates into Florida. The company operated until 2003.

(Top) Arthur Ungar with his wife, Marcella, and daughters, Bertha [Abess] and Marcella [Hofmayer-Werblow], Miami, 1927; (bottom) Ungar Buick dealership automobile plate holder, Miami, 1940s.

Arthur Ungar (1884–1969) opened his Ungar Buick Company in 1919 just as the war clouds were lifted and Miami was on the brink of a wild land boom. Despite the depressed economy in 1930, he continued to grow into one of the nation's largest Buick dealerships. Ungar sold his franchise in 1959. The computer building at the University of Miami is named for Arthur Ungar, and the family continues to be active in the community.

Louis Pallot, founder of Norton Tires, Miami, 1924.

Born in Lithuania in 1895, Pallot came to the US in 1910. He named his business in downtown Miami for Norton, his son with Gertrude, and did well with the new highways going south. Family members including Norton and Ronald Pallot and Howard Katzen joined the company. They were among the first to rent cars to tourists. Norton Tires became the largest independent tire dealer in the US. After seventy years in business, the family sold their company with forty Florida stores to the Goodyear Tire and Rubber Company.

Sam Behr became a tire celebrity, Orlando, 1985.

Stanley Hanin started Allied Discount Tires in Orlando with advertising help from his friend Sam Behr. The business grew from one tiny store in 1976 to forty-one stores in 1989 when he sold Allied to Dunlop. Behr's unique ads made him famous, and he never used a script! A shoe store owner himself, Behr sold tires on the air for Allied for fourteen years.

Ted Arison founded Carnival Cruise Lines in 1972, Miami, 1979.

Arison (1924–99) was born in Israel. After serving in the British Army during World War II, he assumed ownership of the family's Israeli business, M. Dizengoff and Co., where they were ship owners and general agents for several lines. In 1954 Arison moved to the US, and in 1966 he moved to Miami as manager of a passenger shipping company. He helped with the formation of Norwegian Caribbean Lines and in 1972 acquired his own ship, the *Mardi Gras*, which was the start of Carnival Cruise Lines, now the world's largest cruise company. Arison also headed the campaign to bring professional basketball (the Miami Heat) to south Florida in 1988 and was the chief benefactor of the New World Symphony. His son Micky now controls the Heat and Carnival. His daughter Shari is owner of Arison Investments in Israel.

Within the industry and in shipping for more than forty years, Richard D. Fain has been chairman and CEO of the world's second-largest cruise company, Royal Caribbean Cruises, since 1988. The company is based in Miami, where Fain is currently chairman of the University of Miami Board of Trustees. He and his wife, Colleen, have a large collection of Purim *groggers* (noisemakers).

With its newest fleet of ships, Norwegian Cruise Lines (NCL) is the third in size. Russell Galbut of Miami Beach is the first Jewish chairman of NCL, which bought Prestige Holdings, the owner of Oceania and Regent. Galbut says, "We are proud that NCL offers the finest kosher dining on all our ships."

Lori Goodman Baer became the executive director of the Port of Palm Beach in 2005.

Baer, a graduate of Florida State University, has worked in the port industry since 1982, with twelve years at the Port of Miami. During her tenure, dealing with homeland security issues was an almost daily occurrence. The first female head of the port, she said her most important achievement was launching a study about dredging the port's channel.

Carolyn Kurtz (inset), Florida's first female harbor pilot, Tampa, 2010. *Photo by Jorge Viso.*

Kurtz has brought ships into the Port of Tampa for more than two decades. From the pilot boat, she snugs up to the immense incoming vessels, jumps to the ship's dangling rope ladder, and climbs up thirty feet, as shown in the photograph. Then she takes control of the ship from the captain, telling the crew how to make it safely through Tampa Bay's forty-two-mile channel, the state's longest. She graduated from the US Merchant Marine Academy in 1986 and is one of twenty-three pilots working for the Tampa Bay Pilots Association—and the only woman. Preventing collisions and groundings requires familiarity with the coastline, weather, and tides, as well as knowledge of propulsion systems, rudders, radar, GPS, and the hull designs of the various ships. Kurtz sings in the choir for Congregation Schaarai Zedek.

Deborah L. Hecker is chief pilot at Philadelphia International Airport for American Airlines.

Hecker, of Merritt Island, began her flying career in 1994. She was the first person in the history of American Airlines to be dual qualified as a pilot and flight attendant. Hecker founded the Keep Flying Scholarship, a program providing financial assistance and flight school scholarships for women in aviation. She successfully balances her roles as a pilot, wife, and mother. During the Gulf War, she worked on a moshav in Israel.

CHAPTER 4

Entertainment, the Arts, and Culture

Entertainment

Over all of Florida's history, tourists have been present—drawn by its climate, hundreds of miles of beaches, theme parks, and entertainment venues. Jews have played important roles in creating this tourist mecca.

Howard Roland (center) of Orlando as the Big Bad Wolf at a Disney employee training and orientation, Disneyland, California, 1969.

Roland moved to central Florida with his family in 1970. He was the vice president of Corporate Contracting and Purchasing and an officer of the Walt Disney Company overseeing Disneyland, the Magic Kingdom, Epcot, and Euro Disney. During the opening of the Magic Kingdom, Roland's name was imprinted on a window on Main Street for his work on the Contemporary and Polynesian Hotels. He was a member of the Tourism Development Council and president of the Center for Drug Free Living. Upon retiring in 1995, Howard headed the Construction Oversight Committee for Orange County Public Schools.

Circus clown Lou Jacobs was the first living person to have his portrait appear on a US postage stamp, Sarasota, 1966.

Lou Jacobs came to the US from Germany in 1923. He was a master clown who performed for Ringling Brothers and Barnum & Bailey Circus for sixty years (1925–85). Circus performers have long argued that Lou Jacobs made more people laugh in live performances than anyone else in history. His sketches became clown classics. His most famous innovations were his unique makeup and fully functional, midget-size car into which he stuffed his more than six-foot body. Jacobs was a founder of the Clown College in Florida where he taught for twenty-three years. He died in 1992 in Sarasota, where he lived.

Feld Entertainment, Palmetto, 2016.

Feld Entertainment is the global leader in live family entertainment with as many as five thousand performances on six continents in more than seventy countries. The global headquarters in Palmetto is the second-largest building in Florida (after NASA's Cape Canaveral facility). The family-owned company with three thousand employees began in 1967 with the purchase of the now defunct Ringling Bros. and Barnum & Bailey Circus, then expanded into additional live shows, such as theatrical, Disney on Ice, Disney Live, Nuclear Cowboyz, and motor sports. They are now developing multiple properties into mobile pop-up attractions.

The Arts and Culture

At its best, the arts can be nothing more than a means of forgetting the human disaster for a while.
—Isaac Bashevis Singer

Music

Violinist George Orner, Jacksonville, 1928.

Accomplished violinist George Orner was a teacher and director of the Jacksonville College of Music. He was a founder of the orchestra that is now known as the Jacksonville Symphony, one of Florida's longest-standing orchestras.

Violinist David Cohen played a major role in establishing the Van Wezel Performing Arts Hall, Sarasota, 1990.

Child prodigy David Cohen came to Sarasota in 1948. He was cofounder of the Florida West Coast Symphony and, in its early years, its business manager, president, and concertmaster. When he was Sarasota's mayor (1964–66), he identified the need for a new arts venue. Cohen obtained a major grant from the Lewis and Eugenia Van Wezel Foundation and envisioned on Sarasota Bay the Van Wezel Performing Arts Hall, designed by William Wesley Peters, a Frank Lloyd Wright protégé. Cohen was a very respected civic leader, and the David Cohen Rehearsal Hall is named in his honor.

Lewis Van Wezel made his fortune in the diamond business and sold it before he and Eugenia retired to Sarasota in 1937. Lewis became active in civic and cultural circles, served as chairman of the local draft board in 1942 and in 1962 received the Citizen of the Year award.

Irwin Hoffman, founding conductor of what is now the Florida Orchestra, St. Petersburg, 1987.

Hoffman's (1924–2018) violinist father started him on violin and piano at the age of six. At seventeen, he conducted the Philadelphia Orchestra. He even carried a violin in a tank during World War II. Awarded the post of music director out of two hundred applicants, Hoffman arrived in St. Petersburg in 1967 and merged the Tampa and St. Petersburg orchestras. He memorized his symphonies and conducted without a score or baton, keeping musicians on track with hand gestures and facial expressions. His wife, Esther Glazer, often soloed, and their four children were required to study an instrument. After nineteen years in Florida, Hoffman went on to conduct orchestras in Colombia, Costa Rica, and Arizona.

Opera singer Elinor Rosenthal Ross, Tampa, 1968.

A Tampa native (born 1932), Elinor Ross used her gift of a dramatic soprano voice to advance to stardom at the Metropolitan Opera in New York. Ross enjoyed a successful national and international career. Her repertoire included roles such as Abigail, Lady Macbeth, Amelia, Leonora, Elisabetta, Aida, Gioconda, Santuzza, Maddalena, Tosca, Donna Anna, Medea, and Norma. She was forced into retirement in 1979 due to illness.

Judy Drucker, president and founding artistic director, Concert Association of Florida, Miami Beach, 1992.

Drucker (1928–2020) studied piano, first under her mother, Lillian, and then at the New York College of Music. She also studied voice at the Juilliard School and the Curtis Institute of Music. A graduate of Miami Beach High School, she was a coloratura soprano with the Coral Gables Philharmonic Symphony in 1948 and has performed on Broadway; with the Greater Miami-Dade Opera, now known as the Florida Grand Opera; and at the Palm Island Latin Quarter on Miami Beach. In 1967 impresaria Judy Drucker organized the first concert at Temple Beth Sholom on Miami Beach and began bringing world-famous performers. Fifteen years later, Drucker formed the Concert Association of Florida. Friend and confidante to classical music stars from Itzhak Perlman to Luciano Pavarotti, she put south Florida on the cultural map, bringing 126 concerts. In 2008 the State of Florida officially declared a portion of Biscayne Boulevard in Miami outside the Adrienne Arsht Center "Judy Drucker Boulevard."

Miami Beach's New World Symphony founder Michael Tilson Thomas featured on a poster from a performance in Monte Carlo, France, 1995.

In 1987 conductor, pianist, and composer Michael Tilson Thomas founded the New World Symphony on Miami Beach with Ted and Lin Arison. The mission was to have a place for postconservatory musicians to refine their classical music and business skills. More than one thousand alumni have moved on to professional music careers around the world. Thomas is a grandson of Boris and Bessie Thomashefsky, founding members and stars of the Yiddish Theater in America. The Arisons contributed $40 million to this youth symphony and set up a foundation, now run by their granddaughter Sarah. Their new building, designed by renowned architect Frank Gehry, opened on Miami Beach in 2011, featuring an exterior seven-thousand-square-foot wall on which they broadcast concerts to the public.

Steve Goldman congratulates composers Leigha Arnick and Justin White, finalists at the 2013 National Young Composers Composium (NYCC), Orlando, 2013.

Steve Goldman, internationally acclaimed for computer innovations, has lived in Orlando since childhood. He studied composition at Interlochen and received the 1997 Composer Guild's first-place award for orchestral composition. He started the NYCC in 2005 as a competition for young composers ages thirteen to eighteen. The annual National Young Composers Composium (NYCC) attracts close to one hundred entrants from all over the US. Usually six winners are selected—three for full orchestra and three for ensemble pieces. The culminating event for finalists is the Composium—part concert, part rehearsal, and part master class—with a professional orchestra, most recently under the baton of Christopher Wilkins, former conductor of the Orlando Philharmonic. Goldman is devoted to philanthropy in the arts and science, technology, engineering, and math (STEM) education. In the 1990s he persuaded Orlando Mayor Glenda Hood that the city needed a first-class orchestra and then, as chair of the fledgling Orlando Philharmonic, he provided the financing to get the orchestra under the umbrella of United Arts. Recently, Goldman collaborated with the University of Central Florida to establish a chair in composing music.

Eric Jacobsen conducts the Orlando Philharmonic Orchestra, Orlando, 2016. *Orlando Philharmonic Orchestra.*

When Eric Jacobsen was named the primary conductor and music director of the Orlando Philharmonic Orchestra in 2015, he became the third Jewish orchestra conductor/music director in central Florida. He was preceded by Hermann Herz (1967–70) and Sidney Rothstein (1982–86) as principal conductors of the predecessor Florida Symphony Orchestra (FSO). In 1979 violinist Arthur Tabachnick and his wife, cellist Shirley Tabachnick, became the FSO concert master and principal cellist. She retired from the orchestra in 1988 and he in 1990.

Visions—from left to right: Talia Osteen, Amy Turner, and Andra London cut their third CD, *Visions Light of Dawn*, Orlando, 1999.

These young women became an ensemble when their Orlando congregation's cantor Allan Robuck noticed that each of them displayed exceptional vocal talents during their *bat mitzvah* training. Visions, the female Jewish pop trio from Congregation Ohev

Shalom, made a mark on contemporary Jewish music from 1998 to 2010. They performed in more than 150 concerts at synagogues, federations, Jewish summer camps, the Jewish Federation National General Assembly, national conferences for Lions of Judah and Hadassah, and the Maccabi Games in 100 cities in the US and abroad. Visions has released four CDs and a documentary.

Matitiahu Braun performs, Oviedo, 2011.
Photo by Rachel Heimovics Braun.

Israeli-born violinist Mati Braun spent thirty-eight years with the New York Philharmonic. Upon retiring in 2006, he moved to Orlando, where he taught violin, viola, and chamber music. He performs throughout the area as a recitalist. His most recent CD, *Voices of Time: Works for Solo Violin and Solo Viola* (MSR) has been called "veritable master classes in both violin and viola" by Phil's Classical Reviews. Howard Goldstein of *BBC Music Magazine* called it "one of the most memorable collections of string playing I've heard in a long time."

Dance

Miami City Ballet founder Toby Lerner Ansin (center) with Miami City Ballet dancers, Miami Beach, 1997.

In 1985 Ansin had a conversation with ballet legend Edward Villella to hear his ten-year plan to begin a ballet company. Toby Ansin decided ballet was what south Florida needed to round out its cultural life and enticed six friends to join her in supporting the cause by each contributing $1,000. Today, the Miami City Ballet is universally admired as one of the world's preeminent interpreters of the choreography of George Balanchine. Its repertory of more than one hundred ballets, including twelve world premieres, was built upon the Balanchine repertory, style, and technique. It then expanded to include beloved classical works of importance and exciting new choreography by contemporary and groundbreaking artists. Miami City Ballet School, founded in 1993, is one of the largest dance training programs in the nation.

Harriett Lake's legacy: "I want to be sure that 100 years from now, people can still see *Swan Lake*," Orlando, circa 2015.

Rendering of new Orlando Ballet Centre, 2018.
RSVP Rob Schaeffer Visualization and Planning.

Philanthropist Harriett Lake (1922–2018) donated the funds to turn the Orlando Ballet's dream into the reality of a new world-class, 38,000-square-foot facility in Loch Haven Cultural Park. Lake called herself a "philanthropy junkie" and supported more than 150 charities annually.

Harriett met Hymen Lake in Miami Beach, and they married in 1950. They settled in Orlando in 1962 to manage Hy's properties and became very involved in the civic and Jewish communities. Harriett's legacy is her support for the arts, including the University of Central Florida (UCF) Conservatory Theater, the Harriett and Hymen Lake Cultural Center at the JCC, the Harriett Theatre at Mad Cow Theatre, Harriett's Theatre at Seminole State College, Harriett's Bar at the Orlando Shakespeare Theater, and Harriett's Ladies Lounge at the Dr. Phillips Center for the Performing Arts. The *Orlando Sentinel* named her Central Floridian of the Year in 2014.

Art

Arnold Newman, creator of "environmental portraiture," Miami Beach, 1940s.

In 1992, when I was negotiating the lease for the building that was to become the JMOF, I dealt with congregation president Ed Newman and found out that his older brother, Arnold Newman (1918–2006), was the famous photographer. Arnold showed artistic talent at a young age and graduated from Miami Beach High School in 1936. Then he went to the University of Miami for art classes for two years while working full time to help support the family. In 1941 Arnold went to New York.

Newman became nationally renowned—pioneering a style that places the subject in a carefully composed setting, capturing the essence of their work and personality. Newman received many international awards. His work has appeared in *Life*, *Look*, *Vanity Fair*, the *New Yorker*, and *Harper's Bazaar*, among many others, and is included in the collections of museums and private collectors worldwide. I got to know Newman personally. He told me, "I love people. I love them! They interest and intrigue me more than anything else. It's not how famous they are. It's the way they live their lives, what they do with their lives."

In 2000 I went to New York and while walking through the snow in Central Park, convinced him to exhibit at the JMOF his fifty-three portraits of significant Jews taken over six decades—with his personal anecdotes. I had to book *One World, One People* several years out, and he kept calling me to say, "I will not live that long." He did—and appeared at the opening—and when he died, he left that collection to our museum. I have heard it said that there isn't a photographer alive today who is not influenced by Arnold Newman.

Sculptor Frank Eliscu designed and created the Heisman Trophy, Sarasota, 1980.

Eliscu (1912–96) began his sculpting career at the age of seven when he took the tallow from the Shabbat candles into the tub and molded it into horses' heads. He went on to create the glass panels above the doors of the Library of Congress, national monuments, important museum pieces, many works for Steuben Glass, President Gerald Ford's inaugural medal, and more, including many exhibitions. When he moved to Sarasota, he became a city institution, designing sculptures for the Van Wezel, the Ringling Museum of Art, Temple Emanu-El, and Temple Beth Sholom, as well as Henry Landwirth's Give Kids the World program in Orlando. In 1935 Eliscu created the Heisman Trophy (the highest honor in college football). The Heisman Committee invited him to speak at the fiftieth anniversary of the Heisman ceremonies. Eliscu was presented many national awards for his distinguished use of sculpture in collaboration with architects and owners of significant buildings.

***Last Sunset*, acrylic on Masonite by Edna Glaubman, Miami, 1986.** *Loan of the Estate of Rod Glaubman.*

Edna Glaubman (1919–86) and her family were driving from New York to settle in Miami in 1958 when a catastrophic accident altered their futures. Saddled with an extremely disabled son and enormous medical bills, Edna's artistic talents produced the financial support for the family of four. She quickly became part of the Coconut Grove arts scene, a founder of their arts festival, and was selected to exhibit in the premier art shows in south Florida. Architect Morris Lapidus hired her to produce original art for the rooms at his Americana Hotel in Bal Harbour, and then she got commissions for the Fontainebleau and Eden Roc Hotels and others. Glaubman's art graced the music playbills in Miami and charity events. Private collectors and commissions kept her busy for more than twenty years. She used diverse techniques and subjects to produce mixed media (primarily acrylics) paintings, drawings, and lithographs—but only when her handicapped son slept.

This survival story of creativity and will transitions to the survival of Glaubman's artworks. After she died, her art remained in storage at her South Miami home until the arrival of Hurricane Andrew in 1992. Quick action by friends got the collection to a nearby home with electricity. It was scheduled to be moved to New York on September 13, 2001. The September 11 tragedy rerouted the collection to Delray Beach. A few years later, Edna's son Rod moved the collection to New Orleans where he created a gallery—with an opening date of August 27, 2005—just in time for Hurricane Katrina! The collection remarkably survived and has been brought back to Miami for private showings and exhibits.

***Klezmer* by Polish immigrant Chaim Goldberg, Boca Raton, 1980s.**

Chaim Goldberg (1917–2005) was a Polish painter, sculptor, and engraver. He was known for being a chronicler of Jewish life in the *shtetl* Kazimierz Dolny, where he was born, and as a painter of Holocaust era art. His interest in art began in childhood as he explored the riverbanks and looked for shapes that lay hidden within the rocks. He started sculpting the heads of animals from the rocks, which he gifted to friends. His large family lived in a tiny cottage built by his cobbler father. They slept on the floor to accommodate Klezmer musicians and other travelers, whose stories were inspirations for his primitive, expressive paintings and then his life-size sculptures. He served in the Polish army and lost most of his family in the Holocaust. Following World War II, he and his wife, Rachel, emigrated to Israel, where he continued his art. Then they moved to America in 1967 and finally to Boca Raton in 1986. He built a spacious studio and was very prolific. In 1997 there was a large exhibition of his works on the Jewish Federation campus, and Florida discovered Goldberg. He was driven by a sense of history and urgency to retrieve the memories of his Polish past while being torn to respond to the new world in which he was living.

The work of William Pachner was infused by the pain of the Holocaust. *Landscape of the River Sola,* 1966. *Florida Holocaust Museum and Ann & Charles Pachner.*

Sola was a river near Auschwitz concentration camp into which ashes from the crematoria were disposed. Widely known as Tampa Bay's leading artist for much of the second half of the twentieth century, William Pachner (1915–2017) immigrated from Czechoslovakia to the US in 1939 to pursue an art career. He worked as an illustrator and cartoonist for several magazines, including *Esquire*, where he became art director. After the war, when he learned that more than eighty members of his family were murdered in the Holocaust, he dedicated his life to expressing deep emotions through fine art. In the 1970s he established a home and studio in Tampa where he taught at art centers and had many solo art shows. His artworks are in private and public collections throughout the country. With the theme of the Holocaust and using symbolic images, Pachner called his art "the ultimate defiance against Hitlerism."

Yaacov Heller in his Boca Raton gallery, 2006.

Globally-acclaimed American sculptor, artist, and jewelry designer, Heller set up a studio and foundry in 1972 in Israel, where I first found him and bought a sculpted bracelet. When we opened the JMOF, he had settled in Florida and created *mezuzot* for doors and an iconic museum pin to sell in our store. His inspiration often comes from the Bible as he produces works in a variety of media including pewter, silver, bronze, and gold. Yaacov Heller has been commissioned to create works for world leaders, and many of his world-renowned sculptures are in Florida. One is a seven-foot bronze at the Boca Raton Museum at Mizner Park. His current projects include sculpting memorials to the Holocaust and other genocides, especially on college campuses.

Mel Alexenberg's acrylic painting on canvas, *Miami Beach Eruv*, 1999.

This painting shows a generic Miami Beach Art Deco building with an *eruv* seen as the posts and cord at the top. Over the front door, the Hebrew text means "A restored *eruv* [*eruv takin*] is the world restored [*tikkun olam*]." The digitized Rembrandt angel represents electronic age messengers drawing out the beauty of European and Islamic cultures, rather than the anti-semitism that plagues them. The painting was exhibited at the Yale University Art Gallery.

Mel Alexenberg, former dean of visual arts at the New World School of the Arts in Miami (1990–2000), is an artist and art educator best known for his explorations of the intersections between art, science, technology, and culture through his artworks, teaching, writing, and blogging. His current artworks deal with the interface between digital technologies, global systems, and Jewish consciousness. He has written many art books, and his artworks are in the collections of more than forty museums worldwide from the Metropolitan Museum of Art in New York to the Israel Museum in Jerusalem. He and his artist wife, Miriam Benjamin, now live in Israel.

One of the largest artworks in the world, Michele Oka Doner's *A Walk on the Beach*, Miami International Airport, 1998.

Born on Miami Beach to an artist mother and judge and mayor father, Doner absorbed the natural world around her. She said, "Miami Beach is primal in my work. It was a place that fascinated and nurtured me, with the forces of nature, the dramatic thunderstorms, the extraordinary light." The breadth of her art encompasses sculpture, public art, furniture, jewelry, and functional objects, and her works are in collections worldwide.

In Florida, Michele Oka Doner is best known for *A Walk on the Beach*—the one-and-a-quarter-linear-mile floor in Terminal D, Level 2, at Miami International Airport. It is seen by 40 million travelers annually and is composed of more than nine thousand bronzes embedded in terrazzo with mother-of-pearl. In 2016, for Miami City Ballet's production of George Balanchine's *A Midsummer Night's Dream*, Doner designed her first sets and costumes, inspired by images of undersea creatures photographed at the Marine Invertebrate Museum collection at the Rosenstiel School of Marine & Atmospheric Science at the University of Miami. The images were also the subject of her Regan Arts book, *Into the Mysterium*.

***Alef* by Cuban-born Baruj Salinas, who lives in Miami, 1999.**

Using the first letter of the Hebrew alphabet to symbolize new beginnings in new lands, Baruj Salinas engraves another imprint of the eternal commencement that is always different, generating changes in light, color, and life itself. Born in Havana, he studied architecture at Kent State University, Ohio, before moving to Spain. His body of work consists of collage and painted depictions of architectural motifs, landscapes, and organic shapes that dissolve in and out of abstraction. Salinas has held important exhibitions throughout the US and the world. He lives and works in Miami and has crafted an illuminated manuscript *The Torah Project*, recently shown at JMOF-FIU.

Bradley Arthur's Kol Ami Star Garden Memorial, Tampa, 2007.

Bradley Arthur, a world-famous sculptor born in Tampa and raised on Miami Beach, is a member of Congregation Kol Ami in Tampa. He designed and created the Jewish star sculpture at the front entrance, using stainless steel and six colors of granite on each side that represent the Twelve Tribes of Israel. His career as a sculptor began in 1970, at seventeen, after attending a metal sculpture program at the Coconut Grove School of Art. After graduating with a degree in fine arts from the University of South Florida, he worked and traveled and enjoyed a series of apprenticeships with several metal, bronze, and marble sculptors in France, Italy, and New York.

His award-winning, text-based artwork has been exhibited in more than a dozen solo shows and more than one hundred group exhibitions, including the Grand Palais in Paris and the Lincoln Center in New York. Arthur has lectured on the Artists Authorship Rights Act, copyrights, and the Visual Artists Rights Act (VARA) of 1990. His work is listed in the Smithsonian Institution's inventory of American Painting and Sculpture. A number of his sculptures are now part of the collection of the Yale University Art Gallery.

Janet Echelman's work has been installed in thirty-seven cities on four continents. Here she is creating her floating net sculpture for St. Petersburg's new Pier District, 2019. *Photo by Bruce Petschek.*

Rendering of Janet Echelman's *Bending Arc* sculpture (428 feet by 76 feet) for St. Petersburg, 2019.

"I chose this title for my largest permanent piece to date because it is about inclusion, embracing everyone to come to this place," said Tampa native Janet Echelman. This place is downtown St. Petersburg on the waterfront. The billowing net sculpture will require eighty-four miles of twine and more than a million knots woven into the custom-colored polytetrafluorethylene fiber. Her first in Florida, it is scheduled to be installed in late 2019.

Echelman is a fourth-generation Floridian in the Rippa pioneer family who came from Romania to Key West in the 1880s (see Mendel Rippa page 43), and then some went to Tampa. She creates experiential sculpture at the scale of buildings that transform with wind, water, and sunlight. Echelman says, "My art shifts from being an object you look at to a living environment you can get lost in." Her work intersects sculpture, architecture, urban design, material science, structural and aeronautical engineering, and computer science. Her TED (technology, entertainment, design) talk "Taking Imagination Seriously" has been translated into thirty-five languages. Oprah ranked Echelman's work number one on her "List of 50 Things That Make You Say Wow!," and she received the Smithsonian American Ingenuity Award in Visual Arts, honoring "the greatest innovators in America today." The recipient of many awards, Echelman was named an Architectural Digest Innovator for "changing the very essence of urban spaces."

Literature

Nobel Prize winner in literature Isaac Bashevis Singer at award ceremony with his wife, Alma, Stockholm, Sweden, December 10, 1978. *Photo by Gilles Vauclair.*

Polish born I. B. Singer (1904–91) came to the US in 1935. One of the best storytellers of the twentieth century, he wrote mostly in Yiddish and was known for his romantic and legendary tales, some of which had a Florida setting. His works, a combination of religious morality and social awareness laced with personal desires and supernatural elements, were translated into English and many other languages. Best known as a writer of short stories, Singer also published at least twenty novels, fourteen children's books, memoirs, essays, and articles. A street in Surfside, where he lived, is named Isaac Singer Boulevard in his honor and so is a city square in Lublin, Poland. A full academic scholarship for undergraduate students at the University of

Miami is also named in his honor. The JMOF-FIU has a collection of his personal items.

Journalist, novelist, and screenwriter McKinlay Kantor received the Pulitzer Prize for *Andersonville,* Sarasota, 1940.

McKinlay Kantor's father was a Swedish Jew, descended from a long line of rabbis. Kantor (1904–77), given the name Benjamin at birth, began his career helping his mother edit a newspaper; she was a McKinlay. Kantor moved to Sarasota in 1936. During World War II, when he was a war correspondent, Kantor entered the Buchenwald concentration camp as it was liberated on April 14, 1945. Over the next decade, that experience informed his research for and writing of *Andersonville* (1955), his novel about the Confederate prisoner-of-war camp. Noted for his limited use of punctuation, he wrote forty-three books, several set during the Civil War, and received the Pulitzer Prize in 1956. Two of his books have a Florida setting: *The Noises of Their Wings* (the Everglades) and *Beauty Beast* (north Florida).

Syd Hoff was a prolific children's book author, illustrator, and cartoonist, Miami Beach, circa 1999.

Syd Hoff (1912–2004) was best known for *Danny and the Dinosaur*, an enduring best seller for beginning readers. This story of a boy who rides on the back of a brontosaurus out of a natural history museum has been translated into a dozen languages and has sold more than 10 million copies since it appeared in 1958. Hoff got the idea when one of his daughters was stricken with a disability, and he drew pictures to divert her during physical therapy. His signature style was the use of simple, appealing shapes outlined with a thick, fluid ink brush. He sold his first cartoon to the *New Yorker* at age 18 and from 1931 to 1975, contributed 571 cartoons. Many of his tales involved escapist fantasies and animals, such as Sammy the Seal, who is let out of the zoo and attends elementary school. Hoff's animal characters come to the conclusion that although the grass may look greener outside the circus or beyond the peddler's wagon, there's no place like home. He also starred in a brief series of television shows in the 1950s, *Tales of Hoff*, in which he told a story and drew cartoons while on the air. Hoff said, "The best humor has to do with events that people can identify as having happened to them, or something that has been in the subconscious." In 2013 his former home on Miami Beach was designated a Historic Literary Landmark, one of only 18 in Florida, and there is a Syd Hoff Children's Writer Residency program on Miami Beach.

Elaine Lobi Konigsburg received two Newbery Medals from the American Library Association, Jacksonville, 1968.
Photo by Ron Kunzman

Howard Camner, "Best Poet in Miami," Miami, 1990s.

Originally a chemist, E. L. Konigsburg (1930–2013) lived in Jacksonville since the 1960s and wrote and illustrated twenty children's books and young adult fiction. Gleaning ideas from observing people and reading, she is one of only six writers to win two Newbery Medals for the "most distinguished contribution to American children's literature." The first was for *From the Mixed-up Files of Mrs. Basil E. Frankweiler* (1968), which chronicles the adventures of siblings who become involved in solving a mystery while hiding out at New York's Metropolitan Museum of Art. That novel became a feature film in 1973, with Ingrid Bergman as Mrs. Frankweiler and a made-for-television movie in 1995 with Lauren Bacall. The second medal was for *The View from Saturday* (1996), which centers on four sixth graders who form a successful Academic Bowl team, aided by the coaching of a paraplegic teacher.

Miami native, born in 1957, Howard Camner is the author of the acclaimed autobiography *Turbulence at 67 Inches* (2009) and seventeen poetry books including the Pulitzer Prize–nominated *Poems from the Mud Room*. He was a founding member of the Literary Outlaws in New York and was the featured performer with the West End Poetry Troupe. His books are in prominent literary collections worldwide including royal libraries throughout Great Britain and historical archives throughout the US. He is a regular contributor to several publications including *Poets & Artists*, the *Taj Mahal Review*, and the Bristol Banner anthology series. He was named "Best Poet in Miami" in the *New Times* newspaper's "Best of Miami" readers' poll edition of 2007 and was inducted into the Miami Dade College Hall of Fame for Literary Arts. Camner received the Albert Nelson Marquis Lifetime Achievement Award in 2018.

Will Eisner, "Father of the Graphic Novel," had a career that spanned nearly seventy years, Fort Lauderdale, 1950s.

Will Eisner was active from the dawn of comic books to the advent of digital comics. The son of Jewish immigrants, Eisner's (1930–2013) early life experiences growing up in New York tenements became the inspiration for much of his graphic novel work. He published his first comic in 1935 in *Wow, What a Magazine!* where he met Jerry Iger. They created the Eisner-Iger Studio in 1936, where they employed such people as cocreator of Spider-man and the Fantastic Four Jack Kreutzberg (later Jack Kirby), artist Lou Fine, creator of Batman Bob Kahn (later Bob Kane), and artist Mort Meskin. Among Eisner's early characters were Sheena, Queen of the Jungle; Dollman; and Blackhawk. At this shop, Eisner famously turned down a crude submission called "Superman" by creators Jerry Siegel and Joe Shuster. In 1940 Eisner created his most famous character, the Spirit, the lead feature in an innovative format: a sixteen-page color comic book that was inserted in Sunday newspapers.

Eisner produced the first successful graphic novel, *A Contract with God* (1978). This work revolutionized the art form, now America's fastest-growing literary genre. Eisner then created twenty-plus additional graphic novels. In 1988 the comics community created the Will Eisner Comic Industry Awards, presented annually at Comic-Con International.

Other Floridian Jews who were instrumental in creating comic book characters include Allen Bellman of Sub-Mariner and the Human Torch; Martin Nodell of Green Lantern; Sheldon Moldoff, a ghost artist of Batman; and Jay Morton, who penned the *Superman* phrases "Faster than a speeding bullet" and "Look up in the sky. It's a bird. It's a plane. It's Superman!" in Miami's Fleischer Studios (owned by Max and Dave Fleischer). Morton was the principal script writer for *Superman* in the 1940s, responsible for sixty-plus plots.

Brad Meltzer is a *New York Times* best-selling author, Miami, 2018. *Photo by Andy Ryan.*

Known for his thorough research, Brad Meltzer is best known for his fiction thrillers and mysteries (*The Escape Artist*, *Inner Circle*, *The Book of Fate*, *The Fifth Assassin*, *The President's Shadow*, etc.). He says, "There are stories no one knows. Hidden stories. I find those stories for a living." He's one of the only authors to have ever had books on the best-seller list for nonfiction (*History Decoded*), advice (*Heroes for My Son and Heroes for My Daughter*), children's books (*I Am Amelia Earhart* and *I Am Abraham Lincoln*), and even graphic books (*Justice League of America*). His books have been translated into twenty-five-plus languages. Meltzer is also the host of *Brad Meltzer's Decoded* on the History Channel and *Brad Meltzer's Lost History* on H2. Meltzer helped find the missing September 11 flag that the firefighters raised at Ground Zero at the World Trade Center site, making national news on the fifteenth anniversary of the attacks. He has worked with numerous organizations throughout Florida to promote literacy and is responsible for helping save the life of his Miami eleventh-grade history teacher. When she told Meltzer in 2015 she needed a new kidney, Meltzer asked his one hundred thousand Facebook fans to find her a new kidney—they did!

Producers

From 1940 on, for twenty years, Lou Walters owned the Latin Quarter nightclub at 159 Palm Island, the hottest address in American nightlife, Miami Beach, 1950s

Father of TV's Barbara Walters, Lou Walters opened the nightclub that was a mecca for big-name entertainers who performed for the winter crowds. With his partner, E. M. Loew, owner of Loew's Theaters, he booked the top bands, singers, and comedians. After the Latin Quarter, Walters moved his show to the Carillon on Miami Beach, 1959 Hotel of the Year, where his elaborate productions were considered the best on the beach for several years.

His daughter Barbara Walters went to public school on Miami Beach from 1939–42. She is known for a variety of television programs, including *Today*, *The View*, *20/20*, and the *ABC Evening News*, where in 1976 she was the first female coanchor of a network evening news program.

"Selection, service, and ambiance" is the mantra of independent bookseller and Miami Book Fair and movie producer Mitchell Kaplan, Coral Gables, 2011. *Photo by Gerald Hoberman.*

On the way to becoming a lawyer, Mitchell Kaplan changed course toward his love of books. In 1982 he opened his first independent Books & Books in Coral Gables, where famous authors make appearances. His first reading and signing was with Isaac Bashevis Singer, whose *Collected Stories* had just been published. Kaplan has nearly forty years of experience expanding, while national booksellers are failing. In 1984 he cofounded, with Miami Dade College, the Miami Book Fair, which has an annual attendance of about two hundred thousand. In 2011 Mitchell Kaplan won the National Book's Literarian Award for Outstanding Service to the American literary community.

Kaplan loves to read, has a consistent relationship with editors and agents, had a vision of making movies from his favorite books, and is now half of the film and TV production firm Mazur-Kaplan Company. Kaplan's sister Marcy Ross, president of Skydance TV, introduced him to Paula Mazur. They produced *The Man Who Invented Christmas* in 2017. Next, he suggested *The Guernsey Literary* and *Potato Peel Pie Society* for 2018. The company has numerous projects in various stages of development and production.

Josh Shader, TV producer and writer, Orlando, 2014.

Josh Shader is a fifth-generation Jew in the Orlando Shader family that you met in part 3, chapter 1. Moving to Los Angeles in 1999, he became part of the *American Pie* franchise. He says it was a thrilling way to jump into the entertainment industry. "Learning that I could make a living coming up with scatological humor was interesting to say the least." Shader is the proudest of his unscripted television Starz series *The Chair*. He won the Television Critics Association Award for Best Reality Series, got rated 100 percent by Rotten Tomatoes, and won a Directors Guild Award.

Mitch Glazer, movie producer, writer, and actor, Miami, circa 2012.

Mitch Glazer was born in Key Biscayne, graduated from Miami Beach High School in 1970, and then went to college. Glazer wrote for a music publication and settled in Hollywood, California, to write and act in movies. He became a film and TV producer with a long list of credits, most notably for Starz TV series *Magic City* based on his life growing up in Miami (2012), *The Recruit* (2003), *Lost in Translation* (2003), *Great Expectations* (1998), and *Scrooged* (1988) with Bill Murray. Glazer had been nominated for several major awards in the industry.

Theaters

Biscayne Plaza Theatre, Miami Beach, circa 1930.

PLAZA THEATRE

SOUTH END WASHINGTON AVE. -:- MIAMI BEACH, FLORIDA

EDGAR B. PEARCE
Managing Director

JACOB SCHACHTER
Program Director

— proudly presents —

IN PERSON -- ON THE STAGE

STARTING TUESDAY, FEBRUARY 7th, — One Week Only

THE EMINENT YIDDISH ACTOR
AND DIRECTOR OF THE YIDDISH ART THEATRE

MAURICE SCHWARTZ

מאריס שווארץ

STARRING IN JACOB GORDON'S

"GOD, MAN and DEVIL"

„גאָט, מענטש און טייוועל“

DRAMA IN 3 ACTS — 4 SCENES

New Adaptation and Direction by:
MAURICE SCHWARTZ

Stage Manager:
MORRIS STRASSBERG

Characters In Order of Appearance:

LEIZER BOTCHEN	YUDEL DUBINSKY
ZIPE	OLA SHLIFKO
PESSIE	BERTHA GERSTEN
FREIDA	CHARLOTTE GOLDSTEIN
MOTEL	ANATOLE WINOGRADOFF
DOBBE	JENNIE CASHER
CHATZKL DROCHMA	MORRIS STRASSBERG
HERSH DEBROVNER	GUSTOW BERGER
ARIEL MAZIK	MAURICE SCHWARTZ

Place of Action:
In a small town, Dubrovne — under Czarist Russia.
Between Scenes 3 and 4, an interval of one minute.

Biscayne Plaza Theatre program, Miami Beach, circa 1944.

Jacob Schacter managed the first Yiddish theater on Miami Beach. Some of the stars he booked who performed in Yiddish were Jenny Goldstein, Moische Oischer, and Mollie Picon. Some said, "It was like taking the Catskills mountains…and bringing [them] down to the South." Schacter then had a radio career, with *Yiddish Program*, and the broadcasts originated from a studio atop the Blackstone Hotel on Miami Beach.

Mitchell Wolfson founded movie theater chain WOMETCO (Wolfson-Meyer Theater Company) with his brother-in-law Sidney Meyer, Miami, 1925.

A son of Rosa and Louis Wolfson from Key West, Mitchell (1900–83) came to Miami in 1917. Sidney Meyer was a Twentieth Century Fox moving picture representative in Florida, who married Mitchell's sister Zenia. Wolfson controlled WOMETCO (Wolfson-Meyer Theater Company) for fifty-eight years until his death. He was the first Jewish mayor of Miami Beach (1943) and abruptly resigned to "fight the Nazis," as he wrote in a letter to his sister. Lieutenant Colonel Mitchell Wolfson led the siege upon the National Socialist Party's Munich headquarters.

While he served, he wrote his children, "Be fair to your employees, associates and the public. Insist on what is right and just for yourselves, but also grant the same justice to others." He often said that helping to build Miami Dade College was his proudest achievement; 80 percent of his foundation goes there.

Wolfson's first WOMETCO theater became Florida's first television station, Miami, 1926.

In 1949 this theater was converted to a studio for Wolfson and Meyer's TV station, WTVJ-6, Florida's first and the nation's sixteenth TV station. WTVJ carried shows from all the networks (NBC, CBS, ABC, and DuMont). Wolfson and Meyer's company grew to include other theaters, radio, and TV stations, the Miami Seaquarium, and other industries, which have helped make Florida a leisure capital. An investment firm took over WOMETCO in 1984 in a deal worth $1 billion, the largest corporate sale in the history of south Florida at that time. Assets included 104 movie theaters, 6 television stations, 46 cable TV systems, the Seaquarium, Citrus Tower, vending machines, and one of the largest Coca Cola bottlers in the nation. In 1994 Cobb Theaters bought out the WOMETCO chain that would later merge into Regal Entertainment Group.

Stuart Omans, founder of the Orlando Shakespeare Theater (OST), at its original site on Lake Eola, Orlando, 1989.

Omans took a temporary leave as chair of the University of Central Florida English department in 1987 to "bring Shakespeare to the kind of people the playwright reached in his own time." Disney World and the City of Orlando built the amphitheater at Lake Eola for the annual performances. Omans served as the Orlando Shakespeare Theater's (OST's) founding director during 1989–94. The OST is now housed in the Lowndes Shakespeare Center in Loch Haven Park.

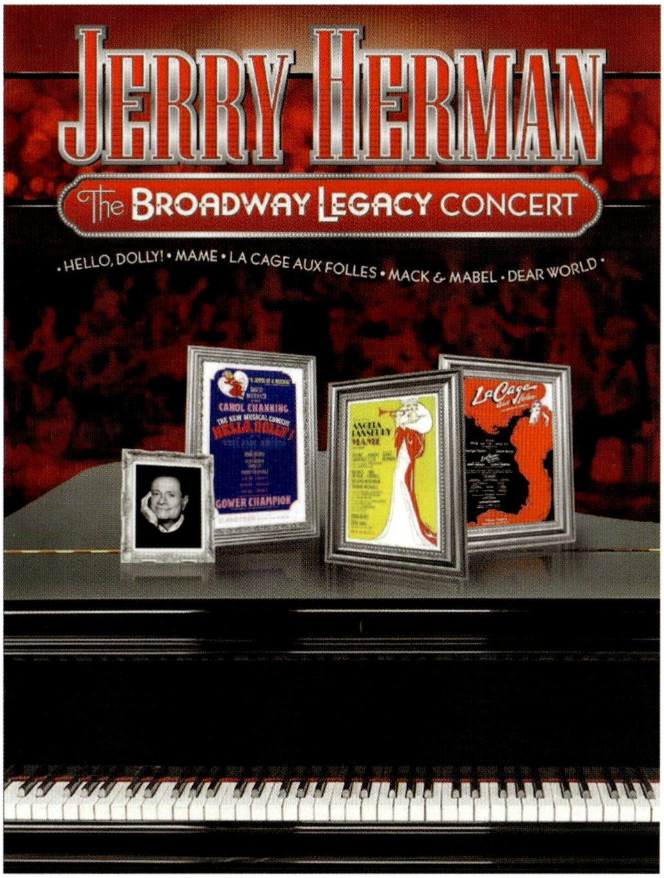

Jerry Herman Ring Theatre at the University of Miami, honors composer and lyricist Jerry Herman, Coral Gables, n.d.

Jerry Herman (1931–), known for his work in Broadway musical theater, composed the scores for *Milk and Honey* (about Israel), *Hello Dolly!*, *Mame*, *La Cage aux Folles*, and others. Many of his show tunes have become pop standards. In 1953 he graduated from the University of Miami, where he produced, wrote, and directed a college musical called *Sketchbook*. It was scheduled to run for three performances, but the show created an instant patron demand and ran for an additional seventeen performances. He's been nominated five times for the Tony Award and won twice. In 2009 Herman received the Tony Award for Lifetime Achievement in the Theater. He received the 2010 Kennedy Center Honor. Jerry Herman lives on Miami Beach.

Adrienne Arsht Performing Arts Center, opened in 2006, Miami, 2008.

This is one of the largest performing arts centers in the nation with 570,000 square feet, nearly 5,000 seats in three halls, and more than 300 annual performances. Business leader Adrienne Arsht donated $30 million to the construction costs. Arsht began her law career in 1966, briefly joined the legal department of Trans World Airlines, and then started her own title company—all before she moved to Miami in 1996 to run her family-owned bank, TotalBank. As chairman until 2007, she grew the bank from four locations to fourteen, then sold the bank for $300 million. A philanthropist to University of Miami and others, in 2004, Arsht became the first woman in Miami-Dade County's United Way Million Dollar Roundtable. Arsht was the first woman to receive the Carnegie Hall Medal of Excellence in 2017.

Dr. Phillips Center for the Performing Arts, opened in 2014, Orlando, 2017.

This new center is named for philanthropist and citrus magnate Dr. Philip Phillips, who you met in part 3, chapter 1. The center is within walking distance of the house he and his wife, Della, owned nearly 100 years ago. In his day, Dr. Phillips hosted many concerts, bringing acclaimed musicians from all around the world to play on his front lawn for the entire Orlando community to enjoy. Housed on a 9-acre, 2-block site, this center is scheduled for completion in 2020 with 5,125 seats in 4 halls and arts education spaces. The goal is to enhance city life and create a vibrant gathering place for socialization and cultural enrichment. It has been named one of *Travel + Leisure* magazine's "25 New Tourist Attractions Worth Adding to Your Bucket List" and one of *Southern Living* magazine's "50 Best Places in the South Now."

Museums

You already know the Jewish Museum of Florida–FIU from the introduction. The JMOF opened the same year as the Wolfsonian (1995), and the Bass already had a presence, so there are now three museums on Miami Beach founded by Jews. Both the JMOF and the Wolfsonian are part of Florida International University, which also hosts the Patricia and Phillip Frost Art Museum on its campus. Miami's Phillip and Patricia Frost Museum of Science also reflects that couple's vast commitment to Florida's cultural life.

Miami Jewish collectors of contemporary art have contributed a major impact to the international art scene. The Rubell Family Collection (RFC), comprised of more than five thousand artworks, opened in 1993 in a forty-five-thousand-square-foot facility in Miami's Wynwood Arts District. The goal of Mera and Don Rubell with their son Jason is to expand the RFC's public mission inside the paradigm of a contemporary art museum. It is now one of the world's largest privately owned, publicly accessible contemporary art collections.

Opened in 1999, the Margulies Collection at the Warehouse is located in a forty-five-thousand-square-foot retrofitted warehouse, also in the Wynwood Arts District. The warehouse presents seasonal exhibitions from the collection of Martin Z. Margulies, as well as educational programs and special exhibitions and an international loan program.

Some other Floridian Jewish collectors include Richard Levy (Judaica), Florence and Robert Werner and Myra and Sheldon Palley (glass), Ruth and Marvin Sackner (language-based artworks), and Jay Kislak (rare books, manuscripts, and historic artifacts).

Jews are or have been directors of many museums in Florida, including Jo Ann Arnowitz (Jewish Museum of Florida-FIU), Carolyn Bass (Florida Holocaust Museum), Arthur Blumenthal (Cornell Fine Arts Museum, Rollins College), Diane Camber (Bass Museum of Art), Jeremy Chestler (Art Center South Florida), Bonnie Clearwater (Museum of Contemporary Art and Nova Southeastern University Art Museum), Jolene Fabricant (Florida Holocaust Museum), Elizabeth Gelman (Florida Holocaust Museum), Susan Gladstone (Jewish Museum of Florida-FIU), Joel Hoffman (Vizcaya Museum and Gardens), Sharon S. Horowitz (Holocaust Memorial Miami), Pam Kancher (Holocaust Memorial Resource and Education Center), Rositta Kenigsberg (Holocaust Documentation & Education Center), Cathy Leff (Wolfsonian-FIU and Bakehouse Art Complex), Irvin Lippman (Nova Southeastern University Art Museum and Boca Raton Museum of Art), R. Andrew Maass (Florida Holocaust Museum and Tampa Museum of Art), Avi Mizrachi (Holocaust Memorial Miami), Dahlia Morgan (FIU Gallery), Jordana Pomeroy (Frost Museum of Art at FIU), Larry Rosenzweig (Morakami Museum and Japanese Gardens), Ellen Saltpeter (Institute of Contemporary Art), David Schaefer (Florida Holocaust Museum),

Chana Sheldon (Museum of Contemporary Art), Mindy Shrago (Young at Art), Debbie Spiegelman (Miami Children's Museum), Susan Suarez (Holocaust Museum of Southwest Florida), Larry Wasser (Florida Holocaust Museum), Naomi Wilzig (World Erotic Museum), Tess Wise (Holocaust Memorial Resource and Education Center), and Marcia Jo Zerivitz, LHD (Jewish Museum of Florida).

The Bass Museum of Art (left) and the Wolfsonian-FIU are museums on Miami Beach.

Opened in 1964 in an Art Deco building as a showcase for a collection of old masters, modern paintings, textiles, and sculptures donated by the retired sugar baron John Bass and his wife, Johanna, the Bass belongs to the City of Miami Beach. Now a contemporary art museum, it completed a major renovation in 2017.

Miamian Mitchell "Micky" Wolfson Jr. (1939–) founded his museum (right) in 1995 to preserve his 180,000 objects, including furniture, decorative arts, paintings, books, prints, and ephemera from the period 1885–1945. The museum uses them to illustrate the persuasive power of art and design, to explore what it means to be modern, and to tell the story of social, political, and technological changes that have transformed our world. It encourages people to see the world in new ways and to learn from the past as they shape the present and influence the future. The 1927 Mediterranean revival building was originally the Washington Storage Company.

During World War II, Abraham Rattner used his talents to help with the war effort; this became a poster, 1940.
Leepa-Rattner Museum of Art and SPC Foundation, Inc.

This artwork by Rattner is titled *Save Liberty: Buy US War Bonds*, gouache on board, 37 ½ x 27 ½ in. (1997.1.1.345). Opened in 2002, the Leepa-Rattner Museum of Art is located on the Tarpon Springs campus of St. Petersburg College. It was established by artist, educator, and author Dr. Allen Leepa and his wife, Isabelle, with support from St. Petersburg College and the State of Florida. The initial gift to the museum included works by Leepa's stepfather, renowned figurative expressionist artist Abraham Rattner; Rattner's second wife, Esther Gentle, a printmaker, sculptor, and painter; and abstract expressionist artist Allen Leepa. Also included was an extensive collection of works by notable twentieth-century artists such as Pablo Picasso, Marc Chagall, Fernand Léger, and Henry Moore.

Abraham Rattner (1893–1978), known for his richly colored paintings often portraying his Jewish heritage, served in the US Army in France during World War I, remained after the war, and stayed in Paris until

1940. He became part of the modernist group there, close to Picasso and writer Henry Miller, with whom he took a road trip around the US. He lived in New York City for the remainder of his career.

Art collectors and founders of the Institute of Contemporary Art (ICA), Norman and Irma Braman beside Picasso's *The Lovers* (1923), Miami, 2017.
Estate of Pablo Picasso/Artists Rights Society (ARS), New York, Max Reed for the New York Times.

Norman Braman was having lunch with his friend, real estate developer Craig Robins, and said, "I'd love to have a museum." Robins said, "I have this piece of land." It was that simple for Irma and Norman Braman to birth this $75 million museum—37,500 square feet, with a jigsaw pattern of color-changing triangular glass panels on the main facade—that opened in 2017 in Miami's Design District, offering free admission. The focus of the Institute of Contemporary Art (ICA) is on emerging artists who have yet to receive much institutional exposure or mid-to late career artists whose work is being discovered for the first time in America. Referencing the Picasso in this photograph, Braman says he is continuously drawn to it. "It could be a contemporary painting today. The color is incredible." His collecting philosophy is "If you have the opportunity to have the best of the artist, then if you overpay, it doesn't matter. Eventually the market will reward you. If it raises the value of our collection, we go for it."

Internationally significant Jay Kislak Collection of Rare Books, Manuscripts, and Historic Artifacts given to the University of Miami and Miami Dade College, Miami, 2017.

Jay Kislak (center) pictured at the landmark $30 million gift announcement with Dr. Eduardo J. Padrón, president of Miami Dade College (left), and Dr. Julio Frenk, president of the University of Miami (right).

"For 500 years, Florida has been a focal point of global exploration and cultural exchange," Jay Kislak said. "I'm thrilled that Miami's top two institutions of higher education, along with the Library of Congress in Washington, DC, will now be using our Collections to reveal the fascinating and important role of our community in world history." Each institution received a first edition of the famous 1493 letter of Christopher Columbus, in which the explorer described his New World discoveries to King Ferdinand and Queen Isabella of Spain.

Entrepreneur Jay Kislak (1922–2018) made his mark in real estate and establishing what would become one of the country's largest privately held mortgage banks. A Miami resident for more than sixty years, he was a lifelong collector, focused particularly on Florida and the Caribbean, exploration, navigation, and the early Americas. In 2004 he and his foundation donated to the Library of Congress more than four thousand items, including the 1516 Carta Marina Navigatoria, the first printed navigational map of the world by the celebrated German mapmaker Martin Waldseemüller. The Kislak Collection forms the basis of a major exhibition and extensive scholarly and public programs at the Library of Congress.

CHAPTER 5

Healing Sciences

Florida Jewish professionals have contributed to the quality of life in the fields of medicine, dentistry, and pharmacology, as well as building hospitals and medical schools.

Dr. Louis Sims Oppenheimer practiced medicine and surgery in Florida, 1884–1939, Tampa, circa 1900.

The 1977 *Journal of the Florida Medical Association* features an article, "Culture Among the Sandspurs," about Dr. Oppenheimer (1854–1939), referring to him as the "Dean of the Florida Profession." A son of Orthodox German immigrants who devoted their entire lives to educating their children, Louis began violin, English, German, and French lessons at the age of six. He went to medical school in Louisville, Kentucky. When Henry Plant began building his railroad from Georgia into Florida in 1884, Oppenheimer heard there were few physicians and drugstores. He boarded the train; rode it to the end of the line, which was Bartow; began his medical practice; opened the first drugstore there; and married the music teacher Alberta Dozier in 1888. They had six gifted children. In 1891, when Henry Plant opened his all-electric-five-hundred-room hotel in Tampa, he invited Dr. Oppenheimer to move there as the house physician. He served as a translator at the hotel and president of every medical society he joined. His X-ray equipment was the first in Tampa. He performed the first appendectomy in Tampa (1896), and his life saving efforts led to histology as a required subject for medical students. When the Spanish-American War broke out in 1898, Oppenheimer wrote the US War Department about the advantages of the embarkation of troops from the Tampa Bay Hotel and port—and helped win the contract for the city. Dr. Oppenheimer had many famous patients, such as Theodore Roosevelt, William Jennings Bryan, and Thomas Edison.

Dr. Mozart Lischkoff was president of the Escambia County Medical Society in 1929 and 1936, Pensacola, circa 1925.

His Polish father, Alex Lischkoff, settled in Pensacola in 1883 and started a jewelry business. Alex married Frances Forcheimer in 1889, and Mozart was one of their three children. Mozart graduated Tulane Medical School around 1906 and also studied in Europe. During World War I, 1st Lieutenant Mozart Lischkoff, MD (medicinae doctor), was in the medical corp. He became a specialist in throat, nose, eye, and ear diseases. In 1918 Lischkoff was selected King Priscus Carnival at Mardi Gras, acknowledging his strong civic involvement.

M. Ervin Wahnish, DDS (doctor of dental surgery; shown with his wife, Jackie), was the first-known Jewish dentist in Orlando, circa 1943.

Dr. Wahnish, nativc of Tallahassee, was a son of tobacco grower Alfred Wahnish, who you met in part 3, chapter 1. He opened his dental office in Orlando after his service in the US Army during World War II. He was one of the first to enter the field of high-speed dentistry and was instrumental in bringing this subject to Florida dentists through clinics and lectures. In 1959 Wahnish was elected president of the Central Florida District Dental Society, and in 1977 he patented an idea for a tooth implant.

Following World War II, Dr. Samuel and Sarah Webber Kaplan opened a medical practice in Venice, 1950.

US Army 2nd Lieutenant Sarah Webber (1919–2005) served in the Army Nurse Corps during World War II. Afterward, she married Dr. Kaplan (1915–98), and they settled in Venice, where Samuel was the first Jewish doctor in the area. Sarah was his nurse for thirty-plus years. Practicing medicine until 1998, Samuel used the *mohel* and *shochet* knives, passed down from his father, to perform Jewish ceremonies in Venice, Sarasota, and Miami. Those knives are on exhibit at the JMOF-FIU. Their three children live in Venice.

US Navy Pharmacist's Mate 3rd Class Sorrell Wolfson became a nationally renowned researcher in pediatric hematology and oncology, Tampa, 1946.

This Tampa-born son of Mildred and Abe Wolfson enlisted in the Navy during World War II, where he was assigned as a corpsman on an aircraft carrier. This spurred his interest in medicine. After being discharged, Wolfson used his GI Bill to attend college and medical school and opened his practice in Tampa.

Mount Sinai Hospital was an outcome of antisemitism, Board of Trustees meeting, Miami Beach, 1951.

Seated left to right are Fannie Selig, Mitchell Wolfson, Joseph Stein, Sam Blank, Leonard Wien, Abe Goodman, Max Orovitz, Baron de Hirsch Meyer, Harry Sirkin, William Singer, Dr. Morris Goodman, Arthur Ungar, and Herbert Scher. Standing left to right are Samuel Gertner, Leonard Abess, Carl Weinkle, Monte Selig, Stanley Myers, Sam Friedland, and Jack Ablin.

When Jewish doctors returned home to Dade County from World War II, they were denied staff privileges in hospitals. So a group of Jewish leaders decided to create their own hospital and received their charter from the State of Florida in 1946. The first facility was Alton Road Hospital. Three years later, more space was needed, so the group purchased what once was Carl Fisher's restricted Nautilus Hotel from the City of Miami Beach at a cost of one dollar per year for 20 years. Max Orovitz was the founding chairman for three decades. Today, the 55-acre medical center with 672 beds, 650 physicians, and 5 satellite locations throughout Miami-Dade County is the largest employer on Miami Beach and the largest independent nonprofit hospital in south Florida. It is a state-of-the-art medical facility and teaching hospital that continues to expand and is renowned for its leadership in medicine, especially cardiac care.

The Dauer Family was responsible for the creation of the Florida Medical Center, Lauderdale Lakes, 1970s.

During World War II, scientist, educator, and philanthropist Dr. Maxwell Dauer was assistant medical director for the top secret Manhattan Project (the atomic bomb project). In the early 1960s, Dr. Dauer; his wife, Reva; and their sons, Roger and Edward, moved to southeast Florida after Dr. Dauer was appointed chief of the Division of Radiophysics in the Department of Radiology at the University of Miami (UM) Medical School. In 1968 Dr. Dauer purchased forty-seven acres of undeveloped land in west Broward County that only a few decades earlier had been swampland. On a portion, he developed the Florida Medical Center (1973) and Memorial Hospital (1978).

After Maxwell retired, his son and radiologist Dr. Edward Dauer (UM Medical School, 1975) and his wife, Joanne, a former critical care nurse and hospital administrator, took over and built the practice into one of the largest groups in Florida. Edward, a noted scholar who holds degrees in medicine and biomedical engineering, is an author and a member of the full-time faculty of UM's College of Engineering. Dauer was on the Florida State Board of Medicine for eleven years, serving two terms as chairman. He is an avid collector of vintage 1950s and 1960s automobiles, stamps, and currency.

Dr. Marshall Warren Nirenberg (right) receives the Nobel Prize in Physiology or Medicine from King Gustav of Sweden, with Princess Christina (center), Sweden, 1968.

The Nobel recognition was for deciphering the genetic code and describing how it operates in protein synthesis. Nirenberg (1927–2010) developed rheumatic fever as a boy, so in 1937 the family moved from New York to Orlando for the climate. He began his scientific career by catching bugs. Nirenberg graduated from Orlando High School (1944) and received his bachelor's and master's degrees in zoology from the University of Florida where he was a member of the Pi Lambda Phi Fraternity. He received his PhD in biochemistry from the University of Michigan (1957). That year, he joined the staff of the National Institutes of Health (NIH) as chief of biochemical genetics and remained there for the rest of his career. When I interviewed him at NIH in 1988, he was a congenial mix of serious and spirited, and when he died, his wife donated meaningful artifacts from his Nobel work and prize presentation to the JMOF-FIU.

Dr. Richard Hodes (right), 1979 president of the Florida Medical Association, on Air Force One with US President Jimmy Carter, 1980.

A prominent Tampa physician, Dr. Hodes was a leader in the Florida House of Representative for sixteen years, helped fashion the Medicaid legislation, and was instrumental in drafting plans to consolidate health, institutional, and welfare services. He served as president of the Hillsborough County Medical Association and first chairman of the Department of Anesthesiology of the University of South Florida College of Medicine. Dr. Hodes portrayed US Senator David Levy Yulee for the opening event of the JMOF in 1995.

Dr. Gregor Alexander holds a premature baby in the world's largest neonatal intensive care unit under one roof, Winnie Palmer Hospital, Orlando, 2015.

Neonatology pioneer Dr. Alexander has treated premature infants in Orlando since 1975. Opening at Orange Regional Medical Center, moving to Arnold Palmer Hospital in 1989, then going to Winnie Palmer for Women and Children in 2006, the Alexander Center for Neonatology has cared for more than forty thousand critically ill newborns. Dr. Alexander believes success is based on treating both the physical and emotional needs of these babies and their families.

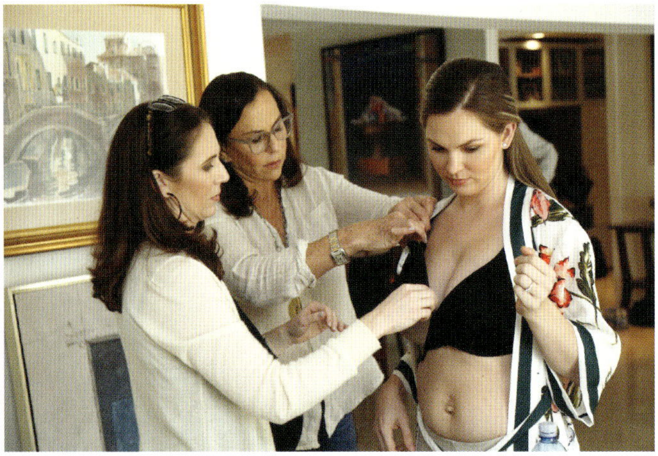

Cofounders Rachael Sablotsky Kish (left) and Noreen Gordon Sablotsky (center) demonstrate their Imalac nursing/pumping bra, Nurture, Miami, 2018.

Noreen Gordon Sablotsky of St. Petersburg and then Miami is a proven leader in the pharmaceutical and medical devices industry. In 1987 she cofounded (with Steven Sablotsky) Noven Pharmaceuticals for the development and commercialization of transdermal drug delivery systems, the most notable being estrogen replacements and a dental anesthetic patch. Currently, she and her daughter Rachael have developed the first nursing and pumping bra that enhances the results of breast pumping for lactating women. The Nurture by Imalac features an attachable massage cup designed to mimic the motion of hand expression that radically increases the efficiency of breast pumping.

In 1987 Dr. Phillip Frost founded Ivax Corp., the world's top producer of generic drugs, Miami, 1987. *Photo by Michael Price.*

Dr. Frost was chair of the Department of Dermatology at Mount Sinai Medical Center (1972–90) and chairman of the board of Key Pharmaceuticals (1972–86). Ivax, a public company, was acquired by the Israeli company Teva Pharmaceutical Industries in 2006. The University of Miami's Music School, Florida International University's Art Museum, and Miami's Museum of Science all bear his name and the name of his wife, Patricia.

Hill Dermaceuticals is the only company in nongeneric pharmaceuticals in the US that has a single owner, Jerry Roth, Sanford, 2017.

After college, Roth worked for a small Tampa company and learned to understand markets. In the 1970s he began his own company, developing and marketing products for skin diseases. A generous donor to Orlando's Roth Family JCC, Jerry Roth received a University of Central Florida honorary doctorate for his support of its academic and athletic programs. In 2002 UCF did a study that showed it would cost $130 million to build a new stadium. Jerry researched pre-engineered facilities on his own, and UCF found a successful way to use his plan and build it for around $54 million.

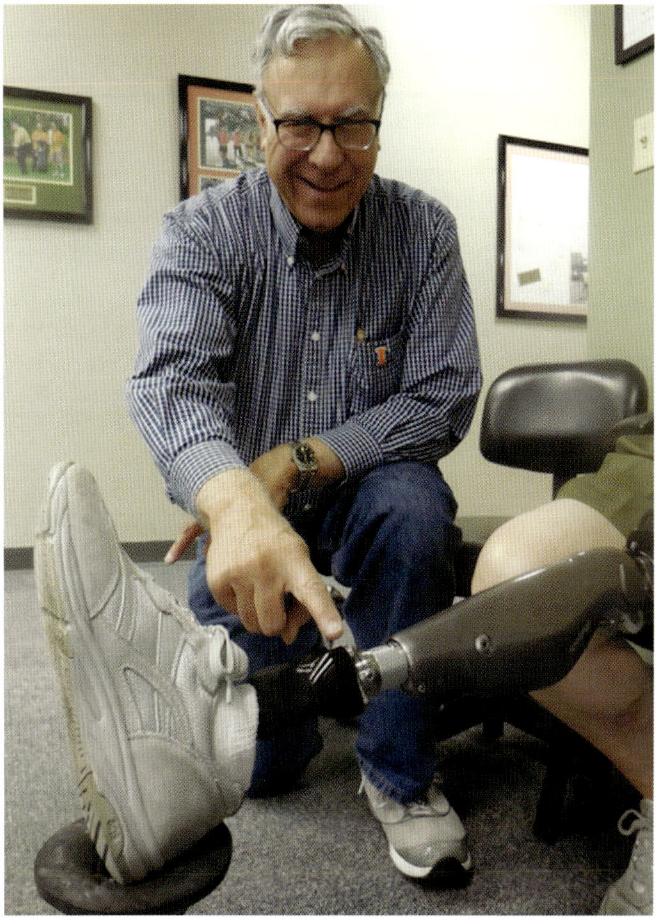

Dr. Les Kramer developed prosthetic foot and socket technologies, Orlando, 2016.

Dr. Kramer had a forty-five-year career with Westinghouse (Siemens), Lockheed Martin, and various independent contractors for which he directed advanced materials research, bringing thousands of high-tech jobs to central Florida. He is credited with seventy publications and fifteen patents. Kramer developed advanced materials concepts for prosthetics including prosthetic foot and socket technologies. Two of the 2013 Boston Marathon bombing victims were able to walk again using artificial feet manufactured by his company, TaiLore Made. Kramer's Lake Mary–based enterprises design and distribute the prosthetics.

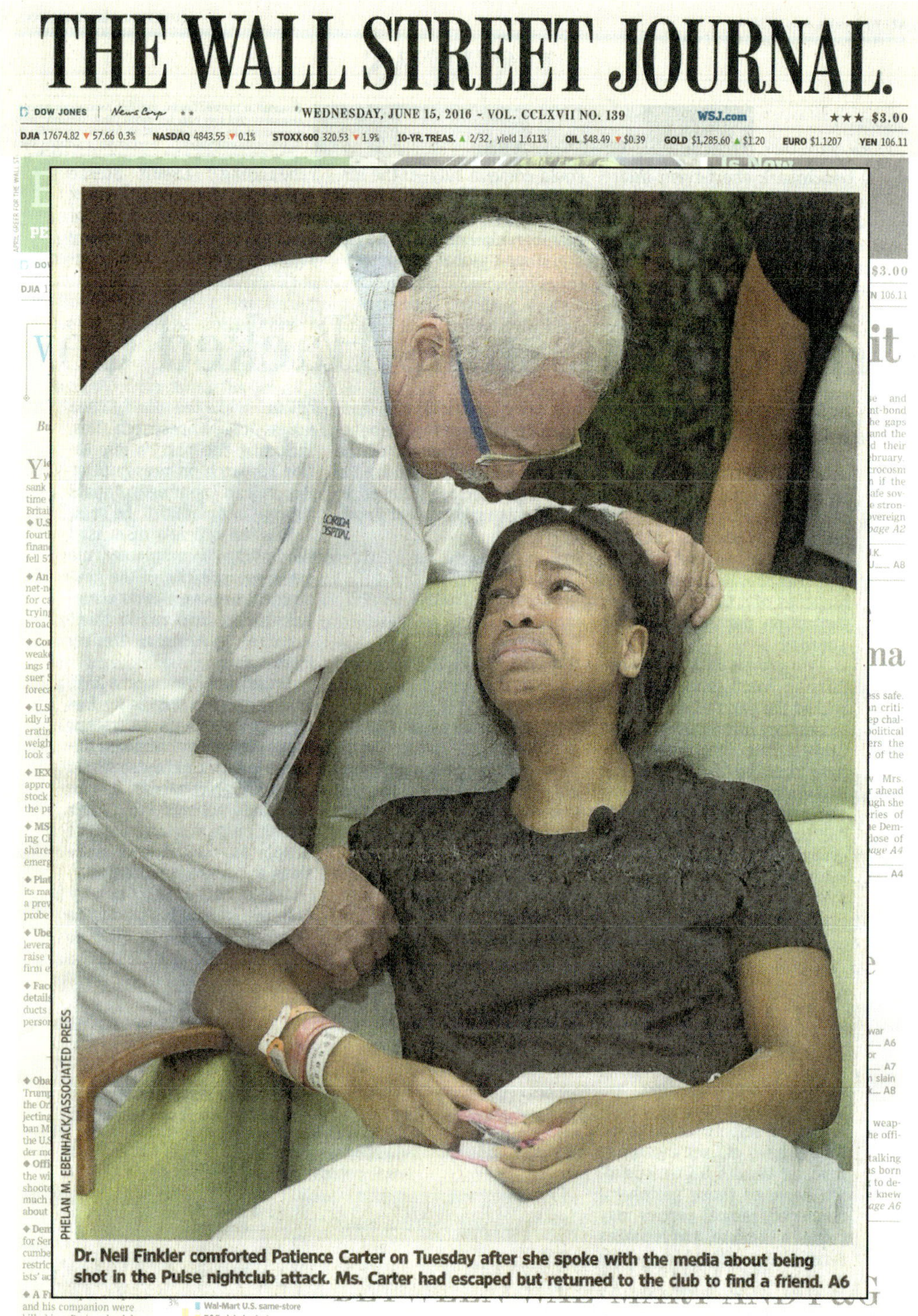

Dr. Neil Finkler, chief medical officer of Florida Hospital Orlando, comforted Patience Carter, a twenty-year-old college student shot in the leg during the Pulse massacre, Orlando, 2016. Wall Street Journal, *June 15, 2016.*

National and international media covered the Pulse massacre for weeks, showing the world not only the horror of the event but also the kindness of Orlando in response. Twelve patients were transported to Florida Hospital from the Pulse nightclub. Dr. Finkler came to Orlando with his wife, Tina, and three children in 1992 to found Florida Hospital Cancer Institute's Gynecology Oncology Program.

CHAPTER 6

Florida Jewish Techies

In 1974 Sidney Stark was named vice president and general manager of the Orlando Division of Martin, Orlando, 1960.

During World War II, Stark worked with Charles Lindbergh on airplane design and later was selected as one of a group of engineers to review German missile documents. Stark was key to winning business for Martin Orlando. In 1956 he became chief engineer for the newly formed Orlando Division. He led the Bullpup, Lacrosse, Pershing, and Sprint programs. In 1974 he was awarded the US Army's Outstanding Civilian Service Award. Stark was head of Martin Orlando until 1976, guiding the division out of a deep recession and helping to secure contracts to develop Patriot missiles that were later deployed to intercept Scud missile attacks in Israel.

Leonard Arnowitz (left), chief engineer of the Vanguard rocket project for Martin, Cape Canaveral, 1960.

Vanguard was the prototype for much of what became the US space program. When Arnowitz became part of the Vanguard project in 1958, he moved his family to central Florida. He and a handful of other Jewish residents built the first synagogue at the Space Coast for 103 families, and he served as president. Congregation board meetings often took place during lunch at the testing facility. Despite the difficulties experienced with buying kosher meat, which had to be sent by bus from Miami, the Arnowitz family kept a kosher home. In 1962 Arnowitz moved to Orlando to work on the Pershing missile under Sidney Stark. He published extensively and held several patents. His son Gary and his family live in south Florida.

NASA astronaut wearing space suit and backpack designed by Harry Kaplan, Cape Canaveral, 1970.

Harry Kaplan of Melbourne contributed to the design of the space suits and backpacks for the life support systems of the astronauts. He received many awards, including the "Silver Snoopy" in 1973 for his work on Apollo 17, presented by the astronauts.

Sheryl Sandberg is chief operating officer of Facebook, Miami, circa 2015.

As a mother, businesswoman, author, activist, and tech pioneer, Sandberg has been a role model and inspirational leader for many. She grew up in North Miami Beach where the 1987 high school yearbook lists Sandberg in the National Honor Society. Sandberg's post-Miami life is well documented. At Harvard, she majored in economics and cofounded an organization called Women in Economics and Government. After graduating summa cum laude, she became a research assistant at the World Bank, working for one of her professors, Lawrence Summers. She returned to Harvard for a master of business administration degree and became chief of staff in the late 1990s for Summers when he was assistant secretary at the US Treasury Department. When Summers became Treasury secretary in 1999, Sandberg, just twenty-nine, continued as his chief of staff.

In 2001 Sandberg decided the internet was the future—first at Google for six years, now as number two at Facebook since 2008. *Forbes* ranked her the fifth most powerful woman in the world. Sandberg founded Leanin.org, a nonprofit named after her best-selling book of the same name, to support women's empowerment.

Option B, written after her husband, Dave Goldberg, died, was released in 2017 and focuses on grief and resilience. Sandberg has reached the heights of success in business while still finding time to speak about the need for women to support each other. And that's what she practices—maintaining a circle of women friends from middle and high school in North Miami Beach, their relationships forged while riding bikes or camping out for concert tickets.

Martin Uman (left), shown with Ben Franklin's equipment at the Franklin Institute, is a lightning expert, Philadelphia, 1970s.

A Tampa native and 1953 valedictorian of Plant High School, Martin Uman (1936–), wrote *All About Lightning* and other books and hundreds of articles on the subject. One of nature's most awesome phenomena, lighting has intrigued man since earliest times. Uman is an internationally known expert in lightning research at the University of Florida. In 1975 he founded Lightning Location and Protection Inc. He was awarded the Gold Medal as Florida's Scientist of the Year in 1990. In 2001 he received the American Geophysical Union John Adam Fleming Medal for "outstanding contribution to the description and understanding of electricity and magnetism of the earth and its atmosphere."

Myron Uman joined the National Research Council, 1975.

In 1986 Myron Uman (1939–), brother of Martin, was appointed executive director of the research panel advising NASA on the redesign of the shuttle's booster rockets following the *Challenger* accident. He was given the NASA Public Service Medal, and in 1989 the astronauts presented their own "Silver Snoopy" to Uman and the panel. Currently living in West Palm Beach, he is a consultant to government and industry on applications of current scientific and technical understanding to environmental and energy issues.

In 1977 Steve Goldman founded Distributed Processing Technology (DPT), the first company to develop and manufacture storage controllers for the computer industry, Orlando.

Kim (front center) and Alison (far right) Mandell Knapp with their staff at Maynard Electronics to service the computer industry, Casselberry, 1987.

Goldman is a world-recognized expert and pioneer in computer storage technology. In the 1980s he helped create computer interface standards for the American National Standards Institute (ANSI). Distributed Processing Technology created more than three-hundred highly skilled and professional jobs in Orlando. DPT invented the PM2554 caching and PM3754112 RAID (Redundant Array of Inexpensive Disks) disk controllers that increase storage speed and decrease the risk of data loss. The US Department of Commerce's E Flag award recognizes America's exporters and was presented to DPT. Goldman served as interim CEO of the Orlando Science Center and created "Wired Science," a STEM program that teaches through sound, graphics, animation, and video. His web-based animated math and physics learning project, "Why U," attracts tens of thousands of global subscribers.

In 1981 the Knapps started Maynard Electronics in their Lake Mary home. Because personal computers were unreliable, they saw a business opportunity making products for IBM (International Business Machines) PCs. Maynard Electronics produced the first IBM-compatible hard drive system, expansion cards, CPU accelerators, and the first multithreading tape backup, improving backup time over competitive products. Maynard Electronics employed one-hundred-plus high-tech and skilled personnel. Later sold and then merged, it is currently a division of Symantec Corporation.

Steve Sinofsky, president of the Windows Division at Microsoft, speaking at the company headquarters, 2009.

Orlando native Sinofsky joined Microsoft as a software design engineer in 1989 and moved up the company ladder to become president of the Windows Division at Microsoft (2009–12). He was responsible for the development and marketing of Windows and Internet Explorer, as well as online services such as Outlook.com and SkyDrive. Sinofsky is currently a board partner at Andreessen Horowitz, where he serves on the board of investments. Sinofsky also coauthored the book *One Strategy: Organization, Planning, and Decision Making* (John Wiley & Sons, 2009).

Mitchell Laskey is holding a BIS (Brijot Imaging Systems) concealed weapons detection camera, Orlando, 2011.
Gulf Coast Business Review.

Laskey relocated his software-based health-care company Dynamic Control Corporation (DCC) to Central Florida in 1982 to hire workers with technical skills. This resulted in four hundred new jobs in Lake Mary. As CEO of BIS (Brijot Imaging Systems), he testified before Congress on the use of advanced technology for various Homeland Security initiatives including passenger screening for airports. He was the driving force behind the Florida Angel Nexus Fund, focusing on high-growth potential technology and life science companies in Florida.

Aaron Fechter invented the Rock-afire Explosion show that includes the keyboard-playing gorilla, Fatz Geronimo (left), Orlando, 2011. *Photo by Seth Christie.*

Aaron Fechter attended Orlando schools, experimented with electronics, studied piano, and loved the Beatles. After graduating from the University of South Florida, Fechter started a career in Orlando as an engineering entrepreneur. In the 1980s he founded Creative Engineering and invented the Whac-A-Mole, the animatronic characters featured at Showbiz Pizza Place (later Chuck E. Cheese's). The Rock-afire Explosion show was installed in two hundred Showbiz Pizza Place restaurants, entertainment centers, and amusement parks around the world. In 2011 it was released on iTunes. In recent years, this show performed as the backup band for Cee Lo Green in Las Vegas and appeared in *Just Go with It* starring Adam Sandler and *Keanu* starring Keegan-Michael Key and Jordan Peele.

CHAPTER 7

Architecture

The unique design hallmarks of distinguished Florida Jewish architects that blend their professional training and heritage with the environment are all over Florida buildings. Some who have already been mentioned in other chapters of this book include Henry Hohauser, Morris Lapidus, and Kenneth Treister.

Roy Benjamin, who designed two-hundred-plus movie theaters, with granddaughter Phyllis Benjamin, Jacksonville, 1960.

Designed by Roy Benjamin in 1934, the Colony Theatre on Lincoln Road is an Art Deco classic, Miami Beach, 2014.
Photo by Karel Miragaya, 123RF.com.

This theater opened in 1935 as a movie house and has evolved into a full-blown 417-seat performing arts center much sought after today for its prime location and beautiful Art Deco trappings. It recently underwent a 3-year $6.5 million renovation. Architect Roy Benjamin (1887–1963) was a descendent of a family (you met in part 1, chapter 1) who settled in Florida in 1865. He moved from Ocala to Jacksonville in 1901, where he began his professional career. Benjamin was a prolific designer of movie theaters and apartment buildings throughout Florida and other parts of the South. Among his earliest was the Arcade Theater in Jacksonville in 1915, which was proclaimed to be the South's largest and best-equipped movie house with 1,250 seats. The Opera House (originally 1926 Edwards Theater) in Sarasota was the site for the world premiere of Cecil B. DeMille's *The Greatest Show on Earth* on January 31, 1952. He designed a theater in Lake Worth (1940) that now is the home for the Palm Beach Cultural Council. Benjamin served on the national board of the American Institute of Architects as a theater specialist. In the 1920s he designed the first skyscraper in south Florida in Lakeland, a 10-story marble arcade building. Benjamin retired in 1945.

Norman M. Giller helped reshape South Florida's landscape using his MiMo (Miami Modernism) style to design ten-thousand-plus structures during his sixty-year career, Miami Beach, circa 1952. *Giller & Giller Architects Archives.*

Norman M. Giller designed the Carillon Hotel that is now the Carillon Spa, rendering, Miami Beach, 1957–58. *Giller & Giller Architects Archives.*

The career of Jacksonville native Norman M. Giller, FAIA (Fellow of the American Institute of Architects; 1918–2008) was unique in that he wore many hats: architect, military veteran, banker, civic leader, and author. In 1944 he received his degree in architecture from the University of Florida. His first architectural position was with Henry Hohauser at fifty cents per hour. Giller started building his Miami Beach practice right after serving in World War II when the postwar building boom was in full gear and architects in high demand, designing for both government and private construction.

His influence can still be seen in the use of sleek lines, flat roofs, and geometric patterns of tile, metal, and glass in many buildings. During the 1960s, Giller went international, opening offices in Central and South America. Norman Giller & Associates became the nation's tenth largest-in-volume firm. In the late 1970s, he added to the firm his son Ira D. Giller, architect and general contractor.

This is the team that was responsible for the transformation of the JMOF-FIU buildings from two synagogues to a museum. I worked closely with Norman on the creation of the JMOF as he was the founding president, my creative mentor, and a smart businessman. The 1983 Norman M. Giller Bridge, connecting Aventura and Sunny Isles, is believed to be the only bridge named for a living architect. Giller served as chairman of the Florida State Board of Architecture and president of the American Institute of Architects, South Florida chapter. A culmination of his many civic leadership positions was being named by the Miami Beach Chamber of Commerce, the 1995 Man of the Year. Norman and granddaughter Sarah Giller Nelson compiled his works in *Designing the Good Life* in 2007.

Alan Berman (inset), an architect responsible for scores of prominent Central Florida buildings, designed this award-winning, three-story triplex, Winter Park, 2003.

This building won a Grand Aurora Award, which is a design competition of the Southeast Building Conference, a program of the Home Builders Association. Alan Berman (1930–2018) graduated in architecture from the University of Florida and at first practiced in Miami Beach where his father, George Berman, was a developer. One of Alan's first jobs was to design the roadside sign for Sunny Isles's Ocean Palm Motel, the first motel with two levels of guest rooms (1950–2009), developed and owned by his father—and designed by Norman M. Giller. Alan's midcentury modernist sign became a beloved local landmark. He met his wife, Florida native Marcia Gibbs of Deland, when their parents arranged a blind date. (You met her father, David Gibbs of the Live Oak Gibbs family, in part 3, chapter 2.) For nearly four decades, Berman designed central Florida office buildings, shopping centers, hotels such as the Sheraton Maitland and Sheraton World Hotel at SeaWorld Orlando and many iconic modern, custom homes.

Marketing brochure for Kinneret I, designed by Ernest Rapp, Orlando, 1967.

Left to right: Jerry Bornstein, Murray Schwartz, architect Ernest Rapp (standing), and Elliott Zerivitz signing Kinneret II mortgage, Orlando, 1978.

The design skills of Ernest Rapp (1919–2008) helped him flee the Nazis and fueled his career in architecture in the Orlando area. When the Germans invaded his native Austria, he was a design student in high school, working on plans for an Irish company, which brought him to Ireland. He then came to New York, where he graduated from Columbia University in architecture and met his wife, Sylvia. In 1956 they resettled in Orlando where his designs dot the entire area—from the State Office Building to restaurants and senior citizen high-rises such as Kinneret, Lucerne Towers, Magnolia Towers, Orlando Central Towers, Baptist Towers, and Calvary Towers. He also designed similar buildings in Miami, Jacksonville, and out of state.

CHAPTER 8

Real Estate, Development, Builders, and Their Support System

The developers and builders and those in allied industries represented here are a tiny sampling of the number of Jews who have helped shape our state from swampland. Certainly, one of Florida's earliest developers was a Jew who you've already met—Moses E. Levy. Location was what must have been on the mind of Mr. Levy in 1820 when he began purchasing one hundred thousand acres in north central Florida. Since then, Jews have been involved in every aspect of the development of Florida. As risk-takers with various enterprises, they purchased land for development; built residential, office, and retail communities; designed buildings as well as subdivisions and cities; provided the financing for development; sold building materials; and argued before zoning boards and city and county commissions on behalf of development. The roles of Floridian Jews have made an indelible imprint and helped transform Florida from the South's least populous state one hundred years ago to the powerhouse that it is today.

Henri Levy, developer of Surfside and Normandy Isle, named for the region in his native France, looking over his land before clearing, Miami-Dade County, 1924.

Henri Levy moved his family to Miami Beach, "a lush tropical paradise," because a daughter had whooping cough. During a rainstorm, he ducked into the office of a real estate broker and emerged with enough land to develop two communities. This was north of Carl Fisher's property, where as a Jew he was free from restrictions and was allowed to make the purchase. Levy was also one of the moving forces behind the creation of the Seventy-Ninth Street Causeway (also known as the John F. Kennedy Memorial Causeway).

William "Bill" Horvitz holding photograph of his father, Samuel Horvitz of Hollywood Inc., 1985.
Sun-Tattler, *July 4, 1985, Hollywood Historical Society.*

In 1929 Samuel Horvitz acquired thousands of building lots in Hollywood-by-the-Sea and proceeded to develop the financially troubled city. Horvitz had been introduced to the exotic outback of southeast Florida at the outset of the 1920s when he opened a branch of his Highway Construction Company of Ohio in Miami and began paving streets and laying sidewalks in the area. By the late 1930s, Hollywood Inc. was building and selling single-family homes. By 1954 the company built its first planned residential community of several hundred homes.

Following the death of Samuel in 1956, one of his sons, Bill Horvitz, began the business's second major residential community, Hollywood Hills, featuring five thousand single-family homes. Subsequent generations of family members continued developing large swaths of Hollywood. There followed other huge, successful developments such as Emerald Hills, the first totally master planned community by Hollywood Inc., which brought it national prominence. When Bill Horvitz sold his company to developer Michael Swerdlow in 1988 for $300 million, he continued his lifetime support of worthy causes.

Russian immigrant Morris Cooper (center, holding street sign) created Cooper City, Broward County, circa 1962.

Cooper came to America in 1910 and quickly began a Horatio Alger rise to success. Along with a partner, Cooper founded the Imperial Shirt Company, which became a major clothing manufacturer with nine factories. With his wife, Clara, Cooper began investing in Broward real estate at the end of the 1930s, before moving there in the late 1950s. He established Cooper Colony Estates, which became the nucleus of the incorporated Cooper City in the early 1960s where he was the major landholder and developer.

Jacksonville's Lonnie Wurn was a Polish immigrant who made important contributions to his city, n.d.

In the era following World War II, Wurn's Peninsula Realty Company was responsible for the construction of 3,500 homes in Jacksonville, including Sans Souci, Jacqueline, Arlington, Fort Caroline, and Granada and also in St. Petersburg. Wurn (1911–2008), attorney, great promoter of his city, and avid swimmer until age ninety-six, provided Jacksonville University with an Olympic-size swimming pool and the City of Jacksonville with a swimming pool, recreation buildings, park, and boat ramp and dock on the St. Johns River, among other things.

Dudley Greenhut (left center) of Greenhut Construction chats with naval officers involved in a Naval Air Station project, Pensacola, 1975.

Austrian-born Adolph Greenhut and his wife, Sarah, settled in Pensacola in 1886. He was mayor in 1913 and a civic and Jewish community leader. His son Dudley, born in Pensacola in 1909, began Greenhut Construction as a family-run premier contractor in 1946 and ran the company until 1990. His son Bill is presently CEO with grandson Ryan Greenhut as president. Greenhut has completed over 1,200 projects worth more than $1.5 billion in 60 years, including more than 20 hospitals, 50 churches, dozens of schools, Florida's Senate and House of Representatives Office Buildings in Tallahassee, Pensacola airport, several missile test sites, bank buildings, automobile dealerships, newspaper buildings, and a golf complex. Greenhut Construction, a leader in energy and environmental design (LEED), has also been a lion in the area of giving while the Greenhuts have headed many important institutions, including a hospital, university foundation, and several charitable foundations.

Arnold Rosen and Leonard Miller combined portions of their first names to form the Lennar Corporation, listed on the New York Stock Exchange, July 27, 1972.

Beginning fourth from the left, from left to right are Muriel Rosen, Arnold Rosen, Sue Miller, Leonard Miller, and Stuart Miller. Arnold Rosen (1900–2001) began building homes in Miami in 1946 on land his father had purchased for fifty dollars a lot, using the first Veterans Affairs financing in Dade County. When he developed Coral Way Village and built two hundred homes, it had the county's first private central sewer system. After he teamed up with Leonard Miller (1933–2002), Lennar grew to become the nation's largest home builder (2017), branching out to mortgage companies, title companies, lending, and commercial management. Stuart Miller succeeded his father as CEO of Lennar. In 2018 Lennar announced that Amazon's Alexa would be included in all the thirty-five thousand new homes built that year.

Arnold and his wife, Muriel, contributed largely to the community. Leonard Miller and his wife, Sue, focused on improving education. Leonard chaired the University of Miami's board of trustees and donated funds to create the Miller Center for Contemporary Judaic Studies. After his death, his family donated $100 million to UM's medical school, now the Miller School of Medicine.

Ben Tobin (inset) purchased from the US Navy, renovated, and ran (until 1971) the seven-hundred-room Hollywood Beach Hotel, Broward County's premier hostelry, 1945.

On the way to creating a huge development portfolio, Russian immigrant Tobin started the second bank in Hollywood in the late 1950s and then sold it to Abe Mailman. He was an owner of the famed Empire State Building in New York (1950). In 1965 he developed Hillcrest, a Hollywood golf and country club, where he lived. Tobin's real estate empire stretched across the US and included shopping centers and prime downtown properties. He was an ardent Zionist and well-known philanthropist. Ben Tobin and his partners formed a company, known today as UNICO Properties Inc. that owns and manages more than seventeen million square feet of office space in the northwest US. Tobin's son and grandson are involved in this business.

Developer and banker Abraham "Abe" Mailman (left) with his friend Ben Tobin, Hollywood, circa 1967.

Mailman, a successful Canadian industrialist, came to Hollywood in 1950, becoming one of southeast Florida's most important bankers, developers, and philanthropists. He created the city of Miramar in 1953 to provide four thousand affordable homes for working people. He then developed the Three Islands property in Hollywood and Hallandale. He played a large part in shaping the Broward Jewish community. With a $1 million gift, he created the Mailman Center for Child Development at UM's Jackson Memorial Hospital. He donated eleven acres for Temple Beth El of Hollywood and founded the A. L. Mailman Family Foundation and the Mailman Family Center at Nova Southeastern University.

Joseph Weinfeld (right) and Gabriel Luff were the first real estate investors in acreage in Collier County, 1957.

When Weinfeld and Luff found out Jews were not welcome in Naples, they bought land anyway—in the middle of a swamp! They sold the lots and helped build the Jewish infrastructure there, including the elimination of "gentiles only" restrictions. Both served as president of the small Jewish Community Center of Collier County that started in 1965.

Brothers Jack and Jules Freeman developed the city of San Carlos Park in Lee County on the west coast and other properties, 1954.

In addition to developing the largest orange grove in the world (in Arcadia), the Freemans learned to build roads, dig canals, design land areas, and create lakes and service facilities for their new city. Today, San Carlos Park has about 25,000 residents. Jack told me that three Jewish developers are responsible for transforming cattle ranches for the population of Lee County: the Freemans, the Rosens, and Lee Ratner (Lehigh Acres). "In the Jewish spirit, we saw a desert and made it bloom. People came and continue to enjoy the fruits of our labors," said Jack Freeman. The Freemans accumulated, developed, and sold 89,000 acres or 139 square miles. (To compare, Manhattan is about 34 square miles.) Jack wrote *Florida Pioneer to Land Baron*.

Brothers Leonard and Julius "Jack" Rosen of Gulf American Land Corporation developed the city of Cape Coral, a planned community in Lee County, 1957.

The Rosens came from Baltimore to Miami in 1954. From an 11-story building that they built there, they assembled 114 square miles of wooded real estate on the western tip of Lee County. From the raw acreage to heavy equipment needed to develop the land and dredge and build canals, to the construction of buildings and the maintenance and operation of utilities and recreational facilities, the Rosen team employed 2,000 people. Cape Coral has 400 miles of canals and now is home to more than 180,000 residents. Leonard was an active leader in the Miami Jewish community.

In 1958 Nathan Gumenick developed the first high-rise apartments on Miami Beach, the fourteen-story Southgate Towers, Miami Beach, 1966.

Mortgage lenders snickered at this project saying there was no need for year-round apartments on Miami Beach! Gumenick split his time between Richmond, Virginia, and Miami Beach and developed a vast array of properties in Miami-Dade County. Third-generation Randy Gumenick directs operations now. Nathan and his wife, Sophia, were large community benefactors to places including Temple Israel, the University of Miami, and Mount Sinai Medical Center, which boasts the Sophia and Nathan S. Gumenick Ambulatory Care Center.

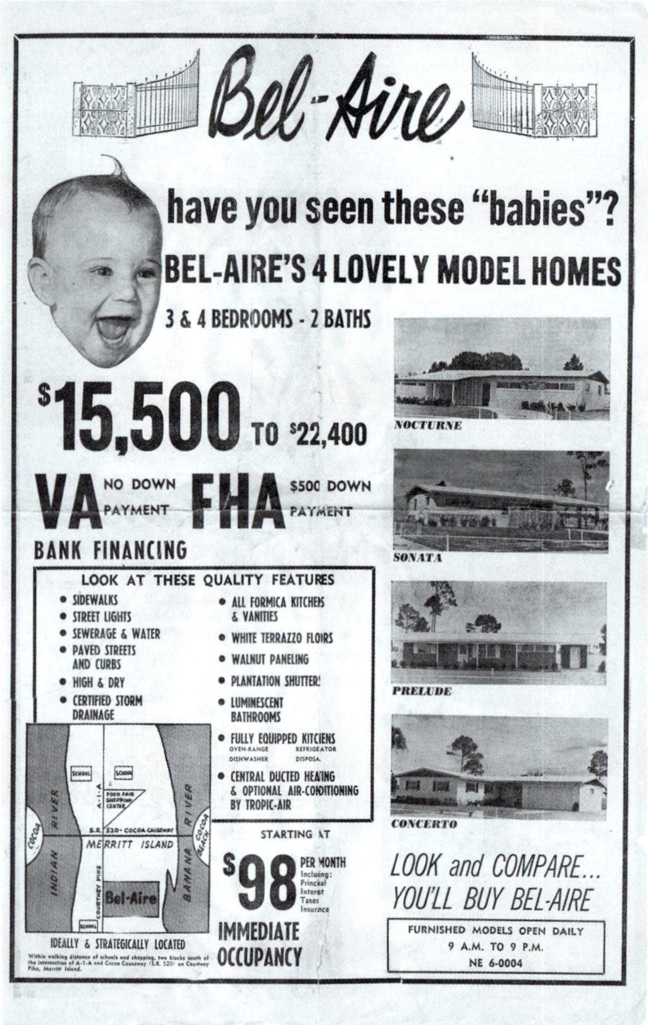

Ad for Bel-Aire Homes, founded by Norman Rossman and Bill Goodman, features Lauren Goodman, Orlando, 1962.

Bill and Gloria Goodman came from Detroit to Orlando in 1957 to retire from a building career. The arrival of Martin Marietta Aerospace Co. created an immediate housing shortage, and builders quickly grasped the opportunity. Polish immigrant Goodman joined with Norman Rossman who had come to Orlando from Miami Beach. In sixteen years, Bel-Aire built about ten thousand houses, strip centers, office buildings, and shopping malls in central Florida. Rossman served on the Airport Authority (1977–81) when it designed and built the first phase of the Orlando terminal. Rossman and Goodman were leaders in the Greater Orlando Jewish Federation, and Rossman, whose heart was in Israel, remembered going to Winter Garden to monitor KKK meetings for the community.

Greater Construction Corp. groundbreaking ceremony for a new subdivision, Greater Hills, Orlando, 1988.

From left to right are John Lowndes, Lake County Commissioner Don Bailey, Lester Mandell, Robert Mandell, Lake County Commission Chairman Chick Gregg, Lester Zimmerman, unknown, and Lake County Commissioner Tom Windram. Greater, formed by Lester Mandell, his uncle Lester Zimmerman, and Jack Lazar, has been one of the most productive home builders in central Florida since its 1965 inception. Developers of the Springs, a planned community in Seminole County, they were among the first builders along State Road 434. Greater later branched into commercial and utilities development, building the Greater Mall in Casselberry and Sanlando Utilities. Greater built more than sixteen thousand homes in twenty-five communities in Deltona, St. Cloud, Winter Garden, Clermont, Windermere, and the Orlando area. The company was sold in 2005.

Business success provided an excellent platform from which the two Lesters became major leaders in the Orlando Jewish community. Lester's son Robert Mandell became chairman and CEO of Greater and got involved nationally and internationally. He served as US Ambassador to Luxembourg; serves on the board of the Smithsonian Museum of Natural History, among others; and in 2019 was appointed to the board of directors of the Corporation for Public Broadcasting.

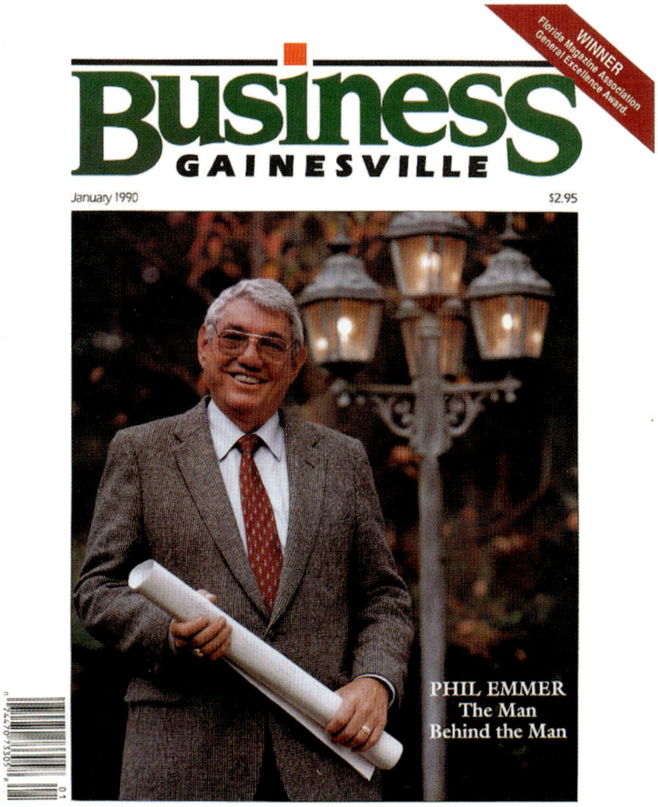

Phil Emmer, chairman of Emmer Development Corp, on a magazine cover, Gainesville, 1990.

Phil (Philip I.) Emmer (1928–2018) attended Sunday School in the synagogue that became the JMOF-FIU. He began as a home builder in the Miami area in 1954, then moved his business to Gainesville in 1960. He was one of the nation's largest developers of US Department of Housing and Urban Development (HUD) turnkey public housing programs. Emmer experienced great success developing land; building homes, apartments, condominiums, retirement communities, and camper resorts; and managing real estate management companies. While the homes were reasonably priced, values have skyrocketed in Gainesville and throughout Florida, pushing resale prices to soaring heights. His company has built eight thousand homes in fifteen Florida counties and branched into more high-end projects. Emmer involved himself in many community and charity endeavors, especially those assisting youths.

Adolph Berger (left) and Leonard Miller founded Pasadena Homes in 1959.

Broward County was still small with a significant agricultural element when brothers-in-law Adolph Berger and Leonard Miller built six homes in the West Hollywood area, mostly under Federal Housing Administration financing. They then took a big step purchasing sixty lots in Pembroke Pines and formed Pasadena Homes. (Berger had once lived in Mt. Vernon, New York, on a street called Pasadena Place—and the duo liked the name.) Their models were $12,500 to $15,950. Thousands of homes in subsequent years arose on land Berger and Miller developed from barren, swampy surface in Pembroke Pines, Davie, and Cooper City. Their largest project was Pembroke Lakes in 1971, and their office became the city hall of Pembroke Pines.

In their careers, Berger and Miller built more than 10,000 units and developed more than 3,500 acres. Berger was president of the South Florida Builders Association, and Miller was president of the Florida Homebuilders Association. Miller was named by President Jimmy Carter to the National Institute of Building and Sciences. Both were deeply involved in the Jewish community and with their colleges, including the Leonard Miller Center for Holocaust Studies at the University of Vermont and Berger's support for Hillel at Dartmouth.

Mel Sembler founded the Sembler Company that has been family owned and operated for more than fifty years, St. Petersburg, 2018.

The company began developing in the St. Petersburg area in 1962, with shopping centers and stand-alone drugstores. Later, Sembler moved into developing big-box stores and marketplaces and leasing and managing retail properties. Corporate headquarters remain in St. Petersburg, with two sons, Greg and Brent Sembler, in leadership, along with Craig Sher, and they have expanded to south Florida, Puerto Rico, Georgia, the Carolinas, and beyond the Mississippi River. The Sembler Company has developed more than 353 projects in 27 million square feet and exhibited a strong commitment to community by sponsoring many events. Mel Sembler has been US Ambassador to Australia and Italy.

Whisper Walk, a fifty-five-plus community developed by Oriole Homes in 1993, near Boca Raton, n.d.

Robert Levy founded Oriole Homes in Boca Raton in 1963. Levy had a connection to start building homes with Jacob Friedman from Baltimore—so the name "Oriole." The company was among the first to dramatically change the residential landscape of south Florida and elsewhere in Florida, building more than twenty-five thousand homes in seventy communities. His sons Richard and Harry A. "Hap" Levy bought raw land, developed it, and built houses. Their projects included "active adult luxury" single-family homes, apartments, and villas. The largest development is Villages of Oriole in Delray, which has about three thousand homes. Hap Levy was president of the Holocaust Documentation & Education Center (Hollywood, FL) for fifteen years. Third-generation Mark Levy led the company until the economic downturn forced its liquidation in 2008.

Seaside founder Robert Davis (second from left) with grandfather Joseph (J. S). Smolian and grandmother Bertha Smolian, Seaside, circa 1946. *Debbie Abrams.*

The brochure reads, "Seaside is a renowned Florida beach town where picket-fenced cottages line brick streets leading towards sugar-white beaches and clear Gulf waters." And so it is! In 1946, on one of the family's summer pilgrimages to the shore, Robert Davis's grandfather J. S. Smolian bought eighty acres near Seagrove Beach on Florida's northwest coast. Robert, who recalls walking the tract as a child with Smolian, grew up to become an award-winning builder in Miami in the 1970s. When he considered plans for the Seagrove property, he thought about the idyllic family vacations and reviving that area's building tradition. Davis invited Miami architects Andres Duany and Elizabeth Plater-Zyberk to help him plan a community that would resemble a small town. The movie *The Truman Show* starring Jim Carrey was filmed in Seaside in 1996–97. Robert's wife, Daryl, is the founder of Seaside's downtown retail development and co-founder of Seaside.

Tibor Hollo (inset), founder of Florida East Coast Realty (FECR), which built Florida's tallest building, Panorama Tower, Miami, 2018.

Hungarian-French Auschwitz survivor Tibor "Ted" Hollo (1927–) arrived in New York in 1945 with eighteen dollars. He got into contracting, and by 1956 his company was one of the ten largest in the country. He moved to Miami that year and formed Florida East Coast Realty (FECR), believing the future of the city was in vertical, downtown residential living. The company's redevelopment of Miami's decaying waterfront neighborhood north of downtown, known as the Omni area, provided the first sparks of energy in a location now on fire with huge development projects.

FECR's high-rise projects in the Brickell Avenue area, beginning in the 1970s, dramatically transformed the culture of what was a neighborhood of single-family homes. In 2018 Hollo opened his $800 million, 85-stories Panorama Tower, the tallest building in Florida at 868 feet, with a 2,000-car parking garage. To top that, he is working on an even taller One Bayfront Plaza at 92-stories and 1,049 feet—the maximum Federal Aviation Administration approval. The Towers by Foster + Partners is another planned development expected to rise to 1,049 feet that was recently announced, with FECR also part of that development team. FECR has built more than 60 million square feet. Tibor Hollo and his wife, Sheila, are major philanthropists and involved in the community.

RMC Property Group, left to right: Michael J. Leeds, president Susie Levin Rice, and CEO Mitchell F. Rice in front of a Publix grocery, Tampa, 2006.

Mitchell Rice and his wife, Susie Levin Rice, have a portfolio of 120 properties comprising 7.7 million square feet throughout Florida. RMC Property Group has developed or redeveloped 20 Publix-anchored shopping centers and developed 100 freestanding Walgreens drugstores, in addition to other projects. The company had humble beginnings in 1972, when Susie's dad,

Leonard Levin, and uncle Richard Levin began with apartments and shopping centers in Tampa.

In the 1980s Susie joined the family business and took it to another level so that in 1996 the company was ranked number one in their field by the *Tampa Bay Business Journal* and retained that position for years. Mitchell Rice cofounded FOG Development Inc. in 1993 to acquire land and develop commercial projects. In 2002 RMC and FOG merged. The firm developed two vertically integrated mixed-use projects: the Broadway Promenade in Sarasota and the Paramount on Lake Eola in Orlando. Susie and Mitchell Levin are very involved in their community.

Stephen Ross, founder & CEO of the Related Companies who is building Hudson Yards in Manhattan, shown dedicating Stephen M. Ross Football Field, Miami Beach, 2011.

Ross graduated from Miami Beach High School in 1958, where he played offensive tackle for his football team. He attended the University of Florida, then graduated from the University of Michigan to which he's donated $300 million for their Stephen M. Ross School of Business. In 1972 Stephen M. Ross founded the Related Companies with a $10,000 loan from his mother. Ross owns 60 percent of the company, which was valued in 2017 with $50 billion in assets.

Stephen Ross is one of America's wealthiest individuals, and his company is the nation's largest privately held real estate developer. "I surround myself with the brightest people possible by creating an environment where they can learn, grow, and really be part of things," Ross recently said. "I want to be known as someone who made cities better and built a great company that does quality work." In 1996 Ross built his first mixed-use project in Palm Beach. In 2000, in West Palm Beach, his company opened City Place, a $600 million, seventy-two-acre mixed-use project that combines entertainment and more than seventy retailers with residential centers, designed in a retro style in what was once a dormant downtown. Then he built the $1.7 billion mixed-use Time Warner Center that opened in 2003 in New York.

From the reputation he created on that job, he now has one thousand projects around the world—including the largest private real estate development in the history of the US. With a $25 billion price tag, Ross is transforming the last vacant part of Manhattan—Hudson Yards on the western edge next to the Hudson River—into a twenty-eight-acre city-state of shopping centers, restaurants, apartments, and office buildings. The vertical shopping experience opened its first section in March 2019 with a $200 million sculpture of staircases. Ross owns 95 percent of the Miami Dolphins National Football League (NFL) football team and has a home with wife, Kara, in Palm Beach.

Miami native Craig Robins is a real estate developer, entrepreneur, and art collector who transforms neglected neighborhoods, circa 2018.

In the 1980s Robins's energies were devoted to revitalizing South Beach. His current focus is the Miami Design District, where he converted an eighteen-block area of abandoned warehouses into a neighborhood devoted to creative businesses and art museums. The neighborhood inspired the founding of Design Miami/ and Design Miami/ Basel, design fairs that Robins owns in partnership with the producers of Art Basel, MCH Swiss Exhibition.

Crescent Heights, the nation's leading urban real estate firm, maintains its central office in Miami-Dade County, 2018.

In 1989 partners Sonny Kahn, Russell Galbut, and Bruce Menin began to specialize in the development, ownership, and operation of architecturally distinctive mixed-use high-rises in major cities across Florida and the US. The company has developed more than thirty-eight thousand residences nationwide, resulting in more than $12 billion in sales. Its buildings are found on both coasts of the US with concentrations in Los Angeles, San Francisco, San Diego, and Seattle as well as Chicago, Florida, and New York. The company introduced the first residential developments in South Beach, helping to spark the renaissance of the Art Deco District. Russell Galbut and Bruce Menin are cousins whose roots go back ninety-three years on Miami Beach when their grandparents Al and Bessie Galbut arrived. (You met them in part 2, chapter 5.)

Alan Ginsburg, real estate developer and founder of the CED Companies, is one of the region's largest landlords and philanthropists, Orlando, 2008.

Ginsburg has been involved in the real estate business for more than forty-five years, developing affordable housing. After moving to Florida in 1980, he founded the CED Companies that develop, build, and manage multifamily apartment communities. CED has grown to become a leader in the Housing Tax Credit program and has built more than forty thousand affordable apartment units across the country. Philanthropist Alan Ginsburg says, "Never forget the importance of the community in which you are creating new development and give back as much and as often as possible." And he does just that.

In 2018 *Winter Park Magazine* recognized him for donating more than $35 million to community organizations, including Florida Hospital, the University of Central Florida's College of Medicine Harriet F. Ginsburg Health Sciences Library, and the Jeffrey & Diane Ginsburg Center for Jewish Student Life at Central Florida Hillel and the Northview dorm. He has also provided a scholarship endowment at Rollins College and made significant contributions in the Jewish community. Ginsburg received the Benemerenti Medal, the highest honor a layperson can receive from the Holy See, which is really rare for a Jew!

Joseph Cayre founded Midtown Equities, which is developing Midtown Miami, 2018.

Born to Syrian Jewish parents who had a souvenir shop on Miami Beach (1949–61), Cayre made hundreds of millions of dollars in the movie and video industries and, later, the Manhattan real estate market before entering the Miami real estate scene in 2000. He is the lead partner in Midtown Miami, one of the most ambitious projects being developed by Midtown Equities, and has his four sons in the business. With huge doses of vision and energy, Cayre describes his Midtown Miami as a $2.3 billion, fifty-five-acre mega-project with three thousand condominiums, five hundred apartments, a hotel, more than six hundred thousand square feet of retail, and two hundred thousand square feet of office space and public green spaces—all transformed from what had been an abandoned, crime-ridden former rail yard. Cayre's portfolio includes the World Trade Center in New York, a few Ritz-Carltons, and landmark buildings in Los Angeles, New York, Chicago, and Washington, DC.

Jeffrey Vinik launched Water Street Tampa, one of the biggest downtown development projects in the country, Tampa, 2018. *Rendering courtesy Strategic Property Partners.*

Partnering with Microsoft billionaire Bill Gates, Vinik has begun construction for a $3 billion, fifty-acre waterfront district that will feature a million square feet of retail, offices, homes, hotels, culture and education centers, and thirteen acres of parks and public spaces. The first phase, scheduled for completion 2020–21, will include the region's first five-star hotel and twenty-one other buildings. Twenty high-rise cranes and three thousand construction workers are on the site. The project also includes the $164.7 million University of South Florida Morsani College of Medicine and Heart Institute. Vinik owns the Tampa Bay Lightning ice hockey team and Amalie Arena.

Suppliers and Engineers

Civil engineer Alexander Brest (center) built two thousand miles of roads, the first missile-launching platform at Cape Canaveral, and many military installations around Florida, Jacksonville, 1979.

Born to Polish immigrant parents, Alexander Brest (1894–1996) worked his way through a civil engineering degree, became a successful businessman, and in the process helped change the face of Jacksonville. Lt. Col. Brest taught civil engineering at the University of Florida, and in 1924 formed Duval Engineering and Contracting Co. Brest was a philanthropist nonpareil, including support for an art gallery, planetarium, park, and baseball facility in Jacksonville.

Samson Companies, left to right: Gordon Owens (manager), Sam Levine (principal), and Murray Levine (principal), Miami, 1963.

They are standing next to a stack of concrete blocks and in front of the ready-mix concrete batching plant. In the late 1930s, Russian born Jacob and Ida Levine moved to Miami Beach with their children: Estelle, Murray, Sam, and Frances. When Murray and Sam returned from World War II, they decided to be a part of the postwar building market and started Mursam Block Company to supply concrete blocks for residential and commercial projects in south Florida. In the 1950s, the name changed to Samson Concrete, referencing both the popular movie of that time and the strength the name Samson denoted in the Bible.

Samson opened state-of-the-art plants, supplying ready-mix concrete and blocks. Other members of the family founded Banner Supply Company in the mid-1950s, which today remains one of the largest independently owned drywall and building material distributors in Florida. Ahead of their time, the Levine brothers began vertically integrating related businesses. They dug the rock that was used to manufacture the concrete in a large quarry (Coral Aggregates Corp.), started a trucking division to transport the rock, and developed, built, and operated residential and commercial real estate projects through Samson Realty & Development Corp., which went public in 1958. Samson Concrete and Coral Aggregates were sold in the mid-1960s. The Levine family continues to be deeply involved in the Jewish and civic communities.

Harvey Kobrin in his office as president of Kobrin Builders Supply Inc., Orlando, 1970.

Kobrin Builders Supply was founded in 1955 by Jack and Sara Kobrin. In 1959 their son Philip joined the company, and their son Harvey joined in 1962, after graduating from the University of Florida. When Jack passed away in 1974, Harvey took over the business, committed to the same uncompromising integrity as his parents. Harvey built the wholesale building supply company (mostly wallboard and plaster) to more than $100 million annually in sales with seven locations throughout the state. Kobrin was the first supplier for Disney World in the early 1970s and then provided 90 percent of their building materials and 100 percent to Universal Studios as well as to the major home builders in central Florida, the Orange County Convention Center, the airport, city hall, and many large hotels. The company was sold in 2013 to Foundation Building Materials. Harvey's son, Scott, is a home builder in Orlando and Volusia County.

Mark (left) and Sy Israel celebrate the fiftieth anniversary of Universal Engineering Sciences, the largest family-owned geotechnical company in the US, 2014.

Sy Israel started his environmental engineering company by working out of his car, inspecting the bottom of septic tanks in Merritt Island. The largest firm of its kind in the state provides geotechnical engineering, construction material testing, building inspection and plan review, threshold inspection, and drilling services to the real estate and construction industries. Sy says his company "is the kidneys of the development business because you don't see what we do, but we recycle, clean, and process things." His son Mark became president in 2001 and in 2018 was named to *Florida Trend*'s "Florida 500" list. The Israels are a major Jewish philanthropic family in central Florida and for the State of Israel.

Gopman Consulting Engineers has serviced some of south Florida's most notable high-rises, Miami, 2006.

Known as "High-Rise Herby," Herbert Gopman has designed and inspected buildings all over the world. His work is seen extensively in Florida, where he has lived since 1944. Gopman received a bachelor's degree in architectural engineering from the University of Miami in 1954 and opened the firm in 1967. Gopman serves developers, architects, contractors, and homeowners. He has worked from design to inspection with multilevel shopping complexes, schools, and parking garages.

CHAPTER 9

Politics and Law

The Torah insists, "Justice, justice shall you pursue." Rabbinical teachings include the phrase "*Tikkun Olam*, Repair the World." Jews are taught a passion for justice for the poor, the weak, and the despised and are encouraged to create meaning out of confusion and chaos. Because of their poor treatment in Europe, Russia, and other places around the world, when Jews settled in America—and in Florida—they felt the human potential and human desire to make life better for everyone. Floridian Jews who became attorneys and those who chose to run for public office were respected as well educated, trustworthy, good in business, and effective communicators.

German immigrant Charles Slager, first-known Jewish politician on Florida's west coast, served as Tampa's postmaster, sheriff, and tax collector (1871–73).

An impressive number of Jews have been engaged in the professions of politics and law in Florida, beginning with US Senator David Levy Yulee in the 1830s. In the nineteenth century, some other Florida

Jews involved in politics (not including mayors, listed later) were Isadore Blumenthal, Hillsborough County commissioner (1871–73); Philip Dzialynski, Polk County commissioner (1872); Jacob Raphael Cohen, Orlando Town Council member (1875); Herman Levy, Newnansville clerk of court and treasurer (1883); and Edward Blum, Tarpon Springs postmaster and commissioner (1887).

In the current era, we find that Jews have served Florida and the nation at many levels of the executive, judicial, and legislative branches of the government.

Robert E. Rubin as US secretary of the treasury, 1995.

United States Cabinet

Robert E. Rubin graduated from Miami Beach High School where he was class president and known to be both laid back and intellectual, Miami Beach, 1956.

Robert E. Rubin's signature on $100 bill, series 1995.

Robert E. Rubin (1938–) was sworn in as the seventieth US secretary of the treasury on January 10, 1995, and served four years. He is a lawyer, banker, and economist who believes "all is uncertain." As a fourth grader, he moved with his family to Miami Beach from New York. On his first day in his new school, his classmates elected him president of their class. Following Miami Beach High School, he graduated summa cum laude in economics from Harvard. After Yale Law school, he practiced law in New York and then was hired by Goldman Sachs & Co. to handle arbitrage. He was there for twenty-six years, where he rose to cochairman.

In 1993 President Bill Clinton asked Rubin to serve as his assistant for economic policy and a member of the National Economic Council at the White House. Rubin felt that financial crises were periodically inevitable. Referred to as "the man who Wall Street trusts," he was an executive at Citigroup for ten years and chaired the Council on Foreign Relations during 2007–17. He is currently active as a founder of the Hamilton Project, an economic policy think tank that produces research and proposals on how to create a growing economy that benefits more Americans.

United States Ambassadors

To date, five Floridian Jews have served as US ambassadors:

- Mel Sembler, Italy 2001–5 and Australia and Nauru 1989–93
- Richard Stone, ambassador-at-large for Central America 1983–84 and Denmark 1991–93
- Robert Mandell, Luxembourg 2011–15
- Al Hoffman, Portugal 2005–7
- David Friedman, Israel 2017—hosted a celebration when the US Embassy moved to Jerusalem on May 14, 2018

United States Senators

Two Jews have served as US Senators representing Florida.

(Left) US Senator David Levy Yulee, 1845–51 and 1855–61 and US Senator Richard Stone, 1975–80.

You met David Levy Yulee in part 1 and Richard Stone as the son of hoteliers Lily and Alfred Stone earlier in part 3. The only Jewish US senator to represent Florida since the Civil War, Democrat Richard Stone (1928–2019) served the public for nearly 40 years, beginning as Miami city attorney in 1966. He was a Florida state senator, Florida's secretary of state, and US Senator before he was an ambassador. He also had a law practice in Miami with Jordan Bittel. Strongly principled, he was so passionate about transparency that he removed the inner doors from his office when he was Secretary of State. As a US Senator, Richard Stone was a strong advocate for aid to Israel on the Foreign Relations Committee.

(Note: The following lists were created with the assistance of Rep. Elaine Bloom and Bernie Friedman and with available facts as of January 2019. The author apologizes for any omissions or errors. Dates are either the year appointed, elected, or a span of the entire period. * = Date[s] of term unknown.)

United States House of Representatives

- William Lehman, US representative, Congressional District 13, 1972–92
- Larry Smith, US representative, Congressional District 16, 1982–92
- Peter Deutsch, US representative, Congressional District 20, 1993–2005
- Robert Wexler, US representative, Congressional District 19, 1997–2010
- Ron Klein, US representative, Congressional District 22, 2008–12
- Alan Grayson, US representative, Congressional District 8, 2009–11; District 9, 2013–17
- Debbie Wasserman Schultz, US representative, Congressional District 20, 2005–present
- Lois Frankel, US representative, Congressional District 22, 2013–17; District 21, 2017–present
- Ted Deutch, US representative, Congressional District 19, 2010–13; District 21, 2013–17; District 22, 2017–present

Samuel "Bud" Shorstein, CPA, Jacksonville, 1987.

Floridian Jews have also had significant roles serving politicians. One example is Samuel "Bud" Shorstein, grandson of Esther and Jacob Shorstein who settled in Jacksonville around 1914. Bud Shorstein served Florida Governor Bob Graham as Secretary of Professional Regulation in 1981–82 and in 1985 he was appointed as the Governor's Chief of Staff. When Graham was elected Florida's US Senator in 1987, Bud accompanied him to Washington as his Chief of Staff.

Florida State Executive

David Sholtz's Inauguration Program as Florida's twenty-sixth governor, Tallahassee, January 3, 1933.

David Sholtz (1891–1953) served one term until January 5, 1937. A dynamic public speaker, he took the reins of state government when the worst effects of the Depression were being felt in Florida. He paid the bills, distributed free text books, increased school appropriations, passed a worker's compensation law, and started the Park Service and Citrus Commission. A graduate of Yale and then Stetson Law School (1915), Sholtz established careers in the business and legal fields in Daytona Beach. He served in the US Navy during World War I, as a state representative (1917), as a state attorney (1919–21), as a city judge (1921), and also as National Grand Exalted Ruler of the Elks.

David Sholtz was the son of Russian Jewish immigrants who had traveled to Brooklyn, New York, then to Daytona in 1914. Sholtz's father, Michael, brought the first electric railway to Volusia County and erected the first concrete bridge across the Halifax River in

Daytona Beach. He so loved Brooklyn baseball that he built another Ebbets Field in Daytona Beach as a winter training camp for the team—in 1916—the year they won the pennant as the Brooklyn Robins. The Brooklyn Dodgers had changed their name to the Robins in 1914 in honor of their new manager Wilbert Robinson; the name changed back to the Dodgers in 1932.

Governor David Sholtz (seated, front center), Bayfront Park, Miami, February 15, 1933.

Governor Sholtz hosted US president-elect Franklin Roosevelt (left) for a political rally. Just after Roosevelt gave a short speech from his seat in the car, Giuseppe Zangara attempted to assassinate Roosevelt. Chicago Mayor Anton Cermak (right) died from that bullet. Zangara was swiftly convicted of murder and executed in the electric chair in perhaps one of the shortest periods of time between crime and execution (thirty-two days).

Florida State Cabinet

- Robert Shevin, attorney general, 1971–79
- Richard Stone, secretary of state, 1970–74
- Gerald Lewis, comptroller, 1975–95
- Sidney Levin, secretary of commerce, 1980s
- George Firestone, secretary of state, 1979–87
- Carlos Lopez-Cantera, lieutenant governor, 2014–18
- Nikki Fried, commissioner of agriculture and consumer services, 2019–present

Florida State Judicial

To date, nearly three hundred names of Jewish judges in Florida have been identified. There is a scrapbook of the judges with their biographies at the JMOF-FIU. The earliest Jewish judge I found in Florida was Augustus "Gus" Cohen, who settled in Pensacola before the Civil War and served in the Union army. Cohen was a federal judge who served during 1894–1914. A granddaughter, Frances Cohen, married Mitchell Wolfson of Miami in 1926.

The earliest known Circuit Court Judge was Harry N. Sandler in Tampa, 1935–64. While in the legislature, he sponsored the Homestead Exemption Amendment. In 1976 Miette K. Burnstein was the first woman and first Jewish Circuit Court Judge in Broward County. Miette became the first woman and first Jewish chief judge in Broward in 1985.

There have been five Jews on the Florida Supreme Court.

In the top row from left to right are Arthur J. England Jr. (1975–81), who served as chief justice during 1978–80, and Raymond Ehrlich (1981–91), who served as chief justice during 1988–90. In the bottom row from left to right are Gerald Kogan (1987–98), who served as chief justice during 1996–98; Barbara Pariente (1997–2019), who served as chief justice during 2004–6; and Robert J. Luck who is currently serving as justice (2019–present).

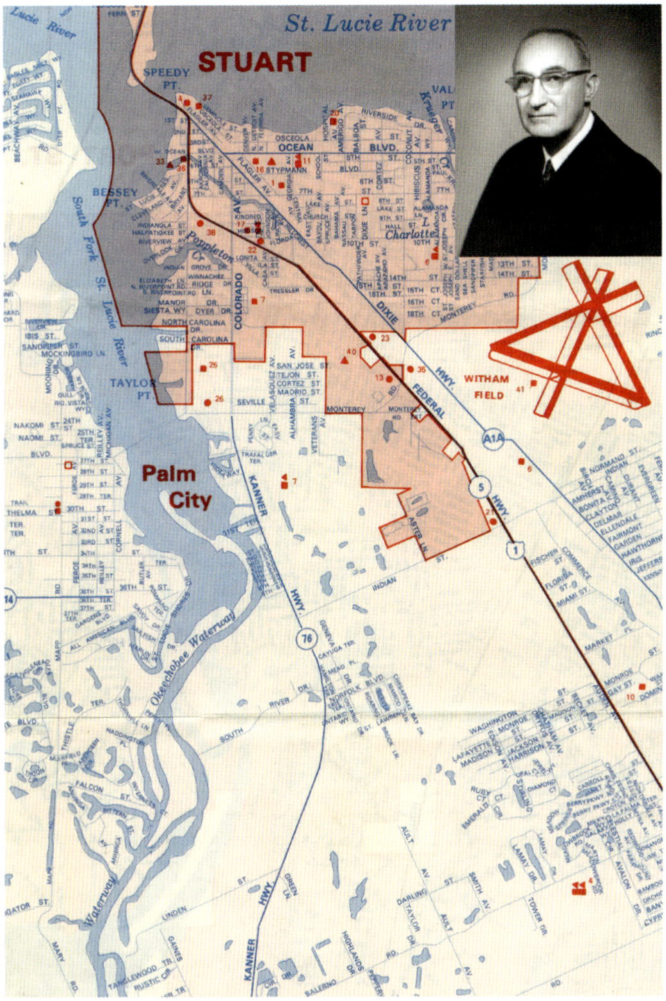

Abram Otto "A. O." Kanner (inset) was honored for his forty years of public service with the naming of Kanner Highway (State Route 76) circa 1945.

Kanner Highway runs 31.5 miles east–west in Martin County. Born in Sanford, A. O. is the first known child to be born in central Florida to a Jewish family that set down roots in the area. (You met him and this family in part 2, chapter 3). Kanner (1893–1967) received his law degree from Stetson. He served as assistant state attorney (1925), state representative (1926–35), state senator (1937–41), and then appellate court judge in the Ninth Judicial Circuit (1941–57). In 1957 A. O. Kanner served as the first chief judge of the newly created Second District Court of Appeal. As a legislator, Kanner fought for roads. His 1933 Kanner Act allowed Florida counties to use gas tax money to avoid bankruptcy and helped lift the state out of the Depression. When he retired, he continued as an associate judge in the Fourth District Court of Appeal at Vero Beach.

List of Florida State Legislators

Those who have served are listed in alphabetical order.

- Mike Abrams, House District 101, 1982–92; District 105, 1992–94
- Alan Becker, House District 103, 1972–78
- Lori Berman, House District 90, 2010–16; Senate District 31, 2018–present
- Elaine Bloom, House District 100, 1974–78; District 104, 1986–92; District 106, 1992–2000; speaker pro tempore of the house, 1992–94 (author of more than one hundred major laws in eighteen-plus years)
- Ellyn Bogdanoff, House District 91, 2004–10; Senate District 25, 2010–12
- Lauren Book, Senate District 32, 2016–present
- Helen Gordon Davis, House District 70, 1974–88; Senate District 23, 1988–92; first woman from Hillsborough County elected to state office
- Peter Deutsch, House, 1982–93
- Ted Deutch, Senate District 30, 2006–10
- Ben Diamond, House District 68, 2016–present
- Murray Dubbin, House District 95, 1963–74
- Katie Edwards, House District 98, 2012–present
- Steven B. Feren, House, 1992–96

- Randy Fine, House District 53, 2016–present
- George Firestone, House Dade & Monroe, 1966; District 110, 1967; District 92, 1968–72; Senate District 36, 1972–78
- Bill Fleece, House Pinellas, 1966; District 53, 1967–72
- Howard Forman, Senate District 32, 1989–2000
- Marcus Frank, House Marion County, 1939, 1949
- Lois Frankel, House District 83, 1986–1992; District 85, 1994–2002
- Michael Friedman, House District 102, 1980–82; District 103, 1982–92
- Dan Gelber, House District 106, 2000–2008, minority leader, 2006–8; Senate District 35, 2008–10
- Joseph Geller, House District 100, 2014–present
- Steven Geller, House District 101, 1988-99; Senate District 31, 1989–2008; minority leader 2006–8
- Ron Glickman, House District 66, 1986–92; District 57, 1992–94
- Harry Goldstein, Fernandina*
- Elaine Gordon, House District 98 and District 104, 1972–94; first female speaker pro tempore, 1984–86; dean of the house, 1992–94
- Ron Greenstein, House District 95, 1998–2006
- Jack D. Gordon, Senate Dade District, 1972–92
- Susan Guber, House District 117, 1986–92
- Tom Gustafson, House District 88, 1976–82; District 94, 1982–90; speaker of the house 1988–90
- Alberto Gutman, House District 105, 1984–92; Senate District 34, 1992–98
- Marshall Harris, House Dade District, 1966; District 108, 1967–72; District 112, 1972–74
- Adam Hasner, House District 87, 2003–11; majority leader 2006–8
- Sally Heyman, House District 105, 1995–2002
- Suzanne Jacobs, House District 88, 1992–2000
- Richard Hodes, House District 68, 1966–82; speaker pro tempore, 1978–80; house majority leader 1980–82; president of the National Conference of State Legislatures 1980–82
- Abram Otto "A. O." Kanner, House Martin District, 1927–36; Senate District 33, 1936–41
- Ron Klein, House District 89, 1992–96; Senate District 28, 1996–2007; minority whip, 1998; minority leader, 2002–4
- Dick Kravitz, House District 19, 2000–2008
- Rick Kriseman, House District 53, 2006–12
- Barry Kutun, House District 99, 1972–82; District 104, 1982–85
- Cindy Lerner, House District 119, 2000–2002

- Curtis Levine, House District 89, 1998–2000
- Gerald Lewis, House District 96, 1965–70; Senate District 43, 1970–72
- Fred Lippman, House District 100, 1978–2000
- Carlos Lopez-Cantera, House District 113, 2004–12; majority whip 2008–12
- Gwen Margolis, House District 102, 1974–80; Senate District 37, 1980–92; first female president of the Florida State Senate 1990–92 and the nation's first female senate president
- Jared Moskowitz, House District 97, 2012–present
- Kenneth Myers, House District 94, 1964–69; Senate District 45 and 39, 1969–80
- Norman Ostrau, House District 96, 1986–92
- Ari Porth, House District 96, 2004–12
- Steve Press, House District 86, 1982–92
- Kevin Rader, House District 78, 2008–10; District 81, 2012–16; Senate District 24, 2016–present
- Nan Rich, House District 97, 2000–2004; Senate District 34, 2004–12, first female leader of Senate Democratic Caucus 2010–12
- Barry Richard, House District 112, 1974–78
- Stacy Joy Ritter, House District 96, 1996–2004
- Irma Rochlin, House District 98, 1984–88
- Harry N. Sandler, House (from Tampa), 1932–35; speaker pro tempore, 1935
- Franklin Sands, House District 98, 2005–13
- Burt Saunders, House, 1994–98; Senate District 37, 1999–2008
- Elaine Schwartz, House District 99, 2006–14
- Robert Shevin, House Dade District, 1964–66; Senate District 43, 1966–70
- David Sholtz, House (from Daytona Beach), 1917–19
- Barry Silver, House District 89, 1996–98
- David Silver, House District 87, 2016–present
- Ron Silver, House District 103, 1978–92; Senate District 38, 1992–present; house majority leader and majority whip
- Art Simon, House District 116, 1982–94
- Emily Slosberg, House District 91, 2016–present
- Irv Slosberg, House District 89, 2000–2002; House District 90, 2002–6, 2010–12; House District 91, 2012–16
- Larry Smith, House Hollywood, 1978–82
- Eleanor Sobel, House District 100, 1998–2002; House District 99, 2002–6; Senate District 31, 2008–12; Senate District 33, 2012–present
- Rick Stark, House District 104, 2012–present
- Paul B. Steinberg, House District 36, 1973–78; Senate 1978–82
- Richard Steinberg, House District 106, 2008–12
- Richard Stone, Senate Dade District, 1967–70

- Jack Tobin, House District 95, 1982–98
- Jim Waldman, House District 96, 2006–12
- Debbie Wasserman Schultz, House District 97, 1992–2000; Senate, 2000–2004; youngest woman ever elected to Florida legislature
- Peter Weinstein, Senate District 29, 1983–92; District 33, 1992–96; majority leader and deputy majority leader
- Sonny Weinstein, House St. Johns District, 1955, 1957
- Eleanor Weinstock, House District 79, 1978–82; District 83, 1982–86; Senate District 26, 1986–92
- Robert Wexler, Senate, 1990–96
- Sherman Winn, House District 105, 1970–72; Senate District 34, 1972–82
- Louis Wolfson II, House District 111, 1963–73
- Leo Wotitzky, House Charlotte District, 1939–49
- Nathan Zelmenovitz, House Okeechobee District, 1953–57

Mayors of Counties, Cities, and Towns

Among those Floridian Jews who have been elected to public office are nearly 200 women and men who have served as mayors in their communities, beginning in 1879 with Henry Brash.

Henry Brash is the first-known Jewish mayor in Florida. He served three terms in Marianna, circa 1888.

This is a different man than the Henry Brash in Apalachicola. This Henry Brash (1857–1928) settled in Marianna in 1870 when he arrived from Germany. In 1894 he moved to Tampa where he was a merchant. He and his wife, Sarah Zelnicker, had five children: Alma, Florence, Isaac, Ruth, and Victor, and they all lived in Tampa.

Herman Glogowski served as mayor of Tampa for four consecutive terms (1886–93). *Tampa Bay History Center.*

German immigrant Glogowski first settled in Gainesville in the 1870s where he had a store and was civically active. In 1883 he married a local Jewish girl Bertha Brown (a cousin of Bertha Zadek Dzialynski, whom you met in part 2, chapter 1). The next year, they moved to Tampa where he opened a clothing store. Glogowski had a talent for people and business and contributed hugely to Tampa's civic and Jewish growth. He served as municipal judge (1880–86), then was elected mayor. He led Tampa through its transitional and formative periods, promoted private investment and development, improved public works and sanitation, and enhanced the fiscal stability of the city. Active on the Tampa Board of Trade, he helped develop incentives to bring cigar factories to town. In 1898–99, he was president of Tampa's first Jewish congregation, Schaarai Zedek.

The City of Miami has only had one Jewish mayor, Abe Aronovitz, 1953–55.

Aronovitz (1899–1960) was raised in Key West, one of the ten sons of Kate and Dave Aronovitz (you met them in part 3, chapter 2). He graduated from Stetson University and moved to Jacksonville where he became interested in politics. He settled in Miami in 1922 because it was developing more rapidly. After serving in World War II, Aronovitz went into law practice. He was an acting state attorney and Miami City attorney in the 1930s. As Miami's twenty-seventh mayor, he battled antisemitism, the police department, and slums and forced Florida Power and Light to cut rates. This was a time when Jews were scarce in public life. This is in contrast to Miami Beach, which has had seventeen Jewish mayors since Mitchell Wolfson in 1943.

Steven L. Abrams, the only Jewish mayor of Boca Raton (2001–8) was also the first Palm Beach County mayor (2013), 2017.

Abrams, a lawyer, was elected three times in Boca Raton, the third time by the most votes in the city's history, and named mayor emeritus when he stepped down due to term limits. As mayor of Boca Raton, he gained national exposure and local respect during the first bioterrorist attack in American history when anthrax was discovered at the American Media Inc. building in 2001. He received the Distinguished Service Medal from the Israel National Police for his leadership during the ordeal. He graduated magna cum laude from Harvard in 1980 and received his law degree from The George Washington University. Prior to moving to Florida, he served as a law clerk in the White House and to Supreme Court Chief Justice John G. Roberts Jr. Abrams was the first Jewish mayor of a Florida county. He is currently executive director of the South Florida Regional Transportation Authority.

List of Mayors of Counties, Cities, and Towns

Those who have served are listed in alphabetical order.

- Norman Abramowitz, Tamarac, 1988–92, 1994–96
- Maynard Abrams, Hollywood, 1966–69
- Steven L. Abrams, Boca Raton, 2001–8; first mayor of Palm Beach County, 2013
- Abe Aronovitz, Miami, 1953–55
- Max L. Bear, Pensacola, 1937
- Joe Berkheim, Gainesville*
- Gene Berkowitz, Tallahassee, 1968
- Anne Bernstein, Palm Shores, 1990–96
- Jack Block, South Miami, 1968–84
- Henry Brash, Marianna, 1879–82
- Shepard Broad, Bay Harbor Islands, 1947–72
- Irving Buchalter, Sunset Beach, 1947–50
- Norman Ciment, Miami Beach, 1981–83
- David Cohen, Sarasota, 1960, 1964–66
- Judy Cuenca, Golden Beach, 1995–?
- Michael Davis, DeLand, 1890s
- Jay Dermer, Miami Beach, 1967–71
- David Dermer, Miami Beach, 2001–7
- Robert Drohlich, Longboat Key, 1995–96
- Morris A. Dzialynski, Jacksonville, 1881–83
- Steven Effman, Sunrise, 1993–96
- Robert Farber, Longboat Key, 1994–95
- Steven B. Feren, Sunrise, 1996
- Samuel Feinberg, Dunnellon, 1917
- Sidney Fischer, Cocoa Beach, 1956–60
- Herman Fishbein, St. Petersburg, 1969

- Michael Fishel, Ocala, 1900–1902
- Lois Frankel, West Palm Beach, 2003–11
- Sandy Freedman, Tampa, 1987–95
- Corinne Freeman, St. Petersburg, 1977–85
- William Friedman, Dade City, 1927-28, 1932–33
- Nathan Friedland, Melbourne, 1965–68
- Malcolm H. Fromberg, Miami Beach, 1983–85
- Edgar "Buddy" Galvin, Hallandale, 1971–72
- Joseph Gardner, Bay Harbor Islands, 1979–82
- Seymour Gelber, Miami Beach, 1991–97
- Dan Gelber, Miami Beach, 2018–present
- Mara Giulianti, Hollywood, 1986–90
- Joseph Glickstein Sr., Neptune Beach, 1930s
- Herman Glogowski, Tampa, 1886–93
- Herman W. Goldner, St. Petersburg, 1961–67, 1971–73
- Stanley G. Goldsmith, Bay Harbor Island, 1982–84, 1991–92
- Susan Gottlieb, Aventura, 2005–2014 (first female and longest-serving Aventura mayor)
- Adolph Greenhut, Pensacola, 1913–16
- Irving Greenhut, Pensacola, 1965
- Evelyn Greer, first mayor of Pine Crest, 1996–2004
- Gabriel Groisman, Bal Harbor, 2016–present
- Dr. Louis Haas, Bay Harbor Islands, 1975–76
- Dr. Leonard Haber, Miami Beach, 1977–79
- C. J. Heinberg, Gulf Breeze, 1961–62, 1968–70
- Fred Holtsberg, Fort Pierce, 1936–37
- Royal Flagg Jonas, North Bay Village, 1951–54
- David Kaminsky, Lauderhill, 1984–88
- Irving Kanarek, Stuart, 1954, 1956
- Neisen O. Kasdin, Miami Beach, 1997–2001
- Rick Kriseman, St. Petersburg, 2014–present
- Hymen Lake, North Bay Village, 1951–54
- Dr. Hal Lenobel, Longboat Key, 1998–99
- Cindy Lerner, Pinecrest, 2008-16
- Philip Levine, Miami Beach, 2013–17
- Josh Levy, Hollywood, 2017–20
- Marcie Liberman, Miami Beach, 1947–49
- Ilene Lieberman, Lauderhill, 1990
- Bernard Liliethal, Palatka Heights, 1880s
- Joseph Mendel, West Palm Beach, 1923–24
- Judge Murray Meyerson, Miami Beach, 1979–81
- Louis Nathan, Miami Shores, 1930

- Theodore R. Nelson, Bay Harbor Islands, 1976–78
- Kenneth Oka, Miami Beach, 1957–59, 1961–63
- Lou Ann Palmer, Sarasota, 1984–85, 1989–90
- Dan Pearl, Sunrise, 1989–93
- Irving Peskoe, Homestead, 1981–86
- Harold Raben, Belle Glade, 1949–50
- Morris Rabinowitz, Graceville, 1961
- Charles Rheinhauer, Ocala, 1906
- Melvin Richard, Miami Beach, 1963–65
- Carol Roberts, West Palm Beach, 1985–86
- Margot M. Roberts, South Palm Beach, 1990s
- Leo Rose Jr., Surfside, 1950s
- Harold Rosen, Miami Beach, 1971, 1974–75
- Harry Rosen, Miramar, 1975–79
- Arthur J. Rosenberg, Hallandale, 1981–83, 1987–89
- Simon Rosin, Arcadia, 1919
- Myron Rosner, North Miami Beach, 2009–12
- Seymour Roth, Indian Harbour Shores, 1985–86
- Bernard Rubin, Fort Pierce, 1957–58
- Philip Rubin, Crystal River, 1932
- Joe Schreiber, Tamarac, 1997–?
- Harold Shapiro, Miami Beach, 1953–55
- Morris Silverman, Florida City, 1932–38
- Scott Singer, Boca Raton, 2018
- Arthur Snyder, North Miami Beach, 1960s
- Gilbert B. Stein, Hallandale, 1989–90
- Estelle Stern, Bal Harbour, 1989–90
- Charles Sussman, Hillsboro Beach*
- Abe Tarapani, Tarpon Springs*
- Edward M. Tavlin, Bay Harbor Islands, 1993–95
- Herb Tobin, Golden Beach, 1982–90
- Harold Turk, Miami Beach, 1949–51
- Sam A. Wahnish, Tallahassee, 1938–41
- Samuel B. Waterman, Hallandale, 1985–87
- Dr. Milton Weinkle, Hallandale, 1972
- Enid Weisman, Aventura, 2016–present
- Sherman Winn, North Miami, 1970s
- Louis Witkovski, Starke, 1884–89 (murdered while in office)
- Mitchell Wolfson, Miami Beach, 1943 (resigned to join the US Army)
- A. Hart Wurzburg, Longboat Key, 1989–90
- Max Wyner, Kelsey City, 1920–22

* dates unknown

Attorneys-at-Law

I have mentioned some names of Jewish attorneys in the early period of Florida history. Among them was David Levy Yulee who was admitted to the bar in 1832. At that time, the term was synonymous with practicing law. The bar first became an organized group in 1889. Florida's first woman lawyer admitted to the bar was probably Gertrude Dzialynski in 1898 (see part 2, chapter 1, the Dzialynski family section).

Burton Young was the first Jewish president of the Florida Bar, 1970–71, Miami, 1970.

The Florida State Bar Association was founded in 1950, the year Burton Young was admitted to the bar. He was the first to serve as president from the University of Miami Law School and also served as president of the Florida Bar Foundation. Other Jews who have served as president of the Florida Bar include L. David Shear (Tampa), Leonard H. Gilbert (Tampa), Samuel S. Smith (Miami Beach), Gerald R. Richman (Miami), James Fox Miller (Hollywood), Alan T. Dimond (Miami), Edward R. Blumberg (Miami), Tod Aronovitz (Miami), Jesse H. Diner (Fort Lauderdale), Michael J. Higer (Miami), Edith Osman (Miami), and Michele Suskauer (West Palm Beach).

Edith G. Osman was the first Jewish woman president and only the second woman president of the Florida Bar 1999–2000, Miami, 1999.

When Osman was president, she organized a project to tell the history of Florida's first 150 women lawyers. Also, Michele Suskauer, daughter of a Holocaust survivor and an attorney in West Palm Beach, was president of the Florida Bar in 2018.

Key West native Reba Engler Epstein Daner was the first-known Jewish woman attorney practicing in South Florida in 1937. University of Miami Law Library expansion dedication, Miami, circa 1990.

From left to right are Congressman Dante Fascell, UM President Edward Foot, Robert Paul, Charles Cobb, Dean of Law School Mary Doyle, Reba Engler Daner, Alex Carlson, William Hoeveler, and Gerald Kogan. Reba Daner (1911–2003) was seven months pregnant as the only woman member of the first full-time graduating class at the University of Miami (UM) Law School in 1930 and was admitted to the bar in 1936. She was a pioneering feminist, balancing family and career. She helped fund the moot courtroom at UM because "I trembled when I first went into a courtroom as a lawyer." Reba was president of Miami's first Hadassah chapter. She retired in 1989 and the University of Miami's Law Library bears her name.

Florida native Paul S. Buchman served as Plant City's city attorney for forty-two years, and Paul S. Buchman Highway honors his contributions, circa 1977.

Buchman (1923–91) was an exemplary citizen, worthy of the state's 1994 designation of the road from Interstate 4 in Hillsborough County to US Highway 301 in Pasco County in his honor. He was educated totally in Florida, including at the University of Florida Law School. Buchman served in the US Army, where he received many medals and had a private law practice while serving as city attorney (1949–91). He performed in leadership positions for two governors on many committees, authored publications, and received awards for his legal public service. His son Kenneth follows him as city attorney in Plant City.

Broad and Cassel, formed in 1946 by Shepard Broad (right) and Alvin Cassel, was Florida's oldest firm that started with Jewish partners and had statewide offices, Miami, 1990s.

As of 2018, the firm was merged as Nelson Mullins Broad and Cassel. The Shepard Broad College of Law was established at Nova Southeastern University in 1974 in recognition of his counsel, community leadership, and financial support. (You met Shepard Broad in part 2, chapter 4.)

I found Alvin Cassel (1914–2000) to be a humorous, kind, gentle, and loving spirit. He worked his way through the University of Florida Law School and served in World War II. Upon his return, he and Shepard Broad formed their partnership on a handshake. Cassel, born in Miami, was an ardent supporter of many organizations, especially the American Jewish Committee, Temple Israel, the Florida Bar Association, and President John Kennedy's Economic Opportunity Program.

Miami's Brickell Avenue and Robert "Bob" Traurig (inset), a cofounder of Greenberg Traurig (GT), Florida's largest law firm founded by Jewish partners, 2009.

Most of the development shown in the photograph is a result of Traurig's legal skills. This "dean of zoning" for nearly half a century advised many developers and builders following World War II to transform vacant lots into bustling hubs of life. Traurig (1925–2018) came to Miami in the 1930s. In 1967, while at lunch in a Miami deli with attorneys Melvin N. Greenberg (1928–94) and Larry J. Hoffman, they saw an opportunity to establish a new breed of law firm for South Florida. Today, Greenberg Traurig (GT) has more than two thousand attorneys and thirty-eight locations on three continents.

Founded in 1947 by Leonard Robbins (right) and Maynard Abrams, the law firm continues today as Abrams Anton, Hollywood.

Both Maynard Abrams (1917–92) and Leonard Robbins (1921–2013) were involved with the Jewish Museum of Florida. Abrams, who served as a mayor of Hollywood, was president of MOSAIC Inc., the forerunner of JMOF, in 1991 until his death. Robbins served on the board of the JMOF for many years. Both moved to Florida at the age of four. Both went to the University of Florida, and both loved flying and served in World War II. However, 1st Lieutenant Leonard Robbins was a B-24 bomber navigator in the European theater, flew fifty combat missions, and earned the Distinguished Flying Cross in 1944. Meanwhile, Abrams served as a flight instructor in Lakeland and ran the Hollywood Airport.

The Fredric G. Levin College of Law at University of Florida was named in 1999 for a $10 million gift by Levin (shown here), 2007.

Pensacola native Fred Levin is in the National Trial Lawyers Hall of Fame. He began practicing law in 1961 in the Pensacola law firm of Levin & Askew that was founded by his brother David and Reubin Askew (not Jewish), who would go on to become Florida's thirty-seventh governor. Levin's most celebrated case was in 1993, when he rewrote the Florida Medicaid Third Party Recovery Act to permit the State of Florida to sue the tobacco industry to recover expenditures for treating illnesses caused by cigarette smoking. The legislation eventually resulted in a $13 billion settlement.

CHAPTER 10

Sports

The story of Florida Jews in sports is largely an underappreciated one, even though Jews are all over the sports pages as team owners, coaches, players, and journalists. Some sports stories have already been told in earlier parts of the book. You may be amazed to know that many Floridian Jews have been national and international champions in their chosen sports, Olympians, All-American players, and Super Bowl participants and that Jewish former NBA players met weekly in south Florida. There was one, in particular, who scored the first NBA basket in 1946 ("Ossie" Schectman). In 2003 the Bucs and Marlins won their national titles in football and baseball, respectively. Nearly two hundred American Jews have played Major League Baseball (MLB) since the 1870s, and many have a connection with Florida. And because the conflict between athletics and Jewish identity runs deep, Jews who find a balance—and excel—are treated like heroes. Here are a few.

Eight professional sports teams in Florida have (or had) Jewish owners. The oldest team, playing since 1966, is the Miami Dolphins, owned by Stephen Ross, Miami, circa 2018.

Miami Heat basketball team owner, Micky Arison (right) shown with Pat Riley, coach for eleven seasons. The first coach in 1988 was Jewish, Ron Rothstein, Miami, n.d.

Stephen Ross owns Florida's oldest professional sports team, the NFL Miami Dolphins, as well as the Hard Rock Stadium that is home to the Dolphins, the University of Miami's Hurricanes, Super Bowls, the annual Orange Bowl for college football, and many global events. Ross had the vision to create a tennis stadium within that football stadium in Miami Gardens; the Miami Open tennis tournament had its inaugural outing there in 2019.

Ted Arison was among those responsible for bringing professional basketball to south Florida with the forming of the NBA Miami Heat team in 1988. His son Micky Arison owns the team today.

Other Florida Jewish team owners include Lawrence DuBow, an original owner/partner of the Jacksonville Jaguars NFL team in 1993. In 2001 Alan

P. Cohen became an owner of the National Hockey League (NHL) Florida Panthers hockey team. In 1995, when Malcolm Glazer bought the Bucs, an article in the *Tampa Bay Times* reported there was a huge amount of hate mail. When the Bucs won the Superbowl in 2003, a community leader was quoted as saying, "Why do they all have such big noses?"

Jews own all three professional sports teams in the Tampa Bay area, February 29, 2016. *Photo by Tom Cawthon, the Poynter Institute.*

From left to right are Tampa Bay NHL Lighting ice hockey team owner Jeffrey Vinik, Tampa Bay NFL Buccaneers football team cochairman Bryan Glazer, and Tampa Bay MLB Rays baseball team principal owner Stuart Sternberg, in St. Petersburg.

MLB Florida Marlins President David Samson with Marlins Owner and CEO Jeffrey H. Loria (center) receiving the World Series Trophy, Yankee Stadium, 2003.

Presenting the trophy is Bud Selig, commissioner of Major League Baseball. Loria sold the MLB baseball team in 2017.

Sportswriter Michelle Kaufman at the Winter Olympics in Sochi, Russia, 2014.

A Miami native of Cuban descent, Kaufman graduated from the University of Miami in 1987. Her career began at the *St. Petersburg Times*, where she covered the Tampa Bay Buccaneers and was one of the only women covering the NFL at that time. She has been at the *Miami Herald* since 1996. She has covered fourteen Olympics, six World Cups, and numerous Wimbledons, French Opens, US Opens, National Collegiate Athletic Association (NCAA) Final Fours, Super Bowls, Pan Am Games, World Series, and NBA Finals. She also teaches a sports writing class at the University of Miami School of Journalism. Her work was published in *A Kind of Grace: A Treasury of Sportswriting by Women*; *Real Sports Reporting*, a sports journalism textbook; and *Nike Is a Goddess: History of Women's Sports.*

JoAnn Mason-Parker stayed in the top five for eight years playing on the worldwide tour for the Women's Professional Billiard Association, Boca Raton, 1991.

JoAnn Mason-Parker began playing pocket billiards at the age of four. Her father, a professional player since the early 1970s, introduced her to the sport, was her first teacher, and led her through victories. At the age of thirteen, she won the National 8-Ball Championship, making her number one amateur in the country. During her ten years as a tour professional, she won numerous events worldwide, even capturing the most prestigious titles: the US Open 9-Ball Championship and the Master's World Open.

Sam Wahnish of Tallahassee, member of University of Florida boxing team, 1914. *Steven Sommers.*

I found others involved in boxing. Edward Feinstein of Miami was captain of the University of Miami boxing team in 1943—at the same time he was captain of their basketball team. Carl Gardner served on the Miami Beach Boxing Commission for twenty years. He also started the Miami Beach Flamingos Baseball Team, and every Sunday morning until he was seventy-five years old, Gardner played softball at Flamingo Park. From 1980 to 2000, everything that happened with Miami Beach boxing ran through Jimmy Resnick, who became one of the first state boxing commissioners (1984–95). Hank Kaplan of Miami was widely regarded as the nation's foremost boxing historian before his death in 2007. Kaplan started a boxing magazine, helped establish the International Boxing Hall of Fame in New York, and was inducted in 2006.

Owner Louis E. Wolfson walking with "Affirmed," his Triple Crown of Thoroughbred racing winner (Kentucky Derby, Preakness Stakes, Belmont Stakes), Ocala, 1978. Florida Horse *magazine.*

The race horse "Affirmed" (1975–2001) was bred by Jacksonville's Louis and Patrice Wolfson (daughter of late Hall of Fame horse trainer, Hirsch Jacobs) and trained at their Harbor View Farm in Ocala. In this sport older than baseball, this title is a first for a Florida Jew. Wolfson moved with his family to Jacksonville at the age of one and was an outstanding business tycoon and humanitarian (see earlier in this part of the book).

Show jumping equestrian Margie Goldstein-Engle, ten-time American Grandprix Association Rider of the Year, Wellington, 1994. HorsePlay *magazine.*

Born in Wellington and raised in Miami, Goldstein-Engle is the winningest rider in the history of US show jumping. She has represented the US at the Olympics and other international competitions, bringing home gold, silver, and bronze medals. In 2001 she was honored by the US Jewish Sports Hall of Fame, and in 2009 she was inducted into the International Jewish Sports Hall of Fame. With more than 195 Grand Prix victories, Goldstein-Engle is a pioneer in this sport as a Jewish female in a field dominated by non-Jews.

Apte Tarpon Fly US postage stamp, limited series, honored the first Jewish backcountry fishing guide in the Florida Keys, Islamorada, 1991.

Miami native Stu Apte was one of the nation's leading fly-fishing authorities. He held forty-four saltwater light tackle and fly rod world records. Apte wrote articles on fly-fishing, appeared on television shows, and produced an award-winning film called *Tarpon Country*. A former US Navy fighter pilot, then Pam Am pilot, he was inducted into the Fishing Hall of Fame in 1969 and the International Game Fish Association Hall of Fame in 2005. He was the founding member of Bonefish and Tarpon Unlimited, an organization that deals with the conservation of the bonefish and tarpon population. Apte developed quite a following as a fishing guide. President Harry Truman and his wife Bess were among his prestigious guests.

Morgan Pressel is a professional golfer on the Ladies Professional Golf Association (LPGA) Tour, Boca Raton, 2008.

Morgan Pressel, born in 1988 in Tampa, started playing golf at age eight and at age twelve became the youngest qualifier in the history of the US Women's Open. Morgan had many accomplishments in her amateur career, including the number one ranking in the US Girls Juniors and Women's Amateur. Coached by her grandfather Dr. Herb Krickstein, Morgan turned professional at age seventeen. She became the youngest woman in history to win a Ladies Professional Golf Association (LPGA) major championship, at age eighteen, which vaulted her to a career-high fourth in the world rankings. In 2015 Pressel came in second at the Swinging Skirts LPGA Classic in San Francisco.

6B—DAYTONA BEACH SUNDAY NEWS-JOURNAL Feb. 9, 1958

NASCAR'S Legal Counsel Recalls

Pioneer Days Of Stock Racing

By BOB DESIDERIO

Attorney Louis Ossinsky finds it profitable to keep one of his biggest clients going around in circles, which isn't so bad as it sounds.

In plainer language, the colorful lawyer is vice president and general counsel of NASCAR, the World's largest stock car racing organization.

This year marks the 10th anniversary of the racing collossus, which Bill France, Bill Tuthill and Ossinsky founded to bring order to a mushrooming, post-World War II sport.

Today, Ossinsky, a senior member of the Volusia County Bar, can recall with justifiable pride: "We expanded from nothing."

Last year, the long haul from nothing had blossomed into an auditor's joy, namely: more than 1,200 races drawing millions of spectators in the U.S. and Canada and a membership of nearly 17,000 active owners, drivers, mechanics, promoters and fans.

Although NASCAR was founded Dec. 10, 1947, it didn't shift into high until the 1948 season, when 975 members participated in 87 sanctioned races.

NASCAR's success story is one that Ossinsky, a self styled "poor boy from Jacksonville," can relish, because he expanded from nothing, too.

[illegible], after a 31 year partnership in law with senior member, Harry A. Horn, Ossinsky has the rugged build which made him a standout tackle in high school and college football.

After being named all state captain for his play at old Duval High School in Jacksonville, Ossinsky went on to play football and study at the University of Georgia. He switched to Stetson, where he continued to not only play football but served as assistant coach, and received his law degree.

Before he finally settled down in partnership with Horn in 1926, Ossinsky had worked at a lot of odd jobs in furthering his education. In high school, he had sold newspapers, and later, even tried his hand at being a correspondent for several newspapers during his Georgia days.

During the 1924-25 season, he was athletic director and coached football and basketball at Seabreeze High School. "In those days, we used to hold our football drills on the beach," chuckled Ossinsky. And in his "spare time," Ossinsky officiated at various athletic contests.

It was in 1933 that Ossinsky began buying his gasoline from another "poor boy," a young fellow from Washington, D.C., named Bill France.

The station was across the street from Ossinsky's Main St. law offices. "We got acquainted," recalls Ossinsky, "and as time went on, I began to represent Bill."

After World War II, France, who had promoted races in a small way in the late 30s, resumed his activities. But things were different.

"Stock car racing showed a lot of promise even then," said Ossinsky," but chaos was the order of the day.

"Races were made up in the most casual way. A promoter would call a few drivers and announce a race. However, it was anybody's guess whether or not he would be around to pay off after the race was over. If the gate was bad, he might skip out; and if the gate was good, he might still take off with the money.

"Conditions were pretty bad for all concerned. The speedways were mostly unfinished, with little thought given to the protection of either spectators or drivers. Drivers competed at their own risk — no kind of insurance or hospitalization was available for them.

The competitive angle was just as helter skelter. All kinds of fuels were used, motors were outfitted with unclassified parts and no reliable records were kept of races for purposes of comparison.

"It's no wonder," sighed Ossinsky, "that racing as a whole was frowned on and was generally looked on with ill will by public authorities."

France and his associates began talking about founding an organization to clean up racing as early as 1946. The next year, saw more groundwork accomplished, and the actual incorporation of NASCAR.

In 1949, NASCAR met and conquered the first big challenge to its authority by putting down a driver's revolt in the Charlotte (N.C.) hearings.

The days of the fly by night promoters and undisciplined drivers were numbered.

Today, NASCAR can count a number of firsts in racing.

"We guarantee the prize money in any NASCAR sanctioned race," began Ossinsky.

"We guarantee hospitalization and insurance benefits.

"NASCAR rules and regulations are enforced through the National Racing Commission.

"Racing is a most hazardous operation at best," admitted Ossinsky, "so one of our greatest concerns is and has been with safety. In turn, this has led to better and safer automobiles for the American motorist.

"For example, in the first Darlington (S.C.) race, more tires blew out that day than possibly ever before in any race. The tire manufacturers were very embarrassed. It has never happened since."

Ossinsky made a thorough research of laws pertaining to speedways which led to further safety features in NASCAR regulations. Classification of tracks, types of races and varying skills of drivers made it possible for NASCAR to name yearly national champions, based on accurate statistics.

Ossinsky found himself traveling all over the country educating promoters and officials in their new responsibilities.

The veteran lawyer modestly discounts his part in making racing as respectable as it is exciting. When you ask him what his specific contributions have been to the NASCAR story, Ossinsky replies: "Oh, you know, all the legal work. Mostly, I just listen to the boys talk and then give them my advice. Sometimes they take it and sometimes they don't."

Ossinsky's counsel must be of a high order.

For in a day when the federal government is talking of legislating such professional sports as baseball and football, and when state Legislatures and cities are sprouting boxing commissions, only the state of New Jersey has thought it necessary to establish an auto racing commission; is a NASCAR's house in tidy, indeed. [illegible]

LOUIS OSSINSKY
. . . as Seabreeze coach

LOUIS OSSINSKY
. . . NASCAR counsel today

In 1948 Daytona Beach attorney Louis Ossinsky Sr. drew up the incorporation papers for the National Association for Stock Car Auto Racing (NASCAR).

Louis Ossinsky, a part-owner, also established the original National Association for Stock Car Auto Racing (NASCAR) safety regulations. Ossinsky served as vice president and general counsel for NASCAR until his death in 1971. He was born in Jacksonville to a family that settled there in the 1880s. In 1920 he was in All-State football from Duval High School. He graduated from Stetson Law School in 1925, where he coached the freshman football team. He was also a well-known basketball referee in the 1920s and 1930s. In 1926 he was the first president of the Judah P. Benjamin Lodge of B'nai B'rith in Jacksonville.

1972 Munich Olympic swimmer Robert Strauss has taught swimming in Miami since 1973 and is director of the Swim Gym, Miami, 2008

Born in Mexico, Robert Strauss started swimming at age two, went to the University of Miami on a swimming scholarship (1971–74), and has since lived in Miami. From its inception in 1984, his Swim Gym has been globally recognized as a leader in the field of aquatic education. By 2018 Strauss had taught more than sixty thousand students, from three months to eighty-plus years old, 90 percent nonswimmers when they started lessons.

Strauss swam in the infamous 1972 Munich Olympic Games for his native Mexico at the age of twenty. On the morning of September 5, the worst tragedy in Olympic history hit. Eight Arab terrorists stormed into the Olympic village and raided the building that housed the Israeli contingent. Two Israeli athletes were killed and nine more seized as hostages. The terrorists demanded the release of more than two hundred Palestinians serving time in Israeli jails, along with two German terrorists. After a day of unsuccessful negotiations, the terrorists collected the hostages and headed for the military airport in Munich for a flight back to the Middle East. At the airport, German sharpshooters opened fire, killing three of the Arabs. A gun battle ensued, killing the Israeli athletes, along with others. Athletic competition was suspended for twenty-four hours. In a controversial decision, International Olympic Committee (IOC) president Avery Brundage declared, "the Games must go on." And so they did.

The day after Robert Strauss completed his swimming competition, he took a trip to the Dachau concentration camp. He returned to the Olympic village on that morning of September 5 and heard machine guns and helicopters and someone screaming, "They're killing all the Jews!" Frightened, he left the village and headed for the train station to go to London to stay with a friend. He watched the Olympics closing ceremonies from there. He returned to Munich just as his team was preparing to leave for the airport to return to Mexico.

Five-time (1984, 1988, 1992, 2000, and 2008) Olympian Dara Torres is arguably the fastest female swimmer in the US, Broward County, 2008. TIME *magazine.*

Torres made the 2008 squad for the Beijing Olympics at age forty-one (while being a mother), becoming the oldest and only swimmer to compete in five Olympic Games for a career total of twelve medals. Torres lived in Broward County and started competing internationally when she was fourteen. In the 1980s, while studying at the University of Florida, she earned twenty-eight NCCA All-American swimming awards and was inducted into the UF Athletic Hall of Fame as a "Gator Great" in 1999. In 2005 she was inducted into the International Jewish Sports Hall of Fame. Torres, a veteran celebrity swimmer for Swim Across America, raises funds for cancer research, is the author of two books, and is a motivational speaker—and she has a fitness app.

1956 Wimbledon doubles champion Angela Buxton lives part time in Pompano Beach, London, 1956.

Englishwoman Buxton was one of the top female tennis players in the world in the mid-1950s. After playing in her first Wimbledon tournament in 1952 and going out on the first round, she realized that she needed to improve and went to California for six months. She was surprised to find out that the Los Angeles Tennis Club would not permit her to play, which she blamed on antisemitism. The turning point in her career was the Maccabiah Games in Israel in 1953, where she picked up two gold medals. In 1956, she teamed up with African American Althea Gibson "because we were both isolated" to win the Wimbledon Doubles Championship. That same year Buxton was a Wimbledon Singles finalist and was ranked number five in the world by *World Tennis Magazine*. She experienced much antisemitism in her career. The exclusive All England Lawn Tennis Club never invited her to join. Buxton joined us at the JMOF to watch the 2008 Wimbledon matches, where we served the traditional strawberries and cream. In 2014 she was inducted into the National Jewish Sports Hall of Fame. Angela Buxton died in 2020.

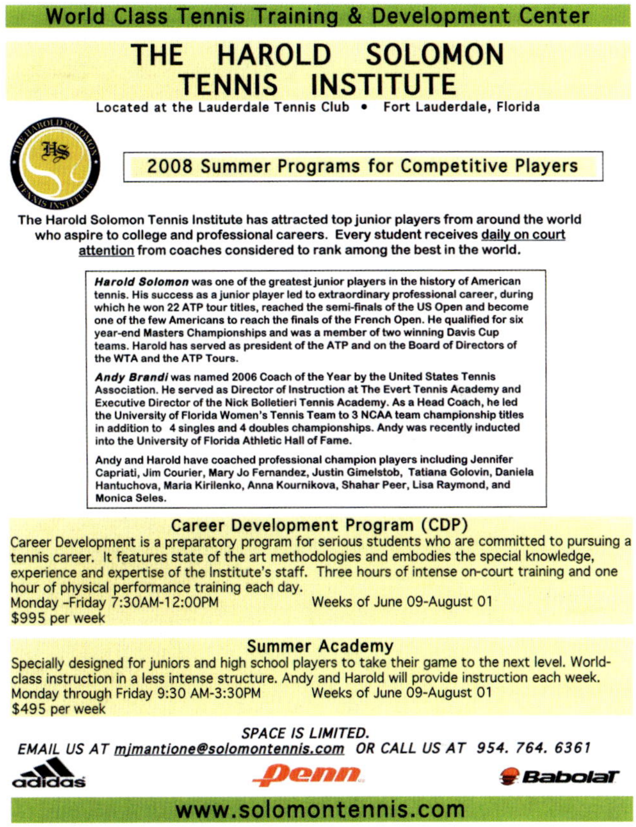

Flyer advertising the program for competitive players at the Harold Solomon Tennis Institute, Fort Lauderdale, 2008.

Harold Solomon has been known as the "Human Backboard" because he played like one and was notorious for frustrating his opponents with his lobs and relentless, methodical returns. He began playing tennis at the age of five and was one of the greatest junior players in the history of American tennis. A seasoned professional tennis player during the 1970s and 1980s with twenty-two singles titles and a French Open finalist, he ranked number five in the world in singles (1980) and number four in doubles (1976). He was president of the Association of Tennis Professionals (1980–83) and was inducted into the US Tennis Association Mid-Atlantic Section Hall of Fame (1994), the International Jewish

Sports Hall of Fame (2004), and the Washington, DC., Sports Hall of Fame (2016). In the 1990s, he began his coaching career in Florida, training champions such as Mary Jo Fernandez, Jennifer Capriati, Monica Seles, Anna Kournikova, Jim Courier, and most recently, Naomi Osaka. His institute, now named Florida Tennis SBT Academy, provides coaching for students who aspire to attain college or professional careers.

Phillip and Robert Soven are World Wakeboard Champions, Longwood, 2010. Wakeboarding *magazine.*

The Longwood-native brothers are wakeboarding superstars and TV stars of *WakeBrothers*, an MTV reality series that chronicles the relationship between their polar-opposite personalities. Since turning professional at age eleven, Phillip is widely regarded as one of the most successful wakeboarders of the past two decades, with his innovative moves and consistent performances. He shattered the record books when he became the first rider in the history of competitive wakeboarding to take home the Pro Tour title, the King of Wake title, and the World Wake Association (WWA) World Series crown all in the same year.

Wrestling champion Boris "The Great" Malenko, Tampa, 1969.

You might have heard that WrestleMania 36 is coming to Tampa in 2020. Before there were major league sports teams in Florida, there was wrestling (in the 1950s through the 1980s) in the building that is now the Glazer Family JCC in Tampa. Weekly matches at the Fort Homer Hesterly Armory attracted sold-out crowds of five thousand fans. One of the top attractions was Russian immigrant Lawrence Simon (1933–94), billed as Boris "The Great" Malenko. Once he was hit so hard that his dentures flew out of his mouth, and his opponent crushed them under his boot. That received so much fanfare that the incident was repeated in matches all over the state. Malenko won more than a dozen Florida wrestling titles including the National Wrestling Alliance (NWA) Florida Heavyweight Championship, and after his retirement, he opened a gym and training center in Tampa. Two of his sons, Joe and Dean, became professional wrestlers. In 2018 Malenko was named a legacy inductee in the World Wrestling Entertainment (WWE) Hall of Fame.

NEW NAME—Workers installed new nameplate for the Jacksonville Ball Park today. The park was renamed in honor of the late Sam W. Wolfson, Jacksonville sportsman-financier.
Journal Photo by Foster Marshall

In Jacksonville, there was a baseball park named for baseball owner Samuel W. Wolfson from 1955–2002.

This was home to all of Jacksonville's minor league baseball teams and hosted other events, including Elvis Presley in 1955. Wolfson was president of the South Atlantic League (1958) and president of the Jacksonville Suns.

Al Rosen, nicknamed "The Hebrew Hammer" and "Flip," won a World Series ring with the Cleveland Indians in 1948.

Al Rosen (1924–2015) excelled in many sports including football, basketball, and boxing and is known as one of the best all-time Jewish baseball players with his friends Hank Greenberg and Sandy Koufax—and he also refused to play baseball on the Jewish high holy days. Rosen was All-City at Miami High and played for Florida Military Academy and the University of Miami. Rosen played third base for the Cleveland Indians baseball team from 1947 to 1956 and was the first unanimous Most Valuable Player in 1953. Rosen is included in several Halls of Fame including the National Jewish Sports Hall of Fame and the International Jewish Sports Hall of Fame. He was an MLB executive with the New York Yankees, Houston Astros, and San Francisco Giants.

Before he was a professional, #52 Neal Walk played basketb all for Miami Beach High School, Florida State Basketball Tournament, Miami Beach, 1965.

Growing up in Miami Beach, Neal Walk (1948–2015) played basketball for Miami Beach High School during 1962–65 and is a member of their Hall of Fame.

The team had mostly Jewish players, and often they were subjected to antisemitic rants. He then played for the University of Florida (UF), where he holds the rebounds record and is the highest-drafted player in their history. He was the first Associated Press (AP) All-American basketball player at UF (two years in a row, 1967–69) and the only Gator basketball player who has had his jersey, number forty-one, retired. He played with the Phoenix Suns, 1969–74, and is considered the best center in their history. After playing for the New York Knicks for two seasons, he played for Israel's Ramat Gan Hapoel.

In 1988 a benign tumor was discovered enveloping Walk's spinal cord. Following surgery, he was left paralyzed. He played wheelchair basketball for the LA Phoenix Samaritans in the National Wheelchair Basketball Association. In 1990 Walk was honored at the White House by President George H. W. Bush as the "Wheelchair Athlete of the Year," and in 2006 he was inducted into the National Jewish Sports Hall of Fame. He closed out his career with the Phoenix Suns in their Digital Archives Department and gave inspirational speeches for charities.

Miami Dolphins #64 Ed Newman played twelve seasons, including three Super Bowls, and became the strongest player in the history of the Dolphins, Miami, 1984.

Ed Newman (1951–) began his football career at Syosset High School in New York and continued it at Duke University, where he was the Atlantic Coast Conference Heavyweight Wrestling Champion in 1970–71 and was named All-Atlantic Coast Conference and All-American. Upon graduation, Newman was drafted by the Miami Dolphins, where he played from 1973 to 1984, during which time he was a four-time Pro Bowl selection. He also became the labor spokesman for his teammates. Newman retired from football following a knee injury in the 1985 season, having played in 167 career games. He is a member of the International Jewish Sports Hall of Fame, the New York Jewish Sports Hall of Fame, and the Duke University Sports Hall of Fame. Syosset High annually presents the Ed Newman Second Effort Award to the football player who demonstrates the most perseverance.

"But I knew that football would not last forever," Newman says. "It was time to prepare for a second career." He went to the University of Miami Law School and graduated in 1987. He had a private practice before being elected a county court judge in the Eleventh Judicial Circuit, where he currently presides. His bailiff is a former Dolphins teammate.

ALAN VEINGRAD DALLAS COWBOYS

Alan "Shlomo" Veingrad (#76) playing for the Dallas Cowboys, 1991.

Born in Brooklyn (1963) and raised in Miami, Veingrad grew to be six feet five and, with a nearly obsessive mind-set, trained to become nearly three hundred pounds of solid muscle for football. He was All-American at East Texas State University, where he was the only Jew on campus in the 1980s. He turned pro and played for seven seasons from 1986 to 1992 as an offensive lineman in eighty-six games for two of the greatest teams in NFL history: the Green Bay Packers and the Dallas Cowboys, with whom he participated in Super Bowl XXVII. He was inducted into the National Jewish Sports Hall of Fame in 2010.

Growing up, he had always sought ways to become a better person, as well as a better athlete, but it wasn't until after retirement that he found meaning in life after football by becoming a Torah-observant Jew. Residing in Boca Raton as an Israel advocate, he travels the country relating his inspirational spiritual journey with humor and poignancy, which includes such positive messages as, "Everything I learned in football can be applied to Yiddishkeit."

First American-born and only Jewish jai alai player Joey Cornblit is a Florida icon who played in front of ten thousand people a night, Miami, 1977.

Jai alai was played for centuries in the Basque areas of Spain and France where it was invented. Joey Cornblit has been classified as jai alai's most popular American player. A Miami native and son of Israeli immigrants, he attended Miami schools. Cornblit said, "Jai alai is a strange game for an American Jewish boy from Miami to owe his comfortable adult life to," but nevertheless, he was the first American to equal the Basque masters of the sport. At age twelve, Cornblit began to beat some professional Basque players at the Miami Fronton, and he turned professional as a senior in high school after returning from a summer in Guernica, Spain, that was spent learning from the Basque masters. In Florida, minors are banned from frontons, but Cornblit bypassed the rules by climbing to the roof and staring through a vent at the game below. After three years of instruction, at age fifteen, Cornblit won a bronze medal at the 1971 World Championships. In 1977 he was the overall winner at Miami's World Jai Alai, the premier palace of the game, and at twenty-two, he was the reigning champion of the game. He retired in 1995 after a twenty-four-year career, and his is the only jai alai jersey to have been retired. Cornblit, who lives in Plantation, was inducted into the Florida Sports Hall of Fame in 2015.

CHAPTER 11

Education

Who are the "People of the Book?" In the seventh century, Muslim leaders identified the Jewish community with this title of respect, and long before that, Hillel the Sage ordained Jews to study. So it comes as no surprise that learning and teaching are integral parts of Judaism's historic culture.

You learned earlier that Moses Levy was instrumental in establishing the territory's earliest free public school, served as the territory's first education commissioner in 1831, and served on a legislative committee investigating the establishment of a University of Florida.

The earliest Jewish school teacher I found in Florida was Bela Cohen in 1887 in Escambia County; she earned forty-five dollars a month. As Florida's institutions of learning burgeoned, so did the presence of Jewish teachers, professors, and administrators, too many to enumerate. Jews continue to serve on school boards and have schools named for them across the state.

Mitchell Wolfson was a founder of Miami Dade College in 1960 in the midst of desegregation with seven black students and Cuban refugees who were arriving. The Wolfson family has contributed about $150 million to educational causes over its history.

Jack D. Gordon served on the Dade County School Board, among other Jews, and was a leader in desegregating the schools—surviving death threats. In 1985 he founded the Institute for Public Policy and Citizenship Studies at Florida International University that bears his name.

Here I will highlight a few Jews who represent the many in enriching education. From innovative preschools and public elementary to high schools to colleges, universities, and graduate schools, Jews have made an important difference. I dedicate this section to all those students and teachers who have been murdered at schools.

Marjory Stoneman Douglas High School teacher Ivy Schamis (center with sunglasses) joins her students at the "March for Our Lives" rally in Washington, DC, March 24, 2018.

Following the February 14, 2018, murder of seventeen people at the school in Parkland, the march brought about a million people into the streets in eight hundred separate youth-led events across the nation. This activism by groups of students led to a national movement focusing on gun regulations, voter registration, and the role of young people in politics. One of the most memorable speeches at the Washington March was by Stoneman Douglas senior Samantha Fuentes. Neither scars nor pain—nor nausea that made her throw up in the middle of a speech being televised around the world—caused her to stop speaking out as an eyewitness to the horror.

Ivy Schamis, who has taught for seventeen years at Stoneman Douglas, teaches a Holocaust class. Her father, Norman Levine, served two terms as president of the JMOF and is a good friend of mine. I have known Ivy for many years. Of that day in 2018, she said, "We were discussing hate groups likely to be on their college campuses and tactics to stand up for what is right. Then, because of the timeliness of the Olympics in Pyeongchang, we turned to discussing the 1936 Olympics in Germany when Jewish athletes could not compete." At that moment, loud shots rang out in the hall, and the students flew out of their seats and tried to shield themselves—some using Schamis's vast collection of Holocaust books.

Fuentes recalled, "I saw the shooter appear emotionless at the glass panel in the door of our classroom. Within seconds, the gunman had broken the glass and was blasting his AR-15 at us. One of his bullets pierced my thigh and shrapnel was lodged in the other leg, as well as in several places in my face, including behind my eye."

The shooter injured four and killed two students in that classroom—in front of Schamis and her students. Five of the seventeen dead were Jewish; a few more had Jewish ancestry. After the shooting, Schamis considered that Jews were the target since the shooter wore backpacks with swastikas and came to the building where she and other Jewish teachers taught. But that ultimately was not the case—he had fired indiscriminately and killed teachers and students of all backgrounds. Schamis asks, "How can this happen, of all places, in a classroom where students were learning how to combat hate? The lessons of the Holocaust were coming alive right there in room 1214. Since that day, the fourth period students have become a symbol of Holocaust Education: loss of innocence coupled with unfailing optimism."

Stanley G. Tate (shown in back center) Florida Prepaid College Program is one of the oldest and largest in the nation, Miami.

Stanley G. Tate of Miami was instrumental in the early development of the Florida Prepaid College Program. Thirty years ago, it was his vision to provide Florida families with an affordable means to save for their children's future college education. Mr. Tate served tirelessly as Board Chairman (1987–2005). More than 1.1 million contracts have been sold for the 529 plans, and more than 460,000 children have used their plan benefits to attend a college or university. In recognition of Mr. Tate's service, Governor Jeb Bush signed House Bill 263 into law on June 26, 2006, renaming the program the Stanley G. Tate Florida Prepaid College Program. Tate has been building homes, apartments, office buildings, and shopping centers in Florida since 1954. He has been deeply involved in civic, Jewish, political, and charitable endeavors.

Paul W. Bell was the first Jewish Dade County Public Schools superintendent and has a middle school named for him, Miami, 1990.

Abraham S. Fischler, EdD, was the second president (1970–92) of Nova University (NSU), Fort Lauderdale, 1992.

As a young man, Bell gave up a full scholarship to law school after a summer job as a camp counselor, realizing his love for children and teaching. A national leader in bilingual education, he served the longest period of his thirty-year career as assistant superintendent for instruction and curriculum and was appointed to lead the nation's fourth largest district in 1990. Bell said, "I have always had the real belief that every child can learn."

Visionary Fischler (1928–2017) led the private university for 22 years, growing it from 57 to 10,600 students. He is credited for making the school the innovative university it is today, recognizing that teaching needs to be paced to the students' abilities. In the mid-1980s he advocated for technology and initiated online learning. "Leaving the world in a better condition than how I found it," was the motto that guided his life. NSU's College of Education bears his name.

Rita Bornstein (center), PhD, was president (1990–2004) of Rollins College, its first woman president, and named president emerita, Winter Park, 2001.

From left to right are Rollins Provost Patricia Lancaster, President Rita Bornstein, and former US Representative Pat Schroeder. Founded in 1885, Rollins is Florida's first recognized college. The college's endowment more than quintupled during Bornstein's presidency. She had been vice president at the University of Miami, where she led what was then one of the largest and most successful fundraising campaigns in the history of American higher education.

Judy Genshaft, PhD, was president and CEO (2000–2019) of the University of South Florida (USF), Tampa, 2010.

With campuses in Tampa, St. Petersburg, and Sarasota-Manatee, the USF system serves 50,500 students in 235 degree programs ranging from undergraduate to doctor of medicine and other health professions. Dr. Genshaft catapulted the USF system to national and international prominence for student success, academic rigor, research and innovation, and economic development. Upon her retirement in July 2019, she gifted $20 million to the school to build a new honors college that will bear her name. This is probably the nation's largest gift by a president back to their university.

Wendy Libby (seated), PhD, became president of Stetson University in 2009, Deland, 2018.

As the first female president, Dr. Libby says her job "has given me opportunities to strengthen Jewish culture and life on the Stetson campus." Since 2009 Stetson increased undergraduate enrollment by nearly 50 percent to more than three thousand students. She hired more than one hundred new faculty members and doubled the endowment fund. As the first female president, Dr. Libby says her job "has given me opportunities to strengthen Jewish culture and life on the Stetson campus." Stetson Law consistently ranks first in the country for trial advocacy and in the top three for legal writing.

Mark B. Rosenberg, PhD, assumed the office of president of Florida International University (FIU) in 2009, Miami, 2018.

As provost and executive vice president for academic affairs at FIU (1998–2005), Dr. Rosenberg spearheaded the establishment of a law school and a medical school. A first-generation college graduate and political scientist specializing in Latin America, Dr. Rosenberg had served as chancellor of the State University System of Florida and is the first FIU faculty member to ascend to its presidency. Under his leadership, FIU has increased enrollment to almost fifty-six thousand students, improved retention and graduation rates by nearly 13 percent, and hired more than five hundred new faculty. Dr. Rosenberg provides leadership to coordinate FIU's emergence as a leading producer of graduates focused on STEM.

CHAPTER 12

Media

Floridian Jews have been involved in all aspects of mainstream media: radio and TV as morning disc jockeys, evening talk hosts, and news anchors or station owners. They have taken part in selling ads and dealing with publicity, and have been magazine editors and owners and newspaper reporters, editors, and owners. For example, Pauline Berman, the nation's first-known woman radio news commentator, had her own program (1930–1933) in Orlando and traveled to Europe (1955) to report on the status of women there.

For a hundred years, there have been Jewish newspapers in Florida to record the events that compile our history and create a sense of community. Louis Mendelson and Morris Gherlerter started the *Florida Jewish News* in Jacksonville in 1924. In 1938 they were bought by Isadore and Teddy Moscovitz and eventually became the *Southern Jewish Weekly*. In Miami, the *Jewish Unity* was begun in 1926, and Louis Shochet started the *Jewish Floridian* in 1928, which lasted for sixty-two years. Today, there are Jewish publications in Miami-Dade, Broward, Palm Beach, Lee, Charlotte and Sarasota-Manatee Counties and in Tampa, St. Petersburg, Orlando, Jacksonville, and Naples.

Journalists say they would rather "tell" the story than "be" the story. This chapter is dedicated to two courageous journalists who *were* the story—Steven Sotloff who was beheaded by the Islamic State of Iraq and Syria (ISIS) on September 2, 2014, and Alfie Kohn who was killed during World War II.

Before his murder by ISIS in 2014, journalist Steven Sotloff (center with black helmet), procures story from Libyan rebels, Al Dafniya front line, Libya, 2011.

Miami native and dual American Israeli citizen Sotloff was the son of Shirley and Arthur Sotloff and the grandson of Holocaust survivors. They encouraged him to be a "voice for the voiceless." He studied journalism at the University of Central Florida and was a freelance journalist who wrote about the impact of conflict on ordinary people in the Middle East for the *Jerusalem Post*, *TIME*, *Foreign Policy*, CNN, and Fox News, among others. He brought out the humanitarian aspect in his powerful stories. Sotloff studied in Israel and studied Arabic in Yemen, then traveled to Egypt, Bahrain, Libya, Turkey, and eventually Syria.

In Libya, he interviewed seven of the Libyan security guards who had been on duty at the US mission in Benghazi on the night of the 2012 attack that killed Ambassador J. Christopher Stevens. His article of personal stories contributed to the national conversation about Benghazi.

Sotloff was kidnapped by ISIS militants after he drove across the border from Turkey into Syria in 2013. He was held for a year before he was beheaded by ISIS, who released an online video of the savage murder. During his year of captivity, Sotloff hid his Jewish faith from his kidnappers but secretly practiced his religion. He smuggled two letters to his family through a former cellmate. "Everyone has two lives," Sotloff wrote. "The second one begins when you realize that you only have one." Many awards have honored Steven Sotloff in memoriam, and there is a journalism scholarship in his name.

Plaque hanging in Student Lounge of University of F lorida (UF) College of Journalism and Communications in memory of Alfie Kohn, killed while getting a story during World War II, Gainesville.

Kohn (1921–44) is the only known UF journalism graduate to be killed in action and the only known Floridian among the forty-five war correspondents killed during World War II. Kohn was posthumously awarded the Purple Heart. After World War II, his parents had his body brought back from France and buried in a military cemetery in Pensacola. A scholarship is named in his memory at UF.

***Tropic* magazine regarding PR man Hank Meyer, Miami Beach, 1970.**

Hank Meyer (1920–99) arrived on Miami Beach from New York in 1938, opened his public relations firm, and convinced the city that they needed a press agent. For nearly half a century, Meyer helped make Miami Beach a major destination as he promoted the sun, surf, sand, and fun. He attracted one hundred television shows to the Beach, including Arthur Godfrey's *Talent Scouts* in the 1950s and *The Jackie Gleason Show* in the 1960s.

Charlie Cinnamon, known as the "Grand sage of publicity for whom all of life had been a stage" was unmatched in his field, Miami Beach, 1990s.

For sixty-plus years, Charlie Cinnamon (1921–2016) was coveted as a news promoter by the world's biggest stars. He was tapped to lead national public affairs campaigns for some of the world's leading cultural organizations and commercial enterprises. Cinnamon was singularly respected by several generations of journalists for his honesty and integrity from the time he started working in the 1940s until his death, which made national headlines. While today's frenetic social media stream and the "fake news" phenomena turn the news industry upside down, Cinnamon's straightforward brand of public relations hearkens back to a time when a handshake meant so much more.

Radio host Larry King (right), who started his career on Miami Beach, is interviewing local personalities at the Flagler Race Track, Miami, 1970.

From left to right are Isadore Hecht, Leonard Abess, Max Orovitz, and Larry King. King was born as Larry Zieger in 1933 in New York to Orthodox Russian Jewish immigrants. He came to Miami Beach in 1957 to start his career in radio broadcasting for $55 a week. Told Zieger was too ethnic, he chose King from a *Miami Herald* liquor ad. Some of his earliest interviews took place at Pumpernik's with Bobby Darin as his first celebrity guest. He was mentored for TV by Jackie Gleason who was filming his show on Miami Beach. In 1978 he left the area to become a talk show host on a national call-in radio show. In 1985 he started *Larry King Live*, which became one of the highest-rated programs on CNN television and ran until 2010. King claims to have interviewed more than forty thousand people.

Joseph Brechner, here in the Channel 9 studio, brought ABC network TV to Orlando, 1958. *Collection of the Historical Society of Central Florida, Inc.*

Joseph and Marion Brechner moved to Orlando to found WLOF-TV, later renamed WFTV-Channel 9. Early on, WFTV produced a variety of local shows featuring news, space education and children's programming. Brechner was one of the first broadcasters in the country to offer on-air editorials, which aired three times daily. He and Marion were broadcasters and powerful advocates for democracy and human freedom, covering civil rights before most other American broadcasters. Since 1981, there has been a Joseph L. Brechner Freedom of Information Endowment at the University of Florida College of Journalism and Communications.

Howard Kleinberg as managing editor of the *Miami News*, Miami, 1968.

When Howard Kleinberg moved to Miami with his parents in 1949, he joined the *Miami News* as a high school correspondent and rose through the ranks, from sports writer to sports editor, managing editor in 1968 to editor in 1976 until the paper closed in 1988. After his home was battered by Hurricane Andrew in 1992, he wrote a diary that became a book. Until retirement, Kleinberg was a syndicated national columnist, an author of articles and books on the social and cultural history of South Florida and a contributor to the *Miami Herald*.

Stan Roberts (center), in the *Orlando Sentinel* newsroom, became managing editor, Orlando, circa 1968. *Orlando Sentinel.*

Roberts moved to Orlando at age six in 1939. He began at the *Orlando Sentinel* as a part-time reporter in the 1960s. By 1967, he was metro editor and from 1970 to 1977, managing editor, a most influential newspaper position. Current events, from civil rights to Watergate, were his passion. When his career took him to meetings at local venues where Jews were not permitted, he singlehandedly effected change and credits the management at the *Orlando Sentinel* with respecting diversity in the workplace. Other Jewish employees at the *Orlando Sentinel* have included sportswriters Jill Cousins and Bill Buchalter and religion writer Mark Pinsky.

***Washington Post* executive editor Martin "Marty" Baron, formerly of the *Miami Herald*, is a native of Tampa, 2016.**

Marty Baron's role as editor of the *Boston Globe* was highlighted in the Academy Award–winning movie *Spotlight*. He was editor of the *Globe* for eleven years. Among the Pulitzer Prizes earned under his leadership, one came from their 2003 investigation into a decades-long coverup of sexual abuse by priests within the Boston Archdiocese. Baron also has held top editing positions at the *New York Times*, the *Los Angeles*

Times, and the *Miami Herald*. Under his leadership, the *Miami Herald* won the Pulitzer Prize for Breaking News Coverage in 2001 for its reporting of the raid to recover Elián González, the Cuban boy at the center of a fierce immigration and custody dispute. Baron has been editor of the *Washington Post* since 2013 and continues to earn Pulitzer Prizes. When I heard him speak in St. Petersburg in 2016, he said, "We will publish what we think the public should know. We do our research and then tell people what we found—tell it straight. People are entitled to know the facts."

Jeff Zucker is a media executive. Since 2019, his titles have put him in charge of much of WarnerMedia's live television coverage. A five-time Emmy Award winner, Zucker graduated from North Miami Senior High in 1982, having displayed journalistic skills that continued as president of the *Harvard Crimson*. Beginning at NBC as a researcher, by 1989, he was producing NBC's *Today Show*. Then he became president and CEO of NBC Universal in 2000. Since 2013, he's been president of CNN Worldwide, where he is attempting to attract younger audiences by focusing on digital storytelling. Zucker says he loves television and loves news, so CNN is the place to be as a relevant twenty-first-century media company.

Miami native Jeff Zucker is president of CNN Worldwide and chairman of WarnerMedia News and Sports, 2018.

PART 4

Tradition! Life Cycles and Jewish Rituals

As Tevye sings in *Fiddler on the Roof,* "Tradition!"

According to a 2013 Pew survey, 78 percent of American Jews practiced Judaism. Despite attempts for annihilation, Jews have maintained their identity for more than four thousand years. Among reasons given for the continuation of Judaism is the celebration of life cycle events and religious observances by Jews from generation to generation throughout the entire world. These include rituals of birth, coming of age, marriage, and death. The Sabbath, the high holy days, and festivals—all perpetuate Jewish life and reinforce Jewish peoplehood. My grandmother (and noted poet Asher Ginsberg) reminded me, "More than Jews have kept the Sabbath, the Sabbath has kept the Jews."

The Rothschild Miscellany, 1985 facsimile of the original 1470 book that is the world's most lavish Hebrew illuminated manuscript. *Artifact on display at the JMOF-FIU, gift of Dr. Sol & Mitzi Center, Miami.*

The original book, commissioned by Moses ben Yekuthiel Hacohen in northern Italy, is on display at the Israel National Museum in Jerusalem. At the time the book was printed in the fifteenth century, Jews in Italy came into contact with all sectors of society and prospered in part due to the Catholic Church's prohibition on Christians lending money for interest. Wealthy Jews became Renaissance men with a taste for letters and art and pleasure in affluent living.

This volume was planned as a sumptuous work to encompass almost every custom of religious and secular Jewish life. The 946 pages with more than 200 detailed vignettes are like a library that contains 70 religious and secular works including the entire Haggadah (Passover *seder* book of prayers and songs) and *siddur* (daily Hebrew prayer book).

It was part of the Solomon de Parent Collection in Trieste from 1832 to 1855 and was then sold to the Rothschild family, who owned it until the Nazis stole it during World War II. In 1950 a Berlin book dealer offered the original book for sale to the library of the Jewish Theological Seminary in New York. When the dealer sent the manuscript to the seminary on approval, the seminary's librarian conducted an exhaustive search to determine both its authenticity and its rightful owner. The search determined the Nazis had stolen the book from the Rothschild family. The ownership dispute was heard by the New York State Supreme Court, which ruled the book should be returned to Baron James de Rothschild. Despite the request of the seminary to keep the rare book there, it was the baron's wish that the original be donated to the Israel National Museum.

This is a rare limited-edition facsimile. The twelve-color replica is one of five hundred made in London in 1985. At that time, the original book was painstakingly disbound, and the copies were produced on parchment with hand-applied silver and gold leaf. The replica is hand bound in Moroccan goatskin with silver clasps.

CHAPTER 1

Births

I mentioned earlier that Virginia Myers was the first recorded Jewish birth in Florida in 1822, and then the family left the state. You met Rachelle Williams and George Dzialynski in part 2, chapter 1; they were born in the 1850s, and their family is still in Florida and still Jewish.

There have been other early births recorded in Florida that might be Jewish, considering their countries of origin and names. But to my knowledge, most of those people listed on the internet either left the state or did not identify as Jewish adults and do not have Jewish descendants in Florida.

***Kiddush* cup, silver coin, repoussé, chased, and engraved, presented by A. Forcheimer to David Gundersheimer for David's *brit milah,* Pensacola, 1879.** *Janice G. S. Brewton.*

The two families represented on this cup settled in Pensacola in the 1850s and have descendants there today. One of the most universally celebrated Jewish ceremonies, traditionally held on the eighth day of a Jewish boy's life, the *brit milah* or *bris* is commanded in the Torah for all Jewish boys in Genesis 17:10 and Leviticus 12:3.

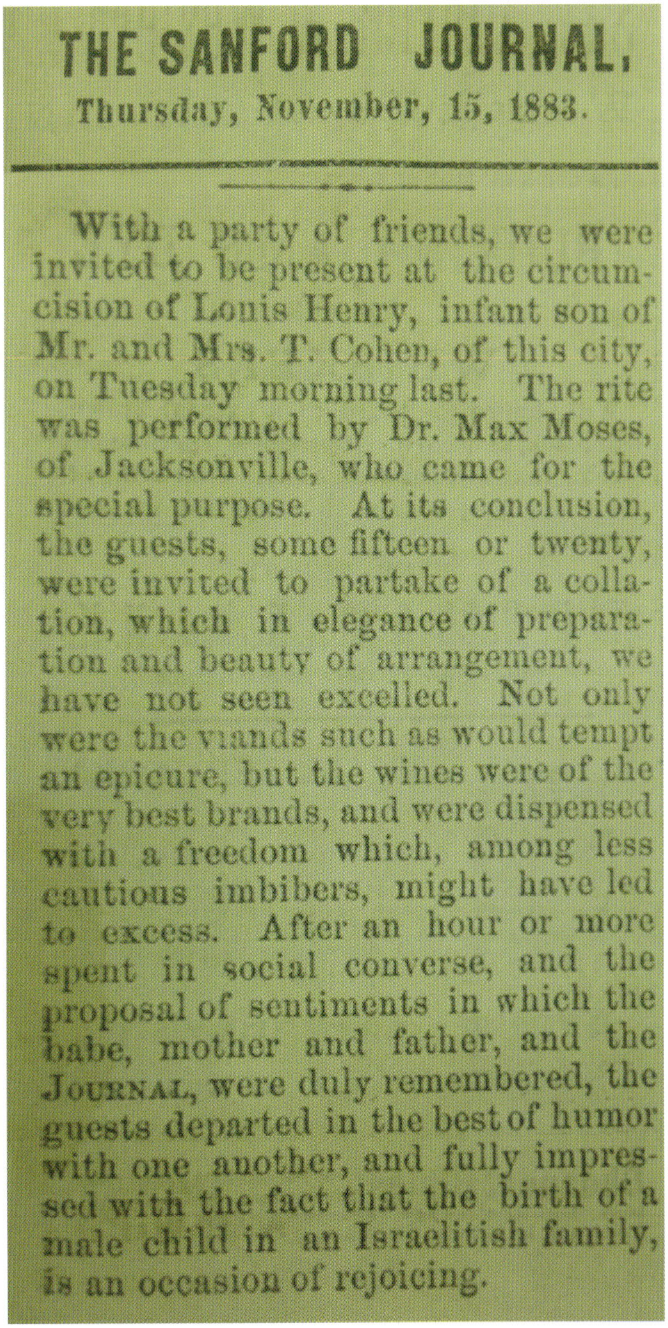

THE SANFORD JOURNAL,

Thursday, November, 15, 1883.

With a party of friends, we were invited to be present at the circumcision of Louis Henry, infant son of Mr. and Mrs. T. Cohen, of this city, on Tuesday morning last. The rite was performed by Dr. Max Moses, of Jacksonville, who came for the special purpose. At its conclusion, the guests, some fifteen or twenty, were invited to partake of a collation, which in elegance of preparation and beauty of arrangement, we have not seen excelled. Not only were the viands such as would tempt an epicure, but the wines were of the very best brands, and were dispensed with a freedom which, among less cautious imbibers, might have led to excess. After an hour or more spent in social converse, and the proposal of sentiments in which the babe, mother and father, and the JOURNAL, were duly remembered, the guests departed in the best of humor with one another, and fully impressed with the fact that the birth of a male child in an Israelitish family, is an occasion of rejoicing.

Article from the *Sanford Journal* about the *brit milah* for Louis Henry Cohen, November 15, 1883. *Sanford Museum.*

Dr. Marx Moses was the first rabbi of Florida's second congregation, Ahavath Chesed, founded in Jacksonville in 1882. He likely traveled by riverboat on the St. Johns River from Jacksonville to Sanford. This article, using the flowery journalistic language of the nineteenth century, gave Dr. Marx Moses an incorrect first name.

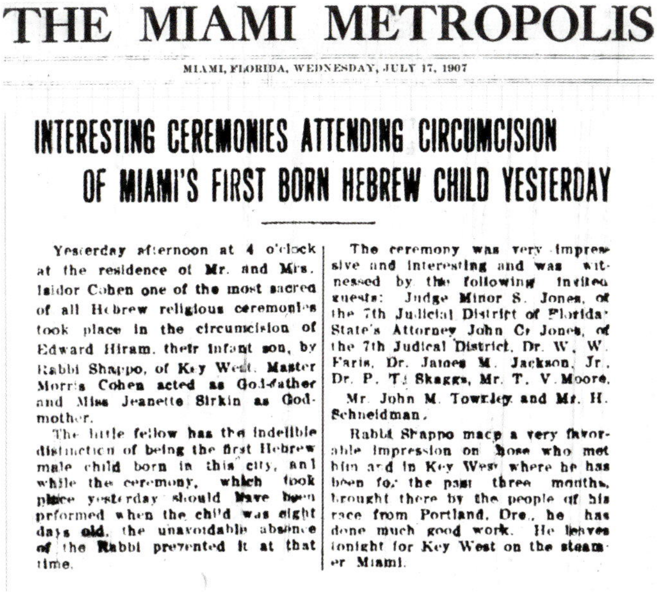

THE MIAMI METROPOLIS

MIAMI, FLORIDA, WEDNESDAY, JULY 17, 1907

INTERESTING CEREMONIES ATTENDING CIRCUMCISION OF MIAMI'S FIRST BORN HEBREW CHILD YESTERDAY

Yesterday afternoon at 4 o'clock at the residence of Mr. and Mrs. Isidor Cohen one of the most sacred of all Hebrew religious ceremonies took place in the circumcision of Edward Hiram, their infant son, by Rabbi Shappo, of Key West. Master Morris Cohen acted as God-father and Miss Jeanette Sirkin as God-mother.

The little fellow has the indelible distinction of being the first Hebrew male child born in this city, and while the ceremony, which took place yesterday should have been performed when the child was eight days old, the unavoidable absence of the Rabbi prevented it at that time.

The ceremony was very impressive and interesting and was witnessed by the following invited guests: Judge Minor S. Jones, of the 7th Judicial District of Florida; State's Attorney John C. Jones, of the 7th Judical District, Dr. W. W. Faris, Dr. James M. Jackson, Jr., Dr. P. T. Skaggs, Mr. T. V. Moore.

Mr. John M. Towrley and Mr. H. Schneidman.

Rabbi Shappo made a very favorable impression on those who met him and in Key West where he has been for the past three months, brought there by the people of his race from Portland, Ore., he has done much good work. He leaves tonight for Key West on the steamer Miami.

When Edward Cohen was born to Ida and Isidor Cohen in 1907, the city's first *brit milah* made front-page news, the *Miami Metropolis*, 1907.

Normally the *brit* is held on the eighth day after birth, but it took three weeks for Rabbi Julian Shappo to arrive by boat from Key West to perform the ritual.

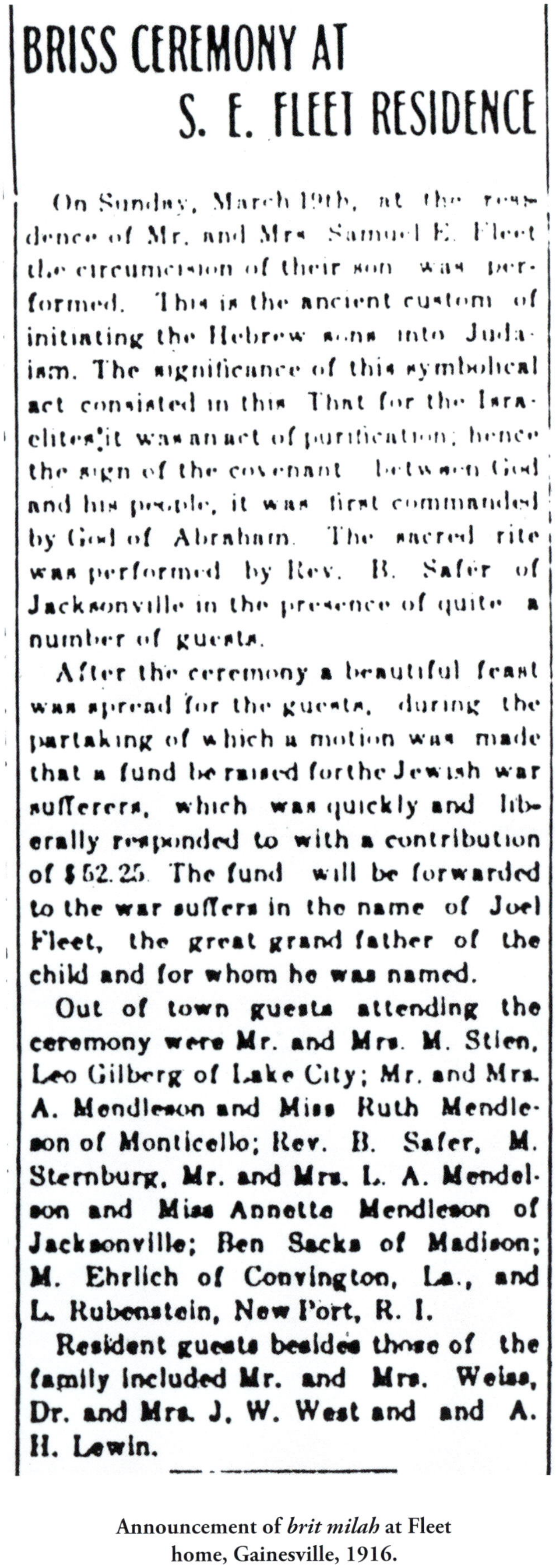

BRISS CEREMONY AT S. E. FLEET RESIDENCE

On Sunday, March 19th, at the residence of Mr. and Mrs. Samuel E. Fleet the circumcision of their son was performed. This is the ancient custom of initiating the Hebrew sons into Judaism. The significance of this symbolical act consisted in this That for the Israelites it was an act of purification; hence the sign of the covenant between God and his people, it was first commanded by God of Abraham. The sacred rite was performed by Rev. B. Safer of Jacksonville in the presence of quite a number of guests.

After the ceremony a beautiful feast was spread for the guests, during the partaking of which a motion was made that a fund be raised for the Jewish war sufferers, which was quickly and liberally responded to with a contribution of $52.25. The fund will be forwarded to the war suffers in the name of Joel Fleet, the great grand father of the child and for whom he was named.

Out of town guests attending the ceremony were Mr. and Mrs. M. Stien, Leo Gilberg of Lake City; Mr. and Mrs. A. Mendleson and Miss Ruth Mendleson of Monticello; Rev. B. Safer, M. Sternburg, Mr. and Mrs. L. A. Mendelson and Miss Annette Mendleson of Jacksonville; Ben Sacks of Madison; M. Ehrlich of Convington, La., and L. Rubenstein, New Port, R. I.

Resident guests besides those of the family included Mr. and Mrs. Weiss, Dr. and Mrs. J. W. West and and A. H. Lewin.

Announcement of *brit milah* at Fleet home, Gainesville, 1916.

Reverend Benjamin Safer of Jacksonville performed this ceremony for Joel Fleet. Indicating the importance of this story in the small community was that this article appeared on page one while a story about a murder was on page four.

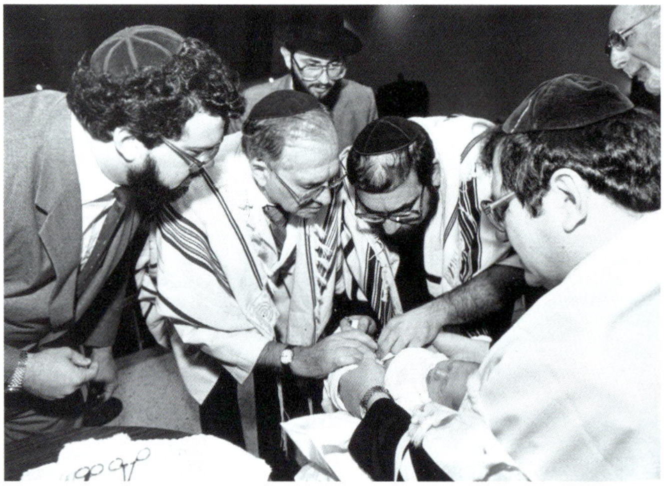

Rabbi Yossi Heber (second from right) performing *brit milah* for his newborn son, Miami Beach, 1987.

Rabbi Heber is assisted by his father-in-law, Rabbi Abraham Seif, known as "Seif the Knife," while his brother Dr. Alan Heber holds the baby on his lap, honored as *sandak*.

***Pidyon haben* of Preston Caudill, grandson of Estelle and Harry Kaplan, performed by Holocaust survivor Max Sattler (center), Cocoa Beach, 1986.**

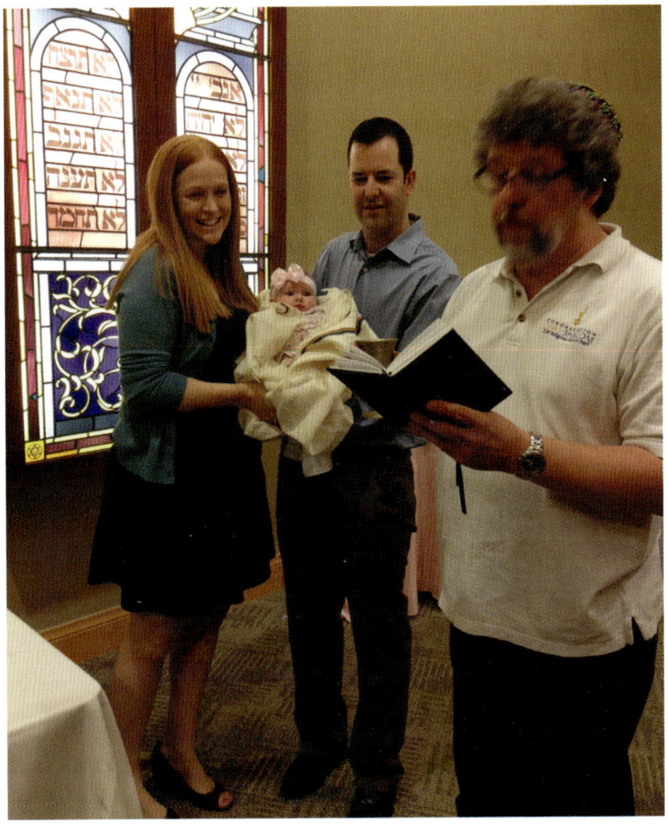

Elana and Dr. Ben Grodin hold their infant daughter Hannah as she is given her Jewish name by Rabbi David Kay during her *simchat bat* ceremony, Orlando, 2014.

CHAPTER 2

Daily and Weekly Rituals

A note about Orthodox Jews—those who adhere to the Jewish traditions in the strictest sense. The first Jews to settle in Florida were not Orthodox in their observance, probably because the frontier did not offer support of this lifestyle. As settlement continued, the Orthodox began to come and build the necessary infrastructure. In current times, the number of Orthodox Jews is increasing, both by new arrivals from other places in the US and by many young Jews already here and attracted to the practice.

Torah (personal-sized) carried by Marcus Vinikowsky Weinkle from Russia to Florida, n.d.

Judaism's most important text is the Torah, or Jewish Written Law. The parchment scroll consists of the five books of Moses, the Hebrew Bible, or the *Chumash* (the Hebrew word for five)—known commonly as the Old Testament—that were given by God to Moses on Mount Sinai and include within them all the Biblical laws of Judaism.

Marcus Weinkle, an Orthodox Jew (you met in part 2, chapter 4), carried this Torah throughout his journey from Russia to Palestine, back to Russia, to New York, and then to settle in Moffitt circa 1902. He took it up and down the west coast of Florida, seeking a *minyan* (minimum of ten people required for public worship). The *yad* shown in this photograph is used as a pointer to indicate the place while reading the Torah as the hand cannot touch the parchment.

Torah scribe (*sofer*) Rabbi Yitzchak Selmar in his workshop, Miami Beach, 1980s.

There are about 305,000 letters in the Torah that are handwritten, copied from another Torah, and each letter is said aloud prior to writing it. Since 1971 Rabbi Selmar has been making and repairing the parchment of the Torah exactly as it was done in ancient days. Each letter of the Hebrew alphabet alone and combined has spiritual significance. If the *sofer* makes one mistake, the Torah is considered impure, and he must start anew.

Generation to generation: Sam Stillman to young Joel Farb, Orlando, 1979.

Although Jews often pray at home, being a part of the community is very important, and some prayers can only be said in a *minyan* that usually congregates at a synagogue. Sam Stillman was a regular for the *minyan* at Orlando's Temple Israel.

Rachel Kanner won a ribbon at the Orange County Fair for this *kippah* she crocheted for her son Aaron, Orlando, 1907.

A skullcap, also known in Yiddish as a *yarmulke* or a *kippah,* is a small, round head covering that observant Jews wear every day and that other Jews wear when studying, praying, or entering a sacred space.

Ritual washing pitcher of Israel Shader, Orlando, circa 1900.

Observant Jews say a blessing while washing their hands before eating a meal. The left hand holds one handle of the pitcher and pours water three times over the right hand. With the other handle, the right hand pours water three times over the left hand. Using two handles ensures that the hand that has been rinsed does not come into contact with the unclean hand.

Hilda Cohen [Saperstein] feeding chickens, Orlando, 1918.

When the Jonas Cohen family was preparing to move to Orlando, Jonas learned how to ritually slaughter poultry so his family would have kosher food.

Rabbi Sholom Blank family on Shabbat, Miami Beach, 1996.

The Jewish week ends with a family event, Shabbat, the Sabbath, just before sundown on Friday evening. The Torah commands Jews to celebrate the Sabbath (Exodus 20:8 and Deuteronomy 5:12). For six days, a Jew may have toiled at the most menial tasks, but on the seventh day, he was commanded to rest. The Sabbath observance includes blessing and lighting candles and blessing wine and *challah*. A fine table is set for the Shabbat dinner.

The commandment to be "fruitful and multiply" is interpreted by the Orthodox to be "boys." Sarah and Sholom Blank of Miami Beach had eleven girls before the first male was born. By 1996 the Blanks had sixteen children.

The *mikvah* makes a Jewish community complete.

A requirement for Orthodox Jews is a *mikvah*, a natural body of water or a gathering of water that has a designated connection to natural water. It must be filled with living waters from a flowing source that has never been dormant, such as the ocean, fresh spring water, rainwater, or even melted snow. The pool, designed specifically for immersion according to the rules and customs of Jewish law, contains about two hundred gallons of water, which is kept under strict hygienic control, cleaned daily, and chlorinated.

The *mikvah* is used (1) by women on their wedding day and then subsequently each month following their monthly menstruation, after counting seven "spotless" days; (2) by men, women, and children as the final stage of conversion to Judaism and non-Jewish adopted children who are taken by their parents; (3) by men, customarily at sacred times, such as before Yom Kippur, on their wedding day, or before Shabbat (some men use the *mikvah* daily before prayer); and (4) to ritually cleanse (*kasher*) new dishes and utensils before use.

Now women from all over the Jewish spectrum appear to be reclaiming this ancient rite of spiritual purity that is more than three thousand years old. According to my research, the earliest *mikvah* in Florida was in Jacksonville in 1921. Today there are more than thirty *mikvaot* in Florida.

The Daughters of Israel Ritualarium, the first *mikvah* in Miami-Dade County, 1944.

Prior to 1944, religious Jews in south Florida used the ocean as a *mikvah*, but this was undesirable when the weather was cold or inclement. Demand increased when honeymooners visited Miami Beach and needed a *mikvah*. Rabbi Moses Mescheloff was involved in the construction and almost went to jail in the process. He relates that during World War II, such construction was a federal offense as one could only build for the war effort; anything else was "unpatriotic." It was hard to find a way to get proper zoning and building permits, so they designed the area as if it were a social hall. Since it was built during the war, materials were scarce. The cost was $35,000 for this white structure that contained a large lobby, hallway, two tiled bathrooms leading to two private ritual pools with rainwater sources, and a caretaker's apartment. By 1970 the building had deteriorated, so it was demolished and rebuilt on the same lot under the guidance of Rabbis Pincus A. Weberman, Berel Wein, and Tibor Stern.

In 1992 the *mikvah* was relocated (below). Since a *mikvah* is symbolic of replenishing the population, the exterior of this *mikvah* has six columns, representing the six million people who perished in the Holocaust. There are two *mikvaot*, with a wall dividing the men's and women's. The ceiling is a two-story rotunda that gives the impression of looking heavenward—with a blue and white clouds-in-the-sky appearance. In 2004 the *mikvah* was named for the Galbut Family matriarch, Bessie D. Galbut.

Bessie D. Galbut Daughters of Israel *Mikvah*, Miami Beach, 2018.

CHAPTER 3

Bar/Bat Mitzvah and Confirmation

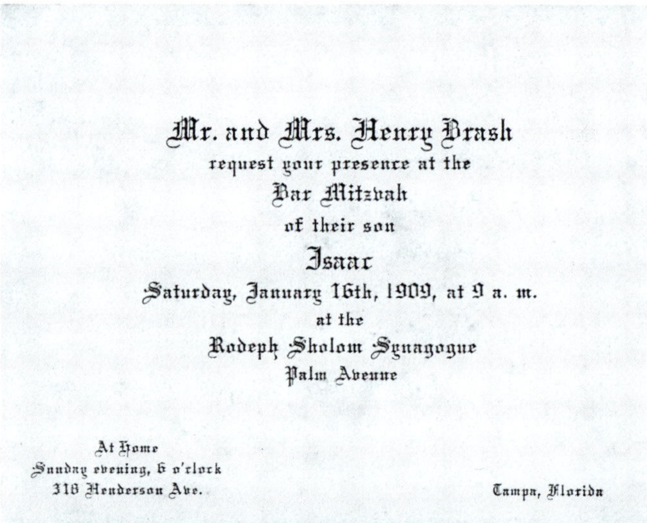

Mr. and Mrs. Henry Brash
request your presence at the
Bar Mitzvah
of their son
Isaac
Saturday, January 16th, 1909, at 9 a. m.
at the
Rodeph Sholom Synagogue
Palm Avenue

At Home
Sunday evening, 6 o'clock
316 Henderson Ave.

Tampa, Florida

***Bar mitzvah* invitation for Isaac Brash, son of Sarah and Henry Brash, Tampa, 1909.**

Milton Gaynor at his *bar mitzvah* in Congregation Beth Jacob (now the JMOF-FIU), Miami Beach, 1930.

German immigrant Henry Brash served as mayor of Marianna during 1879–82. In 1888 he married Sarah Zelnicker, and they settled in Tampa in 1894 where they both became very involved. He was a haberdasher, a founder of Congregation Rodoph Sholom in 1903, and a sixty-three-year member of the Tampa Hillsborough Masonic Lodge #25.

Bessie, Isidore, and their son, Milton, moved to Miami Beach in 1926 where Isidore drove a jitney. In his youth, Milton delivered the *Miami Herald* to help the family. He was a fine athlete and became an officer in the Army Air Corps in World War II. Afterward, he achieved success in the public and private sectors.

Orlando Hebrew Day School class has *bat* and *bar mitzvah* on Masada, Israel, 1983.

Some American families choose to have their children's *bar* and *bat mitzvah* ceremonies on Masada, a site where Jews signed a pact of mutual death rather than surrender to the Romans almost two thousand years ago. Shown left to right, Molly Volpert, Stacy Richman, Hirsh Katzen, Marc Jeser, Ory Schwartz, Gayle Goss, and Matthew Kerstein are confirming the heritage of their ancestors.

Adult *bat* and *bar mitzvah*, Hollywood, 1983.

Those who were unable to be *bat* and *bar mitzvah* at the age of thirteen may do so later in life. Lillian and Sam Mandel both read from the Torah and led the entire service at Temple Solel. Rabbi Robert Frazin conducted the ceremony. The date coincided with the congregation's thirteenth, or *mitzvah*, anniversary.

Rabbi Isaac E. Wagenheim with his Temple Beth El confirmation class, Pensacola, 1902.

This was the first Jewish congregation in Florida, founded in 1876. Families represented in the class are Heinberg, Dannheisser, Friedman, and Guggenheim. Confirmation was a chance for girls to join boys in rites of passage before *bat mitzvah* was initiated in 1922 in the US. Today, confirmation denotes the completion of three years of Jewish education beyond *bat* and *bar mitzvah*.

CHAPTER 4

Weddings

We read in the Torah that Adam was alone in the world and "the Lord said: 'It is not good that man should be left alone; I will make a help mate for him'" (Genesis 2:18).

The Jewish marriage contract, the *ketubah*, was originally instituted at the time of the Babylonian exile around 586 BCE to protect the rights of Jewish married women and to lend more dignity to the marriage. The text, written in Aramaic, assures the woman that her husband will take care of her, provide for her, and cherish her and that if the husband dies or divorces her, she will not be left without financial support.

Ketubah from marriage of Gertrude Israel and Israel Brown, Ocala, 1889. *Hazel Mack, archivist, Congregation Ahavath Chesed.*

> The translation says,
>
> Today...the seventh of the month of Adar Sheni 5649 according to Jewish reconing [reckoning], which is corresponding to the 19 March, 1889 civil reckoning, here in the city of Ocala, in the State of Florida. Mr. Israel Brown son of Julius Brown said to the Virgin Gertrude Israel, daughter of Julius Israel: Be thou my wife in accordance with the laws of Moses and Israel, and I will work for thee, hold thee in honor, love, support, and maintain thee in accordance with the customs of Jewish husbands. Miss Gertrude Israel, on her part consented to become his wife and promised to love and respect him to stand at his side, as a true Jewish wife and to fulfill unto him all the duties, incubent [incumbent] upon a Jewish wife. After these declarations and assurances, I, Joseph Kahn, Rabbi of Congregation Ahavath Chesed of Jacksonville, Fla., have joined together in the Holy Estate of Matrimony, the said Mr. Israel Brown and Miss Gertrude Israel, both of Ocala, Fla., in witness have affixed my signature, the signatures of the said bride and groom and two witnesses. [signed] Gertrude Israel, Israel Brown, Philip Walter, Zee Brown, Rabbi J. Kahn.

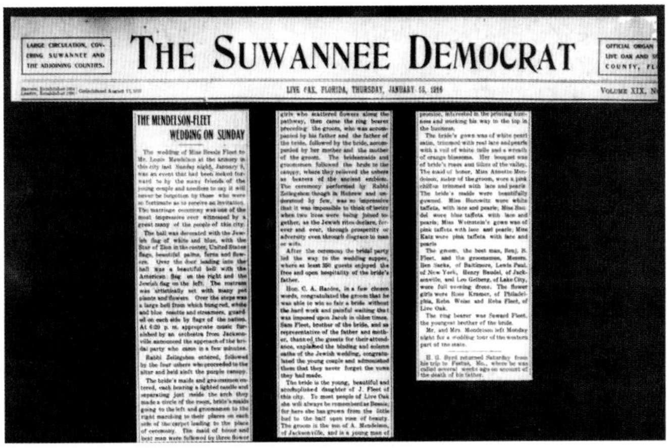

THE SUWANNEE DEMOCRAT

THE MENDELSON-FLEET WEDDING ON SUNDAY

The Suwannee Democrat reporting the Fleet-Mendelson wedding, Live Oak, 1916.

The first-known Jewish wedding in Miami was Rose Seitlin to Max Lehrman, 1913.

The ceremony was held at the home of Morris Zion. Their daughter Nell was the second Jewish girl born in Miami in 1914. The family moved to Fort Lauderdale in 1916. Nell married Louis Gibbs of Live Oak; they settled in Tallahassee. The family still lives in Florida.

(Image at left) The wedding united members of two well established Jewish families in north Florida: Bessie Fleet of Live Oak and Louis Mendelson of Jacksonville. The rabbi and the band came from Jacksonville and relatives came from New York, Philadelphia, and Baltimore to one of the "most impressive [ceremonies] ever witnessed by a great many of the people of this city." Cary Hardee (not Jewish), speaker of the Florida House of Representatives (governor 1921–25), made a congratulatory speech before the 350 Jewish and non-Jewish guests.

The wedding of Rose Gleibman and Aaron Harry Levy took place under the *chuppah* in the Levy orange grove, Orlando, 1917.

Rose Gleibman emigrated from Russia to New York. She came to Orlando to live with her sister Rifka Isen and met Aaron Harry Levy. The entire Jewish community attended the wedding with orange blossoms in the air. Note the Zionist flag crafted as the *chuppah* (wedding canopy), which symbolizes the new Jewish home created by the marriage.

Wedding of Miriam Feit and Saul Rose in Congregation Beth Jacob (now the JMOF-FIU), Miami Beach, 1948.

The ceremony has concluded, and the couple is walking up the aisle to greet their guests. Note: this is not a religious service, so the women and men are sitting together, without a *mechitzah* (divider to separate the sexes during prayer in an Orthodox synagogue). Also, note the *chuppah* on the *bimah*.

European-style community wedding rings. *Artifact on display at the JMOF-FIU, gift of Sylvia and Jack Shorstein, Jacksonville.*

Probably German, late nineteenth century. Silver, architectural ornamentation, hinged, and compartmented to hold a prayer, on paper, for the success of the marriage. The band is inscribed with *mazel tov*. Some Florida congregations own such rings and have adopted this Ashkenazic tradition where each bride borrows the ring for her ceremony.

CHAPTER 5

Holidays

When does the Jewish year begin? As with many Jewish questions, there are at least two answers. The year starts twice. One beginning is in the fall of the year at Rosh Hashanah, which means "head of the year." But Rosh Hashanah occurs in the seventh Hebrew month of *Tishrei*, not the first month. That is *Nisan*, the month of spring—the month of Pesach (Passover).

Many of the Jewish holidays are designated in the Torah. Rosh Hashanah (the beginning of the Jewish Year), Yom Kippur (Day of Atonement), Succot (Festival of Booths), Passover (Festival of Freedom), and Shavuot (Giving of the Torah) are religious and historical agricultural festivals that are observed with special ritual and prayer. Other holidays were added as they took place in Jewish history. Purim and Hanukkah celebrate survival and religious freedom. In present times, we added Yom HaShoah (Day of Remembrance of the Holocaust), Yom HaAtzmaut (Celebrating the Birth of Modern Israel), and Yom Yerushalayim (Jerusalem Day) to commemorate events that happened in this century.

Rosh Hashanah greetings on a postcard, Key West, 1912.

Rosh Hashanah is a time to focus on ultimate spiritual truth and to reach out to family and friends.

5688-1927

לשנה טובה תכתבו

BEST WISHES FOR A HAPPY
AND PROSPEROUS NEW YEAR

CHAS. LUDWIG

Fernandina, Florida

New Year's card, in Hebrew and English, from Charles Ludwig in Fernandina to his fiancée, Anna Kronberg, in Miami, 1927.

Rabbi Irving Lehrman of Temple Emanu-El with students from Lehrman Day School in the *sukkah* (booth) during Sukkot (Festival of Booths), Miami Beach, 1980s.

Practically all societies and cultures celebrate the harvest—the gathering of food that will keep the people alive through the year. The Torah commands that Sukkot begins on the fifteenth day of the seventh month (in the fall following Rosh Hashanah). In Florida, the *sukkah* is made with a roof of palm fronds and decorated with fruits of the harvest. Observant Jews take their meals in the *sukkah* for seven days.

Hillel Community Day School Celebrating Hanukkah (Festival of Lights), Tampa, 1980s.

In 1970 a group recognized the need for a Jewish day school in Tampa. It now has its own ten-acre campus with two hundred students. Here, students are showing their *hanukkiot* (Hanukkah menorahs) used to light the candles for the eight-day celebration of the victory of Judah Maccabee and his heroic brothers over the tyrannical Syrians in 165 BCE. The Syrians were intent on destroying the religious beliefs of the Jews. When the Jews defeated their enemy and entered the Holy Temple to cleanse it, they found enough oil to last one day. Miraculously, the oil burned for eight days—a miracle.

Berkowitz children playing *dreidel* game during Hanukkah, Miami, 1958.

Dreidels (to turn around) are tops that have four Hebrew letters on them, representing the Hebrew saying, *"Nes gadol haya sham,"* meaning "A great miracle occurred there."

Fannie Moss in her Purim Masquerade Ball seashell costume, Jacksonville, 1918.

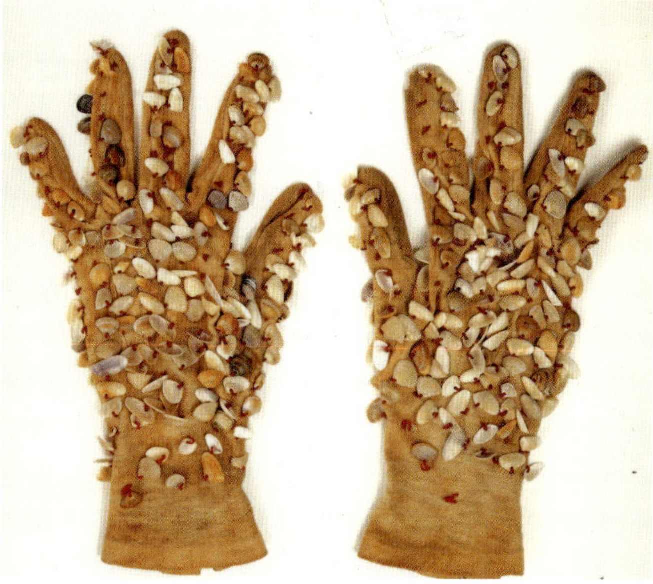

Close-up image of gloves from seashell costume.

After she and her mother spent two months collecting the seashells from Jacksonville Beach, Fannie Moss created this complete outfit for the Purim Ball. The spring holiday of Purim commemorates the saving of the Jews living under Persian rule around 500 BCE. Haman, an evil minister to King Ahasuerus, convinced the king to kill all the Jews in the Kingdom of Shushan on a date chosen by his lottery. The king's Queen Esther was Jewish; she and her uncle Mordechai thwarted the plot. Queen Esther revealed to the king that she was Jewish and asked him to save her people; he did. The Jews of Shushan rejoiced at their deliverance, celebrating their freedom. This is a custom that continues today around the world, with the reading of the *megillah*, costume parties, and merriment. Since 1880, Purim Balls were the social event of the season in the pioneer Jewish communities of Jacksonville, Tallahassee, Pensacola, and Key West.

The sixtieth Pallot family *seder*, held at the Jewish Museum of Florida, Miami Beach, 2010.

First *seder* (Passover meal) at River Garden Nursing Home, Jacksonville, 1949.

The *seder* highlights the supreme importance of freedom. The holiday marks the anniversary of the Exodus of the Israelite people from slavery in Egypt more than 3,300 years ago. *Matzah* is the unleavened bread that is eaten to represent the dough carried by the Israelites when they left Egypt in a hurry, before their bread had time to rise. The term "Passover" refers to the "Lord" passing over the houses of the Israelites who sprinkled the blood of a sacrificial lamb on their doorposts to avoid the tenth plague inflicted on the Egyptians.

The pioneering family member Moses Pallot arrived in Miami Beach in the 1920s, and the first annual Pallot *seder* was held there in 1950. At their 2010 *seder*, there were 129 family members and guests; the youngest was Ellie Jenna Simon, born in 2009, and the oldest present was Phyllis Kamenoff of Orlando, born in 1924.

Together, they sang "Dayenu for the Pallot Family, for what God has done for us in our own time. God brought us out of Europe and the struggles of hard life in Panasheeshok [Lithuania], the small town where our ancestors had settled. Dayenu, that would have been enough. For if God had not brought us out of Europe, surely, we would have perished in the terrible Holocaust brought about by Nazi Germany only 30 years later. God helped us through the early years, and the economic uncertainties in Springfield and Miami. Dayenu, that would have been enough."

Mitchell Horwich, who leads the service, said, "It was great to fill the room in an historic building…and great because we had a lot of children there. Can't do *seder* right without children. When we blow the *shofar* at the beginning—that gets the children's attention!"

CHAPTER 6

Death and Grieving

Death is as much a part of the life cycle as birth. Jews first bury their dead in consecrated ground and then grieve for them during *shiva* (the week of mourning) that follows the burial. The earliest-known licensed Jewish funeral director in Florida was Ed Newman on Miami Beach. Others include Larrie Blasberg, Isaac Gordon, and James Gordon.

Installation luncheon of the Chevra Kadisha, Miami, 1937.

One of the greatest *mitzvot* (good deeds) is caring for the bodies of the dead. The Chevra Kadisha are volunteers who build the coffins, wash the bodies, dress them in the simple white shroud prescribed by Jewish law, and keep vigil until the burial. In the absence of the Chevra Kadisha, these tasks are performed by funeral homes.

Orlando's Chevra Kadisha was formed in 1925 by Morris Wittenstein, who came to Orlando in 1912 from Pittsburgh and was in the dairy business. Wittenstein was very pious, and in preparing for his death, he wrote a letter that he gave to my husband, Elliott, a member of the Chevra Kadisha. The letter, opened at the time of Wittenstein's death in 1975, contained instructions that his wooden leg was to be buried with him so that "when he appeared before the Almighty, he wouldn't be a cripple." He had lost his leg in an industrial accident.

***Yahrzeit* plaques in Congregation Sons of Israel, St. Augustine, 1980s.**

It is Jewish tradition to commemorate the passing of a loved one on synagogue walls. Nameplates are inscribed with English and Hebrew names and the date of death in both the Gregorian and Hebrew calendars. Beside each name is a light that is lit annually on the anniversary of the death and for *yizkor* services.

PART 5

Continuity and Building Community

CHAPTER 1

Cemeteries

To be part of a community is the most urgent historic obligation facing a Jew
—Holocaust survivor and Nobel Laureate Elie Wiesel

Much of my early research in the 1980s on Jews in Florida began in the Jewish cemeteries around the state. There I became familiar with the names of the pioneers and often found their dates and other valuable information. Jewish burial grounds are sacred sites and must remain undisturbed in perpetuity. To show respect for the dead, they are typically the first Jewish organization founded in a community.

Florida's first Jewish cemetery was in Jacksonville in 1857.

(Note: Since this was 1857, I have not been able to find out why this dedication marker says "East Florida," a designation for this colony of the province of Spain, since east and west Florida were merged once Florida became a US territory in 1821 and Florida became a state in 1845.)

Until there was a Jewish cemetery in Jacksonville in 1857, the Chevra Kadisha shipped bodies out of state for ritual burial. In 1857, when six of the twelve Jews in Jacksonville perished in a yellow fever epidemic (including Jacob Munter and Abraham, Henry, and Jacob Dzialynski), the Jacksonville Hebrew Cemetery was established as a separate section of Jacksonville's Old City Cemetery. This was the first Jewish cemetery and the first recorded Jewish communal institution in Florida.

Harry Pepper (left) and Mack Roth founded the Jewish cemetery in Daytona Beach, 1937.

Mack Roth (right) was a major force in Daytona Beach, from the time he arrived in 1914. (You met this family in part 2, chapter 5.) He was also a founder of Temple Israel. When I interviewed him at his office, he was ninety, and there was a stack of cigarette butts piled very high on his desk. I said, "Mack, didn't anyone tell you that smoking is bad for your health?"

He said, "Honey, all my doctors are dead." And he lived to one hundred!

After Jacksonville, Jewish cemeteries were established in Pensacola (1869), Gainesville (earliest stand alone 1871), Ocala (1873), Tampa (1896), Tallahassee (1896), Key West (1891), St. Augustine (1911), Miami (1915), Orlando (1924), St. Petersburg (1924), Sarasota (1932), Fort Lauderdale (1935), Daytona Beach (1937), and then the Palm Beach area (1958). Today there are many Jewish cemeteries throughout Florida. Some are sections within larger cemeteries. Some are stand-alone cemeteries, dedicated solely to Jewish burials. All the Jewish cemeteries preserve memory for their survivors. The Jewish cemeteries are an important resource for genealogists and historians of the local community. They remain a continuing memorial to many who have enriched Florida.

CHAPTER 2

Congregations, Synagogues and Jewish Education

The chartering of a congregation is an important step in formalizing Jewish life. The synagogue is the building in which the congregation meets. It serves three functions: (1) a place of worship, where the community comes together to raise its collective voice to God; (2) education, where learning enhances the ability to understand the commandments of Jewish life; and (3) congregation or assembly, where all may meet to express the joy of life.

The Torah is the most sacred object in Jewish worship. I have been told that Florida Jewish pioneers Robert S. Williams and Moses Endel each brought a Torah with them when they settled in Tallahassee (1865) and Gainesville (1865), respectively. This ensured that Jewish worship would take place on the Florida frontier.

By 1900 there were six Jewish congregations in Florida. The first, Temple Beth El in Pensacola (1876), was followed by Ahavath Chesed in Jacksonville (1882), Rodeph Sholom renamed B'nai Zion in Key West (1887), United Hebrews of Ocala (1888), Schaarai Zedek in Tampa (1894), and B'nai Israel in Pensacola (1899). All remain in existence.

In the twentieth century, more congregations were founded prior to World War II: Rodeph Sholom in Tampa (1903), Sons of Israel in St. Augustine (1908), B'nai Zion renamed Beth David in Miami (1912), Ohev Shalom in Orlando (1918), Schaarai Zedek of St. Petersburg (1921), Temple Israel in Miami (1922), Temple Israel in West Palm Beach (1923), B'nai Israel in St. Petersburg (1923), B'nai Israel in Gainesville (1924), Temple Israel in Daytona Beach (1924), Beth Sholom in Sarasota (1926), Beth Israel in Sanford (1927), Beth Jacob on Miami Beach (1927), Temple Israel in Sebring (1927), Temple Emanuel in Fort Lauderdale (1937), and Temple Israel in Tallahassee (1937).

Today, there are more than three hundred Jewish congregations in Florida, and the number is ever increasing. It is interesting that Boca Raton, which has the largest Jewish community in the state, was late in forming a congregation—Boca Raton Hebrew Congregation, now Temple Beth El—in 1967.

Congregations are identified by a particular branch of Judaism, usually as Orthodox, the most traditional; Reform, the most modern; or Conservative, which follows a middle path. Most congregations in Florida—and all the congregations that predate 1900—are based upon Ashkenazic Judaism, the traditions that arose in central and eastern Europe. Several Florida congregations follow the Sephardic rituals, rooted in pre-Inquisition Spain and Portugal.

Today, about one-third of the Jewish population in Florida belong to a congregation. This breaks down to those households with children. Most of them are in a higher-income bracket, and most are Orthodox.

Florida's first Jewish congregation chartered by the State of Florida, Temple Beth El in Pensacola in 1876.

This Reform congregation's synagogue was twice burned to the ground and rebuilt, first in 1895 and again in 1929.

Rabbi Jacob L. Holdman (right) joins *bar mitzvah* boy Raymon Ordon on the B'nai Israel *bimah* in Pensacola, 1951.

(Note the Torah ark ornament in the photograph.)

Synagogue Torah ark ornament, carved, painted, and gilded wooden pediment depicting the Ten Commandments, Torah crown, and Lions of Judah as guardians, Pensacola, circa 1925.

Gifted by B'nai Israel Synagogue, this ark ornament by an unknown artist, used from the 1920s through the 1960s, is on display in the JMOF-FIU. In 2007 the American Folk Art Museum in New York borrowed it for an exhibit, *Gilded Lions and Jeweled Horses: The Synagogue to the Carousel*. Eastern European artisans who came to America migrated with their woodcarving skills for crafting everything from Judaic Baroque synagogue ark ornaments to carving horses for carousels.

Built in 1888, this is the oldest extant synagogue in Florida: United Hebrews of Ocala, moving day, 1976.

It cost twenty-one dollars in 1888 to cut down the trees and haul off the rocks to prepare the land for construction. The name was changed in 1965 to Temple B'nai Darom, Children of the South. Leon Goldman and Jacob Weiner are carrying the Torahs to move to their new building. This building, with its restored stained glass windows and wooden floor, continues to be used—by a Christian congregation.

Rabbi Ralph B. Hershon with charter members of Congregation Rodeph Sholom (Pursuers of Peace) Ladies Auxiliary, Tampa, August 14, 1917.

The group was organized to preserve Jewish traditional values and heritage and to assist the congregation, primarily in raising funds. Seated from left to right are Mrs. M. Ressler, Mrs. J. Leiter, Mrs. Louis Wohl, Mrs. A. Levine, Mrs. Julius Mairson, Mrs. Ralph Hershon, Paul Losner, Mrs. Max Argintar, Mrs. S. Argintar, Mrs. J. Gordon, and Mrs. L. Ginsburg. Standing from left to right are Mrs. Oscar Steinberg, Mrs. Morris Cracowaner, Mrs. A. N. Goldstein, Mrs. Weil, Mrs. Brodie, Mrs. J. Fleischman, Mrs. Elizabeth Lassman, Mrs. Henry Brash, Rabbi Hershon, Mrs. Herman Juster, Mrs. E. H. Steinberg, Mrs. David Kasriel, Mrs. Max Losner, and Mrs. S. Herscovitz. This photograph was featured in the Tishri/Heshvan 5740 (Fall 1979) issue of *Women's League Outlook*, in an article titled "Reprise…Ladies Auxiliary to Sophisticated Sisterhood" by Helene Wagenheim.

One of the most interesting congregational stories comes from 1903, when Rodeph Sholom, an Orthodox congregation, was founded in Tampa, as a result of an irreconcilable split between the Orthodox and Reform factions at Congregation Schaarai Zedek. The "Reformers" at Schaarai Zedek called a meeting in 1902 to take control. The Orthodox members accused them of "dirty tricks," such as starting the meeting before sundown on Saturday and changing the order of business, knowing the Orthodox would not yet be present, taking a voice vote rather than a roll call to accept three new Reform members to compose a Reform majority, and so on. The case records are 302 pages for *Congregation Schaarai Zedek v. Moses Henry Cohen* (for the Orthodox) in the Sixth Judicial Circuit of the State of Florida. Included are testimonies that reflect the ambivalence of living as a Jew in the South at the turn of the twentieth century. The results were Schaarai Zedek's Reformers taking control of that congregation and then the building and founding of the new Orthodox Congregation Rodeph Sholom.

Rabbis and Jewish Education

Rabbis are appointed by congregations as spiritual leaders and teachers of Jewish law. I am presenting just a few among the thousands who have served Florida communities. Jewish education in Florida, to our knowledge, began in the 1800s with the advent of the first congregations and their programs to prepare their sons for *bar mitzvah*. The first formal Jewish school of record was in Tallahassee around 1880. Today, there are nearly thirty Jewish day schools, hundreds of preschools, after school and Sunday school programs, and about ten colleges or universities offering Jewish study programs. Educational programs also exist for teens and college students that emphasize or take place in Israel. Adult Jewish education is steadily growing as surveys show affiliated and integrated adults alike thirsting for knowledge of their own heritage.

Congregation Ohev Shalom (COS) president Albert Raffeld and Rabbi Benjamin Safer (right) lead the cornerstone dedication, Orlando, 1926.

Jacksonville was the largest Jewish community in Florida until after World War II, when the population swelled in Miami-Dade County. You met Rabbi Safer in part 2, chapter 4, when he arrived in Jacksonville. During and after he served as the first rabbi of B'nai Israel Congregation there (1902–12), Rabbi Safer was a circuit rider who performed *britot* and marriages throughout north Florida from Pensacola to Orlando to Jacksonville and tiny places in between. From about 1931 to 1937, he was the rabbi of Congregation Ohev Shalom (COS) in Orlando.

Rabbi Irving Lehrman (right) and Belle Lehrman with US President Harry Truman, Miami Beach, circa 1948.

In 2011, the year I retired from the JMOF-FIU, the family of Rabbi Irving Lehrman (1910–2005) contributed his archives for me to create an exhibition about his enormous contributions to humanity. Born in Tykocin, Poland, Irving Lehrman came to the US at the age of five. He was the eleventh generation of a famed rabbinic family that goes back to the 1500s. Rabbi Irving Lehrman was hired in 1943 as the spiritual leader for Temple Emanu-El (Conservative) on Miami Beach where he served for half a century. He energized a congregation of 200 families to become 1,500 families. His eloquent, informative sermons attracted so many people that they had to line up around the block to await entrance into the services. Rabbi Lehrman founded the day school (later named in his honor), was a national and international Jewish leader, and was a giant among all clergy.

President Lyndon Johnson appointed him to the White House Task Force on Food, Nutrition and Health and to the White House Conferences on Aging and on Obscenity and Pornography. He was named to the executive committee of UNESCO (the United Nations Educational, Scientific, and Cultural Organization). He was the first Floridian Jew to receive the Benemerenti Medal from Pope John Paul II. Rabbi Lehrman was an active supporter of Israel, was a national and international spokesman for Judaism and Jewish causes, and motivated many of his congregants to get involved in politics and serve in leadership roles in the community. His vision, ingenuity, energy, and inspired leadership built his congregation into one of the largest and most important centers of Conservative Jewry in the US.

Rabbi Lehrman always found time for his family (his wife, Belle, and their children, Rosalind and David) and to read, teach, walk, swim, and draw. He referred to Belle as "My light and my inspiration." Rabbi Irving Lehrman had a huge impact on the Greater Miami, Florida, Israel, and world Jewish communities and the multifaith community and built bridges between races and denominations.

Rabbi Leon Kronish lighting the eternal flame at Temple Beth Sholom, Miami Beach, circa 1947.

Rabbi Kronish (1917–96) joined Rabbi Lehrman on Miami Beach in 1944 and also served his congregation (Reform) for fifty years as a powerful and charismatic leader in both the Jewish and civic communities. A native of Brooklyn, he became a prominent voice in Reform Judaism and national chairman of the State of Israel Bonds drives. Inspired by strong Reform rabbis who taught him, Kronish became a leader for social justice, Zionism, egalitarianism, and Hebrew as a living language. South Florida was a hotbed for the civil rights/desegregation movement, the debate over separation of church and state/prayer in public schools, and the nuclear disarmament and peace movement in the 1950s and 1960s—and Rabbi Kronish influenced these movements. He instituted stimulating and popular adult education classes that helped grow the congregation from 40 families to more than 1,200. Judy Drucker's Cultural and Fine Arts Series were emboldened by Kronish at his temple. His wife, Lillian, was a huge supporter, and they had three children: Jordan, Ronald (who lives in Israel), and Maxine.

Rabbi Joseph R. Narot served Temple Israel of Greater Miami from 1950 to 1980, Miami, 1970s.

Dr. Joseph R. Narot was born in 1913 in Vilna, Lithuania, and immigrated with his family to Ohio where he grew up and was educated. He was ordained by Hebrew Union College in 1940. He served first as assistant rabbi (1940–41), then as rabbi (1941–50) of Temple Beth Israel in Atlantic City, New Jersey. In 1950 he became senior rabbi of Temple Israel of Greater Miami, Miami's oldest Reform synagogue, and served until his death in 1980. He was known for his superb contemporary sermons that attracted five thousand individuals for High Holy Day services held at the Miami Beach Convention Center. He has been described as brilliant, learned, liberal, and outspoken. Boldly speaking out for civil rights and against the Vietnam War, he encouraged his congregation that grew to 1,800 families to live Judaism by being actively engaged in local, national, and world issues. A former editor of the Central Conference of American Rabbis Journal, Narot was the author of numerous books, including *Why I am A Jew*, *For Whom the Rabbi Speaks*, and *Letters to the Now Generation*.

From *rebbetzin* to rabbi: Paula Herskovitz Ackerman of Pensacola was the first woman to serve as a Reform rabbi of a mainstream US congregation, 1950.

Some say that Paula Ackerman (1893–1989) was the single largest impetus in the movement to grant full rights to women in American synagogues: women can now be ordained as rabbis. Raised in Pensacola, she sat every morning on her father's knee as he chanted Hebrew prayers to her. She became the first girl to study Hebrew in Pensacola and went on to teach it because she "just wanted to be around the Temple." She continued to teach also in public school until her 1919 marriage to Rabbi William Ackerman, who was serving Temple Beth El in Pensacola. She was an active *rebbetzin* and teacher for almost three decades, eventually at Temple Beth Israel in Meridian, Mississippi, until 1950, when her husband died. Bereft, the congregation asked her to be their "interim" spiritual leader, which she did for nearly three years. Later, her childhood congregation in Pensacola invited her to serve as their "interim" for six months where she conducted services, preached, taught, and officiated at weddings, funerals, and conversions. In 1986 the Union of American Hebrew Congregations formally recognized her pioneering contribution to Jewish communal life at a special ceremony held at The Temple in Atlanta.

Central Agency for Jewish Education (CAJE) director Gene Greenzweig (left), Abraham "Abe" Gittelson, and volunteer Nancy Lipoff plan a seminar, Miami, 1975.

The Central Agency for Jewish Education (CAJE) was founded in 1945 to enhance Jewish education, identity, and commitment for every age level. One of their programs is "March of the Living," organized to take both youth and adults to Poland to visit the sights of Nazi atrocities and then to Israel to be uplifted. I first met Abe Gittelson when I was director of the Judaica High School in Orlando in 1980, and I arranged for him to train our teachers. Then he was a tremendous mentor to me when I started in this field. He was the educator on our original MOSAIC project team, so we worked together closely. Abe was honored by the Department of Education and Culture of the World Zionist Organization in Jerusalem in 1990 as "Jewish Educator of the Diaspora."

Rabbi Alexander S. Gross Hebrew Academy class, Miami Beach, 1962.

The Hebrew Academy was the first Jewish day school in the southeastern US. It began in 1947 with six students, offering both a secular and religious learning environment. The school now has more than six hundred students through grade twelve.

The Alexander Muss High School in Israel (HSI) winter session group, ancient temple site in Jerusalem, Israel, 1995.

High School in Israel (HSI) is an educational program founded in 1972 by Rabbi Morris Kippur with the Greater Miami Jewish Federation to provide, in Israel, an intense academic experience to Florida high school students. Its unique curriculum is conducted in chronological historical order, on-site where history actually took place, and is designed to introduce students to facts, concepts, and events basic to understanding the development of Western civilization and the history and culture of Israel. HSI grew beyond its Florida roots to be a nationwide program, merged with Jewish National Fund in 2013 and now welcomes students from across North America, Australia, and Europe. The program has more than twenty-six thousand alumni, including my own children.

The Center for Jewish Studies at the University of Florida is the oldest university-level program in Judaic studies in the state (1971). There are also programs at the Universities of South Florida, Central Florida, and Miami; Florida Atlantic University; Florida International University; and Rollins College.

Professor Jack Kugelmass, director, Center for Jewish Studies at the University of Florida (UF), with students, Gainesville, 2019.

CHAPTER 3

Organizations, Jewish Federations, Agencies, Facilities for the Elderly, and Jewish Students on Campus

A unique trait among Jews is the connection to one another—that we care for all Jews wherever they are—emotionally and physically. In my experience, immigrants of most other groups have an allegiance to others from their countries of origin, and Jews expand that to all Jews from anywhere. "We Are One" was the slogan adopted by the United Jewish Appeal (UJA) that raised funds for Jews in need all over the world. I served on the first UJA Young Women's Leadership Cabinet in 1974 and from that day have worn a bracelet crafted from tiny sculpted people connected to each other.

Florida is host to chapters of all the major national and international Jewish organizations—and some very early ones, including B'nai B'rith in 1874. In 1912 Henrietta Szold founded Hadassah, the Women's Zionist Organization of America, and she came to Jacksonville in 1914 to start a chapter there. All the Jewish organizations have a common goal: continuity, which connotes generation to generation of caring from cradle to grave, and passing on the traditions of our heritage.

B'nai B'rith, chartered in Pensacola in 1874, was Florida's first-known Jewish organization. The first annual conference of Florida's B'nai B'rith Lodges, Tampa, 1937.

B'nai B'rith has lodges throughout the state. Established nationally in 1843, this worldwide Jewish service organization is a national and global leader in the fight against antisemitism and anti-Israel bias.

Jewish Congregation Men's Club when Louis Fine (back row, fifth from left) was president, Key West, circa 1887.

Young Men's Hebrew Association (YMHA) on boat outing, Key West, 1908.

First annual outing of the Hebrew Social Club, Jacksonville, 1914.

First United Jewish Appeal radio-thon to raise money in support of Israel's War of Independence, Miami, 1948.

From left to right are Stanley Myers of Miami, president of the Council of Jewish Federations; Henry Morganthau, former US secretary of the Treasury and first national chairman of the United Jewish Appeal; Golda Meyerson (Meir), who became Israel's prime minister (1969–1974); and New York Governor Herbert Lehman, first chairman for State of Israel Bonds.

Prior to the United Nations vote for Israeli statehood on May 14, 1948, Golda Meyerson (Meir) appealed to American Jewry for $50 million so that Israel could defend herself against the Arab states. She often traveled to Florida communities, where she received tremendous support and friendship.

United Jewish Appeal (1939–99) was the fundraising arm of the Council of Jewish Federations, an umbrella organization formed nationally in 1932 to enhance Jewish life and to serve as the central address for each Jewish community. Today, called Jewish Federations of North America, it represents thirteen communities in Florida that each have a mission to sustain and grow a vibrant local community and connect it to the national and international Jewish world. With planning and fundraising, each federation creates other agencies to meet specific communal needs.

In Florida, Jewish Federations exist in these communities (founding date): Jacksonville (1935), Greater Miami (1938), Tampa (1941), Broward County (Hollywood, 1943, and Greater Fort Lauderdale, 1967, with merger in 1996), Pinellas County (1945), Greater Orlando (1947), Sarasota (1959), Palm Beach County

(1962), Volusia and Flagler Counties (1973), Brevard County (1975), South Palm Beach County (1979), Collier County (1981), and Lee County (1984).

Children in front of the Samuel and Helene Soref Jewish Community Center, Sunrise, 1990s.

Jewish Community Centers (JCCs) are the social, cultural, and recreational arm of the community. Trained staff members plan programs that help strengthen Jewish identity and traditions.

JCCs in Florida include (founding date) Tampa (1906), Dave & Mary Alper in Miami (1932), Adolph & Rose Levis in Boca Raton (1972), Roth Family in Orlando (1973), Mandel of the Palm Beaches in Boynton Beach and in Palm Beaches (1974), Michael-Ann Russell in Miami (1977), Samuel & Helene Soref in Sunrise (1977), David Posnack in Davie (1981), Jewish Community Alliance in Jacksonville (1989), JCC of South Florida in Naples (2003), Galbut Family Miami Beach on Simpkins Family Campus (2012), Rosen in south Orlando (2015), and Bryan Glazer Family in Tampa (2016).

Florida's newest JCC (as of this writing) is the Bryan Glazer Family JCC that hosted the Tampa Bay Lightning Ball Hockey Clinic, Tampa, 2017. *Tampa JCCs & Federation.*

These Hungarian refugees found a new home in Miami through the help of Jewish Family Services (JFS) and the National Council of Jewish Women, 1950.

The social service agency Jewish Family Services (JFS) in Miami was founded in 1920 to provide assistance to enrich lives and empower people. There is a JFS in all organized Florida Jewish communities. Youngsters (front) Laslo and Dawn were rescued by Sandor Gnagy, Sandor Funk, and Mrs. Martha Rosza.

Hanukkah luncheon of Bikor Cholim of Beth Jacob Congregation who founded the Miami Jewish Home for the Aged, Miami Beach, 1954.

Members of this committee to care for the sick from left to right are Lena Dubler, Ida Cohen, Anne Frankel, Molly Silverman, Ida Appell, unknown, Lottie Brown, unknown, and unknown.

"Honor thy father and mother that thy days may be long." Jews interpret this fifth commandment to mean that we must collectively not only honor our parents when they are young but also take care of them in the later years—and therein lies a special reward. With 20 percent of south Florida's population being elderly, families and agencies have a mammoth task.

The Miami Jewish Home for the Aged (now Miami Jewish Health Systems) opened in 1940 as a nursing home with a $10,000 gift from a non-Jew, Adam Reiss. It was renamed the Miami Jewish Home and Hospital and led for many years by Judge Irving and Hazel Cypen. The organization grew to include a hospital, assisted and independent living, rehab, Alzheimer's care, and innovative programs. River Garden Hebrew Home in Jacksonville, founded in 1946 by the Ladies Hebrew Sheltering Aid Society (1922), is dedicated to good living for elderly people. Kinneret, a government HUD senior citizen housing project was built in Orlando in 1968 as a 15-story high-rise with 168 rent controlled units; a second building was erected in 1978 with 112 units and a dining room. In 1978 the Joseph Meyerhoff Senior Center began programs and services in Hollywood.

The Joseph L. Morse Geriatric Center was created in 1983 as the Jewish Home for the Aged of Palm Beach County and has progressively added facilities for the full range of services, now as MorseLife Health System. Menorah Manor opened in 1985 in St. Petersburg. Sarasota's Kobernick House opened in 1993 as an independent living rental retirement community, adding Anchin Assisted Living and Memory Support in 1997 and Benderson Skilled Nursing and Rehabilitation in 2011. The Leo Goodman Senior Complex, opened in 1992 in Broward County, offers a variety of services to the elderly: low-cost housing, senior activity center, kosher meals, day care for frail elderly, and an Alzheimer program. The most recent full service facility for the elderly is Sinai Residences, located on the one-hundred-acre south Palm Beach County Federation campus in Boca Raton.

Florida Jewish women are dedicated volunteers to Jewish community organizations. This is the Conference of Jewish Women's Organizations of Dade and Broward Counties, 1954.

In the front row from left to right are Mrs. Matilda Ratner, Mrs. Aaron (Myra) Farr, Mrs. Milton Sirkin, and Mrs. A. Fred Williams. In the back row from left to right are Mrs. Benjamin Appel, Mrs. Irving Weinstein, Mrs. Julian Weinkle, Mrs. Harry Rogers, Mrs. Monte (Fannie) Selig, and Mrs. Irving (Belle) Lehrman.

The Shomrim Society is the largest affiliation of Jewish law enforcement, Miami, 1990.

South Florida Shomrim Society is an example of Jews within a profession organizing "so that Law Enforcement Officers of the Jewish Faith May Join Together for the Welfare of all."

Three Florida women were presidents of national/international Jewish organizations at the same time.

Nan Rich of Weston, national president of the National Council of Jewish Women (1996–99), at the "Stand for Children" Rally, Washington, DC, 1996.

Others in the picture are National Board Member Nancy Ratzan (right), as well as Margie Zeskind and Sheila Silverberg. All were from Miami. The National Council of Jewish Women, established in 1893, is the oldest volunteer Jewish women's organization in America. In the spirit of Judaism, it is dedicated to advancing human welfare and the democratic way of life. The first Florida section was in Miami in 1918. After serving twelve years in the state legislature, Rich is serving her first term on the Broward County Commission.

Pepi Dunay, Dunay (center, in suit), national president of Women's American ORT (1998–2001), during Argentina mission to see the ORT school, Boca Raton, 1999.

The Organization for Rehabilitation through Training (ORT) is recognized worldwide for its network of excellent vocational schools. In 1952 hotelier Jennie Grossinger held a membership tea at her Pancoast Hotel on Miami Beach. Irene Sussman became president of this first Florida ORT chapter. The Florida membership reached its peak of thirty thousand individuals by the 1980s.

Randee Lefkow (in red suit), international president of Jewish Women International, formerly B'nai B'rith Women (1998–2000), during "Light a Candle" Vigil for domestic violence, 1998.

From left to right are Barbara Pollack, Barbara Stein, Randee Lefkow, and Millie Sernovitz.

Dedication of Hillel at the University of Florida (UF), left to right: Louis Ossinsky Sr., Samuel Proctor, and Jerome Kestenbaum, Gainesville, 1952.

Today, there are about 6,500 Jewish students at UF who have the benefits of Hillel, housed in Norman H. Lipoff Hall.

Founded nationally in 1923 and adopted by B'nai B'rith in 1924, Hillel has grown into the world's largest Jewish campus organization. Hillel is on these Florida campuses: Barry College of Law, Eckerd College, Embry Riddle Aeronautical University, Florida Atlantic University, Florida Gulf Coast University, Florida Institute of Technology, Florida International University, Florida State University, Gainesville College, Jacksonville University, Miami-Dade College, Rollins College, Stetson University, Tallahassee Community College, University of Central Florida, University of Florida, University of Miami, University of North Florida, University of South Florida, University of South Florida Sarasota-Manatee, University of Tampa, and Valencia College.

This image below shows one angle of the building with (inset) left to right: Alan Ginsburg, Hank Katzen, Russell Goldberg, and executive director and CEO Aaron Weil. From 2001 to 2013, Central Florida Hillel bounced between apartments, living rooms, and rented buildings. Then the generosity and creativity of Alan Ginsburg, Marc Katzen, and Hank Katzen came together to create NorthView, a state-of-the-art facility across from the UCF stadium. In addition to housing Hillel, NorthView is also home to the Catholic Campus Ministry and is a six-hundred-bed residence hall for UCF. Now home to the Jeffrey and Diane Ginsburg Center for Jewish Student Life at Central Florida Hillel, the six thousand Jewish students at UCF no longer have to be the wandering Jews!

The NorthView Hillel building opened at the University of Central Florida (UCF) in the 2015–16 academic year. *Central Florida Hillel.*

The Alpha Epsilon Phi sorority began in 1938 at the University of Miami, Miami, 1944.

In 1909, when Jewish women were not accepted into campus sororities, a group at Barnard College started a sorority to share common Jewish heritage, values, interests, and friendship. The sorority encourages community service, academic presence on campuses, a positive social presence and reputation, and providing a "college home and family" for each of its sisters. US Supreme Court Justice Ruth Bader Ginsburg is a member of AEPhi.

The Tau Alpha chapter of Tau Epsilon Phi fraternity was founded at UF on February 22, 1925. Thousands of Florida Jewish boys have been part of this fraternity throughout their college years and remain fiercely loyal.

Tau Epsilon Phi (TEP) fraternity, Homecoming Fall Frolics, University of Florida (UF), Gainesville, 1934.

CHAPTER 4

Zionism

In Genesis 12:7, God said to Abraham that "unto thy seed will I give this land."

Passport photograph for the Barbanel family who expressed their Zionist zeal by making *aliyah* from Orlando, 1931.

Zionism seeks to restore the Jewish people to their ancient homeland because it believes that a people without a solid piece of land of its own is doomed to extinction. Throughout the nearly two thousand years of exile, from 70 CE to 1948, "Next Year in Jerusalem" was a prayer and a rallying cry for Jews of the Diaspora. As the modern Zionist movement grew (post 1896), Jewish Floridians joined others in making *aliyah* (immigration to Palestine, later Israel).

Most Jews sense that Israel represents the future welfare of the Jewish people worldwide. The creation of the State of Israel in 1948 was the culmination of the hopes and plans of millions of Jews, including many in Florida. Some helped to ship supplies and arms, some volunteered to fight for the young country, and others conducted fundraising appeals. Today, Jews throughout Florida continue to support Israel by making financial contributions; by visiting, studying, and working there; and by sending their children to study and live there. Some have started businesses there.

From 2013–2019 the Israeli ambassador to the US was Ron Dermer, born (1971) and raised on Miami Beach. His mother, Yaffa, is an Israeli and his father and brother both served as mayors of Miami Beach (see Mayors List).

Miriam Levine had come to Orlando from Pittsburgh in 1912 with her family and married Isador Barbanel in 1917. They and their children were joining the rest of their family who made *aliyah* in 1922—also from Orlando!

Aliyah Bet

Shepard Broad (who you met in part 2, chapter 4), long active in Jewish affairs, was one of seventeen American Jews (and the only one from Florida) who secretly met on July 1, 1945, with Palestine's Jewish Agency chair David Ben-Gurion in the New York home of oil executive and Zionist leader Rudolf Sonneborn. Their mission was to discuss military preparations for the establishment of a Jewish homeland in Palestine. After the eleven-hour meeting, horrified by stories of the Holocaust and determined for Jews to have a homeland of their own, Broad and the others pledged "their lives, their fortunes, and their sacred honor" for what would become the State of Israel three years later. They would discreetly fund raise to purchase arms and ships to bring refugees from the European Displaced Persons camps to Palestine and for Israel's War of Independence. Ben-Gurion stated that this meeting was "the most important day in the history of Israel."

An outcome of the 1945 "Sonneborn Institute" was the purchasing and outfitting of ships for Aliyah Bet (clandestine immigration into Palestine).

Shepard Broad was designated a key person for Aliyah Bet that would attempt to illegally bring about 100,000 refugees to Palestine by sea on more than 60 ships from 1946–1948. Broad organized the purchase and refitting of three ships (the *Hatikvah*, *Geula*, and *Jewish State*) on the Miami River. This is one of Shepard Broad's three ships in Miami: the *Geula*, former US Coast Guard training vessel *Paducah*, carried 1,385 refugees.

A former US coast guard icebreaker, *The Jewish State*, was another ship that Shepard Broad refitted on the Miami River to rescue 2,664 refugees.

The story of one of the Aliyah Bet ships, SS *Exodus*, is well known because of Leon Uris's 1958 book *Exodus* and Leon Preminger's 1960 movie *Exodus*, starring Paul Newman.

Ralph Lowenstein arrived as a Machal volunteer in Israel in 1948 at the age of eighteen.

As a sophomore at Columbia University, Lowenstein made his way to England as an exchange student. He volunteered for the Israeli army in Paris and lived in a DP camp in Marseilles with false papers. He traveled on one of the Aliyah Bet ships, *Pan York*, to Israel and was smuggled into the country to fight in Israel's War of Independence as one of the 1,250 volunteers from the US and Canada (Machal). Resisting his parents' pleas to return home, Lowenstein was assigned as a half-track driver in an armored unit and saw combat ten days later. His unit, the 79th Armored Battalion, spearheaded the action in October 1948 that cleared the Upper Galilee of Iraqi, Syrian, and Lebanese troops, securing it as a part of Israel. "Central to whatever I am or will be," Lowenstein says, "is that Israeli experience. As a very young man, I had the opportunity to put my life on the line for an ideal. Israel did a lot for me."

Lowenstein spent thirty years collecting and building the Aliyah Bet & Machal Archives in Gainesville, which have recorded the data and experiences of the North American volunteers who served. These archives were acquired by the American Jewish Historical Society in New York. He wrote all the materials and directed the construction for the Museum of American and Canadian Volunteers in Israel's War of Independence, on view in the UF Hillel building in Gainesville. He produced the website IsraelVets.com to tell the stories of the volunteers.

The second Jewish dean at the University of Florida, Ralph Lowenstein headed the College of Journalism and Communications (1976–94). His college was a national leader in the transition to digital journalism—the first to introduce computers into the classroom and the first to start a daily internet newspaper. He is the author or coauthor of five books. In 2011 he received the Emma Lazarus Statue of Liberty Award from the American Jewish Historical Society—the society's highest honor, presented to an individual who has demonstrated outstanding leadership and commitment to strengthening the American Jewish community.

Greater Miami Jewish Federation Delegation to Europe and Palestine, 1947.

From left to right are Rabbi Irving Lehrman, President Max Orovitz, and Women's Division Chair Fannie Selig visiting DP camps in Europe. They arrived in Palestine on November 29, the day the United Nations voted for the partition of Palestine into two countries: one Jewish and one Arab. Orovitz was approached by Xiel Federmann from the Haganah to lend him $5,000 in cash. Orovitz agreed—if he could see why the money was needed. Thus, he witnessed the landing of a boatload of "illegal" (Aliyah Bet) immigrants from Europe. The captain had to be handed the $5,000 before he would allow disembarking of his human cargo.

Miami Group, left to right: Sam Blank, Max Orovitz, Sam Friedland, Xiel Federmann, and Dan Ruskin, 1961.

When Orovitz returned to Miami, he engaged Friedland, Blank, Ruskin, I. L. Mintzer, and Louis Stein in creating a joint venture to boost Israel's economy. They funded the construction of the Dan Hotel in Tel Aviv, which opened in 1953. This was the first of many hotels that were built or operated by the Dan Hotel chain, which became the largest in Israel. This private foreign investment provided jobs and attracted tourists to Israel.

The creation of the State of Israel was celebrated statewide from Pensacola (top) to Key West (bottom), 1948.

Esther Weinkle (left) was the national premiere recipient of the Eleanor Roosevelt Israel Humanitarian award, Miami Beach, 1963.

Eleanor Roosevelt had planned to present this award personally, but she died prior to the event. Her son Elliott and other members of the Roosevelt family made the presentation to Esther Weinkle "whose nobility of character, grace, humility, and deep sense of humanity have made her worthy of the cherished tradition of Eleanor Roosevelt and the proud heritage of the Land and People of Israel." Esther and Carl Weinkle were major philanthropists and devoted volunteers to Jewish causes, especially the State of Israel. After he sold his grocery chain (part 3, chapter 3), Carl went into the banking business.

In the wake of the Yom Kippur War in Israel, an emergency Israel Bond campaign was initiated, Miami Beach, 1973.

Mayshie Friedberg and David Rubinstein are filling out forms to purchase Israel Bonds. Floridian Jews joined Jews from all over the country in support of Israel's needs, especially during wartimes.

Ardent Zionist Norman Lipoff (right) with Benjamin Netanyahu before Netanyahu served as Israel's Prime Minister, Jerusalem, 1985.

Norman Lipoff moved with his family from Long Island to Florida in 1950. In 1984 he joined the board of governors of the Jewish Agency for Israel (JAI), the principal link between the Diaspora communities, the Jewish Federations, and Israel and served on the executive of JAI in the 1990s. A tax attorney in Miami for more than forty years, he served as a president of the Greater Miami Jewish Federation and as national chair of the United Jewish Appeal (1990–94). His involvement often takes him to Israel.

Israel Bonds honored Florida State Representative Elaine Bloom at an event coinciding with Purim, Miami, 1987.

Guest speaker US Senator Lawton Chiles said, "Elaine Bloom, like Queen Esther, is always ready to help on behalf of her people." From left to right are Chiles, Honorary National Vice-President of the National Council of Jewish Women Myra Farr, State Attorney Janet Reno, Florida State Senator Gwen Margolis, National Board Member of the American Jewish Joint Distribution Committee and President of Miami's Central Agency for Jewish Education Helene Berger, the Honorable Elaine Bloom, US Congressman Claude Pepper, and 11th Judicial Circuit Court Judge Philip Bloom.

PART 6

Hatred Against Jews = Antisemitism

"Antisemitism is the longest hatred," said scholar Robert Wistrich.

Hatred is perhaps the oldest of human emotions. And the hatred for Jews, antisemitism, is the most persistent, pervasive, and pernicious of all hatreds known in the world. Why? How? Antisemitism is a virus that mutates with each successive generation. It is not monolithic. It adapts to changing social and political situations. It historically occurs in times of great change when people are feeling very anxious and threatened—and Jews are blamed. Recent surveys show that 26 percent of the world hates Jews. That is more than a billion people!

Antisemitism has been the inability to make space for differences among people, which is the essential foundation of a free society. Most current scholars as well as many Christian theologians contend that antisemitism came with Christianity. In his landmark work, *Antisemitism in America* (1994), historian Leonard Dinnerstein (1934–2019) discusses "the plague that refuses to go away." He traced its path in America from colonial times, contending that age-old European bigotry against Jews was instilled in the New World by the earliest settlers, reinforced by successive waves of Protestant and Roman Catholic immigrants and "ingrained as an irrevocable part of the American heritage."

That bigotry surely followed the immigrants to Florida where, in the beginning of Florida's history, Jews were not allowed to settle for 250 years. I discussed in part 1 that during Spanish colonial days, Jews were prohibited from settling in Florida. This was part of the legal framework of the Spanish Inquisition. Once Spain relinquished Florida to Britain in 1763, Jewish settlement began—but the hatred was not halted.

Rabbi Lord Jonathan Sacks of the United Kingdom has said, "Antisemitism is a demonic phenomenon of hatred that has been for 2,000 years. The reason may change, but not the hate. In the middle ages, Jews were hated because of their religion. In the nineteenth and early twentieth century, they were hated because of their race. In the twenty-first century, they are hated because of their nation-state [Israel]."

Israel, nearly three-quarters of a century old, still finds itself the only country among the 193 in the United Nations whose right to exist is routinely challenged and in many quarters denied. There are 102 nations in the world where Christians predominate, and there are 56 Islamic states. But for some, a single Jewish state is deemed one too many. In a recent speech around the time of Passover, Rabbi Sacks referred to the part of the Haggadah that speaks of Jew hatred rearing its ugly head in every generation. "I had only thought this to be applicable to our parents' generation; those who had experienced the Holocaust but not for us who were born and raised after the Holocaust, but now I see things quite differently. The phrase 'Never Again' has come to mean 'Ever Again.'"

Dedication

Burnett Roth (right) receiving a plaque from his brother Nat Roth for his work as president of B'nai B'rith, Miami, 1942.

Burnett "Burnie" Roth, Miami Beach, 2005.

I am dedicating this part 6 on antisemitism and the civil rights portion of part 7 to Burnett "Burnie" Roth (1912–2008), a most unique native-born Jewish Floridian. In my thirty-five years of researching Florida Jewish history, I have not found anyone who has done more to advance tolerance, civil rights, and Zionism in Florida than Burnie—or anyone else who has clipped and saved more than one million pieces of this documented history.

Burnie was born in Daytona Beach, the youngest of nine children of Hymen and Celia Zeiger Roth. He began fighting antisemitism in the third grade, when he protested against the singing of "Onward Christian Soldiers" in the auditorium of Daytona Beach Grammar School. In 1924 he moved with his family to Orlando, where he successfully protested against proselytizing during school assemblies and helped make kosher food available in the Orlando Senior High School cafeteria. He remembered going to Orlando's Albertson Public Library to steal copies of the *Dearborn Independent* and other antisemitic publications so no one could read them.

Burnett was truly one of a kind. He had his own subscription to the *New York Times* when he was ten years old, and at seventeen, he gave a sermon for Kol Nidre services in Orlando entitled "Palestine: Yesterday, Today, and Tomorrow." Years later, he would support Israel's War of Independence by becoming active in Land and Labor for Palestine, heading recruitment of military personnel, and arranging for financing, passports, and transportation.

Burnett was associated with the Anti-Defamation League (ADL) of B'nai B'rith since 1931. He was continuously active with the ADL longer than anyone in the country. A 1925 experience with a black shoemaker who was working in a wooden shack in Orlando helped him realize the importance of racial problems. When he moved to Miami in 1935, he met with community leaders to discuss plans for integration in public schools—twenty years before desegregation became law. Burnett recalls defying Jim Crow laws and attending sit-ins. When I asked if he had any regrets in life, he said, "Two—not being able to join Martin Luther King Jr. in his march on Selma and not initiating the restoration of the Jewish cemetery in Prague."

A graduate of the University of Florida Law School, Burnie fought for human rights for all his ninety-six years. He remembered swastikas appearing on the fronts of Jewish-owned stores in Miami in the late 1930s. He remembered when the German ship *St. Louis* was cruising off Miami Beach in June 1939 and the community rally. Burnie served in World War II. He wanted to see his community function as a democracy without bigotry and with freedom of movement for all. He took on the issues of employment policies, private club restrictions, and apartment and hotel owners' gentile clientele only and whites only policies. After the war, he organized a committee of ten Jewish veterans to visit nearly one hundred hotel and apartment owners on Miami Beach to persuade them to eliminate their restrictive covenants.

When he was Miami Beach vice mayor, he was behind the city's 1947 antihate legislation, the first in the country, creating what would be the blueprint for such laws in years to come. In 1949 the State of Florida passed antidiscriminatory legislation, banning gentiles only and restricted clientele signs.

All his life, he was at the forefront of human rights issues. His collection related to his nearly seventy years fighting hatred in Florida forms a major part of the national archives of the ADL. A portion was donated to the JMOF-FIU to form the Burnett Roth Collection. These items chronicle nearly a century of resistance to bigotry, opposition to tyranny from both the left and the right, education in democracy, and the giving of aid to the oppressed and persecuted throughout the globe.

By the CHAIRMAN:

Question. Have there been any other killings in that county?

Answer. A great many murders occurred right along after that. A merchant by the name of Fleischman was taken from his home at night and carried across the Alabama line and told never to return. He passed up through Georgia and came back to the town of Tallahassee, and started west from Tallahassee; and on his way, within about twelve miles of Marianna, he was killed.

Question. Is Marianna in Jackson County?

Answer. Yes, sir.

Question. By whom was he killed?

Answer. By parties unknown to me. Last April the clerk who succeeded Dr. Finlayson, a man by the name of J. Q. Dickinson, was killed.

Question. By whom was he killed?

Answer. I could not say. I have a manuscript statement, in his hand-writing, of difficulties that occurred there, which statement was found among his papers after his death and handed to me.

Excerpted testimony about the 1869 murder case of Samuel Fleishman in Marianna, Washington, DC, 1871.

This testimony was taken during the Ku Klux Klan Hearings as reported in the US House Report No. 22, vol. 13, 42nd Congress. Some Jews suffered in the violent aftermath of the Civil War. Bavarian immigrant Samuel Fleishman, a resident of Florida by 1850, was a respected merchant in Marianna. He married Sophia Altman (whose brother founded B. Altman & Co. in New York); they had six children. In 1869 he was summoned before a group of vigilantes and told to leave without delay because he had defended blacks and given credit and employment to freed slaves. Fleishman protested, but he was escorted out of town and warned that he would be killed if he returned. Fleishman went to the state capitol in Tallahassee where he asked for state protection. Getting no support, he set out for Marianna as he did not want to abandon his family and business. He was shot and his body found on the road approaching Marianna. His assassins were never apprehended and the $10,000 reward went unclaimed, but many people said, "Ku Klux..." Remarkably, just ten years later, another Jew, Henry Brash, was elected mayor in Marianna.

Max L. Bear (seated center with crown), King of Mardi Gras, Pensacola, 1916. *Pensacola Historical Society.*

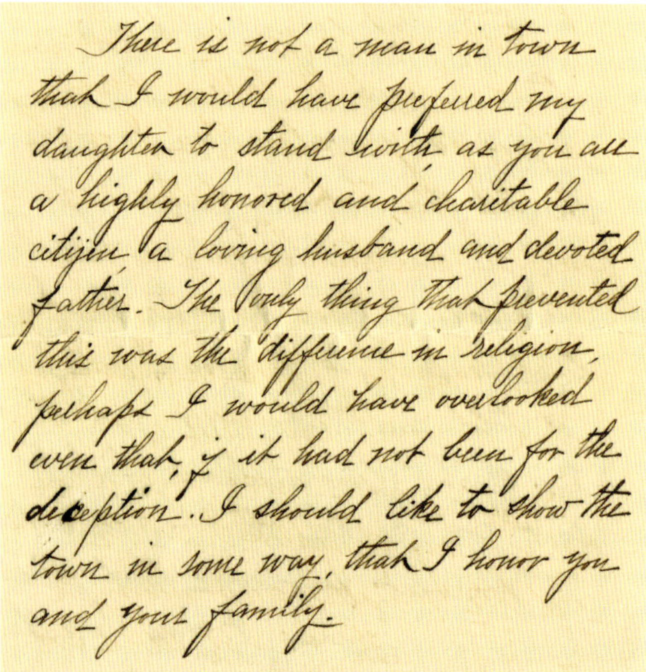

There is not a man in town
that I would have preferred my
daughter to stand with as you are
a highly honored and charitable
citizen a loving husband and devoted
father. The only thing that prevented
this was the difference in religion,
perhaps I would have overlooked
even that, if it had not been for the
deception. I should like to show the
town in some way, that I honor you
and your family.

Part of a nine-page letter from Mrs. William S. Rosascoe to Max L. Bear explaining why her daughter cannot sit as the Mardi Gras queen, Pensacola, March 12, 1916.

In this letter, Mrs. Rosascoe is apologizing and explaining that her daughter would not be queen at the side of Max Bear "on account of difference in religion." Max L. Bear, whose family had already been a part of Pensacola life for forty years, was named king of the prestigious Mardi Gras, indicating the respect he earned as both a civic and Jewish leader. He served in the Spanish-American War, became a principal officer of the Lewis Bear Company in 1901, was mayor (1936–37), was commodore of the Yacht Club, and served as president of his Temple Beth El for forty years!

Restrictive Covenants

Restrictive covenants excluded Jews from owning property in many parts of Florida. Railroad magnate and developer Henry Flagler attached such restrictions that barred Jews from buying property he controlled. On Miami Beach, beginning with the arrival of the first Jewish residents in 1913, Jews were not allowed to live north of Fifth Street because those properties were owned by Carl Fisher who would not sell to Jews. Waterfront hotels on both coasts commonly advertised their resorts to and for gentile clientele. The Tampa side of the once privately owned Gandy Bridge, linking Hillsborough and Pinellas counties, sported an antisemitic sign that some people remember. Sometimes Jews were able to move into towns in Florida only upon approval of the local Ku Klux Klan. Large areas of Palm Beach, Broward, and Miami-Dade Counties in the southeast, and especially Collier County in the southwest, were closed to Jewish settlement until the advent of Jewish real estate developers.

In interviews, Moe Katz discussed the presence of the Klan in Fort Lauderdale and the uneasiness with which Jewish residents viewed the hooded organization. In the 1930s signs on Dixie Highway, the main road into Fort Lauderdale, announced, "Jews Not Welcome." Moe and Mack Katz tore down the signs and informed the police that anyone attempting to insult the members of the Jewish community again would have to deal with them. They only had to go back one more time about those signs, but many Jews arriving in the postwar era attested to the continuing antisemitism in Fort Lauderdale and Broward County.

The Breakers Hotel of Palm Beach was the site of a test case and key target in the battle against the restrictive, antisemitic tourist industry of south Florida. In 1965 this historic, grand hotel was charged under the federal Civil Rights Law with a complaint brought by the Anti-Defamation League. The hotel finally agreed to follow a nondiscriminatory policy.

The successful 1947 film *Gentleman's Agreement*, was a stinging critique of the discriminatory policies of Florida's resorts and hotels. Gregory Peck plays a gentile writer who masquerades as a Jew to expose the practice of "keeping Jews in their place."

Many of the experiences with hotel and housing discrimination were paralleled in social club discrimination, which has been lessened by the passage of legislation and by the efforts of individuals and organizations.

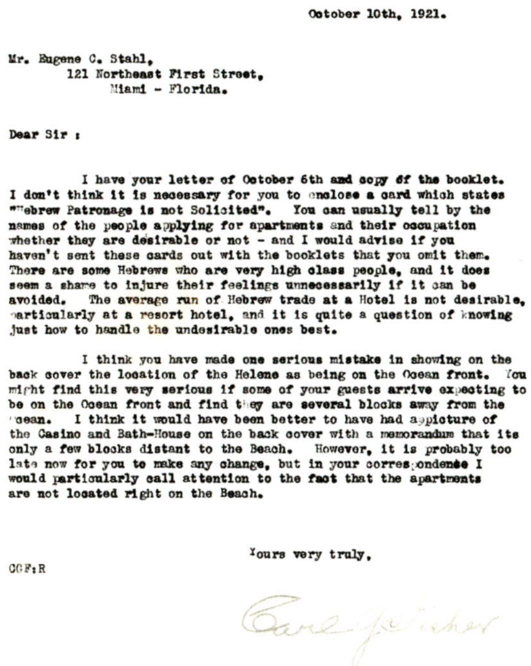

October 10th, 1921.

Mr. Eugene C. Stahl,
121 Northeast First Street,
Miami - Florida.

Dear Sir :

I have your letter of October 6th and copy of the booklet. I don't think it is necessary for you to enclose a card which states "Hebrew Patronage is not Solicited". You can usually tell by the names of the people applying for apartments and their occupation whether they are desirable or not - and I would advise if you haven't sent these cards out with the booklets that you omit them. There are some Hebrews who are very high class people, and it does seem a shame to injure their feelings unnecessarily if it can be avoided. The average run of Hebrew trade at a Hotel is not desirable, particularly at a resort hotel, and it is quite a question of knowing just how to handle the undesirable ones best.

I think you have made one serious mistake in showing on the back cover the location of the Helene as being on the Ocean front. You might find this very serious if some of your guests arrive expecting to be on the Ocean front and find they are several blocks away from the Ocean. I think it would have been better to have had a picture of the Casino and Bath-House on the back cover with a memorandum that its only a few blocks distant to the Beach. However, it is probably too late now for you to make any change, but in your correspondence I would particularly call attention to the fact that the apartments are not located right on the Beach.

Yours very truly,

CGF:R

Introductory letter for "the right kind of Jew" to Miami Beach, developer and hotelier Carl Fisher, 1929.

"I realize that on account of his nationality there may be some objections but if you can possibly get him the courtesy of your golf club I shall be everlastingly grateful to you." Carl Fisher made exceptions for "desirable" Jews and for those "who don't look it"—*if* it was good for business. "You can usually tell by the names and occupations whether they are desirable or not," said Fisher. "The average run of the Hebrew trade at a hotel is not desirable…there are some Hebrews who are very high class people." He wrote, "I would not want my hotel to fall into the hands of Jews."

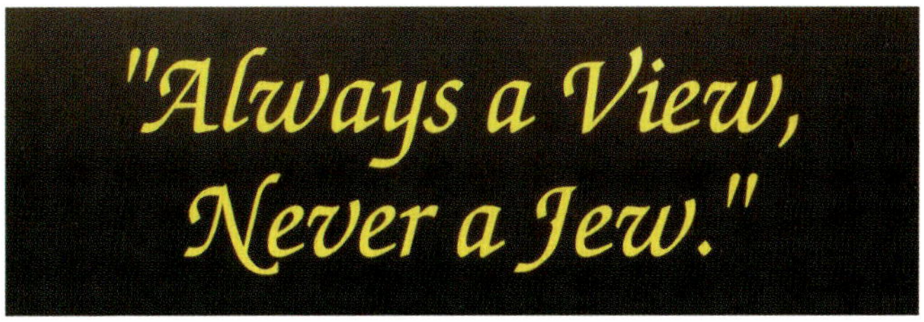

"Always a View, Never a Jew," Gulf Motel, Miami Beach, 1930s.

This bigoted motto was adopted by many of the hotels and apartments on Miami Beach and elsewhere around Florida in the 1940s.

Children at play at Miami Beach Elementary School with a sign on a building in the background: "Furnished Apartments—Monthly Rates—Gentiles Only," 1935.

In 1953 the ADL's survey showed 57 percent of five hundred Florida hotels discriminated against Jews. By 1965 this had been reduced to 5.4 percent.

Hotel Rellim opened for Jews on Pass-A-Grille Beach in response to restricted policies of the area's hotels, St. Petersburg Beach, 1941.

Signs that clearly displayed "exclusive" restrictive policies were common in St. Petersburg hotels. Because there were no places for Jewish visitors to stay in the area, Harriet and Jacob Miller said, "The beaches need to be for everyone" and tried to buy land to build a Jewish hotel. They were thwarted until they used the name "Rellim," which is Miller spelled backward. In 1940 they bought land from Thomas Rowe, who built the nearby luxurious (and restricted) Don CeSar Hotel. Beginning in the early 1950s, their son Irwin Miller ran the Rellim with his wife, Sonya Haliczer. The Rellim was the social hub for the Pinellas County Jewish community for forty years—a winter tourist destination and a summer Jewish beach club. The Rellim was the impetus to a change of policy and signage in the area after 1953. US Vice President Richard Nixon was scheduled to stay at a restricted hotel. When he learned that that would cause him to lose Jewish support, he moved to the Rellim.

"Gentile Clientele" brochure for the Coronado Hotel, Miami Beach, 1940s.

In the 1940s and 1950s, Ellinor Village in Ormond Beach was Florida's largest family resort and had restricted policies, 1950.

Merrill Ellinor printed three hundred thousand marketing brochures with "Restricted Clientele" printed clearly on the cover. German-born Rabbi Henry Okolica (1913–2017) of nearby Daytona Beach's Temple Israel (1946–53) protested this flagrant discrimination policy. He met with Mr. Ellinor, who admitted he had never before encountered a Jew and initially refused to remove the offensive line that meant "We cater only to Christians." After some creative pressure—the possibility of flooding the hotel with false reservations, canceling days before the season began—Ellinor agreed to make the change. At first, "Restricted Clientele" was blacked out. Then Okolica offered to pay 50 percent of costs to reprint the brochures. After receiving the check, Ellinor reprinted and donated that amount to the United Jewish Appeal. Then he said, "This made a better Christian out of me." Today, the property exists as a housing development.

Typical real estate covenants specified that "homes will not be sold to any individual who has one-quarter Hebrew or Syrian blood." This community had a 1948 covenant that no one could buy a lot unless they were a member of the association—that excluded Jews. A Jew who purchased a lot and built a home was refused membership and sued. The attorney was David Catsman. The Florida Supreme Court ruled that any attempt to prohibit property ownership because of race or religion was unconstitutional, a decision that changed the practice of illegal restrictions against Jews.

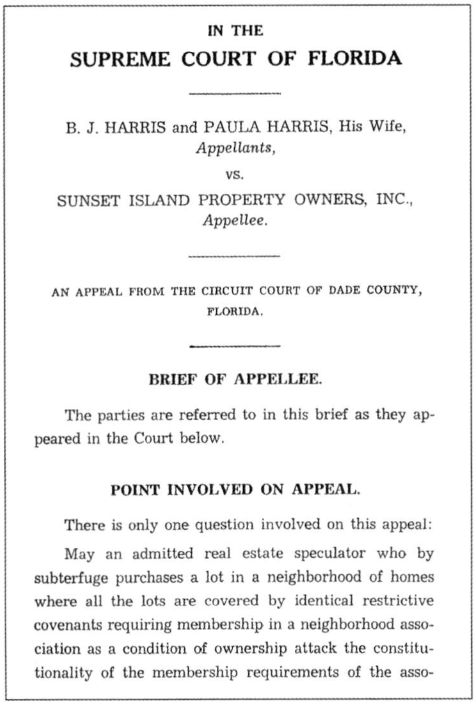
IN THE
SUPREME COURT OF FLORIDA

B. J. HARRIS and PAULA HARRIS, His Wife,
Appellants,
vs.
SUNSET ISLAND PROPERTY OWNERS, INC.,
Appellee.

AN APPEAL FROM THE CIRCUIT COURT OF DADE COUNTY, FLORIDA.

BRIEF OF APPELLEE.

The parties are referred to in this brief as they appeared in the Court below.

POINT INVOLVED ON APPEAL.

There is only one question involved on this appeal:

May an admitted real estate speculator who by subterfuge purchases a lot in a neighborhood of homes where all the lots are covered by identical restrictive covenants requiring membership in a neighborhood association as a condition of ownership attack the constitutionality of the membership requirements of the asso-

Miami Beach's Sunset Island case decided by the Florida Supreme Court, 1959.

Charter members of the 10I Club, Orlando, 1933.

Jewish teens attending Orlando High School formed the 10I Club because they were excluded from the high school fraternities and sororities. There was no Jewish youth group in town, so they made the 10I Club, the name created from the number ten (the number needed for a *minyan*) and the letter *I* from the word *Israelites*. Seated left to right are Irene Braverman [Meyer], Gertrude Haimowitz [Cooper], Pearl Safer [Kramer], Myer Sigal, Florence Wittenstein [Tobias], and Beatrice Lieberman [Lippton]. Standing left to right are Morton Levy, Morris Haimowitz, Maxine Braverman [Lazarus], Dorothy Baker [Gordon], George Wolly, and Abe Kamenoff.

Nation and Race **magazine published by the White Front, Clermont, 1936.**

During the Great Depression of the 1930s, Americans watched Adolf Hitler's rebuilding of Germany after its World War I defeat. Some in Florida embraced Nazism as a viable ideology. In this ironic and unusual image, the Florida Nazi magazine portrays Jews as hypersensitive to any expression of antisemitism. A child plays with a starfish on the beach that happens to take the shape of a swastika. Angry Jews swarm around the offending sea creature. Perhaps the artist experienced some aggressive Jewish opposition to his antisemitic activities.

The slogans "Buy Gentile—Vote Gentile—Employ Gentile" were circulated by the White Front. White Front Rally, Miami, 1939.

Window sticker supporting a boycott of Jewish businesses, Miami, 1938.

Adopting a technique pioneered in Nazi Germany, antisemites in Florida attempted a boycott with these 2.5-inch-diameter stickers on storefronts that appealed to their passions and religious intolerance. This artwork is taken directly from European Nazi sources, with a mangled English-language translation of the original German text. To the credit of the Miami community, gentiles led the effort to remove the offensive propaganda.

Cantor Michael Soloway of Congregation Ahavath Chesed reported the graffiti on his synagogue, Jacksonville, 1961.

This is an expression of antisemitism that continues today. The Florida Legislature passed a hate crime law in 1989. It defines a hate crime as an act committed or attempted by any person or group against another person or group, or their property, which in any way constitutes an expression of hatred toward the victim based on personal characteristics. It is a crime in which the perpetrator intentionally selects the victim based on one of the following personal characteristics: race, color, religion, ethnicity, ancestry, national origin, or sexual orientation.

Bess Meyerson, Miss America, 1945.

Bess Myerson with her parents, Bella and Louis Myerson, Miami Beach, 1946.

In 1945 Bess Myerson (1924–2014) won the hearts of all America—and especially those of the American Jewish community—as the first and still *only* Jewish Miss America. It was right after World War II, and gruesome images of the Holocaust were being revealed. The Jews needed some joy in their lives—a sense of pride—and Bess provided that!

Raised in Sholom Aleichem Cooperative Houses in the Bronx by immigrant parents and a student at Hunter College, Bess was not prepared for the harsh, sexist, antisemitic world of beauty pageants in 1945. Although many Jews changed their names to hide their origins, Miss America 1945 was not among them. When Bess Myerson was asked to become "Betty Merrick" on the final evening of the pageant in Atlantic City, she refused, saying, "If I win this contest tonight, the only people who will really care are my girlfriends from Hunter, my friends from camp, my family, and the families I've grown up with. And if I win and I'm Betty Merrick, they won't know it's me…so I think I have to keep my name: Bess Myerson." And she did win, judged on her musical talent (piano and flute) and intellect. Prejudice raised its ugly head as sponsors and events long associated with the pageant refused to deal with her.

Myerson was known as the "Brainy Miss America." She devoted her life to fighting bigotry and hatred, promoting tolerance among all peoples and civil and human rights. On her initial speaking tour in 1946, Bess said, "A person with a hateful soul can never be beautiful." Her topics ranged from "Women's Role in the Changing World," "Consumerism," "The Middle East...Israel and Its Arab Neighbors," "My Personal Journey from Miss America to Today," "Loving Living Longer," and "The Campus Controversy: Racial and Religious Bigotry" to "Overcoming Ovarian Cancer." And she wrote five books. She established the ADL Campus Journalism Awards for American colleges and universities and served US Presidents Carter, Ford, and Johnson on commissions of vital concern. She also served the City of New York as both commissioner of consumer affairs (1969–73) and cultural affairs (1983–87) when she helped restore the city as the cultural capital of the world. She served in the United Nations, and in 1980 ran for US senator from New York.

Bess had radio and TV shows and a syndicated newspaper column. As a journalist, she was sent to Israel to cover the Eichmann trial in 1961 and the Begin-Sadat meeting in Jerusalem in 1977. From 1958–67, Bess was a panelist for 318 episodes of *I've Got a Secret*, one of the earliest game shows on TV. She received honorary degrees from five universities.

Myerson settled in Florida in 2003 and donated her personal archives to the JMOF.

For more than twenty-five years, I attended the annual conference of the Council of American Jewish Museums (CAJM). In 2001 the conference was in New York City, and the final session was at the relatively new Museum of Jewish Heritage in Battery Park. The last scheduled speaker was Bess Myerson. Usually this is anticlimactic—we have had long days of intense lectures and workshops and are thinking of our trips home and all the things we want to institute from our discussions. When Bess Myerson spoke, she immediately refocused and lifted us emotionally. She inspired us with her stories of the discrimination she faced and her lifetime of fighting hatred. Afterward, I rushed up to thank her, as many did. I told her about the JMOF's upcoming exhibit, *The Art of Hatred*, and asked if she would speak for us at the museum on this topic. She warmly responded, and we began a friendship. She stayed in my condo in North Miami many times, regaling dinner guests of her Miss America stories that reflected her dedication as a Jewish woman to her people.

Bess joined the JMOF's board of directors, and when we planned our expansion and connecting structure between the two former synagogues, she made a contribution to dedicate "Bessie's Bistro" in memory of her parents. When asked what motivated her to contribute $500,000 to the museum, she responded, "The good memories of the happy years my parents, Bella and Louis Myerson, had living in the neighborhood near the museum. They were so proud that I could buy them the house at 1575 Euclid Avenue in the 1970s."

Sergeant Herman D. Adelstein, 1918.

Silver Star presented to Herman D. Adelstein by Florida's US Senator Richard Stone, Lauderhill, 1977.
Jewish War Veterans Archives.

In World War I, Sergeant Herman D. Adelstein of Florida earned the Silver Star, America's second-highest combat medal, for gallantry displayed on the battlefield in France. His superiors blocked the award because he was Jewish. Sixty years later, US Senator Richard Stone, a target of antisemitic campaign ads, finally set the record straight and pinned on Adelstein's long overdue medal. His citation read in part, "*Although enemy machine gun bullets were flying around his gun constantly and shells were landing in the immediate vicinity, he bravely volunteered to help straighten out the ammunition. When the barrage started, he served the piece as gunner and although several men of the platoon were wounded during firing, he continued to perform his duties so effectively and laid on all data so correctly that several direct hits were made on the enemy…and he helped the battery to destroy the enemy machine gun nest and artillery.*" It was signed by General John Hershey.

PART 7

Acculturation

How wonderful it is that nobody need wait a single moment before starting to improve the world.
—German Holocaust victim Anne Frank

Jews who settled in Florida became involved in every aspect of improving the world. First, they labored to become Floridians. The process of acculturating into American and Floridian society is a struggle for balance. Each immigrant ethnic group comes with its own traditions and culture and must face the challenges of integrating. How much of one's own distinctive traditions and culture does one retain? How much does one mix with the new culture?

Each succeeding generation of immigrant families tends to adopt more and more of the traits of their new land. However, by the fourth generation we begin to see three distinctive trends. They are the tip toward becoming more traditional in one's own culture, therefore, withdrawing from the prevailing society; the tip the other way toward assimilation and the diminishing of one's own traditions; or that fine balance of integration into American society without loss of one's own traditions.

CHAPTER 1

Blending Cultures: Becoming Floridians

William Coleman (left) poses on alligator with Mayor J. E. T. Bowden (not Jewish), Jacksonville, 1915.

Louis Moss with alligator, Jacksonville, circa 1920.

Honeymooners Gertrude Katz Moses and David Moses on alligator, West Palm Beach, 1920s.

Brothers Stanley and Milton Weinkle on alligator, Miami Beach, 1931.

In part 2, chapter 4, you met baby Felix Glickstein sitting on an alligator. This was the first "alligator" photograph in the MOSAIC collection, but as I traveled, I gathered many more. For more than a century, settlers, tourists, politicians, and honeymooners have posed enthusiastically with the stuffed or painted varieties as proof of their conquest of the wilderness and their pride in being Floridian Jews. I hope they make you smile!

Rachel Luber Wilck (back right) with Seminoles, Miami, 1927.

When Polish immigrant Wilck was widowed, she bought baby alligators and turtles from the Seminole Indians and shipped them to all parts of the country as Florida tourist souvenirs in the 1920s and 1930s.

Pioneer women experiencing a new thing: Las Olas Beach, later named Fort Lauderdale Beach, 1928.

From left to right are Molly Robbins, Mollie Newman [Spier], Rose Reiss, Sadie Katz, and her daughter Anita Katz [Paris]. Each of these women was instrumental in the beginnings of Temple Emanu-El of Fort Lauderdale, Broward County's first Jewish congregation.

"Fighting Hebrews" was the name adopted for the Suwannee High School soccer team because it had three Jews as their star players, Live Oak, 1922.

This first soccer team of a Florida high school included Isadore Weiss (front row, center) and Sam and David Gibbs (second row, left and right).

Philip Benjamin (left) and Harvey and Ted Wittner enjoy winter warmth in Florida, St. Petersburg, 1932.

I found this same goat cart (or its likeness!) in many pioneer family albums throughout the state!

Louis Fine was the first Jewish Master Mason of the Biscayne Bay Lodge, Miami, 1935.

The Masons are the largest and most widely known fraternity in the world. In Florida, many Jews joined the Masons as the orders offered them a degree of social integration not always available by other routes.

Reba Belle and Joel Mendelson in their Dad's Shrine hats, Jacksonville, 1921.

The Shriners are a spin-off from the Masons, founded more on fellowship and philanthropy than rituals.

Members of the Shrine, Marianna, 1928.

In the front row from left to right are Ben Fleet, William Fleet, and Sam Fleet. In the back row from left to right are Louis Mendelson, Bernard Jacobs, Sam Robbins, and Willie Rosner.

Louis Ossinsky played right guard for Duval High School and was All-State, Jacksonville, 1920.

First Jewish majorette at Fort Lauderdale High School, Nancy Newman [Simon], Fort Lauderdale, 1942.

Her parents, Mollie and Abe Newman, settled there in 1927 in the face of fervent discrimination against Jews.

Congregation Ahavath Chesed formed a Boy Scout Troop in 1915 and continues as the second-oldest troop in Jacksonville, 1920.

The Brownies are second and third graders of the Girl Scouts, Jewish Community Center, Orlando, 1987.

Judge Kenneth Oka's Yiddish campaign poster, Miami Beach, 1957.

Oka (1916–87) was Miami Beach's mayor twice (1957–59 and 1961–63) at a time when Jews were the majority in the city.

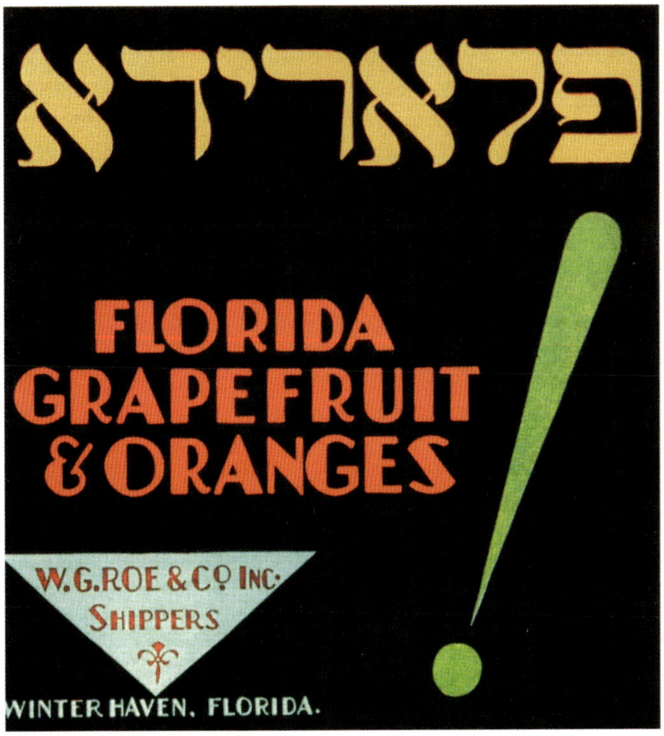

Citrus crate label reads "Florida" in Yiddish, Winter Haven, circa 1930. *Museum of Florida History.*

When I began research into the Jewish history of Florida during the 1980s, I thought a reasonable place to start was Florida's State Archives in Tallahassee. Remarkably, they did not even have a category for "Jews" or "Jewish" among the thousands in their collections. I did find this citrus crate label and then discovered the company did not have Jewish ownership. The (gentile) Roe Company was shipping their fruit to New York and targeting the Jewish market as customers!

In part 2, chapter 1, you met Mena Williams, the first Miss Florida in 1885. There have been two more Jewish women who have served as Miss Florida.

Carol Blum, Miss Florida and third place in Miss America, Miami Beach, 1965.

Mari Wilensky, Miss Florida, Jacksonville, 2005.

A third-generation descendent in Jacksonville, singer Mari Wilensky has participated in pageants since age four and was a top-five finalist for Miss America in 2006.

J. T. Wilensky Jeweler and Optician, Jacksonville, circa 1905.

Mari's great-grandfather Dr. Jacob Tobias Wilensky came from Russia to Jacksonville in 1905 and was the first jeweler and optician there. He and Dora had five children. Dora hosted meetings in her home of the Ladies Hebrew Sheltering Aid Society, which became River Garden Hebrew Home for the Aged.

CHAPTER 2

Military Service

Thousands of Floridian Jews have served the United States in the army, coast guard, marines, navy, and air force.

They displayed courage as officers and regular soldiers, nurses, doctors, and chaplains. The exemplary history of Florida's Jews in the military began in the mid-1800s with the Seminole Indian Wars when Philip Diamond served and West Point graduate Abraham C. Myers was quartermaster. A Florida city now bears his name: Fort Myers. Jews have continued their participation in defense of democracy and freedom, both on the war and home fronts, in the Civil War (1861–65), Spanish-American War (1898), World War I (1917–18), World War II (1939–45), Cold War (1945–91), Korean War (1950–53), Vietnam (1959–75), and the Gulf Wars (1990–2011), which include the conflicts in Iraq and Afghanistan.

Jews have served in the military in a larger percentage than their share of the population. Those who came to America and then to Florida enlisted very often to become accepted, to overcome the concept of the wandering Jew with no loyalty, and to show that they were not cowards. While serving, these Floridian Jews maintained the traditions of their heritage, even when it was challenging.

Some were killed in action in each of the wars, and this section is dedicated to them. At least seven young Floridian Jews made the supreme sacrifice in the Gulf Wars: Army Specialist Daniel Agami (Parkland, 2007), Air Force Airman First Class Elizabeth Jacobson (Riviera Beach, 2005), Army Major Mark Rosenberg (Hollywood, 2008), Marine Corporal Justin Schrage (Indian Harbour Beach, 2004), Air Force Technical Sergeant Timothy Weiner (Lauderhill, 2007), Army Specialist Jeffrey Wershow (Gainesville, 2003), and Army Major Stuart Wolfer (Coral Springs, 2008).

Many earned medals such as the Army Distinguished Service Cross, Army Distinguished Service Medal, Silver Star, Legion of Merit, Distinguished Flying Cross, Bronze Star, Purple Heart, Meritorious Service Medal, Air Medal, and others. The individuals' stories and their character traits are role models for the future generations.

The examples of courageous people portrayed here show the transition from civilians to soldiers, then back to their families—when they were fortunate. They risked their lives for a dream and for our nation. We pay tribute to these extraordinary Americans.

I identified six Jews in Florida who have served at the highest ranks of the US military: US Navy Rear Admiral Ellis Zacharias; US Army Major General

Greater Miami Jewish War Veterans (JWV) Drum and Bugle Corps in Bayfront Park, Miami, 1941.

Jamie S. Barkin, who is also chief of gastroenterology at Mount Sinai Medical Center in Miami Beach, professor of medicine at the University of Miami, and on several top doctors lists (and received a Distinguished Service Medal); US Army Lieutenant General David Fridovich, whose position at the time of his 2011 retirement was the senior green beret and deputy commander of the US military's Special Operations Command in Tampa that directs special operations campaigns (received several Meritorious Service Medals); US Air Force Major General Bernard L. Weiss; US Navy Rear Admiral Paul Becker, who served two years (2007–09) at MacDill Air Force Base, Tampa, as the commanding officer of Central Command's Joint Intelligence Center; and US Navy Rear Admiral Julian Benjamin, a 1944 graduate of Miami Beach High School.

The Jewish War Veterans (JWV) was created in 1896 by Civil War veterans to prove that Jews have proudly served this country since the Revolutionary Era. Richard Schulman is the young boy in the front center.

Ainslee Ferdie (left), past national commander, Jewish War Veterans (JWV), and Angela Mathis, ladies auxiliary, Veterans of Foreign Wars (VFW), Miami, 2004.

David Magidson of Miami also served as JWV National Commander (2006–07) and as president (2008–10) of the board of directors of the National Museum of American Jewish Military History in Washington, DC.

Second Seminole War, 1835–42

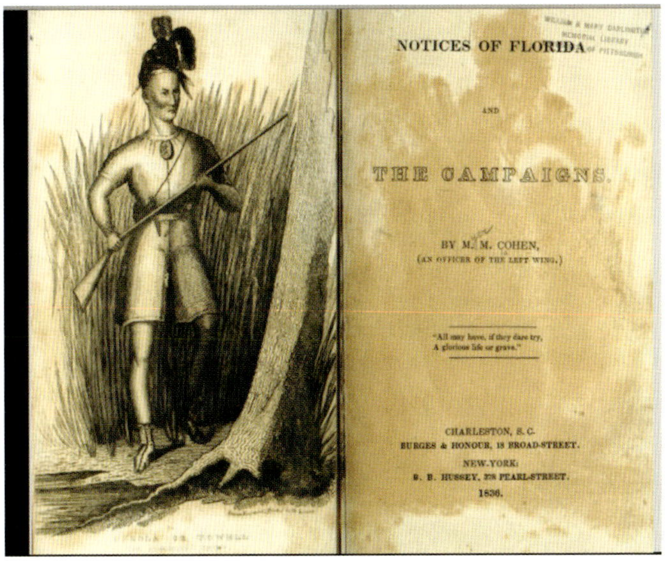

US Army Lieutenant Myer M. Cohen volunteered for the Second Seminole War, was stationed in St. Augustine, and made detailed notes, 1836.

These notes became Cohen's book, *Notices of Florida and the Campaigns*. While using a liberal, romanticized prose style, the book does provide a detailed, in-depth, eyewitness account of the conflict.

Other Jews who served in Florida during the Seminole Wars (1817–18, 1835–42, and 1855–58) include US Army Colonel Abraham Charles Myers (in part 1), Private Philip Diamond, US Army Surgeon Dr. David Camden DeLeon, Colonel Leon Dyer, first Jewish Commodore of the US Navy Uriah P. Levy, and Samuel Noah, one of the first graduates of West Point.

Civil War Confederate Army Lieutenant Michael Levy, Pensacola, 1865.

Civil War, 1861–65

Being a slave state, with secession on January 10, 1861, Florida became one of the founding members of the Confederacy. The Civil War erupted on April 12, 1861.

Pot, pewter, inscribed in center with initials "M & A-L" (Michael and Anna Levy), Pensacola, 1865. *Myron Rosenthal.*

Michael Levy and his brother Julius left Germany for America to avoid conscription in the army. Michael then enlisted during the Civil War, survived the Battle of Shiloh, and was promoted and detailed to the ordnance department. Since he was kosher, he carried his own pot to make hot chocolate. Levy mustered out in Milton, then settled in Pensacola, where he was a founder of Florida's first Jewish congregation. His sons purchased properties in downtown Pensacola that remain in the family.

Confederate Army Lieutenant Albert Moses Luria (1843–62; left) was the first-known Confederate Jew killed during the Civil War, 1860. *Lewis Regenstein, Atlanta, Georgia.*

Albert Moses Luria was born in Apalachicola as the second son of Eliza Matilda and Raphael Jacob Moses (you met Raphael in part 1). At Sewell's Point, in May 1861, an 8-inch shell, with fuse still burning, fell into the company's gun pit. Albert seized it and put it in a tub of water, quenching the fuse and thereby saving his own and his comrades' lives. The company, in recognition of his heroism, had the shell engraved with the history of the incident, added the words, "The pride of his Regiment and the bravest of the brave," and sent it to his parents. He was killed at Seven Pines, while rallying his company after having seized the colors (flags) from the hands of the dying color-bearer.

Confederate Army Lieutenant Joshua Lazarus Moses was the last-known Confederate Jew killed during the Civil War, circa 1863. *Lewis Regenstein, Atlanta, Georgia.*

In addition to losing a son in the Civil War, Raphael Jacob Moses, who served in the Civil War, also lost a nephew. Lieutenant Joshua Lazarus Moses enlisted in the spring of 1861 and died on April 9, 1865, while defending Mobile, Alabama, at Fort Blakely. This was the same day as General Robert E. Lee's surrender at Appomattox.

During my review of the oral histories, I found other Floridian Jews (or those who mustered out in Florida) who served the Confederacy during the Civil War: Matthew Beck, Lewis Blumauer, Jacob Burkheim, Henry Brash, Gus Cohen, Morris Daniels, Morris Dzialynski, Abraham Ellinger, Isador Grunthal, David Miley, Samuel Miley, Saunders Myers, Julius Slager, and Robert S. Williams. (Note: author Daniel R. Weinfeld has done more extensive research and has a list of nearly sixty names.)

Spanish-American War, 1898

United Spanish War Veterans Medal of Emanuel "Manny" Brash, Apalachicola, 1898.

Born in 1868 in Apalachicola to Henrietta and Henry Brash and a lifetime resident, Manny was issued this medal for serving in the armed forces during the Spanish-American War. His father, Henry, had served in the Civil War.

US Army Sergeant Max J. Heinberg Sr., Pensacola, 1898.

A native of Pensacola, Heinberg was stationed in Tampa during the Spanish-American War. Spanish-American War Jewish veterans buried in Orlando's cemeteries are Philip R. Rosenberg, Sol Samuels, Emil Feldman, and Grover Avera.

World War I, 1917–18

When the time came in 1917 to serve their country under arms, no class of people served with more patriotism or with higher motives than the young Jews who volunteered or were drafted and who went overseas with our other young Americans.

—General John Pershing, Commander of the American Expeditionary Forces

Florida Home Guardsman Joseph J. Abramowitz during World War I, Tampa, 1917.

Tampa native Joseph Abramowitz served in the Hillsborough County Home Guard. The departure of Florida's two National Guard regiments of infantry for World War I left the state with no remaining military forces. On May 21, 1917, the state legislature passed a law allowing counties to form Home Guard units composed of white men between ages eighteen and sixty-five. Their activities were largely confined to weekly meetings and drills and participation in patriotic activities.

Pensacola native Private Bertram Dannheisser served as a dentist in the Army Medical Department during World War I, 1917.

After the war, he was a dentist in Pensacola.

World War II, 1939–45

In common with all who fought and died for victory, the Jewish men and women of the Armed Forces were motivated by unity of purpose and animated by faith in the American way of life. The best monument to their memory would be the kind of world to justify their faith and their sacrifice.

—President Harry S. Truman

The United States entered the war on December 8, 1941, following the Japanese attack on the US naval base at Pearl Harbor. Some Floridian Jews killed in action during World War II include Norman Bruce Brown, Alfie Kohn, Meyer Leibovitz, Robert Richter, Marvin Roth, and Isadore Stessel.

On Sunday, December 7, 1941, at Pearl Harbor, US Marine Corps 2nd Lieutenant Arnold D. Swartz was the officer of the guard.

Lieutenant Swartz was seven months into medical school when he was ordered to active duty with the Marine Corps to train as an antiaircraft artillery officer. In late 1941 he was sent to Hawaii. After inspecting the sentries and while waiting for his breakfast on December 7, the Japanese began their attack on Pearl Harbor. "I saw a plane dive that looked like a big red meatball," said Swartz. He organized his men to man the 3-inch gun batteries. Swartz continued, "The Japanese made mistakes by not sending in troops and not destroying the dry docks—and the aircraft carriers were not in port." Swartz made it out alive, only to later participate in the Battle of Midway and the Battle of

Guadalcanal. He was injured, received a medical discharge, and then later settled in Coconut Creek.

US Army Staff Sergeant Abe Stein was assigned to the medical department at Pearl Harbor when the Japanese attack occurred, 1941.

Abe Stein was living in West Palm Beach when he enlisted and chose Hawaii from a photo of a hula girl and palm trees. On that infamous Sunday morning, he carried bodies into the morgue, survived, and then participated in the Allied invasion of Normandy. After the war, he returned to live in south Florida.

US Navy Captain Ellis Mark Zacharias was one of the first to use psychological warfare, Jacksonville, 1941.

Captain Zacharias (1890–1961) said that he predicted in March 1941 that if the Japanese started a war, it would be an aerial attack on a Sunday morning to destroy four American battleships in the Pacific. Zacharias was born in Jacksonville to Teresa and Aaron Zacharias, who settled there shortly after the Civil War to grow tobacco. Ellis was drawn to the waterfront as a child and attended the Naval Academy (class of 1912), the only Jewish graduate of Annapolis for at least a ten-year period.

He was assigned to the battleship USS *Arkansas*, which transported President William H. Taft to see the Panama Canal in 1912. During World War I, he was an engineering officer (USS *Raleigh*) and then a gunnery officer (USS *Pittsburgh*). After the war, Zacharias became an attaché to the US Embassy in Tokyo, where he interacted with high-ranking Japanese military leaders and learned to speak Japanese fluently. In 1934 he became officer in charge of the Far Eastern Office of Naval Intelligence.

During World War II, Captain Zacharias commanded the cruiser USS *Salt Lake City* in the Gilbert and Marshall Islands (and helped escort Doolittle Raiders' bombing raids over Tokyo), was deputy director of the Office of Naval Intelligence, commanded the battleship USS *New Mexico*, and then became chief of staff of the 11th Naval District.

Until his death, Zacharias doubted the need for the atomic bomb (which his nephew Jerrold R. Zacharias, also born in Jacksonville, helped develop at Los Alamos) and believed that Japan might have surrendered without. Because he was skilled in Japanese and had been a close student of Japanese society and culture in the interwar period, he believed in psychological warfare to bring the Japanese to surrender without a shot. Announcing himself as the "official spokesman" of the US, he participated in breaking Japanese morale through his weekly radio broadcasts in Japanese directed at the people on the home islands and specifically to their leaders. In his twelfth broadcast, he said that Japan had already lost the war. "Your progressive defeats and our progressive victories have brought the war to Japan's very doorstep." He suggested surrender in face of total destruction. After the atomic bombs were dropped on August 6 and 9, Japanese Premier Suzuki asked the US, on the air, to spare Emperor Hirohito. Zacharias responded anonymously, and then the Japanese accepted Allied surrender terms on August 15, 1945.

Captain Zacharias was awarded the Legion of Merit with two gold stars, one for his radio broadcasts, and many other medals. After thirty-four years of continuous military service, he was promoted to rear admiral upon his retirement in 1946, the year his autobiography *Secret Missions* was published. He hosted a weekly radio series named *Secret Missions* in 1958 and a television series called *Behind Closed Doors* in 1959.

"Beloved by his men but viewed with suspicion by his superiors, he assuredly was not viewed as a member of the Good Old Boys club in the US Navy," said David A. Pfeiffer, a great-nephew who wrote his biography. When Zacharias died, he was buried in Arlington Cemetery with full military honors in an area reserved for high-ranking war heroes.

Some families sent multiple children to World War II.

Corporal Jack Rubin of Cocoa and Miami Beach landed in Normandy in 1944 and later was captured and became a prisoner of war (POW).

His parents, Romanian immigrants Anna Holtsberg and Isadore Rubin, sent their four children to serve: Harold, Irving, Jack, and Ruth [Elsasser].The Rubins were the first Jewish family in Cocoa, circa 1911, and were major civic activists. While their children were overseas, they received letters written in Yiddish from their grandmother Sarah Holtsberg

Florida Jews who were prisoners of war during World War II, in addition to Jack Rubin, include Jerry Jacobs, Martin King, and Fred Schrager.

Left to right: Henry, Leo, Harold, and Norman Reinhard, the four sons of Beckie and Sam Reinhard, served their nation and all came home, Miami Beach, 1944.

MOSCOVITZ BROTHERS IN THE ARMY

Listed according to age, left to right, are Pfc. Ben Moscovitz; Capt. Isadore Moscovitz; First Lieut. Louis Moscovitz, and Pfc. Abe Moscovitz, sons of Mr. and Mrs. Joseph Moscovitz, 423 West Seventh, Street. All four sons are in the U. S. Army.

Left to right: Ben, Isadore, Louis, and Abe Moscovitz, the four sons of Anna and Joseph Moscovitz, served and all came home, Jacksonville, 1943.

The three sons of Bess and Nathan Rosenblatt served and all came home, Tampa, 1946.

From left to right are Petty Officer Second Class Nathan Rosenblatt Jr., US Navy; Major Charles Rosenblatt, US Army Air Force; and Corporal Frank Rosenblatt, US Army. Charles flew 102 combat missions during World War II and was awarded the Distinguished Flying Cross (twice) and the Air Medal (four times). He also served as a fighter pilot during the Korean War and retired as a colonel after 22 years of service.

Florida native US Army Captain Nellye Israelson, Tampa, 1943.

One example of the many women who served in World War II, Nellye was one of the first women to enlist in the Women's Army Corps. She became an officer, served for three years, and after the war married another soldier, Herbert Friedman. A granddaughter of Julia and Julius Frank, who had settled in Miami in 1896 (you met them in part 2, chapter 4), Nellye, with Herbert, raised Mary [Kramer], Bill, Frances [Williams], and Frank in Tampa. They were deeply involved in all aspects of the civic and Jewish community. Nellye was cochair (with Doris Rosenblatt) of the MOSAIC Tampa task force.

The Signaling Search Light (SSL) was designed by famed architect Morris Lapidus, Miami Beach, 1943.

The Signaling Search Light (SSL) became standard equipment for the Royal and US navies during World War II. When researching for the *Florida Jews in the US Military* exhibit, I was surprised to learn that Lapidus was responsible for this crucial, powerful lamp with a shutter device to flash semaphore messages back to a ship once an invading landing party arrived on shore. US Navy Admiral Hyman Rickover announced the design contest, and US Metal Products entered. US Metal was owned by Russian immigrant Leon Lapidus, who asked his oldest son, Morris, to take a year off from his architectural practice to design the lamp. The Navy required that a prototype be able to withstand the severe conditions of a landing and gunfire and the Lapidus lamp was awarded the production contract.

US Army Corps Chaplain Sidney M. Lefkowitz (center right with *tallit* and no helmet) performed the first Jewish service on German soil following Nazi persecution, Siegfried Line, Aachen, Germany, October 29, 1944.

This *yizkor* service was broadcast from Germany around the world by NBC. Rabbi Lefkowitz served as an Army chaplain from 1942–45. He participated in the D-Day invasion and afterward traveled throughout France and Belgium conducting services. Lefkowitz was the first Jewish chaplain to participate in the liberation of a concentration camp, Camp Dora near Nordhausen, Germany. He was awarded a Bronze Star and ended his career as a major. After the war, Rabbi Lefkowitz served at Congregation Ahavath Chesed in Jacksonville from 1946–73.

US Army 1st Lieutenant Moses Alter with B-29 *Enola Gay* on the day after it dropped the first atomic bomb on Hiroshima, Japan, Tinian Island, Guam, August 7, 1945.

On August 9, the B-29 *Bockscar* dropped the second atomic bomb on Nagasaki, and on August 15, Japan surrendered unconditionally, thus ending the war. As chemical officer, Lieutenant Alter of Miami taught chemical warfare procedures and tactics. Prior to his transfer to the South Pacific, he completed a Chemical Munitions and Material Course for aircraft bombs.

Advertisement for El Al Airlines from *TIME* magazine, January 11, 1963.

Tillie Katz of Jacksonville tells about her son Bill as a child (seen as adult in photograph on table) and then his becoming a bomber pilot during World War II and flying twenty-five missions over Germany. As a group commander in the US 8th Air Force, Captain Katz earned the Distinguished Flying Cross and Air Medal with three Oak Leaf Clusters. In 1948 Katz volunteered for the Israeli Air Force. After the War of Independence, Bill settled in Israel and became chief pilot for El Al Airlines. Always the Jewish mother, she pleads, "If you see him, please tell him to dress warm."

Congregation Ohev Shalom hosted a *seder* for military personnel, Orlando, 1944.

On the home front, Jewish communities all over Florida hosted the troops for holiday observances. More than four hundred women and men attended from the nearby Air Force Tactical Applications Center. The meal was prepared from scratch by the women of the congregation as no kosher food was otherwise available.

Korean War, 1950–53

Many Floridians participated. US Marine Corps Private First Class Tilden Zane of Miami Beach was killed in action near Da Nang.

US Navy Lieutenant Roland Kohen served in the Korean War, Miami, 1950.

After serving in World War II and joining the reserves, Lieutenant Kohen was recalled to active duty in 1950. He was "loaned" to the army due to a shortage of field doctors and medics. Kohen was awarded ten medals including the Purple Heart and the Bronze Star for his actions during the Battle of Chip'yong-ni. When he completed his service, he returned to his medical practice in Miami Beach.

Vietnam War, 1959–75

Navigator Lt. Col. Matthias "Matt" Beerman (left) and his crew flew B-52 combat missions in Vietnam, Orlando, 1967.

Beerman flew a total of one hundred combat missions in three wars—World War II, Korea, and Vietnam.

US Air Force 1st Lieutenant Nathan Tarler, Fort Lauderdale, 1963.

The Lillian and Abe Tarler family moved to Fort Lauderdale in 1939 and were very active in the community. Nathan's *bar mitzvah* was in 1951 at Temple Emanu-El. He went into the US Air Force in 1959 and met his wife, Romelle, while at Homestead Air Force Base. Tarler clocked five thousand hours as a navigator of a C-130 Hercules and was TDY (temporary duty) all over the world. He retired as a major in 1979 and was awarded six medals.

Gulf Wars, 1990–91, 2001–11

Miami native and attorney US Army Colonel Lettie Bien retired after thirty years of service, 2007.

Bien deployed to Iraq, serving in many capacities including senior consultant to the Iraqi Ministry, battalion commander, assistant for Iraqi nation-building issues, coordinator for admissions at West Point, and relocation director for the move of the US Southern Command from Panama to Miami. She is very involved in civic activities in Miami.

As I wrote in the introduction to this military section, at least seven Floridian Jews were killed in action in the Gulf Wars. One was a fifth-generation Floridian Jew.

Gainesville native US Army Specialist Jeffrey Wershow was killed while accompanying US officials on a visit to Baghdad University in 2003.

Wershow served three years (1999–2002) with the Army's 82nd Airborne Division. In 2002 he joined the Florida National Guard and was deployed to Iraq. His unit was one of the first to enter Iraq at the beginning of the war. He was posthumously awarded the Bronze Star and the Purple Heart. Specialist Wershow of Gainesville was the great-great-grandson of Julius and Julia Frank, who settled in Miami in 1896. He was also the great-grandson of former state legislator Marcus Frank of Ocala. You met the Frank family in part 2, chapter 4.

Army team Abramowitz: Brothers (left to right) Alan, David, and Sid followed their dad, Benjamin, and his dad, Reuben, into one hundred continuous years of military service, Melbourne, 1985.

The family has earned a total of thirty-three individual medals. In 1916, fourteen-year-old immigrant Reuben Abramowitz, the Pride of Hester Street in New York, arrived home for supper and found that there were seven people at the dinner table and only six chairs. The next day it was off to enlist for World War I where he was promised "three hots and a cot." His son Benjamin Abramowitz was commissioned in 1955 and became a career soldier, making Florida home in 1964. All three of his sons have carried on the family tradition and served in the army. David's son Jacob had his *bar mitzvah* in the synagogue in Ansbach, Germany, that his great-grandfather Reuben rebuilt and where his grandfather Benjamin had his *bar mitzvah* in 1947—and Jacob was commissioned a 2nd lieutenant in 2009. Others have followed to make duty to country a family motto.

CHAPTER 3

Civil and Human Rights

Jewish women and men returned from the wars and joined others at home as civil rights activists to help create a better world. The humanitarian efforts of Jews are driven by the core value of *tikkun olam* (healing the world), including saving lives and performing acts of social justice. Having the history of slavery in ancient Egypt and global antisemitism right up to today, Floridian Jews are sensitive to injustice. I have introduced dozens of activists throughout the book, and here are some more fine examples. They have marched at the forefront of the battle for civil rights, working to promote equality through school desegregation and integration, the rights of the poor and women, and in more recent years, gay rights and gun control.

Civic Activists

Gun control activist Al Hoffman spearheaded "Americans for Gun Safety Now" following the shooting at Marjory Stoneman Douglas High School, Parkland, 2018.

The group outlined their plan in a *Wall Street Journal* ad. The ultimate objective is implementing a complete ban on assault weapons, which is what Hoffman said was his red line for supporting candidates and lawmakers following the Parkland shooting. Hoffman received the Great Floridians Award in 2005.

Rabbi Israel Dresner (top left) was among civil rights protestors at a segregated motel in what might be the largest mass arrest of rabbis in American history, St. Augustine, June 18, 1964.

Martin Luther King Jr. called St. Augustine, the nation's oldest city, one of the most violent places he had ever visited. Evoking Moses' "Let my people go" plea, King invited rabbis to join him there in a pray-in outside the Monson Motor Lodge and Restaurant to serve as a decoy maneuver for other black and white demonstrators who jumped into the motel's segregated pool. Rabbi Dresner participated with 14 other Reform rabbis while the Civil Rights Act was being filibustered in the US Senate. As a result, the activist rabbis were arrested for unlawful assembly and taken to a 15-by-20 foot cell in the St. Johns County Jail. In the sweltering heat, by the light of one naked bulb hanging in the hallway outside their jail cell, they wrote a manifesto on the backs of pages from a report on Ku Klux Klan activities in St. Augustine. "Why We Went" shared their thoughts that their protest of racial segregation was a rare opportunity to jointly show that "We came because we know that second only to silence, the greatest danger to man is loss of faith in man's capacity to act." They were bailed out for $900 each by the NAACP. Dresner, a close friend of King, was once dubbed "the most arrested rabbi in America." He had been arrested in Tallahassee several years before in a demonstration at a segregated airport restaurant.

Self-described "revolutionary senior citizen," Annie Ackerman of Miami Beach became famous for her crash courses on how to flex political muscles, 1970s. *Miami Herald.*

A civic and consumer activist known as the "Condo Queen," Annie Ackerman also led the fight for senior rights and privileges. Her endorsement was sought by presidential candidates and others who knew of her lifelong commitment to environmentalism and social justice. She was inducted into Florida Women's Hall of Fame in 1986.

"Mother of Miami Beach" Rose Weiss with Mayor Harold Shapiro and the city flag that she designed and crafted, Miami Beach, 1955.

Rose and Jeremiah Weiss and their children moved to Miami Beach in 1919. Outstanding because of her persistent efforts to organize welfare services for the needy of the area, Rose attended every city commission meeting for nearly forty years. During the 1926 hurricane, her home became a Red Cross emergency station, and during World War II, she sold $1 million in war bonds, probably more than any other woman in Florida.

David A. Falk named as King Gasparilla XXX of Tampa to honor his civic contributions, 1938.

The Falk family moved from Key West to Tampa in 1895 and established what became the second-largest retail store in Tampa. David, born in Tampa in 1896, was president of the Florida Retail Merchants Association and a University of Tampa (UT) trustee for twelve years, among many other titles. The one-thousand-seat Park Theater was built in 1928 and renamed the Falk Theater in 1962 in his honor; it hosts UT student productions.

Albert Block (right) presented books to the Leon County school system with Julius Trushin and Amos Godby, Tallahassee, 1947.

Block, who came to Tallahassee in 1932 to help start the Rose Printing Company, was one of the founders of the state's Minimum Foundation Program that guaranteed a basic level of education for every Florida school child. He helped develop the state's community college system and was a community activist. Some other results of his dedication were the first synagogue there, Tallahassee Memorial Hospital, commercial airline service, milk pasteurization, and the Young Democrats Club.

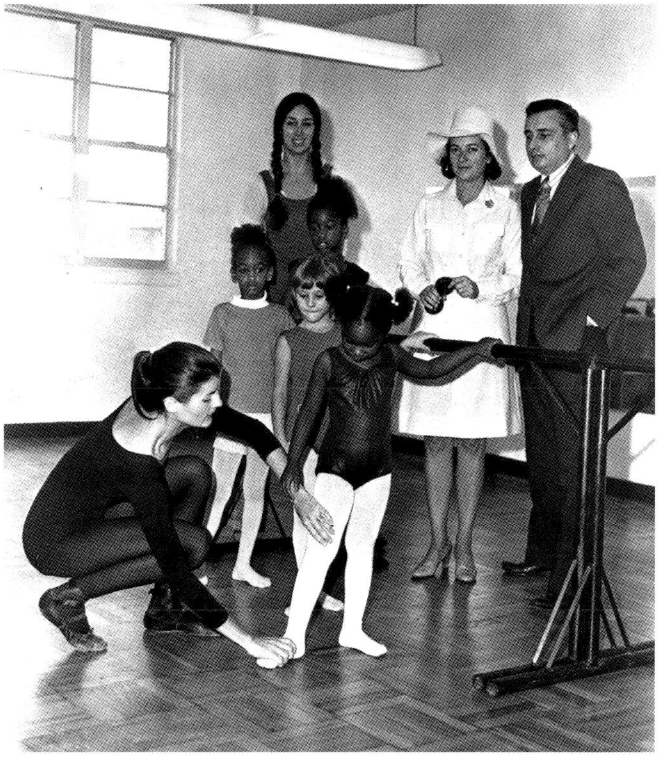

Third-generation Florida native Ruth Wolkowsky Greenfield (in white dress), with her husband, Arnold Greenfield, broke racial barriers with an integrated school, Miami, 1951.

Ruth is with Greater Miami Opera manager Walter Palevova. She founded and directed the first integrated Fine Arts Conservatory for music, art, drama, and dance; it lasted twenty-five years. The *Miami Herald* said that this pioneering color-blind approach was considered scandalous at the time but was a breath of fresh air in the then segregated society. Impresaria and composer Ruth Greenfield founded the free downtown Lunchtime Lively Arts series. For thirty-two years, she taught music at Miami Dade College, Florida's first integrated college, and an auditorium honors her name. You met Ruth's Wolkowksy family in part 2, chapter 4; she is a sister to developer David Wolkowsky, and a third sibling was Edna.

Flossie Gluckman, shown with her husband, Sidney, was an advocate for the poor and elderly, Orlando, 1939.

Long before the Florida Bar Association required pro bono service, Flossie Gluckman supported African Americans in efforts to end discrimination and create equal opportunity. After years of volunteering and raising five children, Flossie headed to law school with one of her sons. After graduation, she established the Neighborhood Law Office and provided free legal advice. Hailed as a trailblazer, Flossie also served as director of Greater Orlando Legal Services. Day after day in the early 1960s, she and a black friend requested seats together at restaurants, got rejected, and tried again until they were successful. In 1964, before school integration, Flossie developed the Wider Horizons summer tutoring program. In 1965 Flossie and Sidney received the Eleanor Roosevelt Humanitarian Award. In 1997 Flossie was honored by the Orlando Human Relations Commission for a "lifetime of dedication and service to human relations progress in Central Florida."

Support for Soviet Jews

Antisemitism was prevalent in tsarist Russia, causing many Jews to emigrate to escape. Others chose to fight on behalf of the 1917 Russian Revolution, believing that communism would end antisemitism. Instead, synagogues were shuttered and free religious practice was forbidden. Judaism was considered a nationality. Jews were denied entry into top schools and jobs.

Jews who applied to emigrate from the Soviet Union were refused permission on the grounds they knew state secrets. Thus, they became known as *refuseniks*. Many refusenik leaders were jailed as "Prisoners of Zion." Not allowed to work, refuseniks were formally viewed by the Soviet establishment as parasites.

Florida's Jewish communities have always supported Jews in need everywhere in the world. From the 1960s to the late 1980s, Jews united to fight for the emigration of Soviet Jews. Soviet Jewry committees formed, and millions of dollars were raised to resettle Jews in Florida, as in the rest of the nation, and in Israel.

The highest form of charity in Judaism is helping a person become self-reliant. This can be with a gift or loan or be done by entering into a partnership with the person to help the individual find employment until she or he no longer needs to be dependent upon others. Jewish Family Services caseworkers worked closely with the new Russian refugees to help them find appropriate jobs.

Speaking out for Soviet Jewry and (inset) welcoming a Soviet family, Lincoln Road Mall, Miami Beach, 1977.

In August 1975, leaders of thirty-five countries including the Soviet Union, signed the Helsinki Final Act, confirming international respect for national borders and urging peaceful dispute resolution. The act also required respect for freedom of thought, conscience, religion, and belief and recognized free movement of people and reunification of families as basic human rights. Though this was not a formal treaty, the document immediately became a powerful global tool to pressure the Soviet Union on human rights violations, including the right to leave. Florida's Jews joined others around the world in pressuring the Soviets to "let their people go!"

One example of Soviet Jewish resettlement in Florida is the Ukrainian Boris Kimlat family, Orlando, 1992.

From left to right are Kostya Kimlat (age ten), Irina Khazina, Inna Shatsman, Boris Kimlat, and Jenya Kimlat (age fifteen). On June 2, 1992, the Orlando Russian Resettlement Committee of Jewish Family Services (JFS) welcomed the Kimlat family. Volunteers greeted the family of five at the airport, provided meals, and readied their furnished apartment with a stocked refrigerator. Soon Boris and Irina found jobs with the help of JFS, and grandmother Inna practiced English daily. By September, she wrote, "Excuse me, my poor English. I and my family became new immigrants in America. I stride into unknowns and not at a young age. I hope that I can be useful to your society, and I want to make friends among you."

In Ukraine, when Boris requested an international passport so that he could leave the country, he was already carrying the internal passport required of all Soviet citizens. The internal passport identified the holder by full name, date, place of birth, social status, and ethnicity. "Jew" was noted instead of "Russian" or "Ukrainian." This "fifth paragraph" or the "fifth line," as it was called, contributed to discrimination against Jewish citizens in higher education, top jobs, and international travel. The ethnicity line was finally dropped from Russian passports in 1997.

Jenya and Kostya became known as Jane and Kevin. Their parents, Boris and Irina, became Bob and Irene. Later the family realized they could be proud Americans while still maintaining their native culture, so they reverted to their original names. Jenya owns her own spa in Longwood and is married with two children who participate at the JCC. Kostya grew up to marry Amy Schwartz in Orlando and become a magician and motivational speaker.

After living in Orlando for twenty-seven years, Boris Kimlat says, "It is through the help of individuals and communities like Orlando that we can flourish as a Jewish family and live the American Dream."

Interfaith

Florida's Jews have worked within their communities with other religious and ethnic groups to create a sense of community and harmony.

Interfaith War Bond drive, Miami, 1940s.

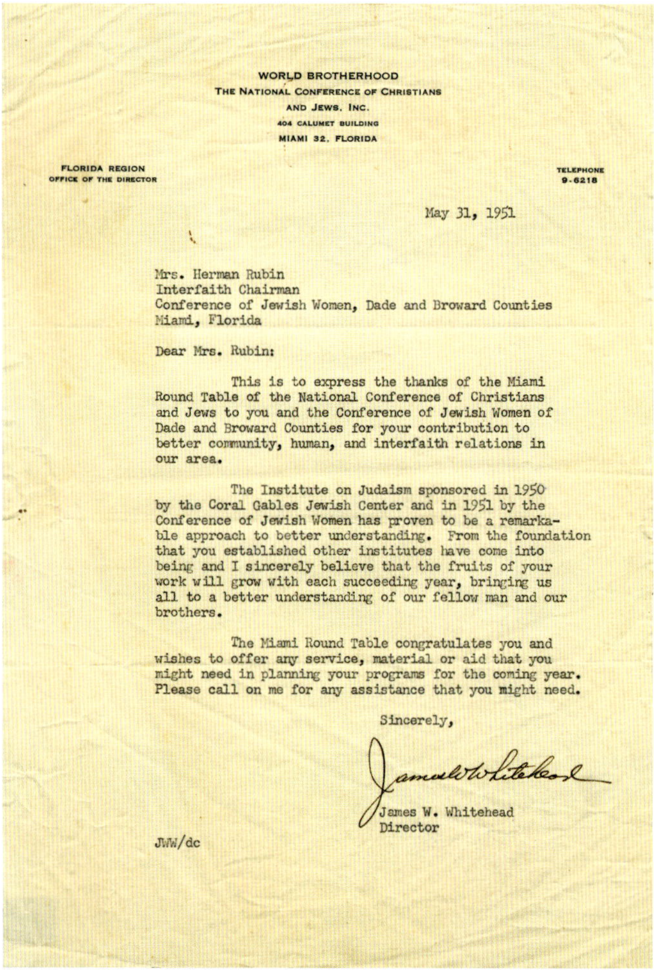

WORLD BROTHERHOOD
THE NATIONAL CONFERENCE OF CHRISTIANS AND JEWS, INC.
404 CALUMET BUILDING
MIAMI 32, FLORIDA

FLORIDA REGION
OFFICE OF THE DIRECTOR

TELEPHONE
9-6218

May 31, 1951

Mrs. Herman Rubin
Interfaith Chairman
Conference of Jewish Women, Dade and Broward Counties
Miami, Florida

Dear Mrs. Rubin:

This is to express the thanks of the Miami Round Table of the National Conference of Christians and Jews to you and the Conference of Jewish Women of Dade and Broward Counties for your contribution to better community, human, and interfaith relations in our area.

The Institute on Judaism sponsored in 1950 by the Coral Gables Jewish Center and in 1951 by the Conference of Jewish Women has proven to be a remarkable approach to better understanding. From the foundation that you established other institutes have come into being and I sincerely believe that the fruits of your work will grow with each succeeding year, bringing us all to a better understanding of our fellow man and our brothers.

The Miami Round Table congratulates you and wishes to offer any service, material or aid that you might need in planning your programs for the coming year. Please call on me for any assistance that you might need.

Sincerely,

James W. Whitehead
James W. Whitehead
Director

JWW/dc

Evelyn Rubin was the Interfaith Chairman of Dade and Broward Counties when this letter was written to her in 1951.

The National Conference of Christians and Jews is a nationwide civic organization that was founded in 1927 to eliminate prejudice, bigotry, and discrimination. They work to build bridges of understanding among all groups through education. The Miami National Conference has been active since 1935.

Rabbi Herbert Baumgard (center) of Temple Beth Am and clergy of various Dade County religious groups gathered for their first interclergy meeting, Miami, 1960s.

Rabbi Solomon Schiff met with the 14th Dalai Lama, Miami Beach, 2010.

During this meeting, the Dalai Lama asked Rabbi Schiff how the Jewish people maintained their faith for two thousand years after they were expelled from their homeland. Rabbi Schiff explained that the many rituals and prayers reinforced the memories of Jerusalem and the hope of return.

Rabbi Schiff has been on the forefront of building interfaith relations since coming to south Florida in 1958. He says that being good citizens, taking part in community affairs, helping one another, and making sure there is no poverty, hatred, or racial intolerance are some of the things people can do to pay back.

Schiff is director emeritus of the Greater Miami Jewish Federation's Mishkan Miami (for spiritual support) and executive vice president emeritus of the Rabbinical Association of Greater Miami, having served both organizations for more than forty years. He received a Papal Medal from Pope Benedict XVI in 2008 for his outstanding service on behalf of interfaith relations.

In 2017 Rabbi Schiff received a Legion of Honor Award from the Chapel of the Four Chaplains. The four chaplains were four US Army chaplains who gave their lives to save other civilian and military personnel as the troop ship SS *Dorchester* sank on February 3, 1943, during World War II. While the chaplains helped other soldiers board lifeboats, they gave up their own life jackets when the supply ran out. They then joined arms, said prayers, and sang hymns as they went down with the ship. These four men were Lt. George L. Fox, Methodist; Lt. Alexander D. Goode, Jewish; Lt. John P. Washington, Roman Catholic; and Lt. Clark V. Poling, Dutch Reformed.

Activist Pauline Berman (1892–1978) said, "Remove hate, bigotry and prejudice, advance good public relations and better understanding among all peoples," Orlando, 1909.

Advancing the Rights of Women

"Modern Matriarch" Anna Brenner Meyers, founding president of the Florida Association for Women Lawyers, is also recognized as a foremost leader in education, Miami, 1950s.

In 2020 we celebrate the 100th anniversary of the 19th amendment to the US Constitution, declaring that the right to vote could not be denied on the basis of a person's sex. Women's Suffrage groups throughout Florida participated in this monumental achievement. Pauline Berman, who settled in Orlando in 1909, said, "Always be planning something," and she did. In 1913, Berman organized Orlando's first civic group for women and was a catalyst for many firsts among women in Florida, including the rights to equality and the vote.

Polish immigrant Anna Brenner Meyers (1896–1983) was a fighter for equal rights for women as a teacher, a lawyer, the first woman and leading member of the Dade County School Board, and a candidate for both circuit court judge and mayor. Meyers traveled around the country gathering information about junior colleges and then had to fight and cajole the other members of the School Board to establish a junior college (Miami-Dade Community College, now Miami Dade College). She was such a leader that, in 1977, a hall at the medical campus and the telecommunication building of the college were named for her. In addition, her name is included on the cornerstones of the original buildings in Kendall. She was president of the International Association of Women Lawyers and is on the list of Great Floridians.

Elaine Gordon represented the underrepresented in the Florida Legislature for twenty-two years and led the fight in Florida for equal rights for women, Miami, 1990.

Gordon (1931–2000) became an advocate for equal rights in 1964 when, as a divorced Miami mother of three young children, she was denied opportunities solely because she was a woman. She was passed over for jobs that were traditionally given to men and could not even establish credit as a single woman. She was a founder of the National Organization for Women and the Florida Women's Political Caucus and introduced the terms *Ms.* and *chairperson* to the legislature. She was inducted into Florida Women's Hall of Fame in 1982.

Advancing the Rights of Gays

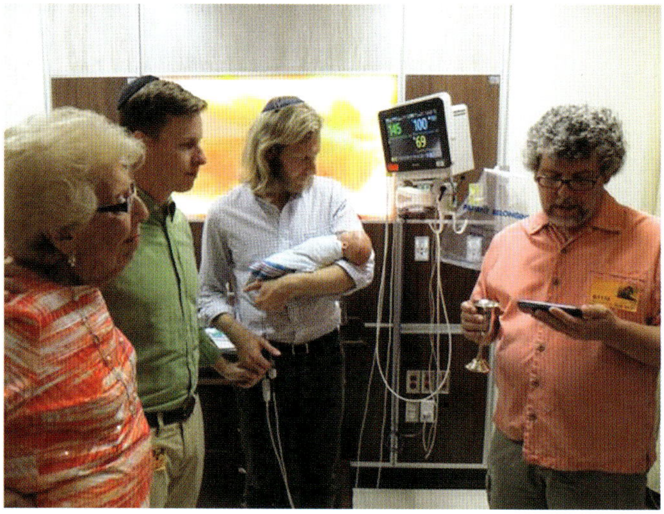

Rabbi David Kay (right) officiated at the *brit milah* ceremony for baby Jack Broffman, Orlando, 2014.

Grandmother Shirley Meltzer and fathers Shane and Matt Broffman (holding the baby) join him in the hospital room. Shane and Matt Broffman celebrated a religious commitment service in March 2011, before same-sex marriage was legal in the US. In 2014 they married in Washington, DC, before Florida law permitted same-sex marriage. Later in 2014, they adopted a son and named him Jack, in memory of Jack Meltzer, Matt's grandfather.

Kaylyn Cooper (left) and Rebecca Stein (center) made history as the first female couple to receive a same-sex marriage license from Orange County, January 6, 2015. *Michele Brennan and Emilie Jones Haller, Photo International.*

Florida voters approved a 2008 constitutional amendment banning same-sex marriage. Declared unconstitutional in 2014, gay marriage was scheduled to become legal in Florida on January 6, 2015. When questions arose whether all court clerks were required to issue licenses, Cooper and Stein filed suit. The Daytona Beach Appeals Court ordered all Orange County courts to issue marriage licenses on January 6. Mayor Buddy Dyer married the couple in a group "Vowed & Proud" civil ceremony outside city hall that same day. They later celebrated a Jewish marriage by Rabbi David Kay (right, in photo) in Orlando under the *chuppah*.

PART 8

Identity

In 1976 author Irving Howe wrote, "Fifty years from now, I am certain, American Jews will still be discussing the problem of identity—indeed is not the discussion the very mark of our identity?" And it continues to be a relentless issue.

Through my initiative and thousands who have joined me over the past thirty-five years, we now have the following three catalysts or instruments for identity discussion through which you can take action.

Collections of the Jewish Museum of Florida–FIU, a partial view, 1999.

The Collections are available to the public for personal research, writing, film, and other purposes to advance greater knowledge of Florida Jewish history. Simply make an appointment with the registrar for access to photographs, oral histories, documents, films, artifacts, books, newspapers, artworks, and other items as described in the introduction. You are also invited to donate items to the Collections for historic preservation. For the first time, there is this archive for the Collective historic memory of Jews in Florida. The museum's website is www.jmof.fiu.edu.

January is Florida Jewish History Month (FJHM); logo created by artist Romero Britto, Miami, 2003.

The concept for Florida Jewish History Month began at the Jewish Museum of Florida. I felt there should be a month for people of every age and background to learn how Jews have been involved in enriching the lives and dreams of all Floridians. No state had a designated month for Jewish history. We worked closely with state legislators to translate the museum's mission to a statewide observance. Senator Gwen Margolis and Rep. Gustavo Barreiro each sponsored companion bills that were passed unanimously in the Florida Senate and House and led to this historic event.

Governor Jeb Bush signed the bill into law on April 17, 2003, designating January, annually, as Florida Jewish History Month. FJHM focuses attention on the contributions Floridian Jews have made in every area of the development of our state—examples of which are illustrated in this book. The museum has a kickoff event annually and lesson plans, a speech, and other resources are available on the website (www.jmof.fiu.edu) for your participation.

JEWISH
AMERICAN
HERITAGE MONTH

May is Jewish American Heritage Month (JAHM). The Jewish Museum of Florida was the birthplace of this national observance, 2006.

During my research to create FJHM, I was astounded to learn there was no national month, as other groups have, to honor the contributions Jews have made to the fabric of our nation. Why? In April 2005, our museum honored US Representative Debbie Wasserman Schultz (District 20) with a Glass Ceiling award as the first Jewish woman from Florida elected to Congress. I posed the question—and she agreed to sponsor federal legislation creating a month to celebrate Jewish contributions.

Immediately, JMOF and Judy Gilbert Gould of the Jewish Community Relations Council of the Greater Miami Jewish Federation collaborated with the staff of Rep. Wasserman Schultz to draft the proposed legislation. Meantime in Washington, Rep. Wasserman Schultz faced a moratorium on the designation of months for national observances—but that didn't slow her down. She tenaciously worked for months to secure 250 sponsors of legislation to waive the rules of the House and allow consideration of a resolution to create a special month. And she did it! During this same time, Judy and I networked with colleagues around the country and within our constituencies to encourage congresspersons to sign. Advocacy in action!

On December 14, 2005, Rep. Wasserman Schultz brought up the resolution in the US House of Representatives, which passed by a vote of 423–0, urging the president to annually proclaim a Jewish American Heritage Month. Pennsylvania Senator Arlen Spector led the effort for unanimous consent in the Senate on February 14, 2006—and the rest is history, again with the boost of advocacy in contacting the president to urge his signing of the proclamation. In April 2006 at the JMOF, it was officially announced that each May would be recognized by the US president as "our month."

This effort took a lot of people! It is my hope that each year the JAHM observance will grow to involve more people to help tell the stories of how Jews have enriched the lives of all Americans. Resources and methods to get involved are on the website www.jahm.us.

National Aeronautics and Space Administration
Lyndon B. Johnson Space Center
Houston, Texas

Certificate of Authenticity
STS-132

This **Jewish American Heritage Month Declaration** was flown for the **National Museum of American Jewish History** aboard the United States Space Shuttle *Atlantis* to the International Space Station. *Atlantis* launched at 2:20 p.m. EDT, May 14, 2010, from Pad 39A at the Kennedy Space Center, Florida. At 8:49 a.m. EDT, May 26, 2010, *Atlantis* landed at the Kennedy Space Center having orbited the Earth 186 times and travelled 4,879,978 statute miles. The flight duration was 11 days, 18 hours, 28 minutes and 2 seconds.

Garrett Reisman
NASA Mission Specialist Astronaut

Certificate of authenticity for the space voyage of the proclamation for Jewish American Heritage Month, 2010.

NASA Mission Specialist Astronaut Garrett Reisman presents the original copy of the JAHM proclamation to Marcia Jo Zerivitz, Philadelphia, August 18, 2010.

In May 2010, Jewish astronaut Garrett Reisman took JMOF's copy of the original Jewish American Heritage Month Proclamation on a 5-million-mile, 186-earth-orbit mission on US Space Shuttle *Atlantis* to the International Space Station and then returned it to us. The JMOF board approved donating this historic proclamation to the National Museum of American Jewish History, now the lead sponsor for JAHM and the site of this historic event.

Conclusion

Jewish students visiting the Jewish Museum of Florida-FIU to learn their history, Miami Beach, circa 2009.

Heather Cohen is proud of her heritage as displayed by her pin, "Kiss Me I'm Jewish," Greater Orlando JCC Nursery School, 1983.

I have shared some highlights from my thirty-five years of collecting photographs and stories of Jewish life in Florida. For Jews—these should strengthen Jewish identity to help ensure Jewish continuity. Remember (from the introduction) Rabbi Irving "Yitz" Greenberg's words, "*If your memories are Jewish, you will be Jewish.*" This book of *centuries of memories* is a vehicle for discussions about Jews in Florida. Young Jews who grow up in Florida, and all those who choose to make Florida home, have this knowledge of what Jews before them have contributed to impact and improve their lives. This history instills pride in being Jewish!

You now know that Jews have made ginormous contributions in every area in the development and success of Florida. Yet, as I write, there is a worldwide resurgence of antisemitism. Jews are still hated—as we have been for 2,000 years. There is a parallel between the ancient forces of xenophobia that drove Jews out of 109 countries, that prevented them from residing in Florida for 250 years after settlement began and even from some Florida cities in modern history—and what is happening today. I used the word "antisemitism" nearly fifty times because that was the driving force that propelled Jews to move from place to place.

I have demonstrated examples of the outstanding achievements and contributions of Jewish people throughout the state. As I discussed in part 6, the Jewish experience in Florida also has a dark side—one of continued prejudice and discrimination. Knowing about the antisemitism that many Jews faced in Florida—and how they persevered against the barriers—is important to better appreciate their accomplishments. Mark Twain observed this in 1899 when writing about the contributions of Jews, "who have done it with his hands tied behind him."

I hope that the content I have shared is meaningful as we are living in a complicated world. Immigrants are demonized and the extremism of racial bigots is easily accessible on social media networks and the internet. Florida has the second-largest number of hate groups in the nation. In fact, the world's first website devoted to the agenda of hatred in cyberspace was launched in 1995 in West Palm Beach—in Florida. On the proactive side to reach the education system, on April 29, 2019, the Florida Legislature unanimously approved measures to address antisemitism in all Florida schools with House Bill 741. It defines antisemitism and requires schools to recognize it as a form of discrimination so that law enforcement can investigate unprotected conduct as hate crimes.

We can each work to stop hateful messages. Hate crimes in the US are rising. Antisemitism is up nearly 60 percent. On college campuses, 54 percent of Jewish students are experiencing antisemitism. More people think that everything Jews do is wrong and all that goes wrong is done by Jews. However, even though we are less than one-quarter of 1 percent of the global population, Jews have been awarded 22 percent of all the Nobel prizes.

In spite of living with this hatred—we Jews are a tenacious, proud, creative, hardworking people. Jews will continue to boast pride in what we have always done and act on what is right for our people, our communities, and our world. We will continue to labor to make this world a better place for everyone—even those who hate us. We will remain minute in number but mighty in our contributions to humanity.

To all my readers, thank you for the time you committed to my book. I hope that you enjoyed my stories to the degree that you remember and share them—and that by absorbing what I presented, you will come to the conclusion that

- Jews have lived in Florida as Jews continuously for more than 250 years,
- Jews have lived all over Florida,
- Jews have enriched Florida in every area of its development,
- Jews have been good neighbors and interacted with other Floridians to improve the quality of life for all peoples, and
- Florida's Jews have maintained their traditions and built institutions to help ensure Jewish continuity for future generations.

Since the story was untold, this is my story of one people who settled in Florida—their issues and their contributions and the places and the times—told through the voices and images I amassed. A personal goal has been to create something good that would outlast me. Hopefully, the Jewish Museum of Florida-FIU and the Collections that I started along with this documentation of Jewish life in Florida will be the impetus to others to continue collecting and sharing the centuries of stories and memories. This will inspire the next generations to be knowledgeable and proud of their heritage, to keep it alive and make their own contributions to advance the human condition. Shalom!

Glossary

Abbreviations: [H] = Hebrew; [Y] = Yiddish

aliyah [H]—Literally, "to ascend." Immigration of Jews to Israel from the Diaspora. See Diaspora.

antisemitism—Two thousand-year-old hatred against Jews. The most persistent, pervasive and pernicious of all hatreds known in the world.

ark—Cabinet in which the Torah scrolls are kept in the synagogue.

Ashkenazim—Jews who came from central and eastern Europe and their descendants. Language is Yiddish. See Yiddish.

bar or ***bat mitzvah*** (plural: ***b'nai mitzvah***) [H]—Literally, "son [bar] or daughter [bat] of the commandment," coming-of-age ritual, traditionally at the age of thirteen for Jewish boys and twelve or thirteen for girls.

beshert [Y]—Destiny.

bimah [H]—Platform from which services are led in a synagogue.

blood libel—Accusation that Jewish people used the blood of Christians in religious rituals that was perpetrated throughout the Middle Ages and (sporadically) into the twenty-first century.

B'nai B'rith [H]—Literally, "children of the covenant." Jewish social service fraternity established in 1855.

brit milah or ***bris*** (plural: ***britot***) [H]—Literally, "covenant of circumcision." Ritual circumcision performed on males eight days old.

bubbe [Y]—Grandmother.

cantor—Synagogue official who sings or chants and leads the congregation in prayer and song. See also *chazzan* [H].

Chabad—Orthodox Jewish movement, also known as Lubavitch. One of the world's best known Hasidic movements, known for its outreach, and one of the largest Jewish religious organizations in the world.

challah (plural: ***challot***) [H]—Braided bread eaten on Shabbat and on most Jewish holidays.

chazzan [H]—Synagogue official who sings or chants and leads the congregation in prayer and song. See also cantor.

Chevra Kadisha [H]— Literally, "holy society." Jewish burial society.

cholent [Y]—Stew prepared on Friday and slowly cooked overnight for Sabbath noonday meal.

chuppah [H]—Canopy under which a Jewish wedding ceremony takes place.

confirmation—Group ceremony usually held on Shavuot that recognizes students (ages fifteen or sixteen) who are completing the religious school curriculum. See also Shavuot.

congregation—Organized group who assemble for religious worship, study and other activities.

consecration—Modern ceremony marking the formal beginning of religious instruction for Jewish children.

Conservative—A major Jewish denomination that views Jewish law as the outcome of the ongoing interaction between God and the Jewish people over the course of history. Term was meant to signify the movement's attempt to conserve Jewish tradition. More traditional than Reform but less than Orthodox.

conversos [Ladino: Judeo-Spanish]—Refers to Jews who converted to Catholicism to avoid persecution during the Spanish Inquisition (1478–1834). Some openly practiced Catholicism but secretly followed Judaism, risking severe punishment or even being burned alive if caught, but continuing to hope for a change, for a better future, for freedom.

Diaspora—Dispersion of a people from their homeland. Refers to Jewish communities and their residents living outside of Palestine or modern Israel. Originating in the sixth century BCE with the Babylonian exile.

eruv [H]—Enclosure, often a wire, around a home or Orthodox community where observant Jews may carry out activities on Shabbat or other holy days that would otherwise be forbidden by religious law. An example is carrying objects.

ghetto—Part of a city in which members of a minority group live. Term meaning "foundry" originally used in 1500s Venice to describe the part of the city in which Jews were forced to live.

goldene medina *[Y]*—Golden land, land of opportunity, the United States.

greener—Recent immigrant.

Haganah [H]—Jewish paramilitary organization in the British Mandate of Palestine (1922–1948) formed by Jews to defend themselves against attacks by the Arabs. Became the core of the Israel Defense Forces (IDF).

Hanukkah [H]—Festival of Freedom or Feast of Lights. Eight-day holiday commemorating the rededication of the Second Temple of Jerusalem after the victory of the Maccabees over Syrian rulers in 165 BCE.

Hanukkah menorah or *hanukkiah* (plural: ***hanukkiot***) [H]—Special candelabra designed with nine candleholders for Hanukkah candle-lighting ceremony. Candles are lit for eight days and the ninth candle is used to light the others.

Hasidic [H]—Relating to or denoting Hasidism, a mystical Jewish movement founded in Poland in the eighteenth century in reaction to the rigid academicism of rabbinical Judaism.

High Holidays—Jewish high holy days of Rosh Hashanah and Yom Kippur, the holiest days in the Jewish calendar.

Irgun [H]—Jewish underground organization that operated in Mandate Palestine (1922–1948) focusing their attention on British military and governmental targets. Vladimir Jabotinsky and Menachem Begin were among the leaders. Some of its members were hung by the British.

kasher [H]—To render kosher. To make proper or lawful. See kosher.

kehillah [H]—Jewish community.

ketubah [H]—Jewish marriage contract.

kibbutz [H]—Communal settlement in Israel, typically a farm.

Kiddush [H] **cup**—Cup often of precious metal that may be engraved or ornamented that holds the wine used for blessings for Shabbat, holidays and other sacred occasions (including weddings) in the home and the synagogue. In many families and congregations, the Kiddush cup is treasured and passed down through generations.

kippah [H]—Small round head covering worn as a symbol of respect and religious observance, sometimes called a *yarmulke* [Y].

kosher—Conforming to Jewish law, especially dietary law. Ritually prepared. Clean or pure. See also *kasher*.

landsmen [Y]—Fellow countrymen.

latke [Y]—Fried pancake, usually potato latke, traditionally eaten on Hanukkah.

Lubavitch—Also known as Chabad. See Chabad.

Magen David [H]—Star or Shield of David, a six-pointed figure consisting of two interlaced equilateral triangles, used as a Jewish and Israeli symbol.

Masada—Young adult Zionist group named after the ancient fortification that was the last Jewish stronghold against the Roman invasion in 73 CE, three years after the destruction of the Second Temple in Jerusalem by the Romans. The Zealots, as they were known, committed mass suicide rather than surrender to the Romans. Today, Masada is one of the most visited tourist sites in Israel.

matzah [H]—Unleavened bread eaten primarily during Passover.

mazel tov [H]—Good luck.

medinat Yisroel [H]—Modern State of Israel.

megillah [H]—Scroll of Esther, part of the Hebrew Bible that is a firsthand account of the events of Purim, the fun-filled holiday that commemorates the rescue of the Jewish people in ancient Persia in 500 BCE.

mezuzah (plural: ***mezuzot***) [H]—Piece of parchment contained in a decorative case and inscribed with specific Hebrew verses from the Torah (Deuteronomy 6:4-9 and 11:13-21) that is attached to the doorpost of a Jewish home.

mikvah (plural: ***mikvaot***) [H]—Ritual bath.

minyan [H]—Quorum of ten adult males traditionally required for public worship. Some congregations count adult women.

mitzvah (plural: ***mitzvot***) [H]—Commandment. Also good works or deeds.

mohel [H]—Person trained to perform ritual circumcision. See *brit milah*.

nosh [Y]—Snack.

Orthodox—A major Jewish denomination, the most traditional of the major movements in Judaism with many different sects all adhering to the central belief that the Torah is the exact word of God without any human influence. With strict observance of Jewish law.

Passover—Joyous spring holiday commemorating the deliverance of the ancient Hebrews from Egyptian slavery. Celebrated for eight days by Conservative and Orthodox Jews and seven days by Reform Jews and in the State of Israel.

pidyon haben [H]—Redemption of the first-born son, by use of five silver coins, from being predestined by his firstborn status to serve as a priest.

pogrom—Organized violent attack, a massacre, against the Jews.

rabbi—Spiritual leader of a Jewish congregation.

rebbetzin [Y]—Wife of a rabbi.

Reform—A major Jewish denomination that emphasizes the evolving nature of the religion, the superiority of its ethical aspects to the ceremonial ones and a belief in a continuous revelation. The most traditionally liberal of the branches of Judaism.

Rosh Hashanah [H]—Literally, "head of the year." The new year on the Hebrew calendar, one of the holiest days of the Jewish year.

sandak [H]—Person who holds the newborn boy on his knees for the circumcision or *brit milah*. See *brit milah* [H].

schmaltz [Y]—Fat rendered from a goose, chicken or any other fowl used for cooking or flavoring food.

seder [H]—Ceremonial meal, usually held on the first and second evenings of Passover, commemorating the exodus of the enslaved Jews from Egypt. See Passover.

sefer (plural: ***sifrei***) [H]—Book.

Sephardim [H]—Jews who originated in Sepharad, Spain or the Iberian Peninsula before the expulsion (1492) or in the Ottoman Empire (non-Europeans) and their descendants. Language is Ladino.

Shabbat [H]—Seventh day of the Jewish week. Jewish Sabbath observed twenty-five hours from just before sundown on Friday night to Saturday night at the appearance of the first stars.

shadkhan [H]—Jewish professional matchmaker or marriage broker.

Shavuot [H]—Holiday celebrated fifty days after Passover on the anniversary of Moses receiving the Ten Commandments on Mount Sinai.

shidduch [H]—A date or match leading to marriage.

shin [H]—Twenty-first letter of the Hebrew alphabet. Stands for the Hebrew word *Shaddai* which means "Almighty."

shochet [H]—Ritual slaughterer, kosher butcher.

shofar [H]—Hallowed out ram's horn that is blown like a trumpet. An ancient musical instrument today blown on Rosh Hashanah and Yom Kippur as part of the prayer service.

shtetl [Y]—Small Jewish town or village formerly found in eastern Europe.

shul [Y]—Synagogue.

siddur [H]—Prayer book.

simcha [H]—Blessing, blessed event.

simchat bat [H]—Baby naming ceremony for Jewish girls.

sofer (male), ***soferet*** (female) (plural: ***soferim***) [H]—Scribe, specially trained scholar who handwrites the Hebrew words on a Torah.

sukkah [H]—Temporary hut where Jews traditionally reside during Sukkot with an open roof made from branches and hanging fruit to celebrate the harvest and to commemorate the Israelites' forty years of wandering in the wilderness. See Sukkot.

Sukkot [H]—Literally, "booths." A weeklong festival when Jews traditionally eat and sleep in a *sukkah*. See *sukkah*.

synagogue—Building used for Jewish worship, study and assembly.

tallit (plural: ***tallitot***) [H]—Prayer shawl.

Talmud—Authoritative collection of ancient rabbinic laws, commentaries and traditions related to the Torah, dating from the second century CE.

tefillin [H]—Small black leather boxes containing Jewish prayers written on parchment and attached with leather straps to forehead and forearm in a prescribed manner. Referred to as "laying tefillin."

tikkun olam [H]—Literally, "repairing the world." The Jewish ideal that each individual acts in partnership with God in behalf of social justice to improve the world.

Torah [H]—Literally, "law, instruction, teaching." A scroll of parchment containing the Five Books of Moses, first five books (Pentateuch) of the twenty-four of the Hebrew Bible. The body of wisdom, Jewish law and ritual tradition.

treif [H]—Not kosher.

tzedakah [H]—Righteous giving, charity.

yahrzeit [H]—Anniversary of a death observed by an immediate family member.

Yeshiva [H]—Orthodox Jewish college or seminary.

Yiddish—Mixture of German, Hebrew, and Slavic. Traditional Ashkenazic language.

yizkor [H]— Memorial service on certain holy days for deceased relatives or martyrs.

Yom Ha-Shoah [H]—Holocaust Remembrance Day.

Yom Kippur [H]—Day of Atonement. Holiest day of the Jewish year.

zayde [Y]—Grandfather.

Zionist—A follower of **Zionism**, the worldwide political movement, rooted in historic yearnings and formally organized in 1897 that worked toward establishing the Jewish homeland in Israel. Today Zionists continue to help Israel develop and prosper.

Main Sources: Joyce Eisenberg and Ellen Scolnic, *Dictionary of Jewish Words* (Jewish Publication Society, 2001); *Merriam-Webster's Collegiate Dictionary*, 11th ed.

Bibliography

atlantajewishtimes.timesofisrael.com/topic/sara-blakely/. Accessed June 3, 2018.

Baker, Aryn. "Murdered Journalist Sought to Give Voice to the Voiceless," *Time*, September 3, 2014.

"Bernard Barker Dies at 92; Watergate Burglar Was a CIA Operative." *Los Angeles Times*, June 6, 2009. Accessed July 5, 2018.

Bettinger-Lopez, Caroline. *Cuban-Jewish Journeys*. Forward by Ruth Behar. Knoxville: The University of Tennessee Press, 2000.

Brennen, Morgan. "Stephen Ross: The Billionaire Who Is Rebuilding New York." *Forbes*, March 7, 2012. Accessed October 10, 2018.

Brown, Canter. *Jewish Pioneers of the Tampa Bay Frontier*. Tampa Bay History Center Reference Library Series No. 7, 1999.

Brown, Joseph. "The Latin Quarter Nightclub." *South Beach Magazine*, May 16, 2004.

Cohen, Isidor. *Historical Sketches and Sidelights of Miami, Florida*. Miami: Privately Printed, 1925.

Cohen, Howard. "The Heart and Soul of Surfside's Sheldon's Drugs, Ethyl Spector Dies at 87." *Miami Herald*, April 22, 2017. (accessed August 11, 2018).

Commissioner of Agriculture of the State of Florida, *Report for the period beginning Jan.1, 1891 and ending Dec. 31, 1892*. Tallahassee: John G. Collins, 1893. Pages 24, 27-28 and errata "page 28, line 13, the signature 'John' Potsdamer should read 'Julius' Potsdamer." (accessed August 20, 2018).

Conversations with Dr. Eugene Lyon, Center for Historic Research, St. Augustine Foundation, 1987.

Davis, F. T. "History of Juan Ponce de Leon's Voyages to Florida." *Florida Historical Quarterly* 14 (1935):7–70.

Davis, William Watson. *The Civil War and Reconstruction in Florida*. New York: 1913, 576, 604.

Dorschner, John. (February 26, 2012) *North Miami Beach High to Facebook's No. 2*. July 26, 2018. https://www.miamiherald.com/news/local/community/miami-dade/article1939532.html.

Emmanuel, Isaac, and Suzanne A. Emmanuel. *History of the Jews of the Netherlands, Antilles*. Cincinnati: American Jewish Archives, 1970.

Freeman, Jack. *Florida Pioneer to Land Baron*. Lake Mary, FL: Self-published, 2004.

Florida Historical Markers, Marker number F-320, Alachua County, David Levy Yulee and Cotton Wood Plantation, Old depot in Archer, 1988.

Glickstein, Natalie. *That Ye May Remember: Temple Ahavath Chesed 1882–1982*. Jacksonville: Byron Kennedy Publishers, 1982.

House Reports, No. 22, vol. 13, 42nd Congress, 2nd Session. 80, 82, 291.

Huhner, Leon. "Moses Elias Levy, an Early Florida Pioneer and the Father of Florida's First Senator." *Florida Historical Quarterly* 19, (1941): 319–345.

Jewishvirtuallibrary.org: Prussia. Accessed June 6, 2018.

Kleinberg, Howard. *Woggles and Cheese Holes*. Miami Beach: The Greater Miami & The Beaches Hotel Association, 2005.

Koren, Dr. Herman. *Histories of the Jewish People of Pinellas County, Florida 1883–2005*. Clearwater: Temple B'nai Israel, 2007.

Korn, Bertram Wallace. *The Early Jews of New Orleans*. Waltham, Mass.: American Jewish Historical Society, 1969.

Liebman, Malvina W., and Seymour B. Liebman. *Jewish Frontiersmen*. Miami Beach: Jewish Historical Society of Southern Florida, n.d.

Loomis, Carol J. "The Larger-than-Life Life of Robert Rubin." *Fortune*, March 13, 2016. Accessed October 17, 2018.

Marcus, Jacob R. *Memoirs of American Jews 1775-1865*. New York, 1955, 146–202, from autobiography of Raphael Jacob Moses.

Medea, Andra. "Jennie Grossinger." *Jewish Women: A Comprehensive Historical Encyclopedia*. March 1, 2009. Jewish Women's Archive, jwa.org. Accessed July 8, 2018. http://jwa.org/encyclopedia/article/grossinger-jennie.

Monaco, Chris. *Moses Levy of Florida*. Baton Rouge: Louisiana State University Press, 2005.

Moore, Deborah Dash. "Jewish Migration to the Sunbelt." *Shades of the Sunbelt: Essays on Ethnicity, Race, and the Urban South*. New York: Greenwood Press, 1988.

Postal, Bernard, and Lional Koppman, *American Jewish Landmarks*. New York: Fleet Press, 1977.

Proctor, Samuel. *Pioneer Jewish Settlements in Florida 1765–1900*. Miami Beach: Proceedings of the Conference on the Writings of Regional History in the South, 1956.

Proctor, Samuel. *Eighteen-Century Florida: Life on the Frontier*. Gainesville: University of Florida Press, 1976.

Redford, Polly. *Billion-Dollar Sandbar: A Biography of Miami Beach*. Dutton, 1970.

Schuster, Goldie Jacobs. Collection of letters and articles about St. Petersburg and Jacobs family history written by Schuster and collected for the *MOSAIC: Jewish Life in Florida* project, 1982.

Sheskin, Ira M. *The 2016 Jewish Federation of Broward County Population Study: A Profile of Jewish Broward County*. Davie: Jewish Federation of Broward County, 2017.

Tebeau, Charlton. *A History of Florida*. Coral Gables: University of Miami Press, revised 1980.

Tebeau, Charlton. *Synagogue in the Central City: Temple Israel of Greater Miami 1922–1972*. Coral Gables: University of Miami Press, 1972.

"How Did Fort Myers Get Its Name." *Sun Bay Paper*, February 16, 2017. Accessed June 17, 2018.

Thompson, Donald H., and Carol Thompson. *Egmont Key, a History*. Charleston, SC: The History Press, 2012.

Treister, Kenneth. *A Sculpture of Love and Anguish: The Holocaust Memorial, Miami Beach, Florida*. New York: S.p.i. Books, a Division of Shapolsky Publishers, Inc., 1993.

Vaughn, Susan. "Auschwitz Survivor Passes Along Gift to Others." *Los Angeles Times*, October 15, 2000. Accessed June 6, 2018.

Whitfield, Stephen J. *Commerce and Community: A Business History of Jacksonville Jewry*. Reprinted from *Southern Jewish History*, volume 12, Southern Jewish Historical Society, 2010.

Whitfield, Stephen J. "Blood and Sand: The Jewish Community of South Florida." *American Jewish History* 82, nos. 1–4 (1994): 73–96. Revised version published in *Jews of South Florida*, ed. Andrea Greenbaum. Hanover, NH: University Press of New England, 2005, 37–52.

Wikipedia contributors, "History of the Jews in Russia," Wikipedia. Accessed April 22, 2018. https://en.wikipedia.org/w/index.php?title=History_of_the_Jews_in_Russia&oldid=837609992.

Zahav, Jonatan. *The Key West Jewish Community-One Hundred Years*. Unpublished, 1987.

About the Author

Marcia Jo Zerivitz, LHD, founding executive director of the Jewish Museum of Florida–FIU, is a native West Virginian who has lived in Florida for more than half a century. She has been a trailblazer in the American and Floridian Jewish communities, serving national, state, and local organizations and has broken the glass ceiling as the first woman in many positions. In 2016 Florida International University awarded her a doctor of humane letters honoris causa for her vision and leadership throughout her life to expand knowledge and enrich collective historic memory.

Among her volunteer positions, she served as president of the Jewish Federation of Greater Orlando (1978–80), on the first United Jewish Appeal Women's Young Leadership Cabinet (1974), as chair of the first Florida Association of Jewish Federations Conference (1979), and on the American Israel Public Affairs Committee's (AIPAC) national council. She has also led missions to Israel.

Marcia Jo transitioned to the Jewish professional world in 1980. Through her experiences, she observed that the Jewish community in Florida had a major challenge—its continuity—and resolved to focus on collecting and preserving, for future generations, the stories and material evidence of the contributions of Jews to the Sunshine State and beyond.

From 1984 to 1992, Marcia Jo traveled 250,000 miles throughout Florida, conducting grassroots research and retrieving the state's hidden, 250-plus-year Jewish history, resulting in a major archive and the *MOSAIC: Jewish Life in Florida* exhibit that traveled to 13 cities (1990–94). She recruited and involved thousands of people in this process.

In 1995, under her direction and planning, this project evolved into the American Alliance of Museums–accredited Jewish Museum of Florida (JMOF) on Miami Beach, housed in two adjacent restored former synagogues that are on the National Register of Historic Places. JMOF—perhaps the first museum in the US to document the history of one ethnic group in a state—preserves and interprets the Jewish experience in Florida in the context of the immigration of all American families. Marcia Jo developed the Collections and presented more than seventy exhibits with five hundred educational programs in sixteen years.

Marcia Jo initiated the legislation for both Florida Jewish History Month (FJHM) each January and Jewish American Heritage Month (JAHM) each May to increase awareness of the contributions of Jews to the quality of life for all.

She wrote (with coauthor Rachel Heimovics) *Florida Jewish Heritage Trail* (which covers 250 sites in 44 cities of Jewish historical significance), published by the Florida Department of State. She authored all Florida entries for *Encyclopedia Judaica* and the photo-documentaries *Jews of Greater Miami* and *Jews of Tampa* for Arcadia Publishing. Her scholarship has been used in exhibitions, films, historical journals, and books; she has been published nationally and internationally.

Marcia Jo retired from JMOF in 2011 and continues to curate exhibits, lecture, research, and write on Florida Jewish history. She was the main on-camera narrator for the 2014 Public Broadcasting Service (PBS) documentary, *A Call to Serve: Florida Jews in the US Military*. In 2017 she curated the exhibit *Kehillah: A History of Jewish Life in Greater Orlando*.

The author resides on St. Pete Beach with her husband, Elliott, whom she credits as her partner on this journey. As a cultural anthropologist, she is credited with an innovative process that gave the world something it did not have: the compelling story of one ethnic group in a hugely diverse Florida.

Index

G

H

M

Q

R

S

T